TRIGILD

DESKBOOK- 5th Edition

Guide to Receivership & Foreclosure

Edited by: Trigild Inc.
9339 Genesee Avenue, Suite 130
San Diego, CA 92121
(858) 242.1222
www.trigild.com

Table of Contents

Trigild Deskbook

The Trigild Deskbook provides a comprehensive but simple source book for lenders' and servicers' dealing with nonperforming commercial loans. We enlisted the help of many attorneys throughout the United States in summarizing the basic rules of foreclosure and receivership.

This Deskbook is not intended to be an exhaustive study of any one state's rules, procedures and intricacies. Nor is it intended for use by attorneys or other legal professionals, and therefore complex analyses are not included and citations have been removed throughout the text and referenced only at the end of each section.

Our thanks to our lawyer-friends who supplied far more material than we could include here. The final material was edited by Trigild staff for brevity and simplicity, and any errors are therefore solely ours. We have not included most procedural and other matters which should be addressed by your own counsel.

We will continue to update and revise the Deskbook on a periodic basis. We therefore welcome and solicit corrections, additions or clarifications from the legal community. We also welcome comments from those in the banking profession, which will help us continue to make this a valuable reference tool.

William J. Hoffman

General Principles

While every state, and Federal, jurisdiction has unique rules and procedures, there are a number of common concepts that apply throughout. A basic understanding of these concepts and definitions will help in reviewing the enclosed material.

Foreclosure

States are generally classified as either *mortgage* states, where the lender holds title to the real property until the loan is paid, or *trust deed* states where title is held by a trustee in the borrower's name.

Most states' foreclosure procedures fall into one or both categories of *judicial* or *non-judicial*. A judicial foreclosure can be broadly described as a lawsuit for non-payment that allows the lender to pursue a deficiency judgment for any amount not recovered in a sale of the property. A non-judicial foreclosure generally allows the lender to take the property as payment in full. Generally, the non-judicial action will be typically quicker and cheaper and most often used when there is no additional recourse available.

You will find that the terms *cure*, *reinstatement* and *redemption* are sometimes used interchangeably and have different meanings in different states. Redemption is used most often to refer to a right of a borrower to redeem a property after it has been foreclosed by judicial action. The redemption period can range from a few months to a year. This redemption, if effective, has an obvious chilling effect on a sale during that period. The concept of reinstatement or cure generally refers to the ability of a borrower to pay any defaulted amount prior to a foreclosure or trustee's sale.

Receivership

Receivership, although even older in law than bankruptcy, is relatively free of specific statutes and codes, and understood by relatively few lawyers and judges. Receivership is frequently confused with bankruptcy by the general public as well as borrowers and creditors. We broadly categorize bankruptcy as laws to protect borrowers from creditors, and receivership as a method for secured creditors to protect the assets which were used as collateral to obtain the loan. In the vast majority of cases receivership will be far less costly than bankruptcy when it comes to professional anad legal fees.

Most states have no specific qualifications for receivers other than that they are a disinterested third party. Some jurisdictions prefer local receivers, but such limitations can often be overcome with specific facts. A very few jurisdictions may still have a list of "approved receivers," but this is fairly rare. Requirements that a Receiver be a citizen of that state are now uncommon, and can usually be met by various arrangements and affilliations.

A Receiver is authorized to act when an Order Appointing Receiver is entered by the court. However, in most jurisdictions the Receiver must file an oath and bond prior to commencing his/her duties. The purpose of the oath is for the Receiver to state that he/she will act responsibly according to the Order. The bond protects the parties in case of any malfeasance by that Receiver. In some cases the lender/plaintiff may also be required to file a bond, most often when the appointment was *ex parte* (see below).

A Receiver's authority and responsibility is governed by the Order Appointing Receiver, and any additional instructions or orders. It is important that the Order include powers to cover all anticipated circumstances, and your lawyer will usually talk with the proposed Receiver for this purpose.

Authority for the Receivers to sell assets in the receivership estate, rather than the lender selling them after foreclosure is being sought more often recently, particularly by CMBS servicers. Some states specifically allow such sales, some prohibit them, and many are virtually silent on the issue. Sale by a Receiver, even if authorized in the original order, should always be made subject to final court approval.

In the case of an emergency (which is determined by each court) lender's counsel may seek an *ex parte* hearing, which shortens the notice period, sometimes to 24 hours. When not available, the hearing will be held according to statutory notice rules and according to the court's calendar.

Most courts distinguish between receivers appointed to take over an entire business entity – often called a *general assets Receiver*, and one appointed to take possession of specific assets which secure the loan and any income generated by those assets – usually called a *rents-and-profits* Receiver. Parties, lawyers and judges often confuse the two. The specific identity of the defendant/borrower in the case heading does not necessarily mean that that entity will be in receivership. Most often the order applies to specific assets which are the lender's security.

A Receiver may also be appointed by way of a *stipulation* between the parties, which makes the court's action most predictable. A stipulated appointment often occurs when the borrower is willing to walk away and the lender does not want a deed in lieu of foreclosure, or to ever take title, for whatever reason.

During downturns in commercial real estate, many persons and companies call themselves receivers in order to supplement other lost income. In the most recent downturn some prospective "receivers" even offer to perform the services for free, in exchange for getting real estate listings, leasing commissions or other benefits. Many states, like California, specifically forbid receivers from making such agreements and require all receivers to swear that no such agreements were even discussed. While these infractions may not be disclosed or even noticed by the court they are potentially very damaging to the lender or servicer. The concept of a receiver is founded on the concept of an independent third party, and having other business relationships with either party virtually removes that detachment which is vital. Receivers should be even more fearful than lenders when it comes to risking a claim of lender liability.

State Court Receivership Basics

Through the appointment of a neutral third party to preserve, manage and/or liquidate a business or particular assets of a debtor -- pending a court's resolution of the claims in the underlying lawsuit -- receiverships offer interest holders and creditors a means of preserving and maximizing the value of their interests. A receiver can be appointed for a broad, general purpose, such as operating and liquidating a business, or for a narrow, more specific reason -- such as preserving real estate or personal property pending a foreclosure sale. Both federal and state courts have powers to appoint and manage receivers. This chapter discusses the procedural and substantive requirements, and related practical considerations commonly encountered in state court receiverships.

State Court Jurisdiction and Venue

A state court's jurisdiction is confined to the territorial boundaries of that state. The primary issue is not whether the court has general subject matter jurisdiction to appoint a receiver, but over what property the court, and thereby the receiver, can exert control. In addition, state venue statutes further govern where the lawsuit for which a receiver will be sought can be filed. For example, many states require that any foreclosure of a secured creditor's interest in real property be maintained in the county or counties in which the property or properties are located.

Procedure and Basis for Appointment of Receiver

The procedure and basis on which many state courts appoint receivers is analogous to what is required to obtain injunctive relief. A receiver can be appointed only as an *ancillary* remedy to the primary claims brought in the underlying lawsuit. As a result, the initial complaint is typically filed asserting primary claims for relief, such as breach of contract and foreclosure, and

Contributed By: Robert Hammeke of Husch Blackwell

a separate motion is filed seeking appointment of a receiver. As with other ancillary motions, a motion to appoint a receiver should be supported by an affidavit verifying the facts and legal basis for the relief sought. It is also advisable to support a motion to appoint a receiver with an affidavit identifying the proposed receiver's qualifications. The moving party should also file, or attach as an exhibit, a proposed order appointing receiver that clearly identifies the proposed receiver's role and responsibilities.

Statutory or Equitable Relief

State courts will apply state statutes and common law equitable principles when determining whether to appoint a receiver. Wide discretion is often provided to the court in deciding the form and evidence required to support an appointment. The statutory guidance provided to the court is also often very broad.

For example, Missouri's general receivership statute provides that:

> The court . . . shall have power to appoint a receiver . . . to keep and preserve any money or other thing deposited in court. . . and to keep and preserve all property and protect any business or business interest entrusted to him pending any legal or equitable proceeding concerning the same, subject to the order of the court.

The factors referenced by many courts when deciding whether to appoint a receiver include: 1) the fraudulent conduct on the part of defendant; 2) any imminent danger of the property being lost, concealed, injured, diminished in value, or squandered; 3) the inadequacy of available remedies; 4) the probability that harm to plaintiff by denial of appointment would be greater than injury to parties opposing appointment; 5) the plaintiff's probable success in the lawsuit and the possibility of irreparable injury to any parties' interests in the property; and 6) whether the interest of the party seeking appointment of a receiver will be protected by the receivership. Given the discretion granted to state court judges and the broad range of circumstances which determine the need to appoint a receiver, the facts of each case will dictate whether certain factors weigh more heavily than others.

Contractual Right to Appointment of Receiver

Most commercial loan security documents -- especially real property mortgages/deeds of trust and related assignments of rents -- grant the secured creditor the absolute right to appoint a receiver upon default by the debtor. Some state courts will simply appoint a receiver based on the parties' contract, while others will merely take the contract into account as a factor that favors appointing a receiver. Some states find that contractual consent to appointment of a receiver serves as a waiver of the defendant's right to challenge the appointment of a receiver.

General Role of Receiver and Who May and Should Act as Receiver

Most states identify few, if any, requirements for qualification to act as a receiver other than that the receiver be neutral and capable. A receiver is an officer of the court and not the representative of any party to the suit, including the party seeking the appointment. As an impartial third party, the receiver is not appointed for the benefit of any person or entity, but simply to protect property interests in specific assets. The court has discretion in whom to appoint as receiver. If there is no strong reason suggesting that the receiver is not appropriate, courts will often appoint a receiver proposed by the moving party. Some courts or judges, however, may have personal preferences -- or an approved list of receivers. It is important, therefore, that the moving party and its attorneys know whether a given court or judge has specific preferences.

Rights and Responsibilities of the Receiver

Order Appointing Receiver

The substantive rights, duties, and liabilities of the receiver are granted, defined, and limited by the order of the court appointing the receiver – an all-important guide and rulebook. Most state statutes provide broad rights, without specific enumerations, with regard to the powers that may be granted a receiver. A draft order appointing receiver should be submitted with the motion seeking appointment of the receiver, and the order should carefully define the assets of the receivership estate, including identification of the real and personal property in the receivership estate. The order should also carefully identify the rights of the receiver. A non-inclusive list of rights that should be considered for the order appointing receiver includes empowering the receiver with the right to:

- access the receivership property, including changing any locks, and the right to seek the sheriff's assistance to gain access;
- operate any business included in the receivership property;
- collect, maintain, protect, insure, sell, liquidate or otherwise dispose of receivership property in the ordinary course of business;
- take possession of bank and other accounts necessary for operation of any business included in the receivership property, and to open, transfer, and change all such accounts into the name of the receivership estate;
- hire professionals and employees to assist the receiver;
- take possession of licenses, permits, or other government issued documents necessary for the continued operation of any business included in the receivership property;
- enter into contracts in the name of the receivership estate necessary to effectuate the needs of the receivership--including contracts to store and protect property and contracts relating to the operation of any business included in the receivership property;
- borrow money from the moving party or other person or entities required to effectuate the needs of the receivership;

- collect any rents or profits relating to the receivership property;
- bring and prosecute all proper actions for the collection of rents, accounts receivable, and contract rights relating to the receivership property;

The order should also identify how expenses are to be paid and what authority or discretion the receiver has with regard to payment of pre-receivership expenses. Additionally, it should include injunctive language precluding the parties or third parties from interfering with the receiver or receivership estate. The order should also identify the receiver's reporting requirements and direct the receiver what to do if a bankruptcy is filed.

It is important to note that a receiver does not generally "step into the shoes of the property owner" -- except for the purposes of protecting and preserving the specific assets covered in the order. Other general obligations and liabilities of the property owner may not be included in the receivership.

Real and Personal Property Sales by Receivers in State Court

Because they have the right to take possession of and preserve a receivership property, courts also have the power to authorize a receiver to market and sell property in the receivership estate. Unless otherwise ordered by the court, the receiver can only sell the right, title and interest of the owner of the property. Note that the sale of goods and inventories as part of the ordinary course of business (as in retailing) do not require special approval. Because a receiver is an officer of the court, a receiver's sale is a judicial sale, and all parties with an interest in the property to be sold must be brought in as notice or defendant parties or otherwise consent to the sale. As with other aspects of the receivership, the court has broad discretion in determining the manner of disposition of the receivership property. In order to provide proper notice, opportunity to be heard, and an effective time, place, and manner for the sale, a state court may look to the state's statutes relating to the judicial sale of property -- either by judicial foreclosure or post-judgment judicial execution. As with other judicial sales, a receiver's sale generally requires confirmation by the state court before the purchaser acquires rights pursuant to such sale.

Sales by Receiver Free and Clear of Liens and Encumbrances

The majority of state courts have held that courts, in the proper circumstances, have the inherent power to authorize the sale of property in its control free and clear of liens. When the court authorizes that receivership property be sold free and clear of liens, the rights of the parties who are lienholders are preserved and transferred from the property sold to the proceeds of the sale -- with the same rank that such rights or liens bore to the original property. Some courts, however, will exercise the discretion to authorize a receiver sale of property free and clear of liens only in limited circumstances, such as only when the property will be sold for more than the amount of the debt owed on the liens on the property. Also, some state statutes empower the appointing court to order a receiver to sell property free and clear of liens if the encumbering liens are disputed and the property is at risk of deteriorating in value pending the lawsuit. State laws and court's attitudes regarding receiver sales free and clear of liens vary, so it is important that a party seeking appointment of a receiver for the ultimate purpose of selling property free and clear of liens know the legal landscape -- as well as the attitudes of any parties holding interests in the property to be sold.

Multi-State Receivership Issues for State Courts

Utilizing a state court to gain control over and manage property located in multiple states presents special challenges. The jurisdiction of a state court is confined to the territory of the state. When a receiver is appointed by a state court, therefore, the receiver is able to take control of the receivership assets only in that state. No uniform law exists through which a secured creditor, by direction of a state court, can gain jurisdiction and control over property located in another state. For this reason, multi-state jurisdiction and control is usually obtained by filing ancillary receivership lawsuits.

To obtain control over property located in a state other than the appointing state, a lawsuit must be first filed in the state in which the property is located. Each court in which a lawsuit is filed and appointment of a receiver sought independently exercises its jurisdiction and may use its state's law and practice. As a matter of comity, state courts often recognize the existence of other primary and ancillary receiverships and cooperate to maximize the management of the collective receivership estate.

Effect of Bankruptcy Filing on Receivership

Under the bankruptcy code, once a bankruptcy petition is filed, all actions involving the debtor or its property are stayed. To protect the exclusive jurisdiction of the bankruptcy court, a receiver with knowledge of the bankruptcy filing must not take any further action with regard to the property of the bankruptcy estate other than to preserve such property. The receiver shall also turn over the property of the bankruptcy estate and file an accounting relating to such property. The bankruptcy court can excuse the receiver from these requirements if this is in the best interests of the creditors of the bankruptcy debtor's estate, but will be cautious in disrupting the debtor in possession's right to possession and administration of property.

Advantages and Disadvantages of Receiverships v. Bankruptcy

One advantage of seeking the appointment of a receiver is the flexibility afforded by receivership law, which is less defined than bankruptcy law and allows the moving party leeway in crafting the scope and course of the receivership. A disadvantage, however, is that bankruptcy law, since it is clearly defined, is more predictable.

Another advantage of receiverships is a greater ability to define and manage the scope of the receivership. A receiver may be appointed to manage all aspects of a defendant's business, to preserve a single piece of property -- or for all things in between. The property to be included in the receivership estate, therefore, can vary depending on the needs of the receivership. The estate created by a bankruptcy case, however, is specific and includes "all legal or equitable interests of the debtor in property as of the commencement of the case."

Another benefit of receivership: a single interest holder or creditor can seek the appointment of a receiver, while the bankruptcy code requires three unsecured creditors to commence an involuntary bankruptcy. Additionally, receiverships offer the moving party more control over the management and administration of the at-issue property. In a Chapter 11, the debtor usually remains in possession, custody and control of the property of the bankruptcy estate, including the right to operate the business of the debtor. However in receivership actions, the moving party has the ability to recommend a receiver with the practical business experience and skills necessary for the receivership. Finally, in those states that recognize the contractual right to appoint a receiver, a receiver can be appointed as a matter of contract.

Bankruptcy has advantages in certain situations as well. In addition to the above-mentioned predictability, bankruptcy law affords other rights that may not be available in receivership. For example, bankruptcy law expressly states when property of the estate can be sold free and clear of interests in the property to be sold, while receivership law is less clear in this regard. Also, the receivership law in many states does not allow a receiver the right to each of the avoidance actions available in bankruptcy. State courts routinely appoint receivers when property is directly at-issue in the case, a suitable receiver is recommended, and the moving party is able to show that the receiver is needed to preserve the property sought to be included in the receivership estate.

If federal jurisdiction does not exist, state court jurisdictional limits will present particular challenges if the property to be included in the bankruptcy estate is located in multiple states.

Additionally, even if a receiver is appointed, the defendant holds the bankruptcy trump card for subsequent use, although the filing may trigger personal guarantees on what would otherwise be deemed non-recourse debt.

Federal Receivership Basics

For secured creditors, a federal receivership can offer the quickest and most cost effective method of gaining control over the collateral upon default. A federal receivership maintains the value of the collateral by allowing the business to continue to operate. The Receiver will preserve and protect the collateral as well as the financial integrity of the business as a going concern. In addition, the Receiver may be able to stabilize the operations to mitigate further potential losses.

Foreclosure actions are generally brought in the county in which the property is located, while state receivership actions are brought in the state in which the property is located. These remedies present logistical issues when collateral is located in multiple counties or states. Federal receivership actions may be commenced in the federal district of the state where the property is located or in the state of the borrower's principal place of business, and the Court will have jurisdiction over the borrower's property no matter where it is located.

Although federal receiverships are grounded in federal common law, there are several federal statutes governing such receiverships.

Appointment of a Receiver

Federal Jurisdiction

In order to initiate an action in the federal court, the federal court must have jurisdiction. Because a secured creditor's enforcement of its rights is not usually based upon a federal question (although federal district courts may appoint receivers in cases initiated by governmental entities for violation of federal laws), diversity and the minimum amount in controversy under Title 28 of the U.S. Code §1332 must exist in order to invoke the jurisdiction of a federal district court.

This means that the citizenship of the secured creditor must be different than the citizenship of each and every borrower and guarantor, if applicable, named in the action. If jurisdiction cannot be obtained, State receivership may be an alternative. If jurisdiction is established, the federal district court then has ancillary jurisdiction to appoint a Receiver, as well as ancillary subject matter jurisdiction over every suit the Receiver may subsequently initiate.

Procedurally, to have a Receiver appointed, the secured creditor will first file suit against the borrower for breach of contract. If there is a personal guaranty of the borrower's obligations to the secured creditor, the guarantor may be included in the complaint as well. Once the breach of contract suit is filed, the secured creditor will then file a motion to appoint a Receiver, supported by an affidavit alleging the basis for the relief requested. In many states, including Michigan, a suit for breach of contract cannot be combined with a count for foreclosure; the secured creditor must decide whether to initiate the suit or begin foreclosure.

The act of appointing a Receiver is analogous to the entry of an injunction; it is an extraordinary remedy that lies in the discretion of the court and should be employed with the utmost caution and granted only in cases in which there is a clear necessity to protect a plaintiff's interest in property.

The following factors are usually weighed by the court to determine whether a Receiver should be appointed:

- the existence of a valid claim by the moving party;
- fraudulent conduct on the part of the defendant;
- imminent danger that property may be lost, concealed, injured, diminished in value, or squandered;
- an inadequacy of the available legal remedies;
- the probability that harm to plaintiff by denial of the appointment is greater than the injury to the parties opposing appointment;
- plaintiff's probable success in the action; and
- possibility of irreparable injury to plaintiff's interest in the property.

Role of the Receiver
Once the Receiver is appointed by the federal court, he/she becomes an officer of the court who manages and operates the property according to the laws of the state where the property is located.

In addition, the Receiver may be sued with respect to any of the acts taken or transactions engaged in while carrying on the business as a Receiver, according to 28 U.S.C §959(a). An action for possession of property held by the Receiver, however, is outside the scope of the section. Generally, the decision of whether to allow a third party action to be brought in a separate action is within the discretion of the court appointing the Receiver.

The court has broad powers and wide discretion to determine appropriate relief in an equity receivership. These broad powers enable the court to effectively supervise a receivership and protect the interests of its beneficiaries. As a court of equity, it has the authority in appropriate circumstances to impose broad stays of all actions against the entities in receivership, except by leave of the receivership court. There is no inherent limitation in receivership law regarding the amount of control that a Receiver may wield over that which the Receiver was appointed. The Receiver may be appointed over an entity or specific collateral.

Effect of Appointment of a Receiver

Control over receivership property. Once appointed, the Receiver is required to post a bond, which vests the Receiver with complete jurisdiction and of all property, personal and real, with the right to take possession of all property over which the Receiver is appointed. The secured creditor will usually request to have Receiver appointed only with respect to its collateral.

Jurisdiction by courts not appointing the Receiver. 28 U.S.C. § 1692 allows nationwide service in a federal receivership, and the territorial jurisdiction of the appointing court extends to any judicial district in which receivership property is found. At least one court has held that 28 U.S.C. §754 is broad enough to include actions initiated by a Receiver appointed outside the United States.

Filing Requirements for Extra Territorial Jurisdiction.
28 U.S.C. §754 states that within 10 days after entry of the appointment order, a Receiver must file a copy of the complaint and the order appointing the Receiver in the district for each district in which property is located. The statute further provides that failure to file such copies in any district divests the Receiver of jurisdiction and control over all of the property in that district. The Court of Appeals for the Ninth Circuit, in S.E.C. v American Capital Investments, Inc., 98 F.3d 1133, 1143 (9th Cir. 1996), has held that a separate 10-day period for filing the complaint and order appointing the Receiver runs from each date on which (a) an interim Receiver is appointed, and (b) a permanent Receiver is appointed.

The majority of courts considering §754, however, have held that failure of a Receiver to timely file the required documents is not fatal and does not divest the court of jurisdiction once the documents are properly filed.

Sales of Assets by a Receiver

The sales of assets by a Receiver are governed by 28 U.S.C. §§ 2001, 2002, 2004. The statutory provisions governing the sale of assets are very specific with respect to certain requirements (e.g. notice provisions, appraisals), but vague with respect to the procedures to be employed in the sales, thereby allowing for flexibility and creativity. In addition, under federal law, there is no right of redemption from judicial sales under 28 U.S.C §2001(b).

Sale of Real Property

A Receiver may use a public sale or a private sale to sell real property. A public sale must occur in the district where the Receiver was appointed, or in some other district, if the court so orders. In addition, the terms and conditions of the sale will be as directed by the court. Notice of a public sale must be approved by the court, and published at least once a week for four weeks prior to the sale, in at least one newspaper in general circulation in the county, state or judicial district where the property is located. A private sale may occur if the court determines that it is in the best interest of the estate. As with a public sale, the terms and conditions of the sale will be as directed by the court. In a private sale, however, the court must appoint three disinterested appraisers to appraise each parcel of property. The originally proposed offer will not be confirmed by the court unless the sales price is two-thirds of the appraised value, or if another offer of at least 10 percent over the original offer is received. Notice of the private sale must also be approved by the court and published in a newspaper of general circulation at least ten days prior to the hearing on the confirmation of the sale.

Sale of Personal Property

The sale of personal property is governed by the same rules as that for the sale of real property, unless the court orders otherwise. 28 U.S.C. §2004 gives the district court discretion as to whether appraisals are required to sell personal property.

Application of the Statutes by the Courts

Courts are generally liberal with respect to receivership sales. Courts have stated that a judicial sale made with notice and in the manner prescribed by law will not be denied confirmation or be set aside for mere inadequacy in price unless the price is so gross as to shock the conscience of the court, coupled with slight additional circumstances indicating unfairness such as chilled bidding.

Receiver's Responsibilities

The role of the Receiver must be defined in the order appointing the Receiver. The order will usually contain provisions relating to, among other things:

- the type and frequency of financial reporting;
- the manner and amount that the Receiver will be paid;
- actions that may be taken by the Receiver without court authority;
- a requirement that utility companies continue to provide service; and
- authorization for the Receiver to take complete possession and control of all books and records as well as cash and cash equivalents.

The Receiver's ability to pursue certain causes of action on behalf of the receivership estate also needs to be considered. Although there is no federal authority for a Receiver to avoid and recover preferential transfers, or avoid unperfected liens, receivers have standing to assert state fraudulent conveyance theories to recover property for the receivership estate. In addition, a Receiver may be able to bring certain actions against third parties that a bankruptcy trustee, debtor in possession or committee cannot.

Contrast to State Receiverships

State court receiverships are governed by state law, under a particular statute, rule or general equitable authority. The state court and/or the governing statute and/or rules prescribe the procedures for initiating the action, the role of the Receiver, the priority of claims and distribution of proceeds in the receivership. The remedy may be invoked not only to oversee the liquidation of an insolvent debtor, but to resolve shareholder disputes and management deadlocks. State court receivers may be granted the authority to operate a business, although more typically, they are empowered only to liquidate assets and distribute proceeds.

Alabama

Foreclosure Summary

Security Instrument	Mortgage
Judicial	Yes (Rare)
Non-Judicial	Yes
Initial Public Notice	Publication
Time Frame	Varies by process; 30-60 Days
Redemption Period	Yes-12 Months
Deficiency	Allowed

Receivership Summary

Ancillary Remedy Necessary	Yes
Ex-Parte	Yes
Approximate Time for Appointment	10-30 Days
Who or What can act as Receiver	No Restrictions Given
Specific Receiver Requirements	No
Is there any approval list for Receivers	No
Out of State Receivers Allowed	Yes

Foreclosure:

I. General Information:

Ala. Code § 35-10-1 (1991) et seq. governs foreclosures in Alabama.

II. Judicial Foreclosure Basics:

Alabama permits judicial foreclosures, though this remedy is rarely used.

III. Non-Judicial Foreclosure Basics:

This is the primary foreclosure remedy practiced in Alabama. The non-judicial foreclosure is used when a power of sale clause exists in a mortgage or deed of trust.

IV. Guidelines for Power of Sale:

See sections X through XI below.

V. Power of Sale Guidelines as Represented in the Security:

Where a power to sell lands is given to the grantee in any mortgage, or other conveyance intended to secure the payment of money, the power is part of the security, and may be executed by any person, or the personal representative of any person who, by assignment or otherwise, becomes entitled to the money thus secured; and a conveyance of the lands sold under such power of sale to the purchaser at the sale, executed by the mortgagee, any assignee or other person entitled to the money thus secured, his agent or attorney, or the auctioneer making the sale, vests the legal title thereto in such purchaser. Probate judges shall index foreclosure deeds by the names of the original grantor and grantee in the mortgage, and also by the names of the grantor and grantee in the foreclosure deeds.

VI. Guidelines for Foreclosure When There is No Power of Sale:

If no power of sale is granted in the mortgage, in our experience, the better practice is to file a judicial foreclosure action.

VII. Foreclosure When Instrument Contains No Power of Sale:

If no power of sale is contained in a mortgage or deed of trust, the grantee or any assignee thereof, at his option, after condition broken, may foreclose same either in a court having jurisdiction of the subject matter, or by selling for cash at the courthouse door of the county where the property is situated, to the highest bidder, the lands embraced in said mortgage or deed of trust, after notice of the time, place, terms and purpose of such sale has been given by four consecutive weekly insertions of such notice in some newspaper published in the county wherein said lands, or a portion thereof are situated.

VIII. Any Additional Satisfaction Permitted Under Continuing Power of Sale:

The sale of any part of the property conveyed by mortgage, either under power of sale contained in the mortgage, or by foreclosure, shall operate as a foreclosure of the mortgage only as to the property sold, and if the mortgage indebtedness is not thereby satisfied in full, the other property contained in the mortgage continues as security for the mortgage debt and there may be a further foreclosure of the mortgage, either by sale under power of sale or by foreclosure. Every power of sale contained in the mortgages hereafter executed shall, unless otherwise expressly provided therein, be held to give a continuing power of sale authorizing the mortgagee or his assignee after the law day of the mortgage to sell the mortgaged property from time to time in separate lots or parcels as it comes into his possession.

IX. Sale Under Power Where Instrument is Silent as to the Place or Terms of Sale:

If a deed of trust or mortgage, with power of sale, is silent as to the place or terms of sale, or as to the character or mode of notice, a sale may be made at the courthouse door of the county wherein the land is situated, after condition broken, for cash to the highest bidder, after 30 days' notice of the time, place and terms of sale by publishing such notice once a week for four consecutive weeks in a newspaper published in the county wherein said lands or property in said mortgage or deed of trust are situated.

X. Notice of Sale and How Notice is Given:

Notice of said sale shall be given in the manner provided in such mortgage or deed of trust or in this Code in the county where the mortgagor resides and the land, or a part thereof, is located; but, if said mortgagor does not reside in the county where the land or any part thereof is located, then such notice must be published in the county where said land, or any material part thereof, is located; provided, that notice of all sales under powers of sale contained in mortgages and deeds of trust executed after July 1, 1936, where the amount secured is $500.00 or more, shall be given by publication once a week for three successive weeks in some newspaper published in the county in which such land or any portion thereof is situated, and said notice of sale must give the time, place and terms of said sale, together with a description of the property to be sold.

For all mortgages executed after December 31, 1988: Notice of said sale shall be given in the county where said land is located. Notice of all sales under this article shall be given by publication once a week for three successive weeks in a newspaper published in the county or counties in which such land is located. If there is land under the mortgage in more than one county the publication is to be made in all counties where the land is located. The notice of sale must give the time, place and terms of said sale, together with a description of the property. If no newspaper is published in the county where the lands are located, the notice shall be placed in a newspaper published in an adjoining county. The notice shall be published in said adjoining county for three successive weeks.

XI. Place and time for Conducting Foreclosure by Power of Sale:

All sales of real estate, under powers of sale contained in mortgages and deeds of trust shall be held in the county where all or part of said real estate is situated. For mortgages executed after December 31, 1988, the power to sell lands must be

 Contributed By: James Woodard of Burr & Forman LLP

exercised at the appropriate courthouse door considered the front or main door to the courthouse, of the county where the mortgaged land or a substantial and material part thereof, is located. The sale shall be held between the hours of 11 A.M. and 4 P.M. on the day designated for the exercise of the power to sell the land.

Relevant Codes, Statutes, and Case Law:
Alabama Code § 6-5-230; Alabama Code § 35-10-1 through Alabama Code § 35-10-3 (1991); Alabama Code § 35-10-6 through Alabama Code § 35-10-8 (1991); Alabama Code § 35-10-13 through Alabama Code § 35-10-15.

Receivership:

I. General Information:

Alabama Code provides that a Receiver may be appointed by the circuit court judge and by the register or clerk in the absence of the judge, upon application in writing. The applicant must post a bond in an amount decided by the judge. Any person who is damaged by the appointment of the Receiver may recover by an action on the bond if the court later vacates the appointment.

A court cannot appoint a Receiver unless a suit is pending. The purpose of a Receivership is intended to prevent injury, waste, or destruction of the property of all parties. Three requirements must be met before a court may appoint a Receiver: (1) a clear legal right to be protected; (2) no other adequate remedy; and (3) a showing that the complainants will otherwise sustain irrevocable damage. The petition for a Receiver will be granted only if there is the reasonable probability that the plaintiff will ultimately succeed in obtaining the general relief sought by his lawsuit.

II. Appointing the Receiver:

A. The Basics:

Since the court cannot appoint a Receiver unless a suit is pending the party seeking appointment of a Receiver should file a complaint, including a count for the appointment of a Receiver. The asking party should also file a separate motion for the appointment of a Receiver.

Depending on the exigencies of the circumstances, it may also be advisable to file a motion for expedited hearing. Courts will generally grant the motion for expedited hearing and direct that service of the motion for appointment of a Receiver be made with the complaint.

A motion for appointment of a Receiver can be filed in conjunction with the complaint.

B. Time Frame for Appointment:
Depending on whether a motion for expedited hearing is filed, anywhere from 10 to 30 days.

C. Can you go in Ex Parte?
A Receiver may be appointed through an Ex Parte motion with the show of good cause. The applicant must convey a strong case of pressing emergency and peril or that giving notice of the hearing to appoint the Receiver would jeopardize the property.

III. Loans and Advances:
Alabama case law recognizes that a Receiver may borrow money pursuant to court order. Though it is not necessary to secure such advances to a Receiver, Alabama law does recognize the use Receivership certificates for such indebtedness.
Although case law recognizes that a Receiver may borrow money, it is advisable to include a provision in the order that states the Receiver is authorized to do so and that it be secured by a first priority lien on the Receivership property.

IV. Sales During the Receivership:
Alabama has no specific statute governing the sale of property by a receiver. As a result, we typically file receivership actions in federal court and follow the federal procedures governing for public or private receiver sales. *See* 28 U.S.C. §§ 2001-2002. Pursuant to these statutory provisions, the receiver would have to petition the court for approval of the sale and the sale procedures.

V. Liens Against Receivership Property:

A. General Information:

Under Alabama law, a receiver's sale is in the nature of a judicial sale, and property sold by such means is generally subject to the liens of record.

In order to properly be "of record," the lien must comply with the statutory requirements provided in Title 35, Chapter 11, Article 5 of the Code of Alabama (1975).

Notwithstanding the foregoing, Alabama Code § 6-6-624 provides, in relevant part, that the appointment of a receiver works to invalidate liens attaching to the receivership property within sixty (60) days prior to such appointment. While this statute has not been the subject of recent litigation, the Alabama Supreme Court has interpreted and applied this statute literally.

B. Dealing with Liens during Receivership:

Alabama law governing the impact of a receiver's sale on liens is not entirely clear. While there is no guarantee that a receiver's sale would be free and clear of liens, a receiver may move for the sale to be free and clear of all liens (although this may result in objections from the junior lien holders). A receiver may also use Ala. Code §6-6-624 as a basis to dissolve liens that attached within the sixty-day time frame prior to his appointment.

Also, federal courts have held that "one having no lien when a receiver was appointed cannot acquire one after the appointment on property in the hands of the receiver, and thus obtain a preference, and this is the rule, even though the right to acquire the lien existed before the appointment."

Thus, provided that federal law applies, a receiver may move to dissolve liens attaching during the receivership.

VI. Owners Associations:

There is no specific Alabama case law or statute dealing with the interaction between receiverships and owners' associations.

VII. Construction Related to Receivership Property:

There is no specific Alabama case law or statute dealing with the ability of receivers to initiate or continue construction on receivership property. In moving to have a receiver appointed, the movant should expressly seek to have the receiver vested with such power, and should also ensure that the order appointing the receiver includes a provision governing the terms of the receiver's construction efforts, including, for example, considerations for construction budgets and/or performance goals.

VIII. Ending the Receivership:

In our experience, the better practice is to file a motion to close out the Receivership as opposed to adding language in the Order Appointing Receiver allowing it to close itself out once the deed has been filed. This way a court order will formally end the Receivership. Also, the court will usually require a final accounting from the Receiver.

IX. Miscellaneous:

A.

It is advisable to include a provision that the Receiver is authorized to market and sell Receivership property subject to prior court approval.

B.

The commencement of proceedings for appointment of a Receiver of a corporation or partnership dissolves all uncompleted attachments and levies of execution made within the proceeding sixty days. (appointment of Receiver for corporation in federal court within sixty days after levy of attachment in state court proceeding dissolved attachment).

Relevant Codes, Statutes, and Case Law:
Ala. Code § 6-6-620 through Ala. Code § 6-6-628 Ala. Code § 35-11-210-218

Brooks v. Everett, 124 So. 2d 100, 105 (Ala. 1960); C.E. Dev. Co. v. Kitchens, 264 So. 2d 510 (1972); Carter v. State ex rel. Bullock County, 393 So. 2d 1368 (Ala. 1981); Ex parte Goodwyn, 149 So. 216 (1933); Grand Lodge, K.P. v. Shorter, 122 So. 36 (1929). Hunter v. Parkman, 34 So. 2d 221 (Ala. 1948); Martin Oil Co., Inc. v. Clokey, 277 So.2d 343 (Ala. 1973; Preuit v. Wallace, 189 So. 887 (1939); Stallworth v. Andalusia Hospital, 470 So. 2d 1158 (Ala. 1985); Dependable Ins. Co. v. Kirkpatrick, 514 So.2d 804, 806 (Ala. 1984) (citing *Barber v. Beckett,* 39 So.2d 17, 19 (Ala. 1949*)); See Pratt v. Deepwater Coal & Iron Co., 134 So. 854, 855 (Ala. 1931) (appointment of receiver for corporation in federal court within sixty days after levy of attachment in state court proceeding dissolved the attachment of the receivership property); Lehman v. Heberle, 9 F. Supp. 100, 101 (D.C. N.Y. 1934); see also U.S. v. Houston, 1977 WL 1295 (E.D. Wis. 1977); Quinn v. Bancroft-Jones Corporation, 12 F.2d 958 (D.C. N.Y.1926).*

Alaska

Foreclosure Summary

Security Instrument	Mortgage
Judicial	Yes
Non-Judicial	Yes
Initial Public Notice	Notice of Sale
Time Frame	7 Months
Redemption Period	No redemption after a non-judicial foreclosure. After the confirmation of a judicial sale the trustor has a one year redemption period; junior lienors have sixty days.
Deficiency	May collect on a deficiency after judicial foreclosure through normal judicial remedies

Receivership Summary

Ancillary Remedy Necessary	Yes
Ex-Parte	Yes
Approximate Time for Appointment	Depends on the Court
Who or What can act as Receiver	No Restrictions Given
Specific Receiver Requirements	No
Is there any approval list for Receivers	No
Out of State Receivers Allowed	Yes

Foreclosure:

I. Non-judicial Foreclosure Summary:

A Notice of Default (NOD) is recorded after the deed of trust is thirty days or more in default. Within ten days, a copy of the NOD must be sent by certified mail to all parties with an interest in the property and posted on the property. A Notice of Sale must be posted in three public places and published once a week for four consecutive weeks. Sale is by outcry auction not less than ninety days after the NOD was recorded.

II. Judicial Foreclosure Summary:

Proceeds as a regular civil lawsuit, beginning with filing and service of a summons and complaint and culminating in a money judgment and a decree of foreclosure and order for sale of the property. Notice of the sale is posted and published as with non-judicial foreclosures, but the sale must be confirmed by the court.

III. Deficiencies:

No further "action or proceeding" to collect a deficiency is allowed after a non-judicial foreclosure except for certain federal agencies with national loan programs, although other collateral pledged to secure the same debt may be realized only if this can be done non-judicially. The foreclosing mortgagee may collect on a deficiency after a judicial foreclosure through normal judicial remedies, although no separate deficiency judgment is entered.

Receivership:

I. General information:

A receiver may only be appointed in connection with an underlying action. Alaska Statute § 09.40.240 provides that a receiver generally may be appointed by a court in connection with any type of action, except an action for the recovery of specific personal property. A receiver may not be appointed where another remedy exists.

II. Appointing the Receiver:

A. The Basics:

A receiver may be appointed in any action, except in an action for the recovery of specific personal property:

1. provisionally before judgment when a party's right to the property that is the subject of the action and is in the possession of an adverse party is probable and where it is shown that the property or its profits are in danger of being lost or materially injured;

2. after judgment, to carry the judgment into effect;

3. after judgment to dispose of the property according to the judgment, to preserve it during the pendency of an appeal, or when an execution has not been satisfied and the judgment debtor refuses to apply its property to satisfy the judgment;

4. when a corporation is insolvent or is in imminent danger of being insolvent, has been dissolved, or has forfeited its corporate rights;

5. when a debtor has been declared insolvent; and

6. in a partnership, to receive distributions that will become due to a judgment debtor in respect of the partnership and to take all other actions the judgment debtor may have taken or that may be required.

Contributed By: Erin Eliasen & Richard Goldfarb
of Stoel Rives

B. Time Frame for Appointment:

This varies by the practice of the particular court and judge. A hearing on the appointment of a receiver is on such notice as the court may prescribe.

C. Can you go in Ex Parte?

Ex parte orders appear to be authorized; however, they are limited in use.

III. Loans and Advances:

No statues or rules govern loans or advances and the Order of Appointment will govern the receiver's authority to obtain loans or issue advances.

IV. Sales During the Receivership:

There are no statutes or case law related to sales during the receivership.

V. Liens Against Receivership Property:

There are no statutes or case law related to sales during the receivership.

VI. Owners Associations:

There are no statutes or case law related to sales during the receivership.

VII. Construction Related to Receivership Property:

There is no formal process.

VIII. Ending the Receivership:

Pursuant to Alaska's rules of civil procedure an action where a receiver has been appointed cannot be terminated except by order of the court. In addition, prior to the court's discharge of the receiver, the receiver will conduct a final accounting of the receivership property and the court will approve that accounting.

IX. Miscellaneous:

Orders granting or denying the appointment or discharge of a receiver are immediately appealable.

Relevant Codes, Statutes or Case Law:
Statutes: Alaska Statute § 09.40.240, Alaska Statute § 09.40.250, Alaska Statute § 32.06.504(a)

Cases: *Sourdough Dev. Services Inc. v. Riley,* 85 P.3d 463 (Alaska 2004)
Mathis v. Meyers, 574 P.2d 447 (Alaska 1978);
First Bank Nat'l of Fairbanks v. Dual, 392 P.2d 463 (Alaska 1964);

Contributed By: Erin Eliasen & Richard Goldfarb of Stoel Rives

Arizona

Foreclosure Summary

Security Instrument	Trust Deed/ Mortgage
Judicial	Yes (Sometimes)
Non-Judicial	Yes
Initial Public Notice	Notice of Sale
Time Frame	Minimum 91 days; typically 120 days
Redemption Period	No
Deficiency	Varies

Receivership Summary

Ancillary Remedy Necessary	No
Ex-Parte	Yes
Approximate Time for Appointment	2- 4 weeks unless ex parte relief is warranted
Who or What can act as Receiver	Corporate/ Individual
Specific Receiver Requirements	Receiver must post bond prior to commencing Duties
Is there any approval list for Receivers	No
Out of State Receivers Allowed	Yes

Foreclosure:

I. General Information:

Deeds of trust are the primary form of security instrument used in Arizona. Unlike mortgages, which may only be foreclosed judicially by civil action (judicial foreclosure), deeds of trust may be foreclosed judicially or by exercising the trustee's power of sale (non-judicial foreclosure). Foreclosure is an available remedy in the event of a monetary or non-monetary default regardless of the form of security instrument.

In addition to the applicable statutory foreclosure process, the loan documents may provide additional notice and cure rights to the borrower and other parties. In particular, especially with larger, multi-property portfolio loans and some multi-family loans, mezzanine lenders, ground lessors and limited partners may be afforded special notice and cure rights under the loan documents.

II. Judicial Foreclosure Basics:

A judicial foreclosure is a civil suit to obtain a court order to foreclose on the collateral. Despite several advantages associated with judicial foreclosures, including the ability to enforce acceleration of the indebtedness, establishing the validity of the security instrument and the underlying indebtedness, and establishing lien priorities, judicial foreclosures are rarely used because they are expensive, time consuming (typically 9-11 months), and lack finality since the mortgagor or trustor and junior lien holders have the right to redeem the property during a period of up to six months after the sheriff's sale.

III. Non-Judicial Foreclosure Basics:

A non-judicial foreclosure is conducted by the trustee and may be held as early as 91 days after recording the notice of sale. Non-judicial foreclosure is relatively inexpensive, it eliminates

Contributed By: Jeffrey Pitcher, Andrew Harnisch
and Daniel Weber of Ballard Sphar

liens junior to the security instrument being foreclosed, and the trustee's sale is not followed by a statutory redemption period. Some of the disadvantages of a non-judicial foreclosure are that there is no judicial determination of lien priority and the secured indebtedness cannot truly be accelerated since a deed of trust may be reinstated by the trustor and junior lien holders at any time up to 5 p.m. mountain standard time on the last business day before the trustee's sale. Reinstatement does not require the payment of principal amounts that would not have been due had no default occurred even though the loan was accelerated.

IV. Power of sale foreclosure guidelines

A trustee's sale guaranty (TSG) is obtained from a title insurance company prior to recording the notice of sale. The TSG provides a schedule of title exceptions as well as the information that is needed for the trustee to prepare the notice of sale and otherwise comply with the statutory notice requirements (e.g. the names and addresses of the parties that are entitled to receive notice of the sale and the names of newspapers of general circulation). The TSG is not a title insurance policy and is meant merely for purposes of the trustee's sale. The premium for the TSG is based upon the unpaid principal balance of the loan and is due when the TSG is issued.

The notice of sale sets the sale date, time and location of the sale and identifies the property to be sold by the trustee by its legal description, tax parcel number and street address. The notice of sale is recorded in each county where the real property is located and mailed, along with a statement of breach, to the trustor, beneficiary, and other parties with an interest in the property or who have requested notice. The notice of sale is also published in a newspaper of general circulation and posted on the property and at the courthouse. The sale may be postponed for successive periods of up to 90 days without the need to record a new notice of sale or repeat the pre-sale notice requirements.

The property is sold at public auction for cash to the highest bidder. The beneficiary may credit bid up to the full amount due under the loan documents. Payment in full is due from the winning bidder by 5:00 p.m. mountain standard time on the next day other than a Saturday or legal holiday. After the sale and payment of bid, the trustee will deliver a trustee's deed upon sale to the winning bidder within 7 business days. If the trustee's deed is properly recorded within 15 days after the date of the sale, the trustee's sale is deemed perfected at the appointed date and time of the sale. Any action for a deficiency judgment must be brought within 90 days of the sale.

In many cases, title coverage under an existing lender's policy continues in favor of the lender, or a subsidiary of the lender, who acquires the property by foreclosure. The coverage is as of the date of the lender's title policy and is usually limited to actual losses or damages not exceeding the lesser of the stated coverage amount and the balance of the secured debt plus interest, foreclosure expenses and protective advances. The lender's policy continues to be subject to the loss rules of the policy, which essentially require the lender to establish an impairment of its security as a result of the claimed title defect.
A lender may elect to purchase a new owner's policy following a trustee's sale if (1) the lender wishes to update the effective date of the coverage, (2) the foreclosure is complicated and/or bankruptcy filings or other events raise questions as to whether a particular title issue affects the property, (3) the issuer of the lender's policy no longer exists or is not sufficiently creditworthy to handle a claim in the amount of the lender's exposure to the property, or (4) the lender takes title to the property in an affiliate that does not fall within the affiliate coverage provisions of the lender's policy. Forty percent of the cost of the TSG is applied as a discount to the premium charged for the issuance of an owner's policy if the owner's policy is issued within one year of the trustee's sale. If the lender sells the property within five years of the issuance of the owner's policy a reduced premium is charged for the owner's policy issued in connection with that transfer. Currently the reissue rate in Arizona is 25% of the premium charged for the first owner's policy.

While the trustee or beneficiary may file and maintain an action to foreclose the deed of trust at any time before the property has been sold under the power of sale, a sale of the property under the power of sale may not be held after an action to foreclose the deed of trust has been filed unless the foreclosure action has been dismissed

V. Power of sale constitutes part of security

A power of sale is conferred upon the trustee of a deed of trust by virtue of the trustee's position and that power may be exercised by the trustee without expressly detailing such power in the deed of trust.

Regardless of any language in a mortgage permitting foreclosure by power of sale, a mortgage must be foreclosed judicially.

VI. No Power of sale foreclosure guidelines

All mortgages must be foreclosed judicially by civil action that is subject to the Rules of Civil Procedure as well as the statutory foreclosure requirements. Competing liens should be identified before preparing the foreclosure complaint. This is accomplished by purchasing a foreclosure title report from a title company. Before filing a foreclosure action, the lender must first comply with all notice and cure requirements under the loan documents and then provide written notice to the debtor that the debt has been accelerated. Although a written acceleration notice may not be required under the loan documents, it is good practice to provide such a notice to the debtor before filing the complaint.

At the time the complaint is filed with the court, a *lis pendens* is filed in the county where the property is located to give notice to subsequent encumbrancers and purchasers of the pending foreclosure action. The foreclosure action should be brought in the county where the real property is located and include all necessary and proper parties (e.g. any person with an interest that was recorded before the notice of *lis pendens* was recorded and that is junior to the security instrument to be foreclosed).

When a security instrument is foreclosed, the court gives judgment for the entire amount due, and directs the mortgaged property, or as much thereof as is necessary to satisfy the judgment, to be sold. A writ of special execution is issued to the sheriff ordering the sale of the property. The sheriff delivers and posts notices of sale identifying the time and place of the sale. The property is sold at the sale for cash to the highest bidder. The lender may credit bid up to the full amount due under the loan documents. Payment of the bid price plus statutory fees is due from the winning bidder within five working days after the sale. The judgment debtor (i.e. the mortgagor or trustor) and junior lien holders have the right to redeem the property during a period of up to six months after the sheriff's sale. The redemption period for the judgment debtor and its successors in interest may be reduced to 30 days if the court determined, as part of its judgment under which the sale was made, that the property was both abandoned and not used primarily for agricultural or grazing purposes. If the judgment debtor or its successor does not redeem the property then, within five days after the expiration of such redemption period, the senior creditor having a lien upon the property may redeem the property, and, failing such, each subsequent lien holder, in the order of its lien priority, may redeem the property within five days after the expiration of the redemption period of the immediately preceding lien holder. If the property is not redeemed, the sheriff will deliver to the purchaser a deed to the property after the expiration of applicable redemption periods.

VII. Foreclosure when instrument contains no power of sale.

A power of sale is conferred upon the trustee of a deed of trust by virtue of the trustee's position and that power may be exercised by the trustee without expressly detailing such power in the deed of trust.

VIII. Additional satisfaction permitted under continuing power of sale.

Not applicable.

Contributed By: Jeffrey Pitcher, Andrew Harnisch and Daniel Weber of Ballard Sphar

IX. Sale under power where instrument silent as to place or terms of sale.

By statute, the sale must be held between 9:00 a.m. and 5:00 p.m. mountain standard time at a specified place on the trust property, or at a specified place at any building that serves as a location of the superior court, or at a specified place of business of the trustee, in any county in which part of the property to be sold is situated.

X. Notice of Sale and How notice of sale is given

The notice of sale is recorded in each county where the real property is located and mailed, along with a statement of breach, to the trustor, beneficiary, and other parties with an interest in the property or who have requested notice. The notice of sale is also published in a newspaper of general circulation and posted on the property and at the courthouse.

XI. Place and time for conducting foreclosure by power of sale.

By statute, the sale must be held between 9:00 a.m. and 5:00 p.m. mountain standard time at a specified place on the trust property, or at a specified place at any building that serves as a location of the superior court, or at a specified place of business of the trustee, in any county in which part of the property to be sold is situated.

Relevant Codes, Statutes or Case Law:
A.R.S. § 1-301; A.R.S. § 12-1281 et seq.; A.R.S. § 12-1621 et seq.; A.R.S. 33-721 et seq.; A.R.S. 33-801, A.R.S. 33-807 et seq.;

Receivership:

I. General information:

Arizona Revised Statutes (A.R.S.) § 33-702(B) provides that a security instrument may include an assignment of rents. After a default under the security instrument or any contract secured thereby, the assignment of rents may be enforced without regard to the adequacy of the security or the solvency of the mortgagor or trustor by the appointment of a receiver. A.R.S. § 33-807(C) provides that the trustee may file an action for the appointment of a receiver. The right to appointment of a receiver is independent of, and may precede, the exercise of any other right or remedy. The superior court may appoint a receiver to protect and preserve property or the rights of parties even if the action includes no other claim for relief (A.R.S. 12-1241).

II. Appointing the Receiver:

A. The Basics:

Appointment of a receiver is statutorily authorized, but the loan documents may add to (or lessen) the authorization and scope of permitted powers and duties of the receiver. A receivership action is independent of foreclosure and is commenced by filing a verified complaint and application for appointment of receiver with the superior court. An order to show cause hearing is usually set for a date that is two to four weeks after the complaint is filed, unless emergency or ex parte relief is requested.

B. Time Frame for Appointment:

An order to show cause is usually entered within two to three days after the complaint is filed and the date of the hearing is typically scheduled for a date that is two to four weeks after the complaint is filed.

A receiver can typically be appointed within two to four weeks if the appointment is uncontested. If the appointment is contested, the time period may be two to three months or more, depending on the need for discovery and the court's trial calendar.

A certificate of appointment is not issued by the clerk of the court until both an oath and bond are filed with the court. The receiver's bond protects interested parties from receiver mismanagement and/or malfeasance. There is no required formula for calculation of the bond amount, but courts generally require a bond in an amount approximately equal to one month's rent or one month's debt service.

C. Can you go in Ex Parte?

In extraordinary situations a receiver may be appointed without notice to the borrower. This typically requires some form of irreparable harm.

D. Receiver's action and reporting:

The receiver may, subject to the control of the court, commence and defend actions. The order may also require that the receiver obtain lender approval prior to commencing and defending actions.

A receivership may be terminated upon motion served with at least ten days' notice upon all parties who have appeared in the proceedings. The court in the notice of hearing may require that a final account and report be filed and served, and may require the filing of written objections.

III. Loans and Advances:

The Arizona Revised Statutes, Arizona Rules of Civil Procedure, and Arizona case law provide only a basic framework for the appointment and powers of a receiver. In general, these sources do not deal with specific powers such as incurring debt and obtaining advances. However, courts routinely approve orders that empower receivers to incur debt and/or obtain secured advances from the lender seeking appointment, subject to court and lender approval. As a result, if the need to obtain credit is anticipated, the party seeking appointment should include such powers in the order appointing the receiver.

The local practice for obtaining secured advances from the lender is for the receiver to issue receivership certificates to the lender reflecting the amount and priority of the receivership advances. These advances can be added to the lender's secured debt.

IV. Sales During the Receivership:

The appointment may permit the receiver to market and sell the property. The right to market and sell the property should be subject to the lender's approval. Any sale of the property should be conditioned on Court approval by motion served upon the borrower and other interested parties. Borrower consent is preferable, but not always required by the court or title underwriter. There are no express statutes or reported Arizona case law permitting or prohibiting receivership sales, but title insurance has generally been available after expiration of the appeal period applicable to the order approving the sale.

Presently, title underwriting standards are fluid with respect to sales by receivers. It is important to involve underwriting in the sales process to approve the proposed sale order and to confirm underwriting requirements. Certain title companies request that the borrower's members (in addition the borrower, the borrower's counsel and the borrower's statutory agent) be served with a copy of the motion to approve the sale. Obtaining written consent from the borrower, and its members, where possible, will accelerate the underwriting process and likely remove any requirements by the title company for appeal periods to expire.

V. Liens Against Receivership Property:

The order may permit the receiver to satisfy or contest liens on the property. Absent such authority, the receiver may ask the court for permission to satisfy or contest liens.

If construction has been performed on the property a title report should be purchased. If there are any recorded or anticipated mechanics' liens, the order can be drafted to include authority for the receiver to satisfy or contest those liens.

VI. Owners Associations:

A receiver is permitted to collect rents and pay the expenses of operating the property including ongoing association fees. The order may provide that payment of association fees that accrued prior to the appointment of the receiver is discretionary.

VII. Construction Related to Receivership Property:

The order may include the rights necessary for a receiver to authorize, oversee and supervise any ongoing or future construction, maintenance or repair of the property. Absent such authority, the receiver may ask the court for permission to engage in such activities.

VIII. Ending the Receivership:

Upon the foreclosure or other disposition of the property, or satisfaction of the underlying loan, the receiver must request discharge and may be required to file a final report and accounting.

The receiver must request discharge and may be required to file a final report and accounting.

Relevant Codes, Statutes or Case Law:
Arizona Rules of Civil Procedure 41(a) and 66; A.R.S. § 12-1241; A.R.S. § 33-702; A.R.S.

Arkansas

Foreclosure Summary

Security Instrument	Deed of Trust, Mortgage
Judicial	Yes
Non-Judicial	Yes
Initial Public Notice	Complaint
Time Frame	Typically 120 Days
Redemption Period	Varies
Deficiency	Varies

Receivership Summary

Ancillary Remedy Necessary	Yes
Ex-Parte	Rare
Approximate Time for Appointment	48 hours – multiple weeks
Who or What can act as Receiver	No Restrictions Given
Specific Receiver Requirements	No Restrictions Given
Is there any approval list for Receivers	No
Out of State Receivers Allowed	Yes

Foreclosure:

I. General Information:

Arkansas has both judicial and non-judicial foreclosure available to foreclose mortgages and deeds of trust, though non-judicial foreclosure is not widely used. After a default under the security instrument, the mortgagee or trustee may either seek judicial foreclosure or non-judicial foreclosure, but not both.

II. Judicial Foreclosure Basics:

In the judicial foreclosure process, the mortgagee brings a suit, and all interested persons must be made parties. If the court issues a decree of foreclosure of the mortgage or deed of trust, the property must be sold under Arkansas law.

Before the sale, notice must be published in a newspaper generally circulated in the county in which the property is situated at least ten days before the sale.

There is no minimum bid for a judicial foreclosure. Traditionally, if the bid "shocks the conscious of the court," it is too low.

Arkansas has a statutory right of redemption for one year after for judicial foreclosures, but that is rarely an issue, as the right of redemption can be waived in the security instrument, so essentially every mortgage and deed of trust signed in the state of Arkansas contains a clause wherein the mortgagor waives his right to redemption.

III. Non-Judicial Foreclosure Basics:

The non-judicial foreclosure statutes are strictly construed, so the statutes should be carefully reviewed and followed. Additionally, several of the Arkansas laws governing non-judicial foreclosures were amended in 2011, so some pre-2011 sources outlining non-judicial foreclosure requirements could be out of date.

Non-judicial foreclosure is only available when the mortgagee is a mortgage company, bank, or savings and loan.

IV. Power of sale foreclosure guidelines

Before the mortgagee can sell the property, the mortgage must be filed in the county where the trust property is situated, and there has to be a default under the security instrument. At least ten days before initiating the foreclosure, the mortgagee must mail to the mortgagor at the property address a copy of the note and mortgage, the name of the holder and location of the original note, information about the availability of loan modification or assistance programs, and, if the default is because of a missed payment, a payment history showing the date of default. Guidelines related to notice required and place and time of sale are listed below.

V. Power of sale constitutes part of security

Under Ark. Code Ann. § 18-50-115, as long as the instrument is recorded, a power of sale is implied. Arkansas statutes provide the guidelines for conducting a non-judicial foreclosure, as indicated below.

VI. No Power of sale foreclosure guidelines

Under Ark. Code Ann. § 18-50-115, as long as the instrument is recorded, a power of sale is implied. Arkansas statutes provide the guidelines for conducting a non-judicial foreclosure, as indicated below.

VII. Foreclosure when instrument contains no power of sale.

Under Ark. Code Ann. § 18-50-115, as long as the instrument is recorded, a power of sale is implied. Arkansas statutes provide the guidelines for conducting a non-judicial foreclosure, as indicated below.

VIII. Additional satisfaction permitted under continuing power of sale.

Under Ark. Code Ann. § 18-50-115, as long as the instrument is recorded, a power of sale is implied. Arkansas statutes provide the guidelines for conducting a non-judicial foreclosure, as indicated below.

IX. Sale under power where instrument silent as to place or terms of sale.

Under Ark. Code Ann. § 18-50-115, as long as the instrument is recorded, a power of sale is implied. Arkansas statutes provide the guidelines for conducting a non-judicial foreclosure, as indicated below.

X. Notice of Sale and How notice of sale is given

Ark. Code Ann. § 18-50-104 describes the contents of the notice and who must receive notice. The mortgagee must file notice of default and intent to sell in the county where the property is located. After recording the notice, the trustee must wait sixty days before selling the property. If applicable, the mortgagee has to certify that the mortgagors who applied for loan modification or forbearance does not qualify under any program offered by the mortgagee or a government agency (if the mortgagee participates in such a program).

At least ten days before the sale, the notice of default and intent to sell must be sent to the property address or mailing address of the mortgagor by certified and first class mail.

The notice of default and intention to sell must include the names of the parties to the mortgage or deed of trust, the legal description and street address of the trust property, the recording information for the mortgage or deed of trust, the default, a statement that the mortgagee intends to sell the property, the time, date and place of sale, and the name and contact information of the party initiating the foreclosure. The notice must also include a conspicuous warning as follows: "YOU MAY LOSE YOUR PROPERTY IF YOU DO NOT TAKE IMMEDIATE ACTION."

Within thirty days of recording the notice of default and intent to sell, the mortgagee must mail the notice to the mortgagor, any successor in interest if the successor's interest is recorded or if the mortgagee has actual notice, any lienholder subsequent to the interest of the mortgagee, when recorded or when the mortgagee has actual notice, and anyone who has properly requested notice under Arkansas law.

The notice must be posted in the newspaper (once a week for four consecutive weeks, but the final publication cannot be more than ten days before the sale), at the county courthouse, and on the internet.

XI. Place and time for conducting foreclosure by power of sale.

Ark. Code Ann. § 18-50-107 governs the manner of sale. The sale has to take place on the same date and at the same time and place indicated on the notice of default and intent to sell. The sale must be between 9:00 a.m. and 4:00 p.m. on a weekday and non-holiday. The sale can take place either at the trust property or the front door of the county courthouse of the county in which the trust party is situated.

Any person may bid at the sale. The sale has to be conducted by a third party licensed to sell real estate and to act as an auctioneer under Arkansas law. The minimum bid has to be at least 2/3 of the indebtedness.

Relevant Codes, Statutes or Case Law:
Ark. Code Ann. §§ 18-49-101 et seq. govern judicial foreclosure.
Ark. Code Ann. §§ 18-50-101 et seq. govern statutory foreclosure.

Receivership:

I. General information:

Arkansas receivership law is governed by Arkansas Rule of Civil Procedure 66.

II. Appointing the Receiver:

A. The Basics:

Under Arkansas law, a receiver is appointed for traditional equitable purposes, and a receiver can be appointed for any lawful purpose. Traditional equitable grounds include appointing a receiver when necessary to save property or money from being lost, removed, or materially damaged. The court has broad discretion in deciding whether a receiver should be appointed.

Contributed By: Melissa Bandy of Mitchell Williams

B. Time Frame for Appointment:

In the circumstance of appointing a receiver when foreclosing a mortgage, the request for receiver is often filed with the complaint, but a separate motion to appoint a receiver can be filed as well. The appointment of a receiver is rarely a means in itself, but it is not a requirement that the appointment of a receiver be ancillary to another cause of action. The request to appoint a receiver must include grounds for appointment. There has to be a prima facie showing that a receiver is required because of a danger that the property will be lost or materially injured, but the court does not have to hold an evidentiary hearing.

The time it takes for a receiver to be appointed varies and depends on the court's schedule. In an emergency situation, it is possible to file an emergency motion to appoint a receiver, and there can be a turnaround as quickly as 24-48 hours.

C. Can you go in Ex Parte?

In rare circumstances, a court may appoint a receiver ex parte. The party asking the court to do so must demonstrate that the circumstances are "exceptional."

D. Receiver's Action and Reporting:

The powers of the receiver do not begin until the receiver takes an oath to faithfully perform his duties and posts the bond.

A receiver may bring and defend actions, take and keep possession of property, receive rents, collect debts, and other actions as authorized by the court.

Under Rule 66(b), the receiver must make a report of his proceedings and actions and make an accounting for receivership money and property every six (6) months or at such other times as directed by the court. Any money or property collected by the receiver must be accounted for and deposited into court or otherwise be subject to the orders of the court. In Arkansas, a receiver is a fiduciary representing the court and all parties in interest.

III. Loans and Advances:

There aren't specific statutes dealing with these issues, but the order appointing the receivers can outline a receiver's ability to do these things.

IV. Sales During the Receivership:

There aren't specific statutes dealing with these issues, but the order appointing the receivers can outline a receiver's ability to do these things.

V. Liens Against Receivership Property:

A receiver takes property subject the owner's liabilities. Appointment of a receiver does not destroy a judgment or execution lien.

VI. Owners Associations:

No information provided.

VII. Construction Related to Receivership Property:

There aren't specific statutes dealing with these issues, but the order appointing the receivers can outline a receiver's ability to do these things.

VIII. Ending the Receivership:

A receiver may be removed for good cause, and the court may appoint a substitute receiver in that case. A receivership may be terminated at the court's discretion when the factual situation that necessitated the creation of a receivership no longer exists.

To end the receivership, the party should file a motion to discharge the receiver and the court can issue and order discharging a receiver.

Relevant Codes, Statutes or Case Law:

Relevant codes: Receivership is covered by Arkansas Rule of Civil Procedure 66. Ark. Code Ann. § 16-117-201 et seq. covers receivers but has been superseded by Rule 66.

There are many Arkansas cases addressing receivers. The list below is a selection of these cases:

Chapin v. Stuckey, 286 Ark. 359, 692 S.W.2d 609 (1985) (Rule 66 superseded statutes; appointment does not have to be ancillary to another cause of action).

Contributed By: Melissa Bandy of
Mitchell Williams

California

Foreclosure Summary

Security Instrument	Trust Deed
Judicial	Yes
Non-Judicial	Yes
Initial Public Notice	Judicial – complaint; Non-judicial – statutory notice of default
Time Frame	Judicial – 1 year or more; Non-judicial – 3 months and 20 days (minimum)
Redemption Period	Judicial – unless deficiency is waived, up to 1 year; Non-judicial – none
Deficiency	Judicial – yes; Non-judicial – no against borrower/trustor, but yes against guarantor

Receivership Summary

Ancillary Remedy Necessary	Yes
Ex-Parte	Yes
Approximate Time for Appointment	At least 16 court days for noticed hearing; at least 1 court day for ex parte
Who or What can Act as Receiver	Individuals
Specific Receiver Requirements	Oath and bond must be filed before receiver commences duties
Is there any Approval List for Receivers	Generally no
Out of State Receivers Allowed	Not prohibited

Foreclosure:

I. General Information:

In California, a defaulted real estate loan may be enforced by two types of foreclosure proceedings: (1) a judicial foreclosure action; and (2) a non-judicial foreclosure sale (also called a "trustee's sale"). For purposes of this discussion, we will assume that the borrower under the loan is also the trustor (the grantor) under the deed of trust securing the loan and that the property covered by the deed of trust is a commercial property.

A judicial foreclosure action, as the name implies, is a lawsuit that the lender files against the borrower in order to enforce its loan. A non-judicial foreclosure sale, which is authorized by the "power of sale" clause typically contained in the lender's deed of trust, is a mechanism that the lender uses to enforce its loan outside of court.

In California, non-judicial foreclosure is pursued to completion much more often than judicial foreclosure because, among other things, (1) a non-judicial foreclosure is generally quicker and less expensive to complete than a judicial foreclosure and (2) there is no post-sale right of redemption following a non-judicial foreclosure as there usually is following a judicial foreclosure. That said, it is not uncommon for a lender to launch both types of foreclosure simultaneously (known as "dual tracking"), using the judicial foreclosure action as a vehicle to obtain a receiver and/or proceed against the guarantor while relying on the non-judicial foreclosure process as the means by which the property is ultimately sold.

II. Judicial Foreclosure Basics:

A judicial foreclosure action is a lawsuit that the lender files against the borrower in order to enforce a defaulted real estate loan. Under California's one-action rule, a judicial foreclosure action is generally the only type of "action" (*i.e.*, court proceeding) that a lender may bring to recover on its secured loan. Unless one of several statutory exceptions applies, a lender's failure to observe this rule may subject the lender to very serious consequences, including in the worst case the loss of the lender's real property security.

A judicial foreclosure action is commenced by the filing and serving of a complaint against the borrower. In many cases, other persons (*e.g.*, certain junior lienholders) will also need to be named in the complaint and served if their interests in the property are to be extinguished or otherwise affected by the action. Failure to do so may result in these persons' interests being unaffected by the judicial foreclosure action.

In a judicial foreclosure action, the lender seeks to have the court determine that the loan is in default and order that the property be sold to satisfy the loan balance. In most cases, the lender will also seek to have the court (1) declare that the borrower is liable for any deficiency resulting from the foreclosure sale, (2) hold a "fair value" hearing to determine the amount of the deficiency and (3) enter a deficiency judgment against the borrower. Once a deficiency judgment has been entered, the lender may proceed against the borrower's other assets in accordance with the law governing enforcement of judgments generally.

Unless a deficiency judgment against the borrower is waived or prohibited, following the judicial foreclosure sale the borrower will generally have a period of one year in which to redeem the property for a redemption price equal to the purchase price at the sale subject to certain adjustments specified by statute. In the unusual circumstance that the proceeds of the judicial foreclosure sale are sufficient to satisfy the loan (including interest thereon) and certain other costs, the applicable redemption period is reduced from one year to three months.

Although judicial foreclosure actions are frequently commenced in California, they are rarely prosecuted to completion. One reason is that such foreclosures are time-consuming (often lasting one year or more) and expensive (at least when compared to non-judicial foreclosures). Another reason is that the borrower's post-sale redemption right makes the property less attractive to third-party purchasers, resulting in lower sale prices.

On the other hand, sometimes there are compelling reasons to pursue a judicial foreclosure action to completion. If the borrower has significant other assets that are not security for the loan, the only way for the lender to reach these assets is through a judicial foreclosure action. In other cases, loan document defects (*e.g.*, a guaranty that is one of the obligations secured by the deed of trust) may make foreclosing through a judicial foreclosure action mandatory if the lender wishes to pursue the guarantor afterwards. Whether any of these special situations applies in a particular case is something that the lender should discuss with experienced local counsel.

III. Non-Judicial Foreclosure Basics:

In California, a non-judicial foreclosure, which is done under a "power of sale" in the deed of trust, is a two-stage process. Stage 1 begins with the recording of a statutory notice of default and continues for approximately three months. Stage 2 starts with the recording and other disposition (*e.g.*, posting, publishing and mailing) of the statutory notice of sale and continues through completion of the sale (which, by law, cannot take place earlier than three months and twenty days after the recording of the statutory notice of default) and delivery of the trustee's deed to the purchaser.

Most non-judicial foreclosure sales in California are handled by trustee companies (including, in some cases, units within title companies) that specialize in providing non-judicial foreclosure services. As a general rule, the company selected to handle the non-judicial foreclosure should be substituted as trustee under the deed of trust prior to commencing the non-judicial foreclosure.

IV. Guidelines for Power of Sale:

In California, a non-judicial foreclosure starts when the trustee records a statutory notice of default (NOD) in the office of the recorder of the county in which the property is situated. To be effective, the NOD must contain certain information specified by law. If the loan has been accelerated by reason of one or more payment defaults and not by reason of one or more other defaults (*e.g.*, a prohibited transfer), the NOD must also contain a rather lengthy statement in a particular form and format. After recording the NOD, the trustee must mail copies of the NOD (with the recording date shown) to the borrower and various other persons specified by law (*e.g.*, certain junior lienholders) within 10 business days for some persons and one month for other persons. In unusual cases, the trustee must also publish or post the NOD.

To continue the non-judicial foreclosure, approximately three months after recording the NOD, the trustee will record a statutory notice of sale (NOS) in the same office where it recorded the NOD. Among other things, the NOS must specify the time and place of the foreclosure sale and describe the property to be sold. If the foreclosure sale is intended to be a "unified sale" in which some or all of the personal property and fixtures that constitute security for the loan are to be sold together with the land, improvements and other real property security, the NOS must also describe such personal property and fixtures in the manner prescribed by law. The trustee must record the NOS at least 20 days prior to the sale date. In addition, the trustee must publish, post and mail copies of the NOS in the manner and/or to the persons prescribed by law at least 20 days prior to the sale date.

In California, a non-judicial foreclosure sale is deemed final when the sale is held and the last and highest bid is accepted. Provided that the successful bidder pays the full amount bid for the property and a trustee's deed is delivered, the sale is deemed perfected as of 8:00 a.m. on the sale date if the trustee's deed is recorded in a timely fashion (generally within 15 days after the sale).

V. Power of Sale Guidelines for Mixed and Multiple Security

Generally, if a loan is secured both by real property and by personal property or fixtures, the lender may use the non-judicial foreclosure process to conduct a "unified sale" of both the real property and some or all of the personal property or fixtures.

Alternatively, the lender may foreclose on some or all of the personal property or fixtures by following the rules set forth in the California Commercial Code (California's version of the Uniform Commercial Code). If the lender wishes to pursue the latter approach, the lender should discuss with experienced local counsel the impact of California's one-action and anti-deficiency rules on that approach.

If the loan is secured by two or more deeds of trust and the lender initially forecloses on one of the deeds of trust by means of non-judicial foreclosure, the lender may foreclose on the other deeds of trust by means of non-judicial foreclosure until the lender's loan (including, for this purpose, the lender's attorneys' fees and other recoverable costs) are fully repaid.

VI. Foreclosure When Instrument Contains No Power of Sale:

In the unusual event that the deed of trust securing a real estate loan does not contain a power of sale clause, the lender must foreclose judicially.

VII. Additional Satisfaction Permitted Under Continuing Power of Sale:

Under California law, the lender may not obtain a deficiency judgment against the borrower following a non-judicial foreclosure sale of the real property security for the loan. The lender may, however, obtain a deficiency judgment against the guarantor if the guaranty is not a "sham" guaranty and the guaranty contains appropriate waivers. In addition, as discussed in part V above, the lender may realize on other security for the loan following a non-judicial foreclosure sale of the property securing the loan, albeit subject to certain limitations.

VIII. Sale under Power of Sale Where Instrument Silent as to Place or Terms of Sale:

In California, a deed of trust typically does not specify the place or the terms of any non-judicial foreclosure sale involving the encumbered property. Instead, that information will be set forth in the NOS.

IX. Notice of Sale and How Notice is Given:

In a non-judicial foreclosure, the NOS must specify the time and place of the foreclosure sale and describe the property to be sold. The NOS must also contain, among other items of information, a statement of the entire unpaid balance of the loan and the lender's reasonably estimated costs, expenses and advances at the time of initial publication of the NOS. In addition, if the foreclosure sale is intended to be a "unified sale" in which some or all of the personal property and fixtures that constitute security for the loan are to be sold together with the land, improvements and other real property security, the NOS must also describe such personal property and fixtures in the manner prescribed by law (which manner will vary depending on whether some or all of the personal property or fixtures will be included in the sale).

The trustee must record the NOS at least 20 days prior to the sale date. In addition, the trustee must publish, post and mail copies of the NOS in the manner and/or to the persons prescribed by law at least 20 days prior to the sale date.

X. Place and Time for Conducting Foreclosure by Power of Sale:

By law, a non-judicial foreclosure sale must be held between the hours of 9:00 a.m. and 5:00 p.m. on any business day, Monday through Friday, in the county where the property is situated. As noted above, this information will be set forth in the NOS.

Relevant Codes, Statutes or Case Law:
California Civil Code §§ 2924-2924k; California Civil Procedure Code §§ 580a, 580b, 580d, 726 & 729.010-729.090; California Commercial Code § 9604.

Receivership:

I. General Information:

To obtain appointment of a receiver under California law, a lender seeking to enforce a defaulted real estate loan must do several things. *First*, the lender must commence a civil action. Unless a civil action is pending, a receiver cannot be appointed. *Second*, the civil action must be one of the types of cases in which a court is permitted by law to appoint a receiver. Under

Section 564 of the California Civil Procedure Code, these types of cases include (1) a judicial foreclosure action and (2) an action by the lender for specific performance of an assignment of rents provision in a deed of trust or a separate assignment document. *Finally*, the lender must satisfy any additional conditions imposed by law. For example, in a judicial foreclosure action the lender must also establish either (a) that the property is in danger of being lost, removed or materially injured or (b) that the condition of the deed of trust has not been performed and the property is probably insufficient to discharge the debt secured by the deed of trust. Significantly, any action by a lender to appoint a receiver pursuant to Section 564 of the California Civil Procedure Code does not constitute an "action" within the meaning of California's one-action rule.

II. Appointing the Receiver:

A. The Basics:

Historically, the most common procedural vehicle used by a lender to secure appointment of a receiver is a noticed motion brought within an action for judicial foreclosure. In some cases, however, appointment of a receiver may be secured on an *ex parte* basis. In those cases, a showing of "irreparable injury" (among other things) is typically required.

B. Time Frame for Appointment:

As noted above, a lender may apply for appointment of a receiver on either a noticed motion basis or an *ex parte* basis. For an application made by noticed motion, generally at least 16 court days' notice is required. For an application made on an *ex parte* basis, courts generally require that the borrower and any other parties be given notice not later than 10:00 a.m. at least one court day before the *ex parte* appearance. In addition, the lender must serve the *ex parte* application on all other appearing parties at the first reasonable opportunity. Absent exceptional circumstances, no hearing may be held unless such service has been made.

C. Can you Appoint Ex Parte?

In California, a lender may secure appointment of a receiver on an *ex parte* basis. To do so, the lender must show in detail, by verified complaint or declaration, (1) the nature of the emergency requiring appointment of a receiver and (2) the reasons why irreparable injury would be suffered by the lender during the time necessary for a hearing on regular notice. Additional showings are also required. If the application for appointment of a receiver *ex parte* is granted, a hearing must be held within 15 (or, in some cases, 22) days to determine why the appointment should not be confirmed.

D. Are There Specific Requirements for Receivers?

By law, the receiver must take an oath and post a bond before the receiver commences his or her duties. The amount of the bond will be set by the court.

E. Is There an Approval List for Receivers?

In California, there is no "panel" of approved receivers from which a court selects a receiver in any given case. Instead, each party appearing at the hearing of an application for appointment of a receiver is entitled to suggest one or more persons for appointment as receiver. Any such suggestion must be made in writing and state the reasons why the person suggested should be appointed. As a practical matter, courts are more inclined to consider for appointment as receiver persons with relevant experience.

F. Is California Friendly to Outside Receivers?

There is no legal prohibition against citizens or residents of other states being appointed as receivers.

III. Order Appointing Receiver:

A. Specific Language for Order Appointing Receiver:

A well-drafted appointment order should contain provisions that specify the receiver's fees, costs and other compensation and that address practical considerations, such as bank accounts, mail, utilities, insurance and other matters affecting the day-to-day operation of the property. In addition, if the lender desires that the receiver have the power to market and sell the property, the appointment order should so provide and should also address important related issues, such as the treatment of liens upon a sale of the property and the distribution of sale proceeds.

B. Do Any Courts Have Specific Requirements for Orders Appointing Receiver?

Some courts prefer that the forms of order submitted to the court be on judicial council forms. In those cases, it will generally be advisable to supplement the provisions of those forms with attachments that address issues which are not fully addressed by the forms. The specific content of these attachments will vary from case to case and from asset type to asset type.

C. Other Information of Interest Regarding Orders Appointing Receiver:

Although the provisions of the California Civil Procedure Code governing a receiver's powers and duties appear to be broadly phrased, these provisions also make it clear that the receiver is operating under the court's ultimate supervision and control. Accordingly, it makes sense for the appointment order to be as specific as reasonably practicable in describing the receiver's power and authority over the property and any rents or other revenues derived therefrom.

IV. Receiver's Action and Reporting:

A. Are There Any Specific Rules Imposed by California Governing a Receiver's Actions or Reporting?

In California, there are a number of specific rules that govern a receiver's actions or reporting. These rules include, for example, (1) rules that limit the types of agreements, understandings or arrangements that a receiver and a lender nominating the receiver for appointment may enter into, (2) rules that require a receiver to obtain court approval before hiring counsel and (3) rules that require the receiver to provide monthly reports to the parties in the case.

B. Are There Any Local Court Rules that a Receiver Should Understand?

In California, civil trial courts are called "superior courts" and are organized on a county-by-county basis. The local rules adopted by California's superior courts vary considerably from one court to another. For example, under the Los Angeles Superior Court Local Rules, an application for appointment of a receiver in a case filed in the central district of that court will be heard by certain "writs and receivers" judges who deal with these sorts of matters on a daily basis, while an application for appointment of a receiver in a case filed in another district of that court will be heard by the same judge who is assigned to the case generally. Before commencing an action to enforce its loan and applying for the appointment of a receiver, the lender should consult with counsel regarding the impact, if any, of the local rules on its litigation strategy (including, in certain instances, the decision of where to file the case).

V. Additional Instructions and Orders:

Because the receiver is an agent of the court and not of any party and operates under the supervision and control of the court, the receiver should request further instructions and, if necessary, orders from the court before taking any action not reasonably within the scope of the receiver's appointment order.

VI. Loans and Advances:

If the property covered by the receivership does not generate sufficient rents or other revenues to preserve and manage the property, with the court's approval the receiver may borrow money for those purposes. With the court's approval, the receiver may also issue receivership certificates as security for the borrowing. These certificates are secured by liens on the subject property and may, to the extent a court order so provides, have priority over other liens. As a practical matter, it would be very unusual for a receiver to borrow money from anyone other than the lender.

VII. Sales During the Receivership:

Although California's case law in this area is not yet fully developed and is subject to change, Section 568.5 of the California Civil Procedure Code generally allows a receiver to sell property that is collateral for a loan, provided that appropriate court orders are first obtained. Courts frequently approve such sales if the borrower and guarantor agree.

If they do not agree, however, the court should still have the ability to order such a sale. But the law is not quite settled: there is a possible conflict between California's one-action and anti-deficiency rules and its receivership laws. Although the California receivership statute expressly provides that an action to appoint a receiver is an exception to the state's one-action rule, it does not expressly state that the receiver has the right to sell mortgaged real property belonging to the current owner to an assuming buyer, while leaving the existing loan and its lien in place.

In the case of the loan is secured by real property, the authors believe that so long as the lender waives any deficiency against the borrower and follows certain other technical steps, including getting appropriate orders from the court, a receiver should be able to sell the real property securing a loan subject to the existing lien. This would allow the existing loan to be modified and assumed by the new buyer of the real property. More importantly, the authors have persuaded certain national title insurers to insure the resulting buyer's, and the lender's, respective titles for such transactions. This theory, its risks and the technical legal requirements for accomplishing such a sale and assumption through receivership are discussed in detail in M. O'Connor and J. Cochran, "Enforcing Defaulted CMBS Loans through Receivership Sales: Risks and Rewards of the Modification, Sale and Assumption Transaction under California's 'One Action' Rule," *CRE Finance World* (January 2011).

VIII. Liens Against Receivership Property:

Under the California Commercial Code, a receiver is treated as a lien creditor for purposes of determining lien priority in any personal property or fixtures included in the receivership estate. As for the real property included in the receivership estate, the extent to which a receiver has a lien superior to that of any subsequent lienholder is governed by court order.

IX. Owners Associations:

The receiver's power and authority with respect to any homeowners' or property owners' association of which the property may be a part is something that should be delineated in the appointment order.

X. Construction Related to Receivership Property:

If the receiver takes possession of an unfinished construction project, the receiver's power and authority to finish construction of the project is likewise something that should be delineated in the appointment order.

XI. Ending the Receivership:

To wind up the receivership, the receiver must present, by noticed motion or stipulation of all parties, the following items for court approval: (a) a final account and report; (b) a request for a discharge; and (c) a request for exoneration of the receiver's surety. If any further compensation for the receiver or its counsel is claim, additional information must be provided.

XII. Miscellaneous:

California law has two statutes not previously discussed that may impact the lender's decision of whether to pursue appointment of a receiver in a case or how long the receivership might last. These statutes, Sections 2924c and 2856 of the California Civil Code, are briefly discussed below.

Right to reinstate the loan. Provided that the default for which the loan has been accelerated is curable, a borrower who has defaulted under a loan repaid in installments secured by

California real property has the right to "reinstate" the accelerated loan. (For example, a borrower has no right to reinstate a loan that has reached its maturity date.)

To reinstate the loan, the borrower must pay to the beneficiary all missed installments, allowable costs and attorneys' fees (both of which are limited by statute), and must cure all other defaults required under the deed of trust and allowed by statute (including, for example, recurring tax and insurance payments). Reinstatement does not require payoff of the entire loan. Once a loan is reinstated, it is "de-accelerated" and returns to its original installment payment status. A borrower (or a junior lienholder) may reinstate the borrower's loan until 5 business days before the date of sale stated in the NOS or, if the sale date is postponed, until 5 business days before the rescheduled date of sale.

Enforcement of guaranties. The extent to which guarantors are protected, as borrowers are, by the procedural protections detailed in California's one-action and anti-deficiency rules has been hotly debated in the courts for years. The enactment of Section 2856 of the California Civil Code, which codified the so-called "Gradsky" waivers, brought some clarity to the issue. It generally allows lenders to pursue guarantors after a non-judicial foreclosure of the real property securing the borrower's loan if their guaranties contain certain waivers described in the statute. (In the absence of such waivers, the lender's rights against the guarantor would be eliminated after a non-judicial foreclosure, though they could be enforced instead through the longer and more expensive judicial foreclosure action.)

Although Section 2856 provides "safe harbor" language for some of the waivers it allows, it does not provide "safe harbor" language for all of the waivers it allows. In addition, if the guarantor's obligations are secured by the deed of trust, then the guarantor will benefit from the same anti-deficiency and one-action protections afforded the borrower under California law. Because the application of the one-action and anti-deficiency rules is based not only on the language of the relevant statutes, but also on the extensive case law in which California courts have heavily interpreted the one-action and antideficiency rules, it is prudent to have experienced California real estate counsel review any and all guaranties prior to initiating foreclosure. A misstep in applying these highly technical laws could result in sanctions, including loss of the lien on the real property collateral for the loan or losing the ability to pursue solvent guarantors.

Relevant Codes, Statutes or Case Law:
California Civil Procedure Code §§ 564-570; California Rules of Court 3.1175-3.1184, 3.1200-3.1207 & 3.1300-3.1312; California Civil Code §§ 2924c & 2856.

Colorado

Foreclosure Summary

Security Instrument	Trust Deed/ Mortgage
Judicial	Yes
Non-Judicial	Yes
Initial Public Notice	Notice of Default
Time Frame	1.5 to 10 months
Redemption Period	110 to 230 days to cure; 8 days post-sale to redeem, more if multiple lienors
Deficiency	Yes

Receivership Summary

Ancillary Remedy Necessary	No
Ex-Parte	Yes
Specific Requirements	Must file Oath & Bond prior to commencing duties
Approximate Time for Appointment	1 day to several weeks
Who or What can act as Receiver	No Restrictions Given
Is there any approval list for Receivers	No
Out of State Receivers Allowed	Yes

Foreclosure:

I. General Information:

Colorado law provides for both judicial and non-judicial foreclosure. The Colorado General Assembly significantly revised Colorado's foreclosure statues, with most changes effective January 1, 2008. In general, the revisions attempt to increase the fairness of the foreclosure process for the borrower by combining the owner's pre-sale cure period and post-sale redemption period, increasing regulation of investors who purchase residential property during foreclosure, and increasing borrowers' access to educational materials regarding the foreclosure process.

II. Judicial Foreclosure Basics:

Judicial foreclosure is conducted as any other civil litigation, following the Colorado Rules of Civil Procedure. Judicial foreclosure is governed by Colo. Rev. Stat. §§ 38-38-100.3 to -705 (2012), and by Colo. R. Civ. P. 105.

III. Non-Judicial Foreclosure Basics:

Non-judicial foreclosure may be commenced with the Public Trustee in the county where the property being foreclosed is located. Non-judicial foreclosures are governed by Colo. Rev. Stat. §§ 38-38-100.3 to -705 (2012), and by Colo. R. Civ. P. 120.

IV. Guidelines for Power of Sale:

A power of sale foreclosure is commenced by filing:

A. a Notice of Election and Demand ("NED");

B. the original evidence of debt, a certified copy of the evidence of debt from a qualified holder, a certified copy of a court judgment, or a lost instrument bond;

C. the original, or a certified or verified copy, of the recorded deed of trust, and all modifications, amendments, or partial releases thereto;

D. a combined Notice of Sale and Notice of Cure and Redemption Rights ("Combined Notice"), unless provided by the Office of the Public Trustee;

E. a mailing list for notification;

F. the affidavit of the holder regarding the identity of the current owner of the property at issue; and

G. the applicable fee.

Those entitled to cure during foreclosure include the property owner; the owner's heirs, guardian, or personal representative if the owner is deceased or incapacitated; certain transferees of the property; any person liable on the evidence of debt; a surety or guarantor of the evidence of debt; or junior lien holders. Colorado has a single pre-sale cure period of between 110 and 125 days after the date of recording the NED (for non-agricultural property) or between 215 and 230 days after the date of recording the NED (for agricultural property). A party entitled to cure must file a notice of intent to cure with the Public Trustee no later than fifteen days prior to the date of sale.

The Public Trustee cannot sell real property without an Order Authorizing Sale from the District Court. The foreclosing party must file with the appropriate District Court, mail, and post at the Clerk's office a copy of the deed of trust containing the power of sale, together with a verified motion and notice that describes (1) the instrument containing the power of sale, (2) the property to be sold, and (3) the default or facts giving rise to the invocation of the power of sale clause. The court clerk sets a hearing date not less than twenty-one nor more than thirty-five days after filing. A notice of such hearing must be posted on the subject property no later than fourteen days before the hearing. The motion for Order Authorizing Sale must be filed with the court to allow sufficient time for the court to hold a hearing or enter the Order Authorizing Sale no later than sixteen days prior to the date of sale, the day prior to last day a notice of intent to cure could be filed. As a guideline, the statutory timeframe requires filing the motion for Order Authorizing Sale a minimum of fifty-one days prior to the date of sale, although allowing additional time is advisable.

The court will hold a hearing if a response is filed no later than seven days before the date set for the hearing. Otherwise, the court will examine the motion, and, if satisfied that venue is proper and that the moving party is entitled to the requested relief, the court will enter an Order Authorizing Sale. A copy of the Order Authorizing Sale must be provided to the Public Trustee no later than 12 noon on the second business day prior to the date of sale. Following sale, a Return of Sale must be filed with the court, and the court will enter an Order Approving Sale to close the action.

V. Power of Sale Guidelines as Represented in the Security:

Colorado law defines "deed of trust" as "a security instrument containing a grant to a public trustee together with a power of sale."

VI. Guidelines for Foreclosure when there is No Power of Sale:

A judicial foreclosure action is commenced by filing a civil complaint naming all parties with an interest in the property, those in actual possession of the property, and those entitled to notice of foreclosure. The complaint should be filed in the District Court where the property, or a substantial part of the property, is located. The collateral (including real property, water rights, mineral rights, or personal property) should be fully described in the complaint by legal description. A Notice of *Lis Pendens* containing the full case caption, nature of the claim, and legal description of the property should be recorded in each county in which any part of the property is located. The court must authorize service by publication on verified motion; service is completed by publishing the summons in a local newspaper for five weeks. The foreclosing party may move for entry of default judgment and entry of a Decree of Foreclosure if no response is filed after thirty-five days of completion of service by publication. Most courts do not require a hearing on a motion for default judgment. If summary judgment motions or trial are required, the Colorado Rules of Civil Procedure will apply to the action. Once a Decree of Foreclosure is obtained, execution is stayed for fourteen days, after which the foreclosing party may deliver the Decree of Foreclosure and a mailing list to the sheriff to begin the sale process.

VII. Foreclosure When Instrument Contains No Power of Sale:

When an instrument contains no power of sale provision, Colorado provides only for foreclosure through a judicial foreclosure action described in the preceding section.

VIII. Any Additional Satisfaction Permitted Under Continuing Power of Sale:

Deficiency judgments are permitted. A party may foreclose on a portion of the property without affecting the lien or power of sale as to the remaining property only if the portion is encumbered as a separate and distinct parcel or lot. A partial release of a deed of trust may occur while foreclosure is in progress.

IX. Sale by Power of Sale when the Instrument is Silent as to the Place or Terms of Sale:

Colorado law provides that a deed of trust containing a power of sale, but lacking provisions regarding the manner in which the power of sale is to be exercised, is neither void nor voidable, and that the deed of trust may be foreclosed either as a public trustee sale or through judicial foreclosure.

X. Notice of Sale and How Notice is Given:

For residential property, at least thirty days after default, and at least thirty days before filing the NED, a holder of the evidence of debt must notify the debtor of the telephone numbers for the Colorado Foreclosure Hotline and the holder's loss mitigation representative. Further, within fifteen days of filing the NED, the holder must personally serve, or post on the property, a statutory federal foreclosure deferment program notice, and the

Contributed By: Lino Lipinsky and
Charles Swanson of
McKenna Long & Aldridge LLP

holder must file an affidavit of compliance within twenty days of filing the NED.

The Combined Notice must contain the information listed in the state statutes, including all information required by the state statutes, statutory advisements regarding cure and redemption, contact information for every attorney representing the foreclosing party, place and date of sale, and complete copies of the statutes listed in the state statutes.

The Public Trustee must record the NED within ten business days after receiving it, and the NED must be made available for public inspection. Within twenty days after recording the NED, the Public Trustee must mail the Combined Notice to those persons and addresses identified by the foreclosing party in the mailing list. The Combined Notice must be mailed again no more than sixty days, and no fewer than forty-five days, prior to the actual sale date. The foreclosing party must provide an updated mailing list as needed. (For judicial foreclosures, the Sheriff must mail a Combined Notice to the mailing list no more than 30 days, and no fewer than sixteen days, after the Sheriff receives the mailing list and a decree of foreclosure or writ of execution.) The Combined Notice must also be published for four weeks (once each week for five consecutive weeks) beginning no greater than sixty days, and no fewer than forty-five days prior to the sale date.

XI. Place and Time for Conducting Foreclosure by Power of Sale:

The place of sale must be the location designated in the Combined Notice, which must be the entrance to, or any room within, the courthouse, or the office of the county Clerk and Recorder, Public Trustee, or Sheriff. The time of sale depends upon whether the property is agricultural or non-agricultural. If non-agricultural: (1) pursuant to a power of sale, between 110 and 125 days after the date of recording the NED; (2) judicial foreclosure, no less than 110 days after the date of recording the Notice of *Lis Pendens* If agricultural: (1) pursuant to a power of sale, between 215 and 230 days after the date of recording the

NED; (2) judicial foreclosure, no less than 215 days after the date of recording the Notice of *Lis Pendens*.

Qualified borrowers may be eligible to defer the foreclosure process for up to 90 days. If (1) the deed of trust is a first lien, and the borrower (2) resides at and occupies the property as a primary residence at the time of filing the NED, (3) has occupied the property as a primary residence since 90 days after the date of the deed of trust, (4) intends to continue to reside at the property, (5) is personally obligated on the debt, and (6) the original principal amount of the debt was $500,000 or less, the foreclosing party must post a notice of deferment opportunity on the property, provide a notice of eligibility to the Public Trustee, personally serve notice upon the borrower, and file an affidavit confirming notice was provided.

A foreclosing party may request an expedited foreclosure process in cases of property abandonment or neglect. If the foreclosing party believes there is a need to protect the property from harm, it may file a motion for order authorizing expedited sale with the Court. If granted, the foreclosure sale may occur between 45 and 65 days after the date of recording the NED. Other specialized timing applies to such expedited proceedings.

Relevant Codes, Statutes or Case Law:
Colo. R. Civ. P. 12, 62, 98(a), 105, 120; Colo. Rev. Stat. §§ 38-38-100.3 to -705 (2012); 2006 Colo. Sess. Laws. 1330 (Senate Bill 06-071); 2006 Colo. Sess. Laws 1434 (House Bill 06-1387); 2007 Colo. Sess. Laws 1830 (House Bill 07-1157); Colo. Rev. Stat. § 38-38-701(4) (2012); Colo. Rev. Stat. § 38-38-801 to -907 (2012).

NOTE: At the time of publication, the Colorado General Assembly was considering significant changes to Colorado's foreclosure procedures. If enacted, Colorado House Bill 1249 would, among other provisions, allow for suspension of foreclosure proceedings during the pendency of a debtor's loan modification application. Practitioners should determine whether HB 1249 had become law.

Receivership:

I. General information:

In Colorado, there are three grounds for the appointment of a Receiver. Colorado law provides for court appointment of a Receiver before, by, or after a judgment to protect property, both real and personal. The receivership may be the sole claim for relief. In addition, a Receiver may be appointed to protect property during the foreclosure process. Lastly, parties may provide for receiverships by contract.

II. Appointing the Receiver:

A. The Basics:

Any party that can establish a *prima facie* right or interest in the subject property may apply to the court for appointment of a Receiver when an adverse party possesses the property, and (1) danger exists that the property or its rents or profits (a) may be lost, (b) removed from the court's jurisdiction, or (c) materially injured; (2) when the court seeks to dispose of the property at or after judgment or preserve it during appellate proceedings; or (3) as other circumstances require under principles of equity. Prior to assuming its duties, the Receiver must swear an oath to execute faithfully its duties, and the Receiver must post a bond. The Receiver's powers are defined and limited by the court's Order of Appointment.

Additionally, if an owner abandons property prior to a foreclosure sale, and the circumstances would warrant appointment of a Receiver but none is petitioned for, the foreclosing party may take possession of the property until the sale, subject to all of the duties and liabilities of a Receiver.

B. Time Frame for Appointment:

Time periods for appointment vary, depending upon the judge, from as little as one day to several weeks.

C. Can you go in Ex Parte?

A court may appoint a Receiver *ex parte* only if: (a) an express clause in the instrument upon which the action is based allows *ex parte* appointment; or (b) the moving party demonstrates the existence of exigent circumstances.

III. Loans and Advances:

No statutes or rules govern loans or advances, and the Order of Appointment will govern the Receiver's authority to obtain loans or to issue advances.

IV. Sales During the Receivership:

A. General Process:

No Colorado statutes set forth a general procedure for receiver property sales. In Colorado, a receiver has only those powers specifically conferred upon it by statute or by the court's order or decree. Thus, the Order of Appointment will determine any applicable process for receiver sales. Such sale must be conducted fairly and impartially by the receiver as an officer and representative of the court, and because there are no statutory restrictions as to time, manner, terms, or notice of sale, such matters are determined in the court's discretion.

While the foreclosure process is generally appropriate to sell property, Colorado statutes specifically authorize receivers appointed in certain types of proceedings, such as those brought to dissolve an entity, to dispose of all or part of the entity's property at a public or private sale upon authorization from the court.

V. Liens Against Receivership Property:

In the context of receiver sales, a purchaser acquires no better title than the receiver possesses. In the context of foreclosure, lienors possess statutory redemption rights.

VI. Owners Associations:

There is no reported Colorado case law specifically addresses special considerations applied to owners associations.

VII. Construction Related to Receivership Property:

No Colorado statute or case law specifies a process for completion of construction in the context of a receivership. Colorado courts do routinely grant receivers the power to manage the property and to hire management and other professionals as necessary. Thus, in an appropriate case, the Order of Appointment will determine any applicable process for construction activity.

VIII. Ending the Receivership:

An action in which the court has appointed a Receiver may not be dismissed except by court order. Thus, the Receiver or another party files a motion to terminate. The movant must send notice to all parties, attorneys of record, and any third parties that might be harmed by the termination. Upon termination, the Receiver should file a final accounting and a motion to discharge the Receiver and the Receiver's bond. The Receiver must give notice to the same parties who received notice of the motion for termination. All receivership monies must be paid out prior to discharge.

IX. Miscellaneous:

A.

A Receiver must post a court-approved bond and swear an oath to execute the Receiver's duties faithfully prior to undertaking its duties.

B.

Nearly all Colorado District Courts require that proposed orders be electronically filed in an editable format.

C.

Orders granting or denying the appointment or discharge of a Receiver are immediately appealable. However, trial courts are given broad discretion over appointment of a Receiver, and the trial court's decision will not be reversed absent a clear abuse of discretion. If a party obtaining appointment of a Receiver is found on appeal not to have been entitled to the appointment of a Receiver, the debtor is entitled to an award of the costs and fees associated with the receivership.

Relevant Codes, Statutes or Case Law:
Rossi v. Colo. Pulp & Paper Co., 299 P. 19, 39-40 (Colo. 1931) (property sold subject to existing liens); *GE Life & Annuity Assurance Co. v. Fort Collins Assemblage, Ltd.*, 53 P.3d 703, 705-06 (Colo. Ct. App. 2001); *Bank of Am. Nat'l Trust Sav. Assoc. v. Denver Hotel Assoc. Ltd. Partnership*, 830 P.2d 1138, 1139 (Colo. Ct. App. 1992); *Zeligman v. Juergens*, 762 P.2d 783, 785 (Colo. Ct. App. 1988); 13 Debra Knapp, Colorado Civil Procedure Forms & Commentary, §§ 66.7 to 66.10 (2d ed. 2005); *Hough v. Lucas*, 230 P. 789, 791 (Colo. 1924) (error to sell property free of existing liens); *Albertson Ranches, Inc. v. Cuddy*, 525 P.2d 1190, 1192 (Colo. Ct. App. 1974).

Contributed By: Lino Lipinsky and
Charles Swanson of
McKenna Long & Aldridge LLP

Colo. R. Civ. P. 66; Colo. App. R. 1(a)(4); C.R.S. §§ 38-38-301 to 306; Colo. Rev. Stat. §§ 38-38-601 to -602 (2012); C.R.S. §§ 7-56-716 (cooperative); 7-80-812 (limited liability company); 7-114-303 (corporation); 7-134-303 (nonprofit corporation).

Connecticut

Foreclosure Summary

Security Instrument	Mortgage
Judicial	Yes
Non-Judicial	No
Initial Public Notice	Complaint
Time Frame	Typically 60 days; 60-150 days
Redemption Period	Dependent upon whether case proceeds as Strict Foreclosure or Foreclosure by Sale
Deficiency	Yes

Receivership Summary

Ancillary Remedy Necessary	Yes
Ex-Parte	Yes
Approximate Time for Appointment	Upon motion at any time during the action
Who or What can act as Receiver	Individual or Company
Specific Receiver Requirements	Receiver must file bond with court before carrying out duties
Is there any approval list for Receivers	No
Out of State Receivers Allowed	Favor CT Receivers

Foreclosure:

I. General Information:

Connecticut law does not provide for any form of non-judicial foreclosure procedure. The Superior Court exercises exclusive jurisdiction over foreclosure actions, as it does for all causes of action, except for those actions over which probate courts are given statutory jurisdiction. The common plaintiff is the party named as holder of the mortgage note and grantee on the mortgage deed, or, in the case of a lien, the named creditor. The owner of the equity is usually the first defendant. Guarantors, co-obligors, mortgagees, collateral assignees, creditors, lien holders, lessees, trustees in bankruptcy, life tenants, and the original maker of the note when the present owner assumed, but the original owner had not been released, should also be listed as defendants.

II. Judicial Foreclosure Basics:

Foreclosure can be either strict foreclosure or foreclosure by sale. Connecticut law grants the court discretion as to entering a judgment of foreclosure by sale or through strict foreclosure. The Courts generally favor a strict foreclosure; however, if there is no equity in the subject premises, the court would entertain a judgment of foreclosure by sale.

III. Strict Foreclosure Guidelines:

In Connecticut the plaintiff must complete a Foreclosure Worksheet to obtain a final judgment of foreclosure, whether it be by strict foreclosure or foreclosure by sale. The worksheet requires the plaintiff to provide the following information at the judgment hearing: fair market value of the premises based on appraisal report, along with oath and affidavit of appraiser, dated within 90 days of the hearing; updated debt; total encumbrances prior to the plaintiff's lien; total encumbrances subsequent to plaintiff's lien; equity in the property; whether the U.S. is a party; whether the owner of the equity is in possession of the property; and whether the owner of the equity is a non-appearing party.

Contributed By: Jamie C. Krapf & Timothy J Fierst of Rosenberg &Estis

If the court decides that strict foreclosure is appropriate, it only needs to set the Law Day. The Law Day establishes a date by which the borrower must satisfy the outstanding debt, and if the borrower does not comply with the Law Day, a second Law Day is set for subordinate lien holders to satisfy the outstanding debt in reverse order of priority. If the debt is not satisfied by either Law Day, the plaintiff takes title to the property.

The elements of a judgment of foreclosure by sale are directed by statute which requires that a person be appointed to have complete responsibility for the implementation of the judgment (known as the Committee). The court sets the date and time for the sale, and also directs whether the property will be sold in parcels or as a whole. The sale is made by public auction. The court also generally appoints the plaintiff's appraiser to re-appraise the property.

IV. Foreclosure by Sale:

The court typically orders the high bidder to put down a deposit at the time of the auction (usually set at about 10% of the appraised value). The deposit should be endorsed over to the Clerk of Superior Court and delivered to the clerk's office as soon as possible. The court appoints a committee to implement the judgment of foreclosure; this committee acts as an arm of the court. The Committee is required to file a motion to approve the sale by the Wednesday following the sale.

The Committee is responsible for: reviewing the appraisal, filing an appearance, reviewing the land records, advertising the sale based on the advertising dates set by the court, obtaining liability insurance for the date of the sale, procuring the foreclosure sign, responding to inquiries, preparing all documents, managing unusual expenses, conducting the sale, and obtaining timely approval of the sale by the court. The Committee also files a committee report to the court prior to seeking approval of the sale. The committee also executes the Committee Deed before asking for the court's approval. If the court approves the sale, the Committee schedules a closing with the buyers. If the sale is not approved, the court may either order a new sale or order a strict foreclosure.

If the sale is approved, the Bond for Deed requires that a transfer of title takes place within 30 days of the date of approval of the sale by the court. The Committee must pay into the court all proceeds from the sale, and the Committee's function officially ends when all proceeds have been paid into court.

V. Non-Judicial Foreclosure Basics:

Non-Judicial Foreclosures are not available in Connecticut.

VI. Guidelines for Power of Sale:

Power of Sale is not available in Connecticut.

VII. Notice of Sale and How Notice is Given:

The sale is uniformly conducted by public auction, although this is not required by any law. The advertising varies depending on the size and substance of the property. Residential properties usually receive two to three notices in a newspaper of general circulation in the area of the property. A sign is usually ordered to be placed on the property. Commercial or more substantial properties often receive greater advertising. The Sunday edition of the Hartford Courant contains a special notice (on the same page as the foreclosure notices) that states the common conditions of foreclosure sales. The court generally appoints the plaintiff's appraiser to re-appraise the property, generally by one week before the sale date.

In general, in order to foreclose on an interest of a party in the subject property, the party must be joined as a defendant in the judicial foreclosure and thereby receives notice of every development in the foreclosure action, including the date, time, and place of the foreclosure sale. Notice of the sale is also published by the Committee in the local newspaper ordered by the Court.

Relevant Codes, Statutes or Case Law:
C.G.S. § 49-24 through § 49-25

Receivership:

I. General information:

In Connecticut, the appointment of a Receiver is not regulated by statute. The Connecticut Practice Book establishes the extent to which the Court may exercise control over and supervise a Receiver's actions. A mortgagee usually seeks the appointment of a Receiver when there is a certain or threatened deficiency. The Receiver holds rents as an arm of the Court, and not as an agent for the plaintiff.

Plaintiff is not entitled to a Receiver as a matter of right and usually has to show that there is a great likelihood of a deficiency resulting as well as threatened waste being committed at the property.

II. Appointing the Receiver:

A. The Basics:

In order to get a Receiver appointed an application is made to the judge before whom the foreclosure action is pending. If the court before which the action is pending is not in session, application may be made to a judge in chambers after notice to the parties in interest, unless the exigencies of the situation dictate otherwise. With the exception of rent Receivers, all appointments not made after notice to interested parties are temporary appointments. No Receiver, temporary or permanent, is qualified to act until it files with either the clerk of the court or the appointing judge, a bond in an amount set by the court. Banks and trust companies, however, are exempt from this bond filing requirement. The amount of a rent Receiver's bond is usually set by multiplying the gross monthly rents by the number of months it is expected will elapse before title becomes absolute in the plaintiff.

The court may, of course, vary the amount of the bond.

B. Time Frame for Appointment:

This is dependent upon the length of time the motion to appoint the Receiver is placed on the court's calendar by the clerk of the court and a hearing is held on the motion. Assuming the motion is granted, the Receiver would be notified by the Court and then he/she would have to qualify to act.

C. Can you go in Ex Parte?

Yes. If the exigencies of the situation so require, the court may appoint a Receiver on an ex parte basis. With respect to Receivers other than rent Receivers, notice of not less than six days of hearing for confirmation of the appointment must be given by mail to all interested parties. Upon the hearing, the court may confirm the appointed temporary Receiver or appoint a new Receiver. The appointment of a temporary Receiver continues until a permanent Receiver is appointed.

III. Loans and Advances:

There are no pre-set laws on loans or advances during a receivership.

IV. Sales During the Receivership:

No information provided.

V. Liens Against Receivership Property:

No information provided.

VI. Owners Associations:

No information provided.

VII. Construction Related to Receivership Property:

No information provided.

VIII. Ending the Receivership:

In general, any party may move at any time for the removal of a Receiver. The court may also remove a Receiver at its pleasure. Usually the Receiver himself moves for discharge when he files his final report. This motion usually also seeks an allowance for the Receiver's fee, an order directing the Receiver to pay the money he is holding over to creditors and may also ask the court to release the Receiver from his bond.

IX. Miscellaneous:

A.

Each order appointing a permanent Receiver (except for rent Receivers) must contain a limitation on the time for the presentation of claims against the estate and direct that the Receiver forthwith give notice thereof, to all creditors, that any claims not presented within such time will be barred.

B.

A Receiver must maintain an escrow account.

C.

Every Receiver, except a rent Receiver, shall, on the first Tuesdays of April and October of each year, file a summary statement of all orders made during the preceding six months and the doings there under. Based upon these reports, the court will make such further orders as are deemed necessary and may direct that the case appear on the short calendar for an order approving the statement.

D.

Every Receiver, except rent Receivers and Receivers of state banks and trust companies, upon an estate which has been in process of settlement for more than four months shall during the first week of April and October of each year, sign, swear to and file with the court a full and detailed account of the condition and prospects of the estate as of the close of the next month. The Receiver must place a motion to approve the report on the short calendar.

E.

Unless the plaintiff can establish that the amount of its debt is greater than the amount which plaintiff will realize from a sale of the property, rents collected by a rent Receiver will ultimately be disbursed by the Receiver to subsequent lien holders and encumbrances. On the other hand, rents collected by a plaintiff pursuant to the terms of loan documents which give the mortgagee the right to collect rents are applied by the plaintiff to the debt.

Relevant Codes, Statutes or Case Law:
Connecticut's General Statutes § 47a-21; Chapter 21 to Connecticut's Practice Book
There are hundreds of Connecticut cases dealing with all aspects of receiverships. *See, e.g; Hartford Federal Savings & Loan Assn. v. Tucker,* 196 Conn. 172 (1985)
Webster Bank, N.A. v. Belinda Company, 2006 WL 538155 (Conn. Super. 2006)
FDIC v. Main Street Properties, 2 Conn. L. Rptr. 234 (Bridgeport 1990)
New Haven Savings Bank v. General Finance and Mortgage Co., 174 Conn. 268 (1978)
New Haven Savings Bank v. Valley View Joint Adventure, 8 Conn. Sup. Ct. Rpts. 410 (Waterbury 1993); *Desiderio v. Iadonisi,* 115 Conn. 652 (1932).

Contributed By: Jamie C. Krapf &
Timothy J Fierst of Rosenberg &Estis

Delaware

Foreclosure Summary

Security Instrument	Mortgage
Judicial	Yes
Non-Judicial	No
Initial Public Notice	Complaint
Time Frame	Approximately six months plus 30 days for court confirmation; longer if contested
Redemption Period	: No statutory authority, but a borrower likely possesses an equity of redemption until the foreclosure sale rather than the end of the 30-day confirmation period
Deficiency	

Receivership Summary

Ancillary Remedy Necessary	No Restriction Given
Ex-Parte	No Rule or Law
Approximate Time for Appointment	Varies
Who or What can act as Receiver	No Restrictions Given
Specific Receiver Requirements	No Restrictions Given
Is there any approval list for Receivers	No
Out of State Receivers Allowed	Can be appointed but there is a rule that states Receiver must be Delaware Citizens

Foreclosure:

I. Description of Procedure:

Typically the method of foreclosure is a suit at law. A writ of *scire facias* sur mortgage is filed in the county in which the mortgaged property is located, which commences upon the filing of a praecipe and complaint with the Prothonotary of the Superior Court. The issuance of the writ is then served and returned just as an original summons is, and the case proceeds like any other civil action. Once judgment is obtained, a writ is directed to the appropriate officer, who subjects the mortgaged property to public sale. Uncontested actions will take approximately six months, plus an additional thirty days after the sale for Superior Court confirmation, upon which the purchaser may take title.

II. Redemption:

There is no statutory authority under Delaware law. However, a borrower is considered as having a right of redemption during which the property can be redeemed by payment of principal, interests, and costs due under the mortgage.

III. Deficiencies:

Again, there are no applicable statutes regarding deficiencies, but one may be recovered by an independent proceeding on the debt instrument that was secured by the mortgage.

IV. Leases:

Leases prior to the recording of the mortgage are not affected by foreclosure sale (absent subordination). Leases subsequent to the recording of the mortgage (or otherwise subordinated) are discharged by a foreclosure sale.

Receivership:

I. General information:

As a general rule, under Delaware law, Receivers may be appointed by statute for a dissolved corporation, or for an insolvent corporation. In addition, Delaware courts have the inherent equitable power to appoint Receivers for solvent entities in certain, limited, situations. In this summary, we will focus on insolvency Receiverships and, to a lesser extent, equity Receiverships.

A. Receivers for Insolvent Entities – When Authorized:

In order to be placed into Receivership in Delaware an entity must be insolvent. Insolvency in this context means "either:

1. a deficiency of assets below liabilities with no reasonable prospect that the business can be successfully continued in the face thereof,' or

2. an inability to meet maturing obligations as they fall due in the ordinary course of business.'" Even where the debtor is insolvent, however, the appointment of a Receiver is only granted where urgent circumstances are present other than the mere collection of a debt and where some truly beneficial purpose will be served by the Receivership proceeding. Insolvency must be shown by clear and convincing evidence.

II. Appointing the Receiver:

A. The Basics:

The procedural aspects of a Receivership proceeding are governed primarily by Rules 148 through 168 of the Delaware Court of Chancery Rules (the "Court of Chancery Rules").

The matter will proceed with the filing of a complaint, the filing of answer or motion to dismiss and litigation will thereafter continue through the entry of a judgment on any count seeking to appoint a Receiver.

The plaintiff has the power to suggest who should be appointed as Receiver, but, ultimately, the Receiver is appointed by the Court. The court has the power to appoint a temporary Receiver during the litigation ("*pendent lite*"), but will only do so under extraordinary circumstances.

B. Time Frame for Appointment:

This would depend greatly on whether the debtor entity contests the relief sought in the complaint and whether it can interpose a reasonable defense to the complaint. One benefit of proceeding in Delaware's Court of Chancery, however, is that the court will often hear these matters on an expedited basis.

C. Can you go in Ex Parte?

The Delaware Receivership rules are silent on this point. If you are unable to obtain the appointment of a Receiver ex parte, the plaintiff may be able to obtain an expedited hearing on whether the court should appoint a Receiver *pendent lite* (pending the outcome of the litigation to appoint a Receiver) or enter other injunctive relief to prevent the debtor from participating in certain allegedly wrongful or harmful conduct while the Receivership proceeding is adjudicated. In addition, the court can, at any time, issue an order for the defendant entity to show cause as to why a Receiver *pendent lite* should not be appointed.

III. Loans and Advances:

There do not appear to be any such laws prohibiting loans or advances. Nonetheless, a Receiver should be very careful to obtain court approval to obtain the same. In addition, the Receiver must make it very clear in the loan documents that the Receiver shall not personally liable for any loan that he or she receives on behalf of the entity in Receivership.

IV. Sales During the Receivership:

No information provided.

V. Liens Against Receivership Property:

No information provided.

Contributed By: Henry J. Jaffe of Pepper Hamilton

VI. Owners Associations:

No information provided.

VII. Construction Related to Receivership Property:

No information provided.

VIII. Ending the Receivership:

Generally speaking, there is a procedure for filing final accounts and obtaining a discharge of the Receiver in the case. Under this procedure, the Register in Chancery sends out a notice to creditors giving them an opportunity to object to the final accounting within a time period fixed by the Court. While, theoretically, it is possible to obtain a waiver of these requirements, it is sound practice for the Receiver to obtain approval of some type of final accounting and a formal discharge.

IX. Miscellaneous:

A.

Court rules provide that a Receiver cannot be appointed unless he or she is a resident of the State of Delaware. However the Court rules also provide that the Court has enormous flexibility and may relieve the Receivers from complying with all or any of the duties and procedures set in specified rules.

B.

Court Rules require all monies in the Receiver's hands to be deposited into a banking institution in the State of Delaware.

C.

The Delaware statute, on its face, generally gives the Receiver broad power to take charge of the company and its business, collect and defend claims and otherwise take various actions. However, certain case law suggests that the Receiver should be careful in not exercising such powers broadly absent approval from the Court. Furthermore, fifteen (15) days notice is needed before corporate assets may be sold – it is a good idea to provide such notice and also obtain court approval for such sales (particularly those sales that are not in the ordinary course of business).

D.

The level of formality of the proceeding may vary depending upon which Chancellor (judge) hears the case. In any event, one can be assured that, if a difficult, time-sensitive or nuanced issue arises, the Chancellor appointed will likely be an experienced and sophisticated jurist and will generally be amenable to hearing and deciding the matter quickly. Delaware courts tend to take care of business quickly and in a high competent manner.

E.

Delaware Receivership law and practice does have a number of attractive features, including the following:

1. Flexibility – Delaware's rules and procedures are extremely flexible, allowing the parties and the court to tailor the procedural requirements of the law to the realities of the case.

2. Outstanding Judiciary and Ready Venue – Delaware's Court of Chancery is the premier venue in the country for resolving corporate disputes and these disputes are generally adjudicated quickly and in an expert manner. Furthermore, the Court of Chancery will have jurisdiction over any entity that is incorporated in Delaware, as so many entities are. Thus, Delaware likely has jurisdiction over a broad array of cases (note that the court has jurisdiction over all personal property of the entity in Receivership and all real property located in Delaware – if real property is located elsewhere, it must be administered in some other jurisdiction and/or proceeding).

3. Receiver's Ability to Reject/Disavow Executory Contracts - It appears that a Receiver has the power to disavow (or, in bankruptcy parlance, "reject")

executory contracts. This is an important power that, typically, may only be exercised in a bankruptcy proceeding. It is good practice to seek an order of the Court allowing such a rejection (or approving a procedure by which rejections shall be accomplished) on notice to the contract counterparty.

4. Receiver May Have an Expanded Power to Sell Assets Free and Clear of Liens - It is clear that, where a property is encumbered by a lien that is subject to dispute and the property subject to the lien is of the type that will deteriorate in value, the Receiver has the power to sell property free and clear of all liens and pay the proceeds to the court. (Apparently, the net proceeds of sale are then paid to the lien holder if its underlying lien and claim are deemed to be valid). Although the Receivership laws do not address whether the Receiver generally has the right to sell property free and clear of liens, statues arguably seem to imply as much.

Relevant Codes, Statutes or Case Law:
Production Resources Group, L.L.C. v. NCT Group, Inc., 863 A.2d 772, 782 (Del. Ch. 2004)
Production Resources, 863 A.2d at 784
Carlson v. Hallinan, 925 A.2d 506, 543 (Del. Ch. 2006)
Dupont v. Standard Arms Co., 81 A. 1089 (Del. Ch. 1912); Conover v. Sterling Stores Co., 120 A. 740 (Del. Ch. 1923); 8 Del. C. § 279; 8 Del. C. § 291-303

Washington D.C.

Foreclosure Summary

Security Instrument	Deed of Trust
Judicial	Yes, but rare
Non-Judicial	Yes
Initial Public Notice	Publication Notice Required
Time Frame	Est. Minimum of 90 days
Redemption Period	No
Deficiency	Yes

Receivership Summary

Ancillary Remedy Necessary	Yes
Ex-Parte	Possible, but not preferred
Approximate Time for Appointment	2 days - 6 weeks
Who or What can act as Receiver	No Restrictions Given
Specific Receiver Requirements	Must post bond to prior to commencing duties
Is there any approval list for Receivers	No
Out of State Receivers Allowed	Yes, Case by Case Basis

Foreclosure:

I. General Information:

Judicial foreclosures are allowed in D.C. but are rare. The more common way to foreclose is through the non-judicial foreclosure process.

II. Judicial Foreclosure Basics:

Yes, but more commonly by power of sale granted in deed of trust. If sold by judicial foreclosure, the court may also enter a judgment in the same action for a deficiency.

III. Non-Judicial Foreclosure Basics:

In order to foreclose, a lien instrument must have been properly recorded and there must be uncured defaults existing beyond any grace period to cure default. Every deed of trust or mortgage encumbering residential real property must be recorded with an information form attached to it, unless note owner has elected to foreclose by judicial foreclosure rather than power of sale foreclosure, and attaches certification to that effect. Notice of Commencement of Foreclosure under Power of Sale shall be on form promulgated by Mayor, recorded within appropriate time limits (30 days), mailed to every borrower and owner within same time limits, mailed to every subordinate interest holder within same time limits, and served upon owner at least 30 days in advance of foreclosure sale auction.

IV. Guidelines for Power of Sale:

There are no official guidelines, but the following is a checklist which covers common practice in D.C.:

A. Review loan documents carefully to determine the following:

1. Notice requirements (including method notice is to be given);
2. Applicable notice and cure periods; and
3. Other special requirements with respect to FNMA/FHLMC, FHA, or VA loans.

B. Prepare and send notice of default to borrower and any guarantors.

C. Prepare and send notice of acceleration to borrower and any guarantors.

D. Appoint substitute trustee(s).

E. Order title report/commitment for the property.

F. Arrange date of sale with lender, auctioneer, and trustee.

G. Prepare 30-day notice of sale (on current Recorder of Deeds form):

1. Send to borrower (and any guarantors) by certified mail and first-class mail.
2. File with the D.C. Recorder of Deeds (retain recordation receipt).
3. Send to all other persons with a record interest in the property by certified mail and first-class mail.

H. If necessary, provide notice of the sale to the Internal Revenue Service of foreclosure sale in accordance with the instructions contained in IRS Publication 796 (notice to be provided no later than 25 days prior to sale date for liens filed 30 days before the sale).

I. Prepare foreclosure advertisement (to be published in a newspaper of general circulation at least five times within the 10 business days prior to the sale).

J. Proof foreclosure advertisement prior to publication. Obtain all issues to ensure that the advertisement actually appears on the dates requested.

K. Order title bring-down to be performed immediately prior to the sale.

L. Check Bankruptcy Court for filing by property owner.

M. Ensure that trustee will attend the sale.

N. Attend auction sale:

1. Qualify and register all bidders.
2. Trustee makes any announcements regarding the property or the sale. Ask whether anyone has questions.
3. Auctioneer reads foreclosure advertisement.
4. Property is sold to the highest bidder.
5. Trustee executes contract with purchaser.

O. At settlement, prepare trustee's deed and, if necessary, seek the release of the IRS's right to redeem.

V. Power of Sale Guidelines as Represented in the Security:

Courts have said: The mortgagee has no title or estate in land, but only a lien for the security of the debt. Under D.C. law, a mortgagor's equity is considered to be the real and beneficial estate. Deed of Trust on realty was equivalent of a mortgage and conveyed legal title to trustees with equitable title remaining in the grantors. Trustee under a deed of trust owes duties both to the note holder and to the borrower.Where mortgage provides that upon default trustees are empowered to sell premises, default gives rise to right in holder to demand sale.

VI. Guidelines for Foreclosure when there is No Power of Sale:

Must commence an action in D.C. courts, which is rarely done.

VII. Foreclosure When Instrument Contains No Power of Sale:

Available, but rarely done.

VIII. Any Additional Satisfaction Permitted Under Continuing Power of Sale:

No case law directly on point. But see Looney v. Quill, 14 D.C. 51 (D.C. Sup. 1883) it discusses different parcels of land subject to a common encumbrance are conveyed to successive purchasers at different dates, the proceeds of the land must be applied in the inverse order of alienation to satisfy the common encumbrance.

IX. Sale by Power of Sale when the Instrument is Silent as to the Place or Terms of Sale:

Must apply to Court for direction.

X. Notice of Sale and How Notice is Given:

See above. Form available on the website of the Recorder of Deeds in PDF format.

Typically notice is handled by auctioneer, although a copy must also be given to Mayor or designee. Copies must be served on owner at current as well as property address. Court decisions also require notice on junior lienholders.

XI. Place and Time for Conducting Foreclosure by Power of Sale:

Sale governed by provisions of deed of trust, custom and practice in the District of Columbia codes.

Relevant Codes, Statutes or Case Law:
D.C. Code § 42-815 through 42-818; 2 D.C. Practice Manual Ch. 23 Real Property, at p. 23-84 (16th ed. 2007).
Vowell v. Thompson, 3 D.C. 428 (1829); In re 5028 Wisconsin Ave. Associates L. P., 167 B.R. 699 (Bankr. D.D.C. 1994); Barbour v. Baltz, 146 A.2d 905 (D.C. Mun. App. 1958); S&G Inv. Inc. v. Home Fed. Sav. & Loan Ass'n, 505 F.2d 370 (D.C. Cir. 1974). Maynard v. Sutherland, 313 F.2d 560 (D.C. Cir. 1962); Jackson v. Finance Corp. of Washington, 41 F.2d 103 (App. D.C. 1930)

Contributed By: Matthew W. Cheney & Monique Amy of Crowell & Moring

Receivership:

I. General information:

Receiverships in DC are governed by statutory and general equitable principals. Pursuant to the DC Statute, a Receiver may be appointed to take possession of:

A. property which has been attached;

B. assets of a bank that has discontinued operations for 60 days or is in liquidation;

C. assets on dissolution of corporations; and

D. rents for master metered apartment buildings when utility payments are delinquent. A Receiver may also be appointed under certain conditions to operate a nursing home or other similar facility in order to safeguard rights of its residents. Until a Receiver has given a bond as required by the terms of his appointment, he cannot dispossess a party in possession.

II. Appointing the Receiver:

A. The Basics:

The Receiver can be sought after a default. The process is similar to Federal Rule of Civil Procedure 66. Courts have equitable power to appoint Receiver for good cause. Appointments made in a commercial context on a case by case basis.

B. Time Frame for Appointment:

Absent a genuine emergency, a hearing can vary from a few days to a few weeks.

C. Can you go in Ex Parte?

Although possible, most judges refuse ex parte appointment of a Receiver unless a genuine emergency exists and there is a good reason for not providing notice. Ex parte orders are subject to swift review and reversal.

III. Loans and Advances:

Generally, loans should be approved by the Court. Any order on funding should include protections similar to those available to

Section 364 of the Bankruptcy Code. The use of future advance provisions in loan documents may provide additional protection.

IV. Sales During the Receivership:

The process is to seek the court's permission, which can be sought in connection with the petition to appoint the receiver or by a separate motion. Applications and orders to sell property should be modeled on those typically submitted pursuant to Section 363 of the Bankruptcy Code. Counsel should be consulted to determine whether an exercise of a power of sale or other foreclosure would be a better strategic option than a sale out of the receivership estate, particularly for commercial property.

There is no statutory authority. Courts will consider applications to sell property on a case by case basis.

V. Liens Against Receivership Property:

Lien issues and priorities can be complicated and counsel should be consulted. A lien search should be conducted early in a matter to help determine priorities and identify any potential issues. Appointment of a receiver does not modify liens or change lien priorities.

VI. Owners Associations:

The receivership does not alter the liens or rights established/obtained by an owners association. Such rights are handled in accordance with applicable state law.

VII. Construction Related to Receivership Property:

In either the original petition for appointment of a receiver or a subsequent application, the party(ies) should seek approval from the court. Such a request would likely include relief modeled after Sections 363 and 364 of the Bankruptcy Code. The use of future advance or other provisions in loan documents may provide additional authority and/or protection.

Contributed By: Matthew W. Cheney & Monique Amy of Crowell & Moring

VIII. Ending the Receivership:

There is no set procedure, but the Receiver shall not be dismissed except by order of the court.

IX. Miscellaneous:

A.

D.C. Courts will look to surrounding jurisdictions for authority when none exists in D.C.

B.

A Receiver may sue to set aside fraudulent transactions.

Relevant Codes, Statutes or Case Law:

D.C. Code § 16-518, 26-103, 28-3103 through 3107, 29-101.91 through 29-101.97, 29 391-405, 32-1411-1420, 42-3303, 43-543, 44-1002.02 through 44-1002.10.

Federal Rule of Civil Procedure 66; Sup. Ct. Civ. R. 66.

Phillips v. Smoot, 12 D.C. 478 (1882); Grant v. Phoenix Mut. Life Ins. Co., 121 U.S. 105 (1887); Cake v. Woodbury, 3 App. D.C. 60 (1894); Wood v. Grayson, 16 App. D.C. 174 (1900); Barley v. Gittings, 15 App. D.C. 427 (1899); Camp v. Canelacos, 131 F.2d 236 (D.C. Cir. 1942).

Florida

Foreclosure Summary

Security Instrument	Mortgage
Judicial	Yes
Non-Judicial	No
Initial Public Notice	Complaint
Time Frame	180-360
Redemption Period	Yes-brief and subject to court procedure
Deficiency	Yes – no one action rule

Receivership Summary

Ancillary Remedy Necessary	Yes
Ex-Parte	Yes
Approximate Time for Appointment	2 days to 4 weeks
Who or What can act as Receiver	An Individual or non-corporation business entity
Specific Receiver Requirements	No restrictions given – except must be neutral, impartial, and cannot be a corporation
Is there any approval list for Receivers	Generally no, but yes with some particular judges
Out of State Receivers Allowed	Depends on the Judge

Foreclosure:

I. General Information:

Florida law does not provide for any form of non-judicial foreclosure procedure. All mortgage foreclosures in Florida must be filed and prosecuted as civil law suits, usually in Florida's Circuit Courts, which are the state trial courts with general jurisdiction in disputes where the amount in controversy exceeds $15,000.00. However, if diversity of citizenship is present and the amount in controversy is in excess of $75,000.00, the action can be prosecuted in federal district court. In general, a mortgage foreclosure suit is treated no differently than any other type of civil suit, and is subject to the same rules governing discovery, including depositions, motion practice, affirmative defenses, counterclaims, trial, and rights of appeal as any other civil action. A hotly contested mortgage foreclosure in Florida can conceivably take more than a year to resolve, not including any subsequent appeal.

II. Judicial Foreclosure Basics:

All foreclosures in Florida are judicial. The plaintiff in a Florida mortgage foreclosure is either the owner/holder of the mortgage and the underlying promissory note or other debt obligation secured by the mortgage or someone with possession of the note and mortgage who is authorized to bring the action. The defendants to the foreclosure suit must include the owner(s) of the property, and usually also include the borrower(s), if different from the owner(s), any guarantors, all junior lienholders, and those tenants whose leasehold or possessory interests arose after the mortgage and whose interests the plaintiff wishes to eliminate.

The identities of the parties-defendant to the suit are determined by a title search, typically called a foreclosure title commitment, obtained from a title insurance agency. The commitment identifies all of the parties to be named as defendants in the foreclosure suit. If the identified defendants are named and served, and the foreclosure is prosecuted to judgment in accordance with Florida law, the title insurance company providing the commitment will then issue a title policy to the plaintiff, or the plaintiff's assignee, if the plaintiff is the winning bidder at the foreclosure sale.

A notice of *lis pendens* is recorded at the outset of the suit in the public records of the county in which the real property is located. Any interest arising after the recording of the notice of *lis pendens*, whether an ownership interest, a possessory interest, or a lien interest, and any unrecorded, non-possessory interest arising at any time, is automatically foreclosed unless the party asserting the interest affirmatively intervenes in the pending foreclosure suit within thirty (30) days of the recording of the notice of *lis pendens*.

III. Non-Judicial Foreclosure Basics:

Non-Judicial Foreclosures are not available in Florida.

IV. Guidelines for Power of Sale:

Power of Sale is not available in Florida.

V. Notice of Sale and How Notice is Given:

A typical judicial foreclosure sale in Florida state court is governed by Section 45.031, Florida Statutes. Per that statute, the date, time and place of the foreclosure sale are generally set in the Final Judgment of Foreclosure. Thereafter, a Notice of Sale is published once a week for two consecutive weeks in a general circulation periodical in the county in which the subject real property is located. The last publication of the Notice of Sale must be at least five days before the foreclosure sale. The foreclosure sales are generally public auctions, usually held at the County Courthouse, and conducted by a Clerk of the Circuit Court.

Section 45.031 provides that the winning bidder must deposit 5% of the winning bid immediately upon closing of the bidding. Most Clerks require by local administrative order that the remaining 95% of the bid amount be paid in cash or cashier's check later that same day, usually at either 2:00 p.m., 4:00 p.m., or 5:00 p.m., depending on the county involved.

The foreclosure sale is automatically confirmed, and the Certificate of Title, the operative deed instrument, is issued by the Clerk to the winning bidder on the eleventh day after the foreclosure sale if no objections to the sale have been filed. If objections are filed within ten (10) days after the foreclosure sale, the Certificate of Title is not issued until the objections are considered and overruled by the Court.

If the foreclosure action is prosecuted in federal district court, consultation with a title company is recommended so that the foreclosure sale procedure is such that a title company would be willing to insure the title. A federal foreclosure judgment in Florida probably needs to address in great detail how and where the sale will be advertised, who will conduct the foreclosure sale – the Clerks of the U.S. District Courts generally do not conduct foreclosure sales – where and when the sale will be held, what the bidding and payment procedure will be, how objections will be dealt with, how the title will be transferred, and how and when the sale will be confirmed by the court.

In general, in order to foreclose an interest of a party in the subject property, the party must be joined as a defendant in the judicial foreclosure, and thereby receives notice of every development in the foreclosure action, including the date, time and place of the foreclosure sale. The primary exception to this requirement that a party be joined in order to eliminate their interest is for parties whose interests are automatically eliminated by operation of the notice of lis pendens, as discussed above.

Receivership:

I. General information:

Perhaps the most important thing to understand about Florida receivership law is that the creditor has NO absolute right to the appointment of a receiver, NO right to select the receiver in the event the court determines that a receiver should be appointed, and NO right to determine the powers and duties of the receiver once appointed. The appointment of a receiver, the selection of the receiver, and the powers and duties of the receiver are all within the sound discretion of the court.

Other than the provisions of Rule 1.620 – providing that the receiver is required to conduct an initial inventory of the receivership property, and subsequent inventories every 3 months unless the court orders otherwise, and Section 660.41, Florida Statutes, which provides in part that a corporation cannot act as a receiver, unless the corporation is a bank or association and trust company incorporated under the laws of Florida, the appointment of receivers in Florida is a creature of common law.

II. Appointing the Receiver:

A. The Basics:

The appointment of a receiver is typically sought via a motion for appointment filed with the court and heard by the judge to whom the underlying foreclosure or other case is assigned. The motion spells out the grounds for appointment. The primary focus of the court is on whether the appointment of the receiver will prevent the subject property from being wasted or subjected to a serious risk of loss. The court has great discretion over whether to appoint a receiver, but the case law generally holds that the mortgagee must show that the secured property is being wasted or subjected to a serious risk of loss, or that rents or revenues from the property are being diverted and the value of the property is less than the mortgage debt. Two grounds for appointment of a receiver often used in other states - (a) the contract / loan / mortgage contains a clause giving the creditor an absolute, unfettered right to appointment of a receiver, and (b) the loan is in default - carry little with Florida courts. Instead, the focus in Florida is on whether the appointment of the receiver will prevent the subject property from being wasted or subjected to a serious risk of loss.

If appointed, the receiver's powers and duties, beyond those specified in Rule 1.620 above, are spelled out in the court's order of appointment.

Not only does the court have vast discretion over the appointment of a receiver, but also over the specific receiver to be appointed. The court is under no obligation to select the Receiver nominated by the moving plaintiff.

The receiver is required to post a cash or surety bond to insure performance of his / her duties. The amount of the bond is discretionary with the court. While not a hard and fast rule, many courts will tie the amount of the bond to the monthly gross cash flow of the property in receivership, or some multiple thereof.

While not common, the court also has discretion to require the plaintiff seeking the receiver to post a cash or surety bond conditioned on the payment of damages to the defendant if the appointment of the receiver is ultimately determined to have been improper. The amount of this bond, when required at all, is discretionary with the court.

B. Time Frame for Appointment:

In general, the time to obtain the hearing on a motion for appointment of receiver is dependent on the schedule of the judge assigned to the underlying foreclosure case. In true emergencies, an expedited hearing can usually be obtained within 24 to 48 hours. Absent an emergency, the time to obtain a hearing may vary from a few days to a few weeks.

C. Can you go in Ex Parte?

Yes, ex parte appointment is possible. But most judges refuse ex parte appointment of a receiver unless a genuine emergency exists and there is good reason for not providing the other parties to the suit with reasonable notice. Ex parte appointments are subject to swift review and reversal, and may also occasion the court to order a larger bond than would be required with an appointment with notice.

III. Loans and Advances:

There are no preset laws or codes so it is important to include such language in the Order Appointing the Receiver. It is common for an order appointing a receiver to allow the receiver to raise money by either issuing receiver certificates, or borrowing directly from the plaintiff or others.

IV. Sales During the Receivership:

In Florida, sales by receivers in real property foreclosures are not the norm. However, because of the degree of discretion afforded courts in appointing receivers, a Florida court can authorize a receiver to sell property during a receivership. There is no specified statutory or common law process for sales of property by receivers. Thus, the process to be followed is determined on a case-by-case basis and is typically spelled out in detail in the order authorizing the receiver sale.

In a real estate foreclosure, as a practical matter, a court is much more likely to allow a sale by the receiver if there are no actively objecting defendants. Thus, if the borrower is agreeable to the process, it is probably more likely to be permitted by the court.

There is some case law, but no real statutory authority, permitting receivers to sell property during the receivership. The court has virtually unlimited discretion in determining whether, and how, to permit the receiver to sell the property. In particular, there is no Florida state law version of a sale free and clear of liens of the type permitted under Section 363 of the Bankruptcy Code.

Within the last 2 years, several title insurance companies in Florida have disseminated bulletins expressing a general reluctance to insure titles obtained via state court receiver sales in lieu of more traditional foreclosure sales. However, it is still possible in some instances to conduct foreclosure sales via receiver, particularly if the borrower consents.

V. Liens Against Receivership Property:

Because Florida does not have a state statutory version of Section 363 of the Bankruptcy Code, an order authorizing a sale of property, especially real property, by a receiver should specifically address how the sale will affect liens. It is a good practice to run a proposed order authorizing a sale of real property by a receiver past the appropriate title insurance company to make sure that the contemplated sale procedure will pass muster with the title company, i.e., that the resulting sale will pass clean and insurable title to the purchaser. Typically, in considering the insurability of a receiver sale of real property in lieu of a more traditional foreclosure sale, the title insurance company will consider, among other things:

A. Whether and how the sale process provides for notice of the sale to junior lienholders, borrowers and guarantors;

B. Whether and how the sale process provides the various defendants an opportunity to object to the sale;

C. Whether and how the sale process provides for the rights of redemption of junior lienholders, the owner and the borrower to be preserved;

D. How the sale process provides for the passage of title to the property to be documented and evidenced in the public records;

E. Whether the order for sale provides for an acceptable confirmation procedure by which the court will enter a post-sale order confirming that the sale was valid and passed good title to the purchaser; and

F. Whether the owner has consented to the sale.

VI. Owners Associations:

A. General Information about Associations and Receivership:

There are no particular statutes regarding the interaction of the receiver with condominium or homeowners' associations. However, in the sub-section below are described a few statutes which are implicated when a receiver is appointed in certain circumstances there enumerated.

B. Dealing with Owners Associations during the Receivership:

It is dealt with on a case-by-case, property-by-property basis. The order appointing the receiver should spell out in detail how the associations are to be dealt with. If the association is developer-controlled, the receiver is typically given more power over the association than if it is controlled by owners of individual units.

Section 718.127, Florida Statutes provides that upon the appointment of a receiver by a court for any reason relating to a condominium association, the court shall direct the receiver to provide to all unit owners written notice of his or her appointment as receiver. Such notice shall be mailed or delivered within 10 days after the appointment. Notice by mail to a unit owner shall be sent to the address used by the county property appraiser for notice to the unit owner.

Section 718.301(1), Florida Statutes provides that when unit owners other than the developer own 15 percent or more of the units in a condominium that will be operated ultimately by an association, the unit owners other than the developer shall be entitled to elect no less than one-third of the members of the board of administration of the association. Unit owners other than the developer are entitled to elect not less than a majority of the members of the board of administration of an association when a receiver for the developer is appointed by a circuit court and is not discharged within 30 days after such appointment.

Section 720.313, Florida Statutes provides that upon the appointment of a receiver by a court for any reason relating to a homeowners' association, the court shall direct the receiver to provide to all members written notice of his or her appointment as receiver. Such notice shall be mailed or delivered within 10 days after the appointment. Notice by mail to a member shall be sent to the address used by the county property appraiser for notice to the owner of the property.

VII. Construction Related to Receivership Property:

This is dealt with on a case-by-case, property-by-property basis. The order appointing the receiver should spell out in detail the logistics for the receiver to complete construction.

VIII. Ending the Receivership:

It depends on the order appointing Receiver. Typically an order terminating the Receivership and providing for the dissolution of the Receiver's bond is entered.

Relevant Codes, Statutes or Case Law:

Rule 1.620, Florida Rules of Civil Procedure; Section 660.41, Florida Statutes

Florida has hundreds of cases governing virtually every facet of receivership law. That's because the appointment, maintenance and dissolution of receiverships is largely a creature of common law. This is one of the reasons that receivers often employ counsel in Florida.

Georgia

Foreclosure Summary

Security Instrument	Security Deed/ Mortgage
Judicial	Yes
Non-Judicial	Yes
Initial Public Notice	Publication
Time Frame	90 days
Redemption Period	No
Deficiency	Yes

Receivership Summary

Ancillary Remedy Necessary	Yes
Ex-Parte	Yes
Approximate Time for Appointment	10 days
Who or What can act as Receiver	Individual or Entity
Specific Receiver Requirements	None
Is there any approval list for Receivers	No
Out of State Receivers Allowed	Yes

Foreclosure:

I. General Information:

The laws of the State of Georgia provide for both judicial foreclosure and non-judicial foreclosure (by a power of sale).

II. Judicial Foreclosure Basics:

The basic forms of judicial foreclosure available in Georgia are:

A. foreclosure in equity (for mortgages, deeds to secure debt or mortgage substitutes deemed to be "equitable mortgages",

B. statutory foreclosure of a mortgage, and

C. foreclosure of a deed to secure debt by execution and levy of a judgment.

III. Non-Judicial Foreclosure Basics:

Non-judicial foreclosure is available in Georgia, provided that a power of sale is granted by the debtor to the creditor in the subject security instrument.

IV. Guidelines for Power of Sale:

Subject to any contractual agreements between the creditor and debtor to the contrary (except for anything to the contrary with respect to the requirements for the notice of sale to the debtor, the advertisement of the sale, the time, place and manner of the sale and the method of transferring title), creditors must comply with the rules governing the following subjects in a foreclosure by power of sale:

A. The timing, form, content and method of delivery of the notice of the sale to be provided to the debtor,

B. The manner of advertising the sale and the content of such advertisement,

C. The date, time and place of the sale,

D. That the sale must be conducted fairly and in good faith, and

E. The method of transferring title to the property. There is no post-foreclosure statutory right of redemption provided to the debtor.

V. Power of Sale Guidelines as Represented in the Security Instrument:

A power of sale is a power that the creditor has to help it exercise rights and remedies against the security for the loan. It is not security for the loan, though.

VI. Guidelines for Foreclosure When There is No Power of Sale:

A creditor may petition a court in the county in which the debtor resides for the foreclosure in equity of the property pursuant to the court's inherent equitable powers. A personal judgment may be awarded against the debtor under this option.

A creditor may file a petition in the superior court of the county in which the property is located in order to foreclose a mortgage at law. The court grants a rule nisi requiring that principal, interest and costs be paid. The rule can either be published twice a month for two (2) months or be served on the debtor thirty (30) days or more before the date payment is to be made. The debtor may respond to the rule by raising defenses at law or in equity, after which time a jury trial will be available.

Judicial foreclosure of a deed to secure debt involves obtaining a judgment from a court of a suit on the note, followed by sheriff's execution and levy of the judgment.

All foreclosure sales conducted by judicially appointed Receivers are subject to confirmation. The debtor and junior lienholders must be made parties to all judicial foreclosure proceedings.

VII. Foreclosure When Instrument Contains No Power of Sale:

The creditor could pursue a judicial foreclosure.

VIII. Any Additional Satisfaction Permitted Under Continuing Power of Sale:

A creditor can pursue a deficiency judgment against a debtor after having conducted a power of sale foreclosure in order to obtain the difference between the outstanding indebtedness under the loan and the amount of the highest and successful bid at the foreclosure sale. This requires filing a confirmation proceeding following a non-judicial foreclosure in which proceeding the creditor must establish, among other things, that the price realized at the foreclosure sale is at least equal to the fair market value of the property at the time of the sale.

IX. Sale by Power of Sale When the Instrument is Silent as to the Place or Terms of Sale:

Where the instrument is silent as to the terms of the sale, the creditor is required to conduct the sale fairly and in good faith.

The sale must be conducted fairly, which requires the creditor to ensure that nothing is done to chill the bidding, which is ultimately a question of fact for a jury to determine based on many considerations. Additionally, there is no requirement that the sale price be at least equal to the fair market value of the property, unless the creditor pursues a deficiency judgment against the debtor.

Only if the security instrument provides authorization, can the creditor purchase the property at the foreclosure sale. However, nothing prevents the current owner from purchasing the property at the foreclosure sale.

The security instrument governs how the power of sale foreclosure proceeds are distributed. If the security instrument is silent as to the application of surplus funds, then equity requires that such funds be paid to the debtor.

The place of the sale, whether or not specified in the security instrument, is required to be the courthouse of the county where the property is located.

X. Notice of Sale and How Notice is Given:

The advertisement of the sale must state the date, time and place of the sale, and a full and complete description of the property to be sold, including a legal description for the real property and a description of any personal property that is collateral pursuant to the security instrument. It is advisable to identify the grantor of the security deed and the current owner of the property. Any person who may be in possession of the property must be identified. If the creditor consents to an assumption of the property, then the new owner must also be identified in the advertisement. Any liens that will continue to encumber the property after the foreclosure sale must also be identified in the notice of sale.

In addition to any contractual requirements between the creditor and debtor regarding the notice of sale, in order to foreclose on either a residential or non-residential loan, the foreclosing creditor must publish an advertisement in the official publication of the county where the subject property is located at least once a week for four (4) consecutive weeks immediately prior to the sale. The Secretary of State of Georgia maintains a list of the official publication for each county in Georgia where the advertisement must be published.

The foreclosing creditor must also provide written notice of the foreclosure to the debtor at least thirty (30) days prior to the foreclosure sale, subject to the waiver of notice by the debtor, which waiver cannot be set forth in the security instrument or be executed contemporaneously with the security instrument. Such notice must include the name, address and telephone number of the person or entity that has the authority to negotiate an amendment to or modification of the security instrument, must contain a copy of the advertisement of sale, and must be sent by registered or certified mail or statutory overnight delivery, return receipt requested to either the property address or to the address(es) designated by the debtor. Actual notice is not required. For "high-cost" residential loans, a creditor must provide notice to the debtor of its intent to foreclose at least fourteen (14) days prior to the publication of the foreclosure advertisement. Also, for such "high-cost" residential loans, an additional notice of default with a thirty (30) day right to cure period is also required to be provided at least thirty (30) days prior to the date on which the creditor intends to accelerate and initiate foreclosure proceedings or other actions to seize the residence.

Notice must also be provided to a guarantor if the creditor seeks to recover attorney's fees in either residential or non-residential circumstances.

XI. Place and Time for Conducting Foreclosure by Power of Sale:

A foreclosure by power of sale must occur between 10:00 a.m. and 4:00 p.m. on the first Tuesday of the month at the county courthouse in which the property is located.

Relevant Codes, Statutes or Case Law:
O.C.G.A.§7-6A-5(11) and (13); O.C.G.A.§9-13-140; O.C.G.A.§9-13-142; O.C.G.A.§23-2-114; O.C.G.A.§23-4-35; O.C.G.A.§44-14-162; O.C.G.A.§44-14-162.1; O.C.G.A.§44-14-162.2; O.C.G.A. §44-14-162.3;O.C.G.A. §44-14-180(1)

Receivership:

I. General information:

The Official Code of Georgia Sections 9-8-1 through 9-8-14 provide for the appointment of a Receiver in a variety of circumstances, and those of most interest to a lender or servicer can be summarized as follows:

A. A Receiver may be appointed to take possession of and hold any assets charged with the payment of debts where there is manifest danger of loss, destruction, or material injury to those interested.

B. A Receiver may be appointed when there is a fund or property with no effective management.

II. Appointing the Receiver:

A. The Basics:

A verified complaint and motion would be filed after the default or action requiring the appointment of a Receiver has occurred. Usually, this process is done with notice to the borrower having charge of the assets, and the other party is able to respond.

Large discretion is vested in the trial judge in granting interlocutory injunctions and appointing Receivers to maintain the status until final hearing. A bond may be required in the discretion of the court.

B. Time Frame for Appointment:

A Receiver's appointment is subject to the court's schedule. Generally, a Receiver is appointed within 10 days of the hearing on the motion to appoint.

C. Can you go in Ex Parte?

Yes. Under extraordinary circumstances, the court may appoint a Receiver before and without notice to the borrower if there is a showing that the collateral is in jeopardy.

III. Loans and Advances:

There are no pre-set laws, codes or case law on such matters.

IV. Sales During the Receivership:

The Receiver can sell property if authorized by a court order.

V. Liens Against Receivership Property:

There are no specific statutes that deal with liens during the receivership and liens are dealt with on a case by case basis.

VI. Owners Associations:

There are no specific statutes that deal with Owners Associations during the receivership and liens are dealt with on a case by case basis.

VII. Construction Related to Receivership Property:

The Receiver would need a court order to permit construction and financing of construction.

VIII. Ending the Receivership:

The order of the court will determine the process to close the receivership. The Receiver is at all times subject to the court's orders and may be brought to account and removed at its pleasure. The Receiver needs to present a final report and there must be an order discharging the Receiver from his duties, unless the court's order allow otherwise.

Relevant Codes, Statutes or Case Law:

Adams v. Blalock, 136 S.E. 146 (Ga. 1926) (affirming appointment of Receiver to manage real estate and collect rents where maker of note was in default of obligations to make payments and was insolvent.) See also Ramey v. McCoy, 189 S.E. 44 (Ga. 1936) ("it is proper to appoint a Receiver to protect property sold on installment payments, the installments not paid, the interest and taxes accumulating.").
Sheffield v. Sheffield, 170 S.E. 83, 84 (Ga. 1933).
Richardson v. Roland, 267 Ga. 34, 472 S.E.2d 301 (Ga. 1996).
O.C.G.A. § 9-8-6 and §23-4-25

Hawaii

Foreclosure Summary

Security Instrument	Mortgage/ Trust Deed
Judicial	Yes
Non-Judicial	Yes
Initial Public Notice	Publication
Time Frame	Typically 60 days; 160-195 days
Redemption Period	No
Deficiency	Yes

Receivership Summary

Ancillary Remedy Necessary	Yes
Ex-Parte	Yes
Approximate Time for Appointment	30 days
Who or What can act as Receiver	No Restrictions Given
Specific Receiver Requirements	No
Is there any approval list for Receivers	Yes, it is a list of commissioners
Out of State Receivers Allowed	Typically, pick from Commissioner List

Foreclosure:

I. General Information:

Hawaii is a mortgage state that recognizes both judicial and non judicial foreclosure of mortgages secured against real property.

II. Judicial Foreclosure Basics:

A foreclosure that does not require a trial involves the filing of a (1) complaint (2) Motion for Summary Judgment which seeks a Decree of Foreclosure (appointment of a commissioner to auction the property) and (3) Motion to Confirm Sale. Hawaii Revised Statutes ("HRS") provide statutory authority for judicial foreclosures.

To be entitled to summary judgment and a decree of foreclosure, the Lender is required to prove four (4) material factual elements:

A. The existence of the Mortgage and Note;

B. The terms of the Mortgage and Note;

C. Default by the Borrowers/Mortgagors under the Note and Mortgage; and

D. The giving of requisite notice (acceleration letter, if any).

III. Non-Judicial Foreclosure Basics:

There are two alternate non-judicial foreclosure statutes in Hawaii. All non-judicial foreclosures in Hawaii are conducted under the original foreclosure statue HRS §§667-5 et seq because the process is significantly simpler than the alternate statute HRS §§667-21 et. Seq.

Non-judicial foreclosures must be performed by or under the supervision of an attorney licensed in Hawaii and physically located in Hawaii.

Any right to a deficiency judgment is waived under a non-judicial foreclosure.

IV. Guidelines for Power of Sale:

A. Mortgage must provide for foreclosure by power of sale.

B. Acceleration/demand letter, if required by the mortgage.

C. Copy of the Note and Mortgage.

D. Default by the Borrowers/Mortgagors under the Note and Mortgage.

E. Notice of Intention to Foreclose Under Power of Sale

1. Served on all parties with an interest in the property.
2. Posted on the property 21 days prior to the auction.
3. Served on the State of Hawaii Director of taxation 21 days prior to the auction.
4. Published in a newspaper of general circulation for 3 consecutive weeks, with the last ad published 14 days prior to the auction.
5. The affidavit of sale must be recorded at the State real property recorder's office within 30 days of the auction.

V. Guidelines for Foreclosure when there is No Power of Sale:

The exact amount of the indebtedness is not required to be proved until after the confirmation of the foreclosure sale since proof of default alone is sufficient to order foreclosure.

VI. Foreclosure When Instrument Contains No Power of Sale:

In such case you must foreclose judicially.

VII. Any Additional Satisfaction Permitted Under Continuing Power of Sale:

Only if permitted by mortgage or note.

VIII. Sale by Power of Sale when the Instrument is Silent as to the Place or Terms of Sale:

Auction is conducted at the particular state circuit court, which has jurisdiction over the property

IX. Notice of Sale and How Notice is Given:

Terms may vary, please contact the author for a copy.

Notice is given on the requirements under the Mortgage which typically provide for personal delivery or by first class mail.

X. Place and Time for Conducting Foreclosure by Power of Sale:

Noon at the State of Hawaii Circuit Court with jurisdiction over the subject property.

Relevant Codes, Statutes and Case Law

The original non-judicial statute under HRS §§667-5 through 667-10 and the alternate non-judicial statute under HRS §§667-21 through 667-42.

Receivership:

I. General information:

Receivership is a provisional remedy which is usually incidental to other relief such as the foreclosure of a real estate mortgage. In such cases, the Receiver is usually appointed to preserve protect and maintain the mortgaged property, to intercept rental income from the property, as in the case of an assignment of rents, to apply to the mortgage debt. If the mortgaged property is being used in the operation of a business as for example, a hotel, a Receiver may be appointed to operate the business pending the sale of the mortgaged property.

There are no specific statutory provisions in the State of Hawaii concerning the appointment of Receivers in foreclosure actions. However, the mortgage documents, particularly in the case of commercial loans, may contain specific provisions allowing for the appointment of Receivers.

Whether or not the mortgage documents contain an authorization for the appointment of a Receiver, the court in its discretion may appoint one on a proper showing that such an appointment would be necessary to preserve and maintain the property for the protection of the rights of the secured creditors.

II. Appointing the Receiver:

A. The Basics:

Once the complaint for foreclosure has been filed, the plaintiff may move immediately for the appointment of a Receiver

B. Time Frame for Appointment:

Unless the situation calls for emergency action, the appointment of the Receiver would normally take approximately one month.

C. Can you go in Ex Parte?

Appointment of a Receiver is discretionary by the court. If the mortgage documents provide for the appointment of a Receiver on an ex parte basis and there is sufficient urgency to justify such an appointment, the court in its discretion may appoint a Receiver without notice to the defendant mortgagor. However, such urgent circumstances are rare.

III. Loans and Advances:

There are no laws in the State of Hawaii concerning loans and advances by a Receiver, however in the usual case the Receiver is expected to advance costs in connection with the duties which he is specifically authorized to perform. If the costs are likely to be excessive or if the receivership continues for an extended period of time, the Receiver may seek approval for interim compensation from the court.

IV. Sales During the Receivership:

No information provided.

V. Liens Against Receivership Property:

No information provided.

VI. Owners Associations:

No information provided.

VII. Construction Related to Receivership Property:

No information provided.

VIII. Ending the Receivership:

In many cases the receivership is terminated when the Receiver becomes the court appointed commissioner. The court appointed commissioner's appointment ends when he files his final statement of disbursements pursuant to the order confirming the sale of the property.

If the appointment of the Receiver/commissioner is to be terminated for some other reason a court order canceling the appointment will be required.

Idaho

Foreclosure Summary

Security Instrument	Trust Deed
Judicial	Yes
Non-Judicial	Yes
Initial Public Notice	Notice of Default
Time Frame	150 days
Redemption Period	Yes
Deficiency	Yes

Receivership Summary

Ancillary Remedy Necessary	Yes
Ex-Parte	Possible
Approximate Time for Appointment	14-45days
Who or What can act as Receiver	No Restrictions Given
Specific Receiver Requirements	No
Is there any approval list for receivers	No
Out of State Receivers Allowed	Depends on the type of property

Foreclosure:

I. General Information:

Under Idaho law, both judicial and non-judicial foreclosures are available. Idaho Code § 6-101 et seq. is generally applicable to the judicial foreclosure process and Idaho § 45-1502 is generally applicable to the non-judicial foreclosure of trust deeds. Under Idaho law, a mortgage may only be foreclosed judicially. A land sale contract may be foreclosed judicially or enforced as a contract.

II. Judicial Foreclosure Basics:

The judicial foreclosure process under Idaho law is relatively quick and streamlined in comparison to many states. All parties with an interest in the property and all issues involved therein may be dealt with in one action. This may include appointing a receiver, resolving boundary disputes, conflicting priority claims, deficiencies and other factual or legal matters that make non-judicial foreclosure inadvisable. Although Idaho's state court system is friendly to the process of judicial foreclosure, it is certainly more expensive and time consuming than a non-judicial approach if that is available. As a result, judicial foreclosure is still typically only utilized when no other alternative exists or where there are legal or factual disputes such as priority issues. Another reason that non-judicial foreclosure is preferred is that the right of redemption exists after the sale of the property in a judicial foreclosure.

Idaho Code governs jurisdiction in state court and governs venue. Venue is proper in any county in which a portion of the at-issue property is located. In the instance in which the property spans multiple counties or the property is cross-collateralized and part of the same loan package, the foreclosing party may choose the preferred county for venue.

Idaho law adheres to the common one action rule. As such, all parties with an interest in the property must be joined as parties to the foreclosure action. Senior lien holders, including governmental entities with liens for taxes and assessments are not necessary parties, however, we recommend joining senior lien holders.

Idaho adheres to notice pleadings, however, with regard to foreclosure complaints, the courts do, as a matter of application, require a certain level of formality, including the assertion of a note and mortgage, property description, the alleged default, the total amounts due, and the complaint should include mention that no other suit is pending for collection of the debt. If there is a prepayment premium at issue, this element should be pleaded separately and citation to the specific agreement clause is advisable. The complaint should always request attorney fees and costs, including the cost of the title report.

Deficiency judgments are available under Idaho law. State Statute limits this remedy to "the difference between the mortgage indebtedness, as determined by the decree, plus costs of foreclosure and sale, and the reasonable value of the mortgaged property, to be determined by the court in the decree upon the taking of evidence of such value." Following the sale if the amount of the indebtedness plus costs exceeds the greater of (1) the fair market value or (2) the proceeds of the sale, at that time the lender should seek a deficiency by motion to the court.

The redemption period for property of more that twenty acres is one year. For smaller tracts, the applicable period is six months.

III. Non-Judicial Foreclosure Basics:

A deed of trust may be foreclosed non-judicially by advertisement and sale following compliance with certain requirements contained with the Idaho statutes. Generally, this is a cost effective and timely approach if it is available. In Idaho we can typically complete the non-judicial sale within 150 days. However, reinstatement may be accomplished if the borrower cures an unaccelerated default within 115 days. Delay is significantly limited in this process since no right of redemption exists. Further, legal defenses to this process are presented via an injunction which is rarely instituted and even more rarely granted. However, if multiple lien holders are involved, the non-judicial process becomes cumbersome and subject to delay.

It is our practice to utilize the judicial process if priority issues are uncovered via the title report. Some of the common mistakes in the process include failure to assure that the deed of trust is properly recorded, failure to have a default properly correlates to a power of sale provision, non-compliant notice of default and violations of the one action rule (i.e. an action on the debt is pending).

IV. Foreclosure When Instrument Contains No Power of Sale:

Idaho law will require use of the judicial process when no power of sale is available.

V. Notice of Sale and How Notice is Given:

A notice of sale must include the names of the grantor, name of the beneficiary, name of the trustee, property description, citation to the mortgage records for the county recorder (i.e book, page, instrument number), the default, owed amounts, date of sale, time of sale, place of sale.

State Law discusses the process by which the sale is conducted. Of course, the sale must comply with the information on the notice and by statute it must occur between 9:00 a.m. and 4:00 p.m. Sales almost always occur at the county courthouse in the county where the property is located or at a title company office located within the county where the property is located.

Notice of the sale must be given 120 days prior to the sale at the last known address of the grantor, any person that formally requested notice, the grantor's successor in interest and any lienholder. State law allows service of the notice on any adult occupant at the property. Three attempts must be made at service and a copy of the notice must be posted each time. The attempted service must also take place at least thirty days prior to the sale date.

Relevant Codes, Statutes or Case Law:
I.C. 11-*410* et seq; Idaho Code § 1-705; Idaho Code § 5-401; Idaho Code § 5-505 is applicable to lis pendens; Idaho Code § 6-108; Idaho Code § 11-401 et seq; Idaho Code § 45-1506

Receivership:

I. General information:

In practice, Idaho courts do not favor the appointment of a receiver. It is viewed as a remedy similar to a preliminary injunction and requires the presentation of significant evidence justifying the need. The Idaho bench generally sees the receivership process as being invasive of private property rights that should not be allowed until the proper conditions or proof is met to allow foreclosure.

A receiver may be appointed by the court in which an action for foreclosure is pending "where it appears that the mortgaged property is in danger of being lost, removed or materially injured . . . ." A receiver should also be appointed in cases where the property is in "imminent danger of great waste or irreparable injury."

II. Appointing the Receiver:

A. The Basics:

The appointment of a receiver varies from court to court. Typically with the filing of a motion for the appointment of a receiver we recommend a particular person that has the appropriate qualifications for the particular case at issue. We typically file an affidavit of the proposed receiver with a CV or resume and discuss why the individual is appropriate for the matter. The selection of receiver, once one is determined to be needed, is very much discretionary with the court and often comes via agreement of the parties.

B. Time Frame for Appointment:

Under normal circumstances and depending on the court's calendar, a motion can be filed and heard within fourteen days. However, the judges tend to take receiver motions under advisement. If that occurs, it could be 30 to 45 days between filing the motion and obtaining an order.

C. Can you go in Ex Parte?

It is possible to approach a motion for receiver in much the same way that we would present a temporary restraining order request or preliminary injunction. That will speed up the above-described time periods. However, this process will have an even higher burden in practice. The waste or injury must be very significant and there must be moving evidence along the same lines. We do not suggest this approach except in the most compelling circumstances.

III. Loans and Advances:

No statutes or rules govern loans or advances, and the Order of Appointment will govern the receiver's authority to obtain loans or to issue advances.

IV. Sales During the Receivership:

No information provided.

V. Liens Against Receivership Property:

No information provided.

VI. Owners Associations:

No information provided.

VII. Construction Related to Receivership Property:

No information provided.

VIII. Ending the Receivership:

A simple motion and order from the court is the appropriate mechanism. It is usually a stipulated motion and no hearing is needed.

IX. Miscellaneous:

Receivership orders in Idaho are somewhat rare and tend to be specifically tailored to the case at issue. It is recommended that the order specifically discuss the fees and mechanism for payment for the receiver.

Relevant Codes, Statutes or Case Law:
Idaho Code § 8-601 et seq. There is very limited and rather unhelpful case law on receivership under Idaho law.

Kelly v. Steele, 9 Idaho 141, 72 P. 887, 888 (1903). *See also* Idaho Code §§ 8-601 and 8-601A (appointment of receiver is appropriate where mortgaged property is in danger of injury; or where corporation is insolvent or is in danger of insolvency; or where income from property is in danger of being lost)

Jones v. Quayle, 3 Idaho 640, 32 P. 1134, 1134 (1893) (Where a party has under his control property in which another party has an interest, and he allows it to depreciate in value, or wrongfully disposes of the same, it is proper for the court to appoint a receiver).

Illinois

Foreclosure Summary

Security Instrument	Mortgage
Judicial	Yes
Non-Judicial	No
Initial Public Notice	Complaint
Time Frame	210 days
Redemption Period	Yes, limited
Deficiency	Varies

Receivership Summary

Ancillary Remedy Necessary	Yes
Ex-Parte	Rare
Approximate Time for Appointment	1 day – few weeks
Who or What can act as Receiver	Individual
Specific Receiver Requirements	Bond
Is there any approval list for Receivers	No
Out of State Receivers Allowed	Generally Yes

Foreclosure:

I. General Information:

The remedy of foreclosure is available in Illinois to enforce the obligations secured by a mortgage or trust deed upon maturity or default. All foreclosure in Illinois is judicial.

II. Judicial Foreclosure Basics:

A. General:

The interest in the mortgaged real estate of all persons made a party in such foreclosure and all non-record claimants given proper notice is terminated by the judicial sale of the property.

B. Reinstatement:

In any foreclosure of a mortgage executed after July 21, 1959, a mortgagor may reinstate the mortgage within 90 days of service of foreclosure action by curing all defaults, other than payment of the principal amount which was accelerated, including costs and expenses. Upon reinstatement, the foreclosure action shall be dismissed and the mortgage documents shall remain in full effect as if no acceleration or default had occurred. The court may enter a judgment of foreclosure prior to the expiration of this period, subject to the right of the mortgagor to reinstate the mortgage.

C. Redemption:

Only an owner of redemption may redeem from the foreclosure and only during the redemption period and only if the right of redemption has not been validly waived.

The redemption period for residential real property, ends on the later of 7 months after the mortgagor has been served with the summons or otherwise submitted to jurisdiction of the court and 3 months after the judgment of foreclosure is entered. For all other foreclosures, the redemption period ends on the later of 6 months after the mortgagor has been served with the summons or otherwise submitted to jurisdiction of the court and 3 months after the judgment of foreclosure is entered.

The amount required to redeem is the amount specified in the judgment of foreclosure and the amount of other expenses authorized by the court which the mortgagee reasonably incurs between the date of judgment and the date of redemption.

Notice of a party's intent to redeem must be given at least 15 days before the redemption period ends and by written notice to the mortgagee's attorney of record. Proof of such notice must be filed with the court.

III. Judicial Foreclosure Guidelines:

A. Notice of Foreclosure:

At least 30 days prior to the entry of a judgment of foreclosure, any person identified in the complaint as a defendant must be given notice of the foreclosure.

A notice of foreclosure is constructive notice of the pendency of the foreclosure to every person claiming an interest in the property if it is recorded in the county where the property is located and it includes:

1. the names of all plaintiffs and the case number
2. the court in which the action was brought
3. the names of title holder of record
4. a legal description of the real estate
5. a common address or description of the location of real estate, and
6. identification of the mortgage sought to be foreclosed

B. Pleadings and Service:

A foreclosure complaint must contain the statements and allegations called for by the form set forth in Illinois code.

C. Real Estate Subject to Senior Liens:

During a foreclosure, and any time prior to sale, a mortgagee or any other lienor may pay obligations on any senior mortgage when due, including real estate taxes. With court approval, a mortgagee or any other lienor may pay any other amounts in connection with other liens, encumbers or interests reasonably necessary to preserve the status of title and may add such amounts to the debt secured by the mortgage.

D. Judgment:

Upon the entry of a judgment of foreclosure, all rights of a part in the foreclosure against the mortgagor are secured by a lien on the property, which has the same priority as the claim to which the judgment relates. The lien is terminated upon confirmation of a judicial sale.

IV. Judicial Sale

Upon entry of a judgment of foreclosure, the property shall be sold at a judicial sale in accordance with the statute and on such terms and conditions as specified by the court in the judgment of foreclosure.

V. No Power of sale foreclosure guidelines

No real estate in Illinois may be sold by virtue of any power of sale contained in a mortgage or any other agreement, and mortgages may only be foreclosed in accordance with the Illinois Foreclosure Act.

VI. Notice of Sale and How notice of sale is given

The mortgagee or other party designated by the court shall file public notice of the sale as follows. The notice of sale shall include:

a. the name, address, phone number of the person to contact for information regarding the property;
b. the common address and other common description or the property;
c. a legal description of the property sufficient to identify it with reasonable certainty;
d. a description of the improvements on the property;
e. the times specified in the judgment, if any, when the real estate may be inspected prior to sale;
f. the time and place of the sale;
g. the terms of the sale;
h. the case title, case number and the court in which the foreclosure was filed; and
i. such other information ordered by the court.

The notice of sale must be published at least 3 consecutive calendar weeks, once in each week; the first such notice to be published not more than 45 days prior to the sale, the last such notice to be published not less than 7 days prior to the sale. It must be published by advertisements in a newspaper in the county where the property is located and separate advertisements in such newspaper.

VII. Other Types of Foreclosure:

A. Dead in Lieu of Foreclosure:

Rather than foreclosing on the property, the mortgagor and mortgagee may agree to terminate the mortgagor's interest in the property after a default in exchange for a deed from the mortgagor. Acceptance of a deed in lieu of foreclosure relieves all personal liability of persons who would otherwise owe payment or performance of other obligations secured by the mortgage.

B. Consent Foreclosure:

In a foreclosure, the court will enter a judgment satisfying the mortgage indebtedness by vesting absolute title to the property in the mortgagee free and clear of all claims and liens, except liens of the US government that cannot be foreclosed without judicial sale, if, before the sale:

1. the mortgagee offers to waive any and all rights to a personal judgment for deficiency against the secured by the mortgage;
2. the offer is made either in the foreclosure complaint or by motion upon notice to all parties not in default;
3. all mortgagors who then have an interest in the property, by response to the complaint or stipulation filed with the court, expressly consent to the entry of such judgment;
4. no other party objects to the entry of such judgment within the proper time for objection; and
5. upon notice to all parties not in default for failure to appear, answer or otherwise plead.

If a party other than mortgagor who has interest in the mortgaged property objects to the entry of the consent judgment, the court, after a hearing, must enter an order providing either:

1. that for good cause shown, the judgment by consent will not be allowed;
2. that for good cause shown, title to the mortgaged property is vested in the mortgagee as requested by the mortgagee and consented to by the mortgagor; or
3. that the objecting party has agreed to pay the amount owed on the mortgaged property and will pay that amount within 30 days after entry of the order and upon payment, title to the property will vest in the objecting party.

VIII. Place and Time for Conducting Foreclosure by Power of Sale:

The judgment will provide the terms for conducting the sale. It may be conducted by any judge or sheriff.

Relevant Codes, Statutes or Case Law:
ILP, p. 238.; 7351LCS 5/15-140lth rough 1402; 7351LCS 5/15-1404 through 1405; 735 ILCS 5/1 5-1502 through 1507; 735 JLCS 5115•1602 through 1603

Receivership:

I. General information:

In general, a receivership in Illinois is not governed by statute but rather by equity practice, as Illinois still has separate courts of law and equity (chancery). Receivership is a remedy to protect, preserve and administer property pending some other form of relief. Accordingly, courts in Illinois will not hear an action solely to appoint a Receiver.

Ordinarily, a party seeking appointment of a Receiver must have some right, claim or interest in the specific property for which receivership is sought.

II. Appointing the Receiver:

A. The Basics:

To request a Receiver, the movant must file an application or motion for relief. It should set forth the particular facts and circumstances that constitute the ground for the appointment of the Receiver and contain a clear statement that the defendant has some particular property or thing in his possession. The request for an appointment of a Receiver does not have as stringent pleading requirements as the requirements for the pleading to commence the suit, but the requestor still must provide facts either in the pleading or at the hearing to warrant the appointment of a Receiver. The motion for appointment of a Receiver should be verified and, if an application for a Receiver is based on allegations of a complaint, the complaint should be sworn to.

B. Time Frame for Appointment:

Once a complaint is filed, a motion to appoint a Receiver can be filed anytime thereafter. Ordinarily a motion can be heard on at least 4 days' notice by mail and 1 day notice by facsimile. A Receiver may be appointed temporarily pending a final determination of the motion. The court has discretion to set the hearing date, which is requested from the court. Requests for emergency hearings usually result in hearings within one business day.

C. Can you go in Ex Parte?

Ordinarily, the court should not appoint a Receiver on an ex parte application, but under exceptional circumstances, it may do so even though no notice has been given to the adverse party. Appointment of a Receiver on an ex parte application is only proper where there is real danger that the property will be wasted or removed from the jurisdiction, or in other exceptional cases.

III. Loans and Advances:

A Receiver has no power to pledge the trust estate for borrowed money in the absence of leave of court, and all persons extending credit to a Receiver do so at their peril.

IV. Sales During the Receivership:

No information provided.

V. Liens Against Receivership Property:

No information provided.

VI. Construction Related to Receivership Property:

No information provided.

VII. Ending the Receivership:

When the Receiver has disposed of the property in receivership according to the court order, his liability and responsibility as Receiver to that property ceases, and the receivership is terminated.

VIII. Miscellaneous:

A Receiver is entitled to compensation for his services up to the time of his discharge. The amount of compensation is at the discretion of the court. The receivership property bears primary liability for the compensation and expenses of the Receiver.

Relevant Codes, Statutes or Case Law:

Receivership is generally a matter of common law in Illinois and many relevant cases have been cited herein. The only relevant statutes are 735 I LCS 5/2-41 5 (Appointment of and actions against Receivers); 65 ILCS 511 I -31-2; 205 I LCS I 0511 Q-1.

Contributed By: John Collen of Tressler LLP

Indiana

Foreclosure Summary

Security Instrument	Mortgage
Judicial	Yes
Non-Judicial	No
Initial Public Notice	Complaint
Time Frame	150 days
Redemption Period	Yes, 3 months
Deficiency	Yes

Receivership Summary

Ancillary Remedy Necessary	Yes
Ex-Parte	Typically No
Approximate Time for Appointment	Varies depending on the judge
Who or What can act as Receiver	No Restrictions Given
Specific Receiver Requirements	Before commencing duties Receiver must file Oath & Bond
Is there any approval list for Receivers	Typically no, some Judges do maintain lists
Out of State Receivers Allowed	Depends on the Judge

Foreclosure:

I. General Information:

A. All foreclosure sales in Indiana are done by judicial action, as there is no power of sale provision in the Indiana Code.

B. Indiana has a right to pre-sale redemption. Pre- sale Redemption occurs between the time the complaint is filed and the date the property is sold. The length of the redemption depends on the date the mortgage was signed and ranges between three (3) months and twelve (12) months, but is typically three (3) months.

C. Mortgagor can waive pre-sale redemption, which results in the lender losing the right to pursue a deficiency judgment.

D. Indiana recognizes and enforces an assignment of rents and leases.

II. Judicial Foreclosure Basics:

A. Filing a Complaint in county where property is located.

1. Complaint must name parties with ownership interest in the property as necessary parties.
2. Complaint should also name all junior lienholders and other having junior claims or interests as proper parties.
3. Request for appointment of a Receiver can be made in connection with the complaint, or by separate motion.
4. Can be combined with suit on note and on guaranties.
5. Can be combined with foreclosure of personal property.
6. A lis pendens should be filed at the same time as filing the complaint.

B. Lender must wait the pre-sale redemption period, typically three (3) months, to execute on a complaint for

Contributed By: Jim Vantine and Lori Purkeyu of
Miller Canfield

foreclosure. The period is twelve (12) months for mortgages executed prior to January 1, 1958 and six (6) months for mortgages executed after December 31, 1957 and prior to July 1, 1975.

C. Court issues order for sale and judgment, which is certified by the Clerk of the court to the Sheriff.

D. The Sheriff schedules and conducts the sale.

1. If the lender desire to postpone the sale another Sheriff's sale request must be filed, and notices reserved and republished.
2. Foreclosure sale process requires publication of the notice of sale once a week for three (3) weeks in a local newspaper. The first notice must be published 30 days before the sale of the sale.
3. Owner of the property must be served with the notice of the foreclosure sale by the sheriff at the time the first notice is published.

E. The owner of the property retains all possessory rights to the property, rent free, until the foreclosure sale.

F. The successful purchaser at the foreclosure sale is entitled to immediate possession of the property following the foreclosure sale and the Borrower no longer has any redemption rights.

G. State statute permits, under certain limited circumstances, the sheriff's sale to be conducted by a private auctioneer on the civil sheriff's behalf.

H. Indiana law requires all expenses of sale and real estate taxes in arrears to be paid first from sale proceeds.

III. Non-Judicial Foreclosure Basics:

Non –Judicial Foreclosures are not available in Indiana.

IV. Guidelines for Power of Sale:

The Indiana Code does not contain a power of sale provision; all sales are by judicial action.

Relevant Codes, Statutes or Case Law:
I.C. 32-29-7 ; I.C. 32-30-10-4

Receivership:

I. General information:

Indiana receivership statute, governs appointment of Receiver.

A. To vacate a fraudulent purchase of property.

B. In actions between partners or persons jointly interested in any property or fund.

C. In all actions in which property, fund or rent and profits in controversy are in danger of being lost, removed or materially injured.

D. In actions in which a mortgagee seeks to foreclosure a mortgage:

1. The court shall appoint a Receiver if at the time the motion is filed the property is not occupied by owner as his/her principal residence and
2. property is in danger of being lost, removed or materially injured;
3. property may not be sufficient to discharge the mortgaged debt;
4. either the mortgagor or the owner of the property has agreed in the mortgage or in some other writing to the appointment of a Receiver;
5. a person not personally liable for the debt secured by the mortgage has, or is entitled to, possession of all or a portion of the property;
6. the owner of the property is not personally liable for the debt secured by the mortgage; or
7. the property is being, or is intended to be, leased for any purpose.

Contributed By: Jim Vantine and Lori Purkeyu of Miller Canfield

8. When a corporation has been dissolved, is insolvent, is in imminent danger of insolvency or has forfeited its corporate rights.
9. To protect or preserve the property during the time allowed for redemption and to secure rents and profits.
10. In other cases as may be provided by law or where, in the discretion of the court, it may be necessary to secure ample justice to the parties.

II. Appointing the Receiver:

A. The Basics:

Receivers are appointed by motion, supported by affidavit and documents. Receivers may not be appointed in any case until the adverse party has appeared or has had reasonable notice of the application for the appointment, except upon sufficient cause show by affidavit.

B. Time Frame for Appointment:

This varies greatly by the practice of the particular court and judge.

C. Can you go in Ex Parte?

Typically not.

III. Loans and Advances:

There are no set laws or procedures for Indiana.

IV. Sales During the Receivership:

Draft a broad order for appointment of Receiver which permits the Receiver to sell, lease or otherwise dispose of property. A sale may be either private or public, and it is necessary to obtain court confirmation of the sale after it has occurred for the Receiver's protection

IC §32-30-5-7(5) specifically permits a Receiver to sell property in his own name. *See, Zumpfe v. Piccadilly Realty Company,* 13 NE2d 715 (1938).

V. Liens Against Receivership Property:

There are no specific statutes relating to the affect of liens upon a Receiver. Generally, a Receiver will take any project subject to existing liens.

VI. Owners Associations:

There are no specific provisions relating to owners associations and a Receiver.

VII. Construction Related to Receivership Property:

The order appointing receiver should be broad enough to permit the Receiver to commence or complete construction, and direct third persons to deliver all plans and specifications to the Receiver. The order should also provide for the Receiver 's ability to borrow any amounts necessary to complete construction.

VIII. Ending the Receivership:

Court may end a receivership at any time. Receiver will be required to file all necessary reports. The Court's approval of the Receiver's report releases and discharges the Receiver.

IX. Miscellaneous:

A.

The Receiver's powers are defined by statute, and including bringing and defending actions; take and keep possession of property, receive rents, collect debts and sell property, and generally do other acts respecting the property as the court may authorize.

B.

Indiana permits an appeal of an order appointing, or refusing the appointment of a Receiver within ten (10) days after the court's decision, without awaiting the final determination of the case.

Relevant Codes, Statutes or Case Law:

I.C. 30-32-5-3; I.C. 32-30-5-7; I.C. 32-30-5-9 through 32-30-5-10; I.C. 32-30-5-14 through 32-30-5-21; IRC 32-30-5

Citizens Financial v. Innsbrook, 833 N.E.2d 1045 (Ind. Ct. App. 2005)

Contributed By: Jim Vantine and Lori Purkeyu of Miller Canfield

Iowa

Foreclosure Summary

Security Instrument	Mortgage
Judicial	Yes
Non-Judicial	Yes (under certain circumstances)
Initial Public Notice	Petition
Time Frame	160 days
Redemption Period	Yes, subject to foreclosure without redemption procedure
Deficiency	Yes (with certain exceptions)

Receivership Summary

Ancillary Remedy Necessary	Yes
Ex-Parte	Yes (in emergency only)
Approximate Time for Appointment	10-30 days
Who or What can act as Receiver	No Restrictions Given
Specific Receiver Requirements	Need to File oath and post a bond
Is there any approval list for Receivers	No
Out of State Receivers Allowed	Yes

Foreclosure:

I. General Information:

There are numerous procedures for the foreclosure of mortgages in Iowa. The procedures vary depending on the type of borrower, the type of property encumbered by a mortgage and whether the lender is willing to waive a deficiency. If the borrower is cooperative, there is a procedure for foreclosing out junior lienholders pursuant to a deed in lieu of foreclosure.

II. Judicial Foreclosure Basics:

In general, mortgages must be foreclosed judicially in Iowa. The foreclosure action must be commenced in the county where the subject real property is situated. Separate actions on a note and mortgage may not be prosecuted in the same county at the same time. If <u>separate</u> actions are brought on the note and the mortgage, the lender must elect which to prosecute and the other must be discontinued at lender's cost. The foreclosure petition and an original notice must be served personally on the defendants. Copies of the loan documents should be attached to the foreclosure petition.

A. Residential

If the subject real property is the residence of the borrower <u>and</u> is a one-family or two-family dwelling ("Residential Property"), the creditor must provide the borrower with a notice of the right to cure the existing default (the "Cure Notice") at least thirty days prior to commencing a foreclosure action or otherwise seeking to enforce the debt. A borrower has a right to cure the default unless the lender has already provided the borrower with a Cure Notice with respect to a prior default within the preceding three hundred sixty-five days. (The lender can, however, accept a voluntary surrender of the subject real property during the cure period).

The borrower has a right to cure the default within thirty days from the date the creditor gives the Cure Notice by tendering either the amount of all unpaid installments due at the time of tender, without acceleration, or the amount stated in the Cure

Notice, whichever is less, or by tendering the performance necessary to cure a default as described in the Cure Notice.

B. Agricultural

If the property encumbered by the mortgage is agricultural land used in a farming operation ("Agricultural Property") and the debt is $20,000 or more, the lender must not only provide the borrower with the Cure Notice, but must also obtain a "mediation release" signed by a mediator selected by the farm mediation service. (The requirement of a "mediation release" can be waived if a court determines after notice and hearing that the time delay required for the mediation would cause the lender to suffer irreparable harm). The "mediation release" (or its waiver by court order) is a jurisdictional requirement to commencing a juridical foreclosure action.

The borrower under a mortgage of Agricultural Property has a right to cure a default unless (a) the lender has given the borrower a Cure Notice with respect to two prior defaults on the same obligation, (b) the borrower has surrendered the subject real property and the lender has accepted the surrender in full payment of the debt, or (c) the lender has given the borrower a Cure Notice with respect to a prior default within twelve months prior to the existing default. The cure notice should be sent to such a borrower by certified mail.

If the borrower has a right to cure the default, the Borrower may tender a cure within forty-five days after the cure notice is given. (The time period for requesting a mediation runs concurrently with the cure period). The borrower can cure the default by paying (a) the amount of all unpaid installments due at the time of payment, without acceleration, plus a delinquency charge of the annual interest rate plus five percent per annum between the giving of the cure notice and the payment; (b) paying the amount set forth in the Cure Notice, whichever is less; or (c) tendering the performance described in the cure notice.

In order to secure a meditation release, the lender must file a request for mediation with the farm mediation service. The farm mediation service is required to send an initial mediation notice within twenty-one days after it receives a mediation request and the initial mediation is required to be held within twenty-one days after the initial mediation notice is sent. If the borrower fails to attend the mediation, waives mediation or the parties fail to reach an agreement at the initial mediation, the mediator must provide the lender with a mediation release. However, if the lender fails to attend the initial mediation or participate in all mediation meetings, a mediation release may not be given.

C. Non-Agricultural

If the subject real property is not Agricultural Property, the lender can choose to foreclose without redemption rights. In order to elect foreclosure without redemption, the lender must include a notice on the first page of the foreclosure petition, the form of which is set forth in the Iowa Code. If foreclosure without redemption is elected, the borrower may file a demand to delay the foreclosure sale at any time prior to entry of judgment. If such a demand is filed, the sale generally is held promptly after the expiration of two months from entry of judgment. However, if the subject real property is Residential Property (and the Petition does not waive a deficiency judgment) the sale shall be held after the expiration of twelve months. The sale shall be held after six months if the petition includes a waiver of a deficiency judgment. If no demand is filed, the sale may be held promptly after judgment. If the lender elects foreclosure without redemption and does not include a waiver of a deficiency judgment, the subject real property is Residential Property and the borrower does not file a demand for the delay of the sale, then the lender is not permitted to seek a deficiency judgment. After the sale where a lender has elected foreclosure without redemption, neither the borrower nor any junior lienholder may redeem the property.

Upon entry of judgment, a special execution issues directing the sale of the property by the county sheriff.

D. Redemption Rights

If the lender does not elect foreclosure without redemption and the property is Agricultural Property or Residential Property, then the borrower may redeem the property at any time within one year from the date of sale and is entitled to possession during the redemption period. The borrower has the exclusive right to redeem the property for the first six months of the twelve month redemption period. Other creditors may redeem the property within nine months of the sale. However, a party that has stayed execution on the judgment is not entitled to redeem.

If the lender does not elect foreclosure without redemption, the lender has not waived a deficiency judgment and the property is not Agricultural Property or Residential Property, the redemption period is one hundred eighty days after the sale. In that situation, the borrower has an exclusive right of redemption for ninety days and creditors may redeem within one hundred thirty-five days.

If the lender has not elected foreclosure without redemption, the lender has waived a deficiency judgment and the property is not Agricultural Property or Residential Property, the redemption period is ninety days after the sale. In that situation, the borrower has an exclusive redemption of thirty days after the sale and creditors may redeem within sixty days after the sale.

If the subject real property is less than ten acres in size, the borrower and lender may agree in the mortgage to reduce the redemption period to six months after the sale if the lender waives a deficiency judgment in the foreclosure proceeding. In that situation, the borrower may remain in possession of the property during the redemption period and the borrower has an exclusive redemption period of three months after the sale. Creditors may redeem the property for a period of four months after the sale.

If the subject real property is less than ten acres in size, the borrower and lender may also agree in the mortgage that if the lender waives a deficiency judgment in the foreclosure proceedings and if the court finds in the foreclosure decree that the owner of the subject real property and those parties personally liable for the debt have abandoned the subject real property at the time of the foreclosure, then the redemption period is reduced to sixty days. In that situation, the borrower has an exclusive period to redeem for the first thirty days after the sale and creditors may redeem for a period of forty days after the sale. If the borrower enters an appearance in the foreclosure, however, there is a presumption that the property is not abandoned.

III. Non-Judicial Foreclosure Basics:

There are two separate methods for the non-judicial foreclosure of a mortgage in Iowa.

A. Non Judicial Foreclosure

The first method is only available if the subject real property is not Agricultural Property. The lender initiates the process by personally serving a notice (the "Non-Judicial Foreclosure Notice") on the borrower, any parties in possession of the subject real property and all junior lienholders. The Non-Judicial Foreclosure Notice must (a) identify the mortgage, including recording information, and provide a legal description of the subject real property, (b) specify the terms of the mortgage with which the borrower has failed to comply, (c) indicate that the mortgage will be foreclosed unless within thirty days of service of the notice the borrower cures the default or files a rejection of the Non-Judicial Foreclosure Notice (the "Rejection") with the county recorder where the subject property is situated and serves a copy of the rejection upon the mortgagee. The Non-Judicial Foreclosure Notice must also contain certain language set forth in the Iowa Code.

If the borrower files a Rejection with the county recorder together with proofs of service that the rejection has been served on the mortgagee, then the Non-Judicial Foreclosure Notice is of no force or effect and the lender must foreclose the mortgage judicially. If the borrower does not file a Rejection, then the lender automatically succeeds to all interest of the borrower in the subject real property, all junior liens are foreclosed and the debt is extinguished, i.e. there is no possibility for a deficiency.

B. Deed in Lieu

A mortgage may also be foreclosed by deed in lieu of foreclosure. In this procedure, the borrower conveys to the lender all interest in the subject real property and the lender must accept the conveyance and waive any deficiency. The borrower and lender must also record a jointly executed agreement (the "Deed in Lieu Agreement") with the county recorder of the county in which the subject real property is situated. The Deed in Lieu Agreement must indicate that the borrower and lender have elected to follow the alternative voluntary foreclosure procedures of the Iowa Code. At the time the Deed in Lieu Agreement is executed, the lender must provide the borrower with the form set forth in the Iowa Code. The form provides the borrower with an opportunity to cancel the Deed in Lieu Agreement within five business days from the date of the agreement.

A lender that agrees to a foreclosure pursuant to these procedures cannot report to a credit bureau that the borrower is delinquent on the mortgage, but may report that the foreclosure procedure was used.

IV. Notice

The lender must also send by certified mail notice of the election to follow such procedures to all junior lienholders, which notice must advise the junior lienholders that they have thirty days from the date of mailing of the notice to exercise any rights of redemption. If a junior lienholder does not redeem, its lien is automatically removed from the property.

Receivership:

I. General information:

A receivership is ancillary to the main action in Iowa and therefore must be combined with another cause of action involving the property that the Receiver is to take possession.

II. Appointing the Receiver:

A. The Basics:

The appointment of a Receiver can be sought either in a petition or through a motion. The party seeking the appointment must show (a) a probable right to, or interest in, the property that is the subject of the controversy, (b) that the property, or its rents or profits, is in danger of being lost or materially injured or impaired, (c) that the appointment will promote the interests of one or more parties to the action, and (d) that the appointment will not unduly infringe upon the rights of any of the parties. In order to qualify, the Receiver must take an oath to faithfully discharge the Receiver's trust and must file a bond with the clerk of court in an amount fixed by the court.

B. Time Frame for Appointment:

A hearing on the appointment is set on such notice to the other parties as the court may prescribe. Thus, it is entirely within the discretion of the court as to when a hearing on the appointment will be held. Generally, it should take ten to thirty days, depending on the court's calendar.

C. Can you go in Ex Parte?

State law provides that the hearing on appointment will be held on such notice to the other parties as the court shall prescribe. However, the court may exercise discretion to appoint a Receiver without notice in an emergency or unusual circumstance.

III. Loans and Advances:

Under Iowa law, a Receiver has the power to bring and defend actions, to take and keep possession of property, to collect debts, to receive the rents and profits of real property, and, generally, to do such acts in respect to the property committed to the Receiver as may be authorized by law or ordered by the court. The Iowa statutes, however, do not speak directly to the Receiver's authority to obtain loans or issue advances. This may be addressed within the Order of Appointment.

IV. Sales During the Receivership:

No information provided.

V. Liens Against Receivership Property:

If there is a contest as to the priority of liens upon the property placed in the hands of a Receiver, the matter should be submitted to the court to determine their priority.

VI. Owners Associations:

No information provided.

VII. Construction Related to Receivership Property:

No information provided.

VIII. Ending the Receivership:

There are no specific requirements regarding the closing of the receivership. The closing of the receivership should be addressed in the Order of Appointment.

Relevant Codes, Statutes or Case Law:

Iowa Code §§ 628.1-628.29 (redemption); Iowa Code §§ 654.1-654.17B (foreclosure of real estate mortgages); Iowa Code §§ 654.18- 654.26 (alternative foreclosure procedures); Iowa Code §§ 655A.1-655A.9 (non-judicial foreclosure of non-agricultural mortgages); and Iowa Code §§ 680.1-680.11(receivership)

Wolf v. Murrane, 199 N.W.2d 90 (Iowa 1972); *Citizens State Bank v. Beucher*, 294 N.W. 717 (Iowa 1940); *Jarl v. Pritchett*, 179 N.W. 945 (Iowa 1920)

Kansas

Foreclosure Summary

Security Instrument	Mortgage
Judicial	Yes
Non-Judicial	No
Initial Public Notice	Complaint
Time Frame	120 Days
Redemption Period	Yes 3-12 months
Deficiency	Yes

Receivership Summary

Ancillary Remedy Necessary	Yes
Ex-Parte	Yes
Approximate Time for Appointment	10 days
Who or What can act as Receiver	Individual or Company
Specific Receiver Requirements	The receiver must comply with the oath and bond requirements of K.S.A. 60-1302
Is there any approval list for Receivers	No
Out of State Receivers Allowed	Yes

Foreclosure:

I. General Information:

Kansas is a mortgage state and requires judicial foreclosure in all instances. Non-judicial foreclosure is not available in Kansas.

II. Judicial Foreclosure Basics:

In Kansas, upon default under the note, mortgage or other loan documents, mortgages are foreclosed upon judicially. The lender will bring an action for breach of note and mortgage and seek foreclosure in such action. Such action should also contain any other claims by lender, including enforcement of guaranties, declaratory judgment on the assignment of rents, and the appointment of a receiver (if applicable).

Kansas is a notice pleading state (K.S.A. 60-208) rather than a fact pleading state. Accordingly, it is just essential in Kansas to provide notice of the claims, but not specifically delineate all facts in the petition. Because most mortgages include a security interest not only in the real estate, but also in personal property, practitioners generally take the approach of using a verified petition. Pursuant to K.S.A. 60-1006, a foreclosure of a security interest in personal property requires the petition to be verified or supported by an affidavit.

In the petition, it is critical to not only name the borrower (and guarantors, if applicable), but also any and all parties claiming an interest in the property, such as second mortgage holders and other junior lienholders. In the petition, the lender should assert that its mortgage is superior to the rights of all such junior lienholders. A title search prior to filing the petition is essential to properly name all of the parties. The petition will typically seek not only an in rem judgment against the property in the foreclosure action, but also a personal judgment against the borrower and guarantors for any deficiency (or carve-out liabilities in the event of non-recourse debt). Many practitioners will not only seek notice via personal or certified mail service , but will also provide notice by publication (for construction notice purposes).

Under Kansas law, both the borrower and junior creditors have a statutory right of redemption. The Kansas statute is fairly detailed as to the time period for redemption, which varies based upon certain circumstances. The general rule is that the borrower's redemption period is 12 months, but is reduced to 3 months if less than 1/3 of the original indebtedness secured by the mortgage has been repaid to the lender. The redemption period may be waived or shortened in the mortgage. K.S.A. 60-2414(a) provides that "(e)xcept or mortgages covering agricultural lands or single or two-family dwellings owned by or held in trust for natural persons, the mortgagor may agree in the mortgage instrument to a shorter period of redemption than 12 months or may wholly waive the period of redemption." Nearly all commercial mortgages include a waiver of the redemption right, which is obviously enforceable by Kansas statute as noted above.

However, such waiver of redemption does not extend to junior lien creditors, which redemption period is typically 3 months. Accordingly, if a second mortgage or other junior liens are involved, a lender must wait 3 months after the foreclosure sale prior to taking title to the property via the sheriff's deed. The ability of a junior lien creditor to redeem the mortgaged property will play into the calculation of the lender's credit bid at foreclosure.

III. Non-Judicial Foreclosure Basics:

Not available in Kansas.

IV. Power of sale foreclosure guidelines

As noted above, Kansas is a judicial foreclosure state, so there is no separate "power of sale" under Kansas law.

V. Power of sale constitutes part of security

Same as above.

VI. No Power of sale foreclosure guidelines

Same as above - Kansas is a judicial foreclosure state.

VII. Foreclosure when instrument contains no power of sale.

Same as above- Kansas is a judicial foreclosure state.

VIII. Additional satisfaction permitted under continuing power of sale.

Same as above- Kansas is a judicial foreclosure state.

IX. Sale under power where instrument silent as to place or terms of sale.

Same as above - Kansas is a judicial foreclosure state.

X. Notice of Sale and How notice of sale is given

The journal entry for the judgment on the foreclosure action should specifically set forth not only a judgment on the indebtedness owed by the borrower (and guarantors, if applicable) and secured by the mortgage, but also set forth lien priorities and redemption rights (if any). The judgment is stayed for a period of 14 days prior to the sheriff's sale. If the borrower fails to pay the judgment in full within such 14-day period, then the lender will direct the sheriff to advertise and sell the property pursuant to a sheriff's sale. The sheriff must advertise the notice of sale for 3 consecutive weeks. The sheriff will not only publish the sale, but personal notice must be provide to all parties in the lawsuit (which must be delivered to the borrower within 5 days after the initial publication.

At the sheriff's sale, the lender will strategize on the amount of the bid based upon the judgment amount and the value of the mortgaged property. A number of other considerations will go into the determination of such bid, including the likelihood of collection against the borrower and/or guarantors for any deficiency amount and whether there is a creditor redemption period (and the likelihood of any junior lien holders to redeem the property). Following the sheriff's sale, the sheriff will file a return on the foreclosure sale with the court, including the purchaser information and amount of bid. If the court finds the proceedings to be "regular and in conformity with law and equity, it shall confirm the same, direct the clerk to make such entry upon the journal and order the sheriff to make to the purchase the certificate of sale or deed and provided for in this article" . The court also has discretion to determine the bid is substantially inadequate and to order a resale.

Once the court confirms the sheriff's sale, the sheriff will issue a certificate of purchase to the successful bidder. After the expiration of the redemption period, if any, the sheriff will issue a sheriff's deed to the successful bidder and title will then vest in the purchaser. The purchaser should obtain an owner's policy of title insurance upon issuance of the sheriff's deed. Further, after the sheriff's sale, the Lender may also commence enforcement of the deficiency amount against the borrower and/or guarantors pursuant to the journal entry of judgment.

XI. Place and time for conducting foreclosure by power of sale.

Not applicable.

Relevant Codes, Statutes or Case Law:
K.S.A. 60-2401; K.S.A. 2406; K.S.A. 60-2410; K.S.A. 60-2414; K.S.A. 60-2415; K.S.A. 60-2416; K.S.A. 60-206; K.S.A. 60-208; K.S.A. 60-303; K.S.A. 60-262; K.S.A. 60-1006.

Receivership:

I. General information:

A receiver may be appointed in a variety of circumstances whose duty it will be to keep, preserve, and manage all property and protect any business or business interest entrusted to the receiver pending the determination of any proceeding in which such property or interest may be affected by the final judgment.

II. Appointing the Receiver:

A. The Basics:

A receiver shall not be appointed unless (a) the petition or application for appointment specifies the general character and probable value of the property or business (and, if real estate, estimated income generated) and (b) notice and an opportunity to be heard (except as to ex parte appointments referenced below).

Most loan documents (typically in the mortgage or in the assignment of leases and rents) provide for the appointment of a receiver. A comprehensive review of the loan documents regarding the contractual provisions for appointment of a receiver is important. However, even absent such provisions, a lender can still point to the Kansas statutes in seeking such appointment if in the best interest of the asset.

B. Time Frame for Appointment:

The notice period for a receivership varies based upon local rules and availability of the assigned judge, but the typical notice period is 10 days. Of course, this time period could be shorter or longer depending upon the circumstances (or no filing period in the case of an ex parte appointment, as provided below).

K.S.A. 60-1305 provides for a 14-day appeal process if a party challenges the appointment of a receiver.

C. Can you go in Ex Parte?

Yes. Kansas statute provides that the judge may "after the introduction of evidence and a record of the proceeding is made, make a finding that immediate and irreparable injury is likely to result, and shall set forth in the order the probably nature of such immediate and irreparable injury."

Most loan documents provide for the appointment of an ex parte receiver upon default. Our experience is that courts will put some weight to the borrower's consent to such ex parte appointment of a receiver in the loan documents when determining whether or not to hold a receivership hearing. The best argument is to show waste and other irreparable harm to the property in seeking ex parte appointment (which is typically supported by an affidavit by the lender and with a structural condition report or other evidence of waste). Courts will also consider financial harm to the property (misappropriation, fraud, mistreatment of tenants, etc.) as a means to appointment the receiver on an ex parte basis. We have found that the courts are more apt to appoint a receiver on an ex parte basis now than they were a few years ago. Of course, this varies on a case-by-case basis, not only on the facts and circumstances surrounding the property and the debt, but also on the individual judge's preferences (as such determination is completely discretionary).

III. Loans and Advances:

Kansas typically includes language in the receivership order which allows receivers to borrow funds on a non-recourse basis if in the best interest of the asset and used for the management and operation of the asset.

IV. Sales During the Receivership:

The Kansas statutes do not specifically provide for the sale of property by a receiver. As mentioned above, K.S.A. 60-1303 provides that a receiver may "perform such acts…as the judge may authorize." Because of that language, we typically include the receiver's power of sale in the receivership order. At times, we have been able to get this language approved. Other times, we have had the court strike the language as enforceable and overreaching under Kansas law or have had borrowers object to this language. Even when we have included this language in a receivership order, we have not had a receiver try to sell property within the receivership period. We have had receivers market the property for sale (to get an indication of the market), but to not try and sell the property until after foreclosure. The ability for a receiver to sell property under Kansas law is still an open issue. Our position has been to continue to seek to include this language in the order and wait for the right circumstance to try and enforce it. As mentioned above, some judges have already said that this was enforceable and overreaching, but there has been no case law or statutory law to support this position adopted in Kansas yet.

Kansas also has the practical issue of whether a title company would insure over a sale by a receiver under Kansas law, even if that right is in the receivership order. The title company may try to require the borrower to consent to the sale by a receiver in order to insure "clean" title.

V. Liens Against Receivership Property:

As noted in the foreclosure section above, the rights of second mortgage holder and junior lien creditors are wiped out and extinguished upon foreclosure (after the applicable creditor's redemption period).

The receivership order should provide that the receiver is not required to pay any liens which are junior or subordinate to the senior mortgage.

VI. Owners Associations:

No separate statutory or case law authority in Kansas. A review of the title work should determine whether or not the liens created under the declaration for the owners association is prior to or subordinate to the senior mortgage. If prior to, then the receiver would have the ability to pay out of the income generated at the property. If subordinate, then the receiver would not need to pay them, as they will be wiped out and extinguished at the foreclosure sale.

Typically, the receiver will pay the association dues on a go-forward basis after the receiver is appointed and the prior unpaid association dues are wiped out at foreclosure.

VII. Construction Related to Receivership Property:

The receivership order should address whether or not the receiver is entitled to complete construction, which may include securing funds to do so. There is no separate Kansas statutory law addressing this issue.

VIII. Ending the Receivership:

The Kansas case law provides that a receivership should be discharged when the sale is confirmed. Despite the Howard case, we have had some courts keep the receiver in place until the redemption period has expired. The receiver will then submit a final accounting for approval by the court and an order discharging the receiver. Again, the Kansas statute is not specific as to how a receiver gets discharged, but we typically notice up the court, provide the final accounting for approval by the court, ask for an order terminating the receivership and returning the receivership bond. This hearing and order is completed as soon as possible after the receiver prepares its final accounting.

As noted above, a final accounting is provided and a hearing with the court to approve the termination of the receivership (and return of the receivership bond). The receiver recovers its compensation out of the income generated at the property.

Relevant Codes, Statutes or Case Law:
K.S.A. 60-1301-1305, et seq.; K.S.A. 60-711 (appointment of receiver for attachments); K.S.A. 58-2343 (assignment of rents of real property; lien; action upon default).

Kentucky

Foreclosure Summary

Security Instrument	Mortgage
Judicial	Yes
Non-Judicial	NA
Initial Public Notice	Unknown
Time Frame	6 Months
Redemption Period	12 Months
Deficiency	Yes, but with Restrictions

Receivership Summary

Ancillary Remedy Necessary	Yes
Ex-Parte	Yes
Approximate Time for Appointment	One day to Three weeks
Who or What can act as Receiver	Not Specified
Specific Receiver Requirements	None
Is there any approval list for Receivers	No
Out of State Receivers Allowed	Yes

Foreclosure:

I. General Information:

Foreclosure actions in Kentucky are in effect suits in equity to enforce a lien against property to satisfy a debt. A lien enforcement action, therefore, is in the nature of a quiet title action resulting in a judicial sale, usually conducted by the master commissioner of the circuit court of the county in which the action is brought.

II. Judicial Foreclosure Basics:

Any party with a right to, title to, an interest in, a claim against, or a lien on the property should be named a defendant in the complaint because the interests of any such parties not named in the complaint will not be affected by the judgment and will remain attached to the property after the judicial sale.

The circuit courts have jurisdiction over lien enforcement actions against real property, and the suit must be brought in the circuit court of the county in which the real property is located.

When the mortgage covers both real property and personal property, secured party may foreclose its interest in both real and personal property under state real property law, or separately, as to the personal property under Article 9, and as to the real property under state real property law.

A notice of *Lis Pendens* must be filed in the county clerk's office upon the filing of the complaint.

The master commissioner of the circuit court conducts hearings when necessary in a disputed foreclosure, reviews motions for judgments and orders of sale, and makes recommendations to the circuit judge regarding judgments and orders of sale. The master commissioner also conducts the judicial sales, and may be appointed by the court to act as a receiver. A licensed auctioneer may also be employed at the request of the mortgage holder to conduct the judicial sale under supervision of the Master Commissioner's office.

III. Non-Judicial Foreclosure Basics:

Non-judicial foreclosure is not available in Kentucky.

Relevant Codes, Statutes or Case Law:
KRS 134.420; KRS 360.040; KRS 382.330; KRS 424.130; KRS 24.140; KRS 424.150; KRS 425.600; KRS 426.006; KRS 426.520; KRS 426.522; KRS 426.525; KRS 426.530; KRS 426.540; KRS 426.571; KRS 426.574; KRS 426.575; KRS 426.576; KRS 426.685; KRS 426.690; KRS 426.700; KRS 426.705; KRS 541.170; KRS 451.180; KRS 451.190

Receivership:

I. Appointing the Receiver:

A. The Basics:

The circuit court, on the request of the plaintiff or other appropriate party supported by affidavit, may enter an order in the case appointing a receiver to preserve the property. The plaintiff's right to request the appointment is based in each of "two separate and distinct" sources: the equitable right now codified in KRS 425.600, and by virtue of a provision to that effect in the loan documents.

The order appointing receiver should be drafted broadly to allow the receiver maximum flexibility to preserve, manage, lease and operate the property, including provision for the receiver to borrow from the plaintiff when necessary to sustain operations. The order should also contain a prohibition against anyone filing suit against the receiver without a prior order of the court granting permission to do so. The order should also limit personal claims against the receiver and professionals to those stemming from misappropriation of funds coming into the hands of the receiver, gross negligence, gross or willful misconduct, malicious acts, or the failure to comply with the court's orders.

An order granting or denying the appointment of a receiver is a final order for purposes of appeal.

B. Time Frame for Appointment:
The appointment is effective as of the date specified in the order appointing the receiver – usually immediately upon entry of the order.

C. Can you go in Ex Parte?
Yes, (a) where the lender is contractually entitled to appointment of a receiver without notice, or (b) even without the contractual right, where there is threat of irreparable injury to the property or fund at issue.

II. Loans and Advances:
There are no specific statutes regarding loans and advances to the receiver, but provision for the receiver to borrow from the plaintiff when necessary to sustain operations may be included in the order appointing the receiver, including receivership certificates to evidence and establish the security and priority for repayment of such loans.

III. Sales During the Receivership:
In certain circumstances, responsibility for the facilitation of the foreclosure sale, usually conducted by the Master Commissioner after the entry by the Court of a final judgment and order of sale, may be delegated to a receiver. It is not clear under current law whether the power of sale can be delegated to a receiver without a final judgment.

IV. Liens Against Receivership Property:
There are no specific statutes regarding liens against property held in receivership. Receivers take possession subject to the liens outstanding against the property.

V. Owners Associations:
There are no specific statutes regarding owners associations in connection with property held in receivership.

VI. Construction Related to Receivership Property:

By provisions in the order appointing the receiver and defining the duties of the receiver during the receivership.

VII. Ending the Receivership:

The receivership is terminated according to the terms of the order appointing the receiver. Typically such a provision includes terminations (a) automatically (unless the court rules otherwise) thirty (30) days after the filing with the court and the receiver of a written demand for removal by plaintiff's counsel; or (b) in the court's discretion upon a motion for cause or upon the courts own motion.

VIII. Miscellaneous:

No party to the action or his attorney or any person with an interest in the action may be appointed receiver. The receiver must take an oath to perform his duties faithfully and must post a bond or present proof of acceptable insurance in lieu of a bond.

Relevant Codes, Statutes or Case Law:
KRS 425.600; KRS 31A.080; KRS 381.420;

Elkhorn Hazard Coal Co. v. Fairchild, et. al., 191 Ky. 276; 230 S.W. 61 (1921); G.B. Brassfield & Son v. Northwestern Mutual Life Insurance Co., 233 Ky. 94; 25 S.W.2d 72 (1930); Louisville Joint Stock Land Bank v. Radford, 295 U.S. 555 (1935); Monin v. Monin, 156 S.W.3d 309 (Ky. Ct. App. 2004); National Bank of Kentucky v. Kentucky River Coal Corporation, 20 S.W.2d 724 (Ky. 1929); Rosenbalm v. Commercial Bank of Middlesboro, 838 S.W.2d 423 (Ky. Ct. App. 1992); Wakenva Coal Co., Inc. v. Johnson, 234 Ky. 558; 28 S.W.2d 737 (Ky. 1930); Wilson v. Jonas, 8 Ky. L. Rptr. 510 (Ky. 1886);. See National Bank of Kentucky v. Kentucky River Coal Corporation, 20 S.W.2d 724 (Ky. 1929); Wakenva Coal Co., Inc. v. Johnson, 234 Ky. 558, 565 (Ky. 1930); see also, Wilson v. Jonas, 8 Ky. L. Rptr. 510, 512 (Ky. 1886).
In Wakenva Coal Company v. Johnson, 28 S.W.2d 737 (Ky. 1930).; Thompson v. BB&T (unpublished) 2009 Ky. App. Unpub LEXIS 369.

Louisiana

Foreclosure Summary

Security Instrument	Mortgage
Judicial	Yes
Non-Judicial	By Executory Process
Initial Public Notice	Petition
Time Frame	120 days
Redemption Period	No
Deficiency	Yes

Receivership Summary

Ancillary Remedy Necessary	Yes
Ex-Parte	Yes if mortgage provides
Approximate Time for Appointment	1-30 days
Who or What can act as Receiver	No Restrictions Given
Specific Receiver Requirements	No Restrictions Given
Is there any approval list for Receivers	No
Out of State Receivers Allowed	Yes

Foreclosure:

I. General Information:

There are essentially two methods to enforce the security rights of a seizing creditor under Louisiana law – ordinary process with pre-judgment sequestration, and executory process.

II. Judicial Foreclosure Basics:

To enforce a mortgage by ordinary process, the seizing creditor would file a petition in the parish where the mortgaged property is located seeking a personal judgment against the borrower/mortgagor, and recognition of the lien of the mortgage. The seizing creditor may also ask that the property affected by the mortgage be seized immediately under a writ of sequestration and that a keeper be appointed, if it is within the power of the borrower/mortgagor to waste the property or the revenue therefrom. The creditor would have to furnish security for a writ of sequestration in an amount to be determined by the court.

There are the usual legal delays for the filing of responsive pleadings. Assuming no exceptions are filed by the borrower/mortgagor, generally a period of thirty to forty-five days will elapse before the answer is filed.

The borrower/mortgagor would be entitled to a trial on the merits which, under present docket conditions, may not be fixed for a year or so after the answer is filed. It might be possible to obtain a summary judgment without much delay if there were no genuine issues as to material facts. In addition, judgment by default may be obtained quickly against the borrower/mortgagor if he fails to file an answer.

Upon obtaining a judgment against the borrower/mortgagor and waiting the necessary delays for application for a new trial, the seizing creditor would proceed to have the mortgaged property seized and sold at public auction by the civil sheriff pursuant to a writ of *fieri facias*. At this stage, the writ of sequestration is dissolved and seizure of the collateral is continued under the writ of *fieri facias*. The keeper (the Louisiana equivalent of a Receiver) would remain in place pending the judicial sale.

Written notice of seizure of the mortgaged property under the new writ for a judicial sale to satisfy the judgment, must be served on the borrower/mortgagor to give him the opportunity to enjoin the sale if he can show that the seizure or judgment is defective, or to reduce the seizure if the borrower/mortgagor can show that the value of the collateral exceeds what is reasonably necessary to satisfy the judgment. Third parties may also intervene in the proceeding at this time to claim a privilege or lien superior to that of the mortgage.

Following seizure, the sheriff publishes two notices of the sale in a local newspaper, the first notice being 30 days prior to the sale, and the second notice being 7 days before the sale. The mortgaged property must be appraised prior to the sale, the borrower/mortgagor and the seizing creditor each having the right to appoint an appraiser.

The seizing creditor must be careful to give notice of the judicial sale to any parties at interest of record under the Mennonite decision.

At the sale, the mortgaged property will not be sold if the highest bid does not exceed two-thirds of the appraised value. In such case, the sheriff must re-advertise for a second sale, at which time the mortgaged property will be sold for cash for whatever price it will bring. The judicial sale of the mortgaged property is subject to superior liens, encumbrances and leases; all inferior liens, encumbrances and leases are cancelled.

The sheriff's commission for the judicial sale is 3% of the adjudication price unless otherwise negotiated by and between the sheriff and the seizing creditor, with court approval. The policy of sheriffs concerning the negotiation of commissions varies from parish to parish and can change in each parish from time to time depending on politics and economics.

There is no right of redemption of mortgaged property adjudicated at the judicial sale.

III. Non-Judicial Foreclosure Basics:

In executory process, the mortgaged property can be seized and sold through an *ex parte* proceeding without a personal judgment against the borrower/mortgagor.

A prerequisite to executory process is that the mortgage be in proper form and contain a confession of judgment by the borrower/mortgagor for the full amount of the indebtedness, including attorney's fees.

To enforce a mortgage by executory process, assuming all of the technical requirements for executory process are satisfied, the seizing creditor would file a verified petition naming the borrower/mortgagor as debtor, alleging the default on the mortgage or note secured thereby, and requesting the seizure and sale of the mortgaged property and the appointment of a keeper pending such sale. The customary form of Louisiana mortgage contains provisions for the appointment of a keeper pursuant to the keeper act discussed more fully below. Certain of the loan documents must be filed with the petition for inspection by the court to verify that the documents are in proper form and satisfy the technical requirements with respect thereto.

After the verified petition and documents are presented to and approved by the court, the court will order the issuance of a writ of seizure and sale. A keeper will be appointed in the order, without the requirement of a bond, if the mortgage contains the appropriate provisions for the appointment of a keeper pending the judicial sale of the collateral. Otherwise, an application must be filed with the court for the appointment of a keeper and a bond will be required in an amount determined by the court.

Upon seizure of the mortgaged property by the sheriff, but prior to the sale thereof, a written notice of the seizure must be served on the borrower/mortgagor. The notice of seizure, which cannot be waived by the borrower/mortgagor, gives the borrower/mortgagor an opportunity to assert certain defenses to the seizure, such as the extinguishment of the mortgage, the legal enforceability of the mortgage, or the lack of sufficient authentic evidence to entitle the seizing creditor to executory process. Defenses to the seizure can be asserted only in an injunction proceeding to arrest the seizure and sale or by a suspensive appeal from the order directing issuance of the seizure and sale.

Following a seizure of the mortgaged property, the sheriff proceeds to advertise and sell the collateral following the same procedure as discussed above in connection with ordinary process, except that an appraisal is not necessary if it has been waived by the borrower/mortgagor in the mortgage. If, however, the seizing creditor intends to pursue borrower/mortgagor for a deficiency judgment to collect any deficiency, the sale must be made with the benefit of appraisal. The rules for the appointment of a keeper, the sheriff's commission and the sale of the property with the benefit of appraisal, are also the same as for ordinary process. Likewise, the seizing creditor must be careful to give notice of the judicial sale to any parties at interest of record under the Mennonite decision.

If the judicial sale does not yield sufficient revenue to satisfy the seizing creditor's claims, the seizing creditor may, by converting the executory proceeding to an ordinary proceeding or by separate suit, obtain a deficiency judgment against borrower/mortgagor for the balance owed, but, as indicated above, only if the mortgaged property has been sold with benefit of appraisal. It should be noted that while the borrower/mortgagor may defend against the action for deficiency judgment on the ground that the appraisal procedure was not followed closely, the borrower/mortgagor is estopped from bringing an action to set aside the judicial sale of the mortgaged property for defects in the executory proceedings once the sheriff's deed is filed for registry.

As in a judicial sale under ordinary process, there is no right of redemption of the mortgaged property adjudicated at the judicial sale under executory process.

IV. Notice of Sale and How Notice is Given:

The sheriff must advertise the sale of the seized property at least twice: the first advertisement must be published 30 days before the sale and the second no earlier than 7 days and no later than one day before the sale.

After the filing of the petition with appropriate exhibits (original note, certified copy of the mortgage and certified copy of borrower's authorization to execute the mortgage) in proper jurisdiction, the court will issue a writ of seizure and sale ordering the sheriff to seize the mortgaged property. A notice of seizure will contain the legal description of the property as well as the sale date and must be served upon borrower as well as filed in the mortgage records.
A certified mortgage certificate will provide lender with all interested parties to whom notices must be served after seizure of the property at least 10 days prior to the judicial sale. If a federal tax lien has been filed against the property, notice must be given to the IRS at least 25 days before judicial sale.

Receivership:

I. General information:

State law dictates that when property is seized pursuant to executory or ordinary process, the parties to a mortgage may designate a keeper (the Louisiana equivalent of a Receiver) of the property, the keeper may be the seizing creditor or its agent and the parties shall also specify the method by which a keeper is to be selected.

II. Appointing the Receiver:

A. The Basics:

A keeper will be appointed in the order, without the requirement of a bond, if the mortgage contains the appropriate provisions for the appointment of a keeper pending the judicial sale of the collateral. Otherwise, an application must be filed with the court for the appointment of a keeper and a bond will be required in an amount determined by the court.

B. Time Frame for Appointment:

Immediately, if the keeper is designated in the mortgage and typically, not longer than one month if the keeper is appointed in a summary proceeding.

C. Can you go in Ex Parte?

Yes, if so authorized in the mortgage.

III. Loans and Advances:

No statutes or rules govern loans or advances, and the Order of Appointment will govern the Receiver's authority to obtain loans or to issue advances.

IV. Sales During the Receivership:

No information provided.

V. Liens Against Receivership Property:

No information provided.

VI. Owners Associations:

No information provided.

VII. Construction Related to Receivership Property:

No information provided.

VIII. Ending the Receivership:

The keeper renders a final accounting and no further action is needed.

IX. Miscellaneous:

The sheriff or other officer seizing property shall have no responsibility for the property seized or the actions of the keeper after custody of the property has been delivered to the keeper, and shall not be entitled to receive any commission on the rents, revenues, or other fruits of the property delivered to the keeper.

Relevant Codes, Statutes or Case Law:
La. R. S. 9:5136 *et seq*.

 Contributed By: Susan M. Tyler of Jones Walker Waechter, Poitevent, Carrère & Denègre,

Maine

Foreclosure Summary

Security Instrument	Mortgage
Judicial	Yes
Non-Judicial	Yes
Initial Public Notice	Notice of Sale/Complaint
Time Frame	75 days/8 months
Redemption Period	None/90 days
Deficiency	Yes

Receivership Summary

Ancillary Remedy Necessary	Yes
Ex-Parte	No
Approximate Time for Appointment	21 to 30 days
Who or What can Act as Receiver	Individual or Corporation
Specific Receiver Requirements	Receiver must be authorized to transact business in Maine
Is there any Approval List for Receivers	No
Out of State Receivers Allowed	Yes, but must be authorized to transact business in Maine

Foreclosure:

I. General Information

14 M.R.S.A. §§ 6101 – 6325 address both judicial and non-judicial foreclosure proceedings.

II. Judicial Foreclosure Basics

The mortgagee commences a judicial foreclosure by filing a Complaint in the Superior or District Court in the division in which the mortgaged premises is located. The plaintiff in a Maine foreclosure action is the owner and holder of the mortgage and the promissory note secured by the mortgage. The named defendant(s) must include the mortgagor(s) and borrower(s), if different from the mortgagor(s). The Complaint should also name the following as parties-in-interest, which are determined by title search: the owner(s), if different from the mortgagor(s) or borrower(s), junior lienholders, junior mortgagees, and other individuals that may have a possessory interest in the mortgaged premises.

After filing the Complaint, a Clerk's Certificate of Foreclosure must be recorded with the Registry of Deeds for the county in which the mortgaged premises is located. The Clerk's Certificate of Foreclosure must bear the title "Clerk's Certificate of Foreclosure" and prominently state, immediately after the title, the street address of the mortgaged premises, if any, and the book and page number of the mortgage, if any. Any party having a claim to the mortgaged premises that has not recorded notice of the claim with the Registry of Deeds as of the time of recording of Clerk's Certificate of Foreclosure need not be joined in the foreclosure action, and any such party has no claim against the real estate after completion of the foreclosure sale, unless that party moves to intervene in the foreclosure action.

The defendant(s) and party(ies)-in-interest must be served with a copy of the Complaint and Summons in accordance with M.R. Civ. P. 4. Once all parties have been served, to obtain judgment, the mortgagee files a Motion for Summary Judgment pursuant to M.R. Civ. P. 56. If any residential tenants reside in the

Contributed By: Fred W. Bopp II, Lauren Weliver and Stephanie A. Williams of Perkins Thompson mortgaged premises, the mortgagee must provide a copy of the judgment to the tenant.

Following the entry of judgment, the statutory redemption period lasts for 90 days. Upon expiration of the redemption period, if the mortgagor has not redeemed the mortgage, the mortgagee may publish the notice of sale. The notice of public sale must be published within 90 days after the expiration of the redemption period for 3 consecutive weeks in a newspaper of general circulation in the county in which the mortgaged premises is located. The notice of sale must state the date, time, place, and terms of sale. The public sale must be held not less than 30 days nor more than 45 days after the first date of the notice of sale publication, and the sale does not need to take place in the county in which the mortgaged premises are located.

After the sale, the mortgagee files a report of sale with the Court that provides, among other things, the deficiency amount and how the mortgagee calculated the deficiency. To execute on the deficiency, the mortgagee must generally file a Motion for Assessment of Deficiency and, once granted, the Court will issue a Writ of Execution for the deficiency amount.

III. Judicial Foreclosure Miscellaneous

The Maine Supreme Judicial Court sitting as the Law Court recently issued its decision in *Bank of America v. Cloutier*, 2013 ME 17, __ A.3d __. *Cloutier* holds that an economic beneficiary (e.g., a loan servicer) can be the named plaintiff in a judicial foreclosure action if the economic beneficiary identifies what entity owns the note and proves that the economic beneficiary has the power to enforce the note. *Id.* at ¶ 21.

IV. Non-Judicial Foreclosure Basics

Non-judicial foreclosure is only available for commercial mortgage foreclosures and where the subject mortgage contains specific statutory power of sale language, including that the mortgage is given primarily for a business, commercial or agricultural purpose. Additionally, an individual cannot grant a power of sale to the mortgagee; only corporations, limited liability companies, partnerships and similar entities may grant a power of sale to the mortgagee.

Prior to commencing a non-judicial foreclosure, a title search and UCC search should be conducted. The mortgagee then selects a sale date, and, at least 21 days before the sale, a notice of sale must be published in a newspaper of general circulation for the county in which the mortgaged premises is located. The notice of sale must be recorded 21 days prior to sale in the Registry of Deeds for the county in which the mortgaged premises are located. Also 21 days prior to sale, a copy of the notice of sale must be sent by registered mail to the mortgagor(s), party(ies)-in-interest, and any residential tenants. The notice of sale must prominently state the street address of the real estate encumbered by the mortgage deed, if any, and the book and page number of the mortgage, if any.

If the mortgagee desires to preserve its right to pursue a deficiency claim, at least 21 days before the sale, a notice of intention to foreclose and of liability for deficiency after foreclosure of mortgage must be sent to the mortgagor(s) and guarantor(s). Within 30 days after the foreclosure sale, the mortgagee or mortgagee's representative must execute an affidavit of the mailing of the notice.

The sale must be held on or near the mortgaged premises. Within 30 days after the sale, an affidavit of exercise of power of sale foreclosure with an attached certificate of publication of the notice of sale must be recorded in the Registry of Deeds for the county in which the mortgaged premises are located.

To pursue a deficiency thereafter, the mortgagee must file a Complaint with the Superior Court with jurisdiction and venue over such an action.

V. Power of sale foreclosure guidelines

14 M.R.S.A. §§ 6203-A – 6203-E provide the procedure for a non-judicial foreclosure, and are discussed in greater detail in Section III, above.

VI. Power of sale constitutes part of security

As indicated above, the subject mortgage must contain specific statutory power of sale language, including that the mortgage is given primarily for a business, commercial or agricultural purpose.

VII. No Power of sale foreclosure guidelines

The mortgagee must foreclose through the judicial foreclosure process.

VIII. Foreclosure when instrument contains no power of sale

Mortgage holders must file an action to foreclose in the Superior or District Court in the division in which the mortgaged premises are located.

IX. Additional satisfaction permitted under continuing power of sale

If the subject mortgage is secured by more than one parcel of property, absent language in the mortgage or related loan documents allowing the mortgagee to conduct separate power of sale foreclosures, it is advisable that the mortgagee utilize one power of sale foreclosure notice of sale that includes all the property that secures the mortgage, rather than the mortgagee attempting to auction the mortgaged premises pursuant to more than one separate power of sale foreclosure notice of sale.

X. Sale under power where instrument silent as to place or terms of sale

The foreclosure sale must occur on or near the mortgaged premises.

XI. Notice of Sale and How notice of sale is given

14 M.R.S.A. § 6203-B provides the procedure for notice and how it is given in a non-judicial foreclosure, and is discussed in detail in Section III, above. 14 M.R.S.A. § 6323 provides the procedure for notice and how it is given in a judicial foreclosure, and is discussed in detail in Section II, above.

XII. Place and time for conducting foreclosure by power of sale

The sale must occur on or near the mortgaged premises and must be commercially reasonable in all respects.

Relevant Codes, Statutes or Case Law:

14 M.R.S.A. §§ 6101 – 6325; 33 M.R.S.A. § 501-A.

Receivership:

I. General information:

The rule is well settled in Maine that loan document provisions providing for the appointment of a receiver are valid and enforceable in arms-length commercial transactions.

Where a loan document does not specifically provide for the appointment of a receiver, there are a variety of Maine statutes that allow for the appointment of a receiver. See 13-B M.R.S. § 1105(2) (providing for a creditor to seek dissolution of a non-profit corporation); 13-B M.R.S. § 1106(2) (providing for a court to appoint a receiver in a judicial proceeding to liquidate the assets and activities of a non-profit corporation) 13-C M.R.S. § 1430(3) (providing for a creditor to seek judicial dissolution of a corporation); 13-C M.R.S. § 1432 (providing for a court to appoint a receiver in a judicial proceeding brought to dissolve a corporation); 31 M.R.S. §§ 1054 (providing for a court to appoint a receiver on application by a judgment creditor when the judgment debtor is a partner of a partnership); 31 M.R.S. § 1383 (providing for a court to appoint a receiver on application by a judgment creditor when the judgment debtor is a partner of a limited partnership).

In particular, 13-C M.R.S. § 1430(3) provides that a corporation may be dissolved by a judicial dissolution in a proceeding initiated by a creditor, if the creditor can establish:

1. The creditor's claim has been reduced to judgment, the execution on the judgment has been returned unsatisfied and the corporation is insolvent; or
2. The corporation has admitted in writing that the creditor's claim is due and owing and the corporation is insolvent.

Additionally, a court in a judicial proceeding brought to dissolve a corporation may appoint one or more receivers to manage and to wind up and liquidate the business and affairs of the corporation. The court shall hold a hearing, after notifying all parties to the proceeding and any interested persons designated by the court, before appointing a receiver. The court appointing a receiver has jurisdiction over the corporation and all of its property wherever located. 13-C M.R.S. § 1432(2)-(4) set forth provisions relating to the need for the receiver to post a bond, the receiver's powers and duties, and receiver and receiver's counsel's compensation and reimbursement for expenses.

Similarly, for a non-profit corporation, a creditor may seek dissolution:

1. When the claim of the creditor has been reduced to judgment and an execution thereon has been returned unsatisfied and it is established that the corporation is insolvent; or
2. When the corporation has admitted in writing that the claim of the creditor is due and owing and it is established that the corporation is insolvent.

13-B M.R.S. § 1105(2). 13-B M.R.S. § 1106(1) provides that a court "shall have the power to . . . appoint a receiver or receivers *Pendente Lite*, with such powers and duties as the court, from time to time, may direct" in a proceeding to liquidate the assets of a non-profit corporation. Additionally, 13-B M.R.S. § 1106(2) provides:

After a hearing and upon such notice as the court may direct to be given to all parties to the proceedings and to any other parties in interest designated by the court, the court may appoint a liquidating receiver or receivers with authority to collect the assets of the corporation. Such liquidating receiver or receivers shall have authority, subject to the order of the court, to sell, convey and dispose of all or any part of the assets of the corporation wherever situated, either at public or private sale. The order appointing such liquidating receiver or receivers shall state their powers and duties. Such powers and duties may be increased or diminished at any time during the proceedings.

13-B M.R.S. § 1106(2). 13-B M.R.S. § 1106(3)-(6) are provisions relating to standards for how to distribute non-profit corporate property, the receiver and receiver's counsel's compensation and reimbursement for expenses, the receiver's power to sue and defend, and the requirement that a receiver be a United States citizen.

Regarding partnerships, 31 M.R.S. § 1054 provides the exclusive remedy for how a judgment creditor "of a partner or partner's transferee may satisfy a judgment out of the judgment debtor's transferable interest in the partnership." 31 M.R.S. § 1054(5). 31 M.R.S. § 1054(1) provides:

> On application by a judgment creditor of a partner or of a partner's transferee, a court having jurisdiction may charge the transferable interest of the judgment debtor to satisfy the judgment. The court may appoint a receiver of the share of the distributions due or to become due to the judgment debtor in respect of the partnership and make all other orders, directions, accounts and inquiries the judgment debtor might have made or that the circumstances of the case may require.

31 M.R.S. § 1383(1) is a similar provision applicable to limited partnerships.

There is scant authority for a plaintiff to seek the appointment of a receiver based on common law. However, at least one Maine case has held that, although a court will not wind up the affairs of a corporation at the request of a creditor without statutory or other authority, it can exercise equitable powers to appoint a receiver to recover corporate property "where corporate property has been abandoned and is exposed to certain injury or loss, or where the corporation has no officers to care for its property; or, where by acts of the directors the corporate property is exposed to imminent peril; or, where the directors have been guilty of a breach of trust, and the property is in danger of future injury or waste, unless withdrawn from the reach of danger

II. Appointing the Receiver:

A. The Basics:

In a typical case, the plaintiff/creditor files a motion for appointment of receiver with the court along with the complaint. The plaintiff should support the motion with one or more affidavits, and the motion and affidavit(s) should detail the specific grounds demonstrating the basis and need for the appointment of a receiver. In the motion, the plaintiff is allowed to specify the name of the desired receiver, and the receiver's fee schedule should also be included. The motion should also describe the specific functions that the plaintiff seeks the receiver to perform. The motion is heard by the judge to whom the underlying foreclosure or other case is assigned.

Unless the plaintiff moves for expedited or emergency treatment of the motion, the court will hold a hearing on the motion generally within twenty-one to thirty days after the motion is filed, after all parties to the proceeding and any interested persons designated by the court are notified, before appointing a receiver. The appointment of a receiver can be hastened by requesting an expedited or emergency hearing on the motion, especially where the plaintiff can allege that the value of the security is being harmed by waste, improper maintenance, and the like. The court may decide not to hold a hearing if the plaintiff is pursuing appointment of a receiver based on the express provisions of its loan documents, and no timely objections are made to the motion.

In its order appointing a receiver, the court will specify the powers and duties of the receiver. The order may be amended from time to time, as necessary. Receivers often employ counsel in Maine, and the order should address this issue if it is contemplated that the receiver will have counsel.

If the court appoints a receiver, some Maine statutes provide, in specific circumstances, that the court may require the receiver to post bond, with or without sureties, in an amount the court directs. A receiver shall in all cases give such bond as the court may direct with such sureties as the court may require.

B. Time Frame for Appointment:

There is no set time limit within which a court must act on a motion to appoint a receiver. The Maine Rules of Civil Procedure provide that, once a motion is filed and properly served, interested parties have twenty to twenty-one days to file a memorandum in opposition, depending on the timing of the filing of the motion providing that (1) any party opposing a motion that was filed prior to or simultaneously with the filing of the complaint shall file a memorandum in opposition no later than the time permitted for filing an answer, which is twenty days after service of the summons and complaint pursuant to and (2) any party opposing a motion made at any other time shall file a memorandum in opposition not later than twenty one days after the filing of the motion. Thereafter, if a memorandum in opposition is filed, the plaintiff has 7 days to file a reply.

Depending on the extent of any opposition to the motion and the corresponding time allotted for the filing of memoranda, a court may act on a motion for appointment of a receiver within twenty-one to thirty days of the filing of the motion, or less, if gross negligence, fraud, or waste can be demonstrated.

C. Can you go in Ex Parte?

No.

III. Loans and Advances:

There is no specific guidance provided by Maine statute, case law, or court rule for a receiver seeking or making loans and advances. The order appointing the receiver should address any relevant authority.

IV. Sales During the Receivership:

The court can authorize a receiver to sell property during a receivership. There is no specified statutory or common law process for sales of property by receivers. The process to be followed is determined on a case-by-case basis and is typically spelled out in detail in either the order appointing the receiver or a subsequent order authorizing the receiver to conduct a sale. Also, there is no Maine state law version of a sale free and clear of liens of the type permitted under §363 of the United States Bankruptcy Code.

In Maine, it has been established that at least in statutory proceedings for the dissolution of corporations the decree of appointment ipso facto vests the title of the real estate in the receiver. However, by statute and common law, receivers are required to seek court approval of any sale of property. In at least one case, a receiver petitioned a court both for the authority to sell certain assets of the corporation and to approve the sale.

An order of the court confirming a sale by the receiver is a final and appealable order. Therefore, by operation of M.R. Civ. P. 62(a), it is not stayed "[u]nless otherwise ordered by the court." Accordingly, if an appeal of an order confirming a receiver's sale is sought, but a stay of the order from the court is not granted, the appeal is subject to dismissal as being moot if the judicial sale is untainted by fraud, unfairness, collusion or mistake.

V. Liens Against Receivership Property:

At the time a complaint is filed that seeks to wind up the business of a corporation and distribute its assets pursuant to applicable Maine statutory law, the entire property of the corporation is considered in *Custodia Legis* and the property from that point on is not subject to seizure or sale on execution.

Furthermore, a recovery of judgment against the corporation in receivership "does not create a lien upon any of the firm property or funds in [the receiver's] hands, and [accordingly,] such property or funds cannot be levied upon by execution or reached by garnishment because it is already in *Custodia Legis*."

Instead, after the receiver has taken possession, any person claiming the property, or any interest therein, may present his claim to the court which appointed the receiver. He may be made a party to the suit in order to establish his claim; Or he may petition to have it heard before a master; Or he may, by express permission of the court, bring a suit for the possession, care being taken to protect the receiver. But the receiver will not be ordered to deliver the property to a claimant until his right is established, in one of these modes. Nor can any claimant bring a suit against the receiver, except by leave of court, without being liable for a contempt, if the property is a part of the subject matter in controversy.

Id. at 282-83; see also Bisbee v. Mt. Battie Mfg. Co., 107 Me. 185, 189 (1910) ("[T]he rights of priority of creditors, existing at the time a bill is filed, are not destroyed by statutory proceedings for winding up a corporation or sequestering its assets. The statutory lien by previous attachment is preserved. The enforcement of it, however, in the usual way is suspended. Lien creditors must apply to the court, which will give effect to liens which existed when the property passed into the custody of the law.")

Additionally, in relation to liens, in Maine, a "[r]eceiver of a corporation holds property coming into his hands by the same right and title as the corporation, and is subject to all equities, including the right of setoff, which existed at the time of his appointment and could have been successfully invoked against the corporation." Cooper v. Fidelity Trust Co., 132 Me. 260, 269 (1934).

VI. Owners Associations:

There is just one statutory provision relating to receivers and owners associations. In the context of unit ownership, the statute provides that if an association forecloses upon a lien it has for sums assessed against one of its unit owners, "the unit owner shall be required to pay a reasonable rental for the unit, if so provided in the bylaws and the plaintiff in such foreclosure shall be entitled to the appointment of a receiver to collect the same." Other than this one example, there are no particular statutes regarding the interaction of a receiver with condominium or homeowners' associations. The order appointing the receiver should spell out in detail how any associations are to be dealt with.

VII. Construction Related to Receivership Property:

There is no specific guidance provided by Maine statute, case law or court rule for a receiver completing construction. The order appointing the receiver should address any relevant issues.

VIII. Ending the Receivership:

M.R. Civ. P. 44(a)(1) requires a plaintiff to seek an order of the court in order to voluntarily dismiss an action wherein a receiver has been appointed. There is no other court rule, statute or case law that requires a specific process for ending the receivership. The order appointing the receiver should specify how the receivership is to be terminated. Typically, the plaintiff will want to obtain (and the court will usually require) an order terminating the receivership.

IX. Miscellaneous

Regardless of the specific powers and duties that are outlined in the order, by statute, the receiver of a Maine corporation has the power to:

1. Dispose of all or any part of the assets of the corporation wherever located, at a public or private sale, if authorized by the court;
2. Sue and defend in the receiver's own name as receiver of the corporation in all courts of this State; and
3. Exercise all of the powers of the corporation, through or in place of its board of directors, to the extent necessary to manage the affairs of the corporation in the best interests of its shareholders and creditors.

Receivers of non-profit corporations are given similar authority by statute, except that they are not granted the authority to exercise all the powers of the non-profit corporation. See 13-B M.R.S. § 1106(2) ("Such liquidating receiver or receivers shall have authority, subject to the order of the court, to sell, convey and dispose of all or any part of the assets of the corporation wherever situated, either at public or private sale."); Id. § 1106(5) ("Receiver to have power to sue and defend. A receiver of a corporation appointed under the provisions of this section shall have authority to sue and defend in all courts in his own name as receiver of such corporation.").

Relevant Codes, Statutes or Case Law:
M.R. Civ. P. 41(a)(1); M.R. Civ. P. 62(a); M.R. Civ. P. 66(d)(3). 13-B M.R.S. §§ 1105, 1106; 13-C M.R.S. §§ 1430, 1432; 31 M.R.S. §§ 1054, 1383; 33 M.R.S. § 581. Morrill v. Noyes, 56 Me. 458 (1863); Chalmers v. Littlefield, 103 Me. 271 (1907); Cobb v. Camden Savings Bank, 109 Me. 178 (1909); Bisbee v. Mt. Battie Mfg. Co., 107 Me. 185 (1910); Fleetwood Pride v. Pride Lumber Co., 109 Me. 452 (1912); Glidden v. Rines, 124 Me. 286 (1925); Cooper v. Fidelity Trust Co., 132 Me. 260 (1934). Hazzard v. Westview Golf Club, Inc., 217 A.2d 217 (1966); Fleet Bank of Me. v. Zimelman, 575 A.2d 731(Me. 1990

Maryland

Foreclosure Summary

Security Instrument	Deed of Trust/ Mortgage
Judicial	Yes, but rare
Non-Judicial	Yes
Initial Public Notice	Publication notice required under MD Rules
Time Frame	Min. of 90 days (more time for residential property)
Redemption Period	No
Deficiency	Yes

Receivership Summary

Ancillary Remedy Necessary	Not required, but not unusual
Ex-Parte	Possible, but not preferred
Approximate Time for Appointment	2-45 days
Who or What can act as Receiver	An Individual
Specific Receiver Requirements	See Restrictions under MD Rules
Is there any approval list for Receivers	No
Out of State Receivers Allowed	Yes, case by case basis

Foreclosure:

I. General Information:

Mortgages of real property in Maryland may be foreclosed under:

A. power of sale, i.e., clause in mortgage authorizing mortgagee or any other person named therein to sell mortgaged property, or

B. assent to decree, i.e., provision in mortgage whereby mortgagor assents to passing of decree for sale of property.

In each case, record holders of at least 25% of mortgage debt must consent or make application for sale, and process, answer or hearing is not required.

All purchasers at foreclosure sale have the same rights and remedies against tenants of mortgagor as mortgagor had, and said tenants have the same rights and remedies against a purchaser as against the mortgagor on the date the mortgage was recorded.If a mortgage so authorizes and required advertisement of sale discloses, a foreclosure sale is subject to tenancies entered into after recording of mortgage. Any lease so continuing shall be unaffected by sale, except that purchaser shall become landlord, as of date of sale, on ratification of sale.

Emergency legislation signed by the Governor on April 3, 2008, effective on all residential foreclosures filed on and after April 4, 2008, provides protections to individual homeowners in the foreclosure process. More time and notice are required before and after a foreclosure sale. Additional regulations are contemplated and were not yet implemented at the time of publication of this guide. Consult a local attorney if residential property is part of your collateral.

II. Judicial Foreclosure Basics:

Mortgages may also be foreclosed by judicial foreclosure where there is neither power of sale nor assent to decree, in same manner as mortgage containing assent to decree, except that (1) process, answer and hearing are required, (2) 25% requirement is inapplicable, and (3) court, under certain circumstances, may

Contributed By: Matthew W. Cheney & Monique Almy of Crowell & Moring order sale before final decree. Action to foreclose mortgage under power of sale may only be instituted by natural person authorized to exercise power.

III. Non-Judicial Foreclosure Basics:

A. Assent To Decree

Where foreclosure is under assent to decree, procedure is substantially the same. Mortgagee files petition to foreclose and files verified statement of mortgage debt together with mortgage or certified copy as exhibit. If default has occurred, the court will enter decree ordering that the property be sold forthwith and appointing trustee or trustees to make the sale. Trustee must give bond and sell property pursuant to the terms, including notice, fixed by court. Sale must be ratified by court.

B. Deed of Trust

Deed of Trust may be foreclosed in same manner as mortgage, except that foreclosure to be made by trustee appointed by deed or successor and the 25% rule is inapplicable.

IV. Guidelines for Power of Sale:

Case law makes it clear that the power of sale must be given to a natural person, not a corporation. Further, that person can be an attorney. The power can be assigned. Where foreclosure is under power of sale, person named in mortgage to conduct sale must do so for county or Baltimore city where property lies. Such person must: (1) docket suit in appropriate court and file verified statement of mortgage debt together with mortgage or certified copy as exhibit; (2) give bond approved by clerk or court and publish notice of time, place and terms of sale; and (3) not less than ten nor more than 30 days before sale (*but see reference above regarding residential foreclosures*), send notice by certified mail, return receipt requested, bearing U.S. Postal Service postmark to mortgagor, present record owner and holder of subordinate mortgage, deed of trust, judgment or other subordinate recorded or filed interest who has filed appropriate request to receive notice. Sale must be ratified and confirmed by court. Failure to give notice to record owner or subordinate mortgagee does not invalidate title of purchaser; failure to give notice to mortgagor does not invalidate sale if person conducting sale gives affidavit or return receipt that such notice to mortgagor has been given prior to ratification by court.

V. Power of Sale Guidelines as Represented in the Security:

Courts have said: "It has repeatedly been held by this court, that a power of sale in a mortgage, conferred on the mortgagee, is a power coupled with an interest and so being, is appurtenant to the estate, and passes to the executors, administrators or assigns, and is not lost by the death or insanity of the mortgagor."

"But where the power is conferred upon a third person, who has no interest in the estate, it is a collateral power."

VI. Guidelines for Foreclosure when there is No Power of Sale:

Follow judicial sale process described above.

VII. Foreclosure When Instrument Contains No Power of Sale:

Follow judicial sale process described above.

VIII. Any Additional Satisfaction Permitted Under Continuing Power of Sale:

Power of sale survives partial satisfaction of debt if additional collateral remains.

IX. Sale by Power of Sale when the Instrument is Silent as to the Place or Terms of Sale:

If instrument is silent, sale must be on "reasonable terms." Terms of sale should be disclosed in advertisement.

X. Notice of Sale and How Notice is Given:

Perhaps the most important, and controversial, topic of foreclosure is notice. Must provide notice of the foreclosure sale to those parties whose interests are about to be foreclosed, including:

A. The holder of a recorded subordinate mortgage, (at least 10 days)

B. Local governments, (at least 15 days)

C. Special Procedures, Internal Revenue Service, (at least 25 days)

D. The holder of any other recorded subordinate interest,

E. The holder or beneficiary of an unrecorded interest where the existence and location of the interest and the holder is reasonably ascertainable.

These groups have an interest in the property which is constitutionally and statutorily entitled to some type of notice. It is no longer necessary that the holder of a recorded inferior interest file a request for notification at the courthouse.

Publish a Notice of Sale in a newspaper of general circulation in the county where the action is pending, at least once a week for three successive weeks. A notice of sale must be given to holders of an interest in the property not less than 15 days before sale and last publication of notice must not be more than 1 week before sale.

XI. Place and Time for Conducting Foreclosure by Power of Sale:

As specified in advertisement and notices.

Relevant Codes, Statutes or Case Law:
MD. Code Ann., Real Property § 7-105; Maryland Rules 14-201 through 14-210; Maryland Rules 14-301 - 14-306.
Powell v. Hopkins, 38 Md. 1, 11-12 (1873); Reid v. Gordon, 35 Md. 174 (1872); Berry v. Skinner, 30 Md. 567 (1869); Dill v. Satterfield, 34 Md. 52 (1871); Harnickell v. Orndorff, 35 Md. 341 (1872); Mackubin v. Boarman, 54 Md. 387 (1880).

Receivership:

I. General Information:

The appointment of a Receiver is not guaranteed. The proposed order should be reviewed by the proposed Receiver.

II. Appointing the Receiver:

A. The Basics:

Appointment is procured by petition to court. Upon default, mortgagee has the right to ask for appointment of Receiver. Receiver and each attorney, accountant or appraiser he desires to employ must inform the court whether he has had certain relationships with or interests in debtor or secured creditor.

B. Time Frame for Appointment:

Absent a genuine emergency, the time for a hearing on a request to appoint a Receiver can vary from a few days to a few weeks.

C. Can you go in Ex Parte?

Ex parte appointment is possible, but most judges refuse ex parte appointment of a Receiver unless a genuine emergency exists and there is good reason for not providing the other parties to the suit with reasonable notice. Ex parte appointments are subject to swift review and reversal.

III. Loans and Advances:

Needs to be approved by the Court. Order should include protections similar to those available to Section 364 of the Bankruptcy Code. The use of future advance provisions in loan documents may provide additional protection.

IV. Sales During the Receivership:

There is no established process other than seeking the court's permission, which should be sought in connection with the petition for the receiver or a separate application.

There is also no statutory authority or well established case law precedent. Courts will consider applications to sell property on a case by case basis.

Contributed By: Matthew W. Cheney & Monique Almy of Crowell & Moring

However, Applications and orders to sell property should be modeled on those typically submitted pursuant to Section 363 of the Bankruptcy Code. Counsel should be consulted to determine whether an exercise of a power of sale or other foreclosure would be a better strategic option than a sale out of the receivership estate, particularly for commercial property.

V. Liens Against Receivership Property:

Lien issues and priorities can be complicated and counsel should be consulted. A lien search should be conducted early in a matter to help determine priorities and identify any potential issues. The appointment of a receiver does not modify liens or change lien priorities.

VI. Owners Associations:

The receivership does not alter the liens or rights established/obtained by an owners association. Thus, associations' rights are handled in accordance with applicable state law.

VII. Construction Related to Receivership Property:

In either the original petition for appointment of a receiver or a subsequent application, the party(ies) should seek approval from the court. Such a request would likely include relief modeled after Sections 363 and 364 of the Bankruptcy Code. The use of future advance or other provisions in loan documents may provide additional authority and/or protection.

VIII. Ending the Receivership:

Removal of Receiver or ending receivership may only be accomplished by application to the Court.

IX. Miscellaneous:

Some courts refuse to appoint a Receiver in all but a few commercial situations.

Relevant Codes, Statutes or Case Law:
Maryland Rules 13-101 through 13-707. Gaither v. Stockbridge, 67 Md. 222 (1887); County Corp. v. Semmes, 169 Md. 501 (1935); Johnston v. Lippert, 96 Md. 584 (1903); Southern Maryland Agriculture Ass'n v. Magruder, 198 Md. 274 (1951).

Massachusetts

Foreclosure Summary

Security Instrument	Deed of Trust, Mortgage
Judicial	Yes
Non-Judicial	Yes
Initial Public Notice	Notice of Sale
Time Frame	75
Redemption Period	None
Deficiency	Yes

Receivership Summary

Ancillary Remedy Necessary	Yes
Ex-Parte	Generally, No
Approximate Time for Appointment	1 Week at the Minimum
Who or What can act as Receiver	No Restrictions Given
Specific Receiver Requirements	To be on the Approved list
Is there any approval list for Receivers	Yes
Out of State Receivers Allowed	Upon a showing of need

Foreclosure:

I. General Information:

Massachusetts General Laws chapter 244 governs foreclosures in Massachusetts.

II. Judicial Foreclosure Basics:

Massachusetts General Laws c. 244 §§ 1-13 govern judicial foreclosure. However, mortgage holders rarely use this procedure.

III. Non-Judicial Foreclosure Basics:

Non-judicial foreclosure is the primary method whereby mortgage holders affect foreclosure in Massachusetts. The subject mortgage must contain statutory power of sale language in order to foreclose in this manner.

One complicating factor in Massachusetts is that a prerequisite to foreclosure against property owned by an individual or series of individuals, including a general partnership of which at least one member is an individual, is a judgment from either Massachusetts Land Court or Superior Court declaring that the individual is not a soldier or sailor as defined by the Service Members Civil Relief Act. This process adds time and expense to the non-judicial foreclosure process.

IV. Guidelines for Power of Sale:

Massachusetts General Laws c. 244 § 14 provides the procedure for non-judicial foreclosure, and is discussed in greater detail Sections X-XI, below.

V. Power of Sale Guidelines as Represented in the Security:

Assignees may exercise the power of sale in the same manner as original mortgagees.

VI. Guidelines for Foreclosure when there is No Power of Sale:

Mortgage holders must foreclose either through the judicial foreclosure process or through peaceable entry if the mortgage lacks statutory power of sale language.

VII. Foreclosure When Instrument Contains No Power of Sale:

Mortgage holders must file an action to foreclose in the Superior Court of the county in which the subject realty lies or exercise peaceable entry. In the absence of power of sale language, the Superior Court will only grant a writ of possession for the collateral realty, and not a sale.

XIII. Sale by Power of Sale when the Instrument is Silent as to the Place or Terms of Sale:

The foreclosure sale occurs at the property that is the subject of the sale.

IX. Notice of Sale and How Notice is Given:

Massachusetts General Laws c. 244 § 14 governs the Notice of Sale. That statutory section requires Notice of Sale by publication at least once a week for three consecutive weeks before the sale, with the first publication occurring at least twenty-one days before the date of sale. That notice must contain the date and time of sale and a description of the property consistent with the statutory form.

Notice of the sale must also be given at least fourteen days prior to the sale to all interest holders that are on title at least thirty days prior to the sale by registered mail.

In order to preserve a deficiency claim, Massachusetts General Laws c. 244 § 17B requires a notice reserving the right to pursue a post-sale deficiency to sent at least twenty-one days before the sale by registered mail to the mortgagee and guarantors, with preparation of an affidavit attesting to compliance with the statutory subsection no later than thirty days after the sale.

X. Place and Time for Conducting Foreclosure by Power of Sale:

The foreclosure sale may occur at the subject property at any commercially reasonable time.

Relevant Codes, Statutes or Case Law:
Massachusetts General Laws chapter 244 controls foreclosures in Massachusetts.

Receivership:

I. General information:

Receivers for distressed commercial properties are available but not commonplace in Massachusetts. There is no specific statute that allows for the appointment of a receiver in this context; the Superior Court's general equitable power and Rule of Civil Procedure 66 govern.

II. Appointing the Receiver:

A. The Basics:

The request for appointment of a receiver is brought by way of a Petition for Appointment of Receiver, which is filed with the Superior Court in the county where the subject property lies. The Petition should contain specific factual bases demonstrating the need for a receiver. The petitioner should file a Motion for Short Order of Notice, which will likely expedite the assignment of the matter for hearing.

The court exercises broad discretion as whether to appoint a receiver or not. Depending on the judge, a default and a concomitant contractual right to the appointment of a receiver may not be sufficient to support appointment without other extenuating circumstances.

B. Time Frame for Appointment:

The court may appoint a temporary receiver within as little as one to three weeks after filing and service of the Petition, depending on the county wherein the matter is pending. However, there is no set time limit within which a court must act on a Petition to Appoint a Receiver.

C. Can you go in Ex Parte?

Generally, no.

III. Loans and Advances:

No information provided.

IV. Sales During the Receivership:

Generally, receivers do not have the power to sell property.

V. Liens Against Receivership Property:

Receivers generally cannot avoid liens.

VI. Owners Associations:

No information provided.

VII. Construction Related to Receivership Property:

No information provided.

IV. Ending the Receivership:

A receivership is terminated through a Motion to Discharge after a final accounting has been submitted and approved by the Court. Mass. Sup. Ct. R. 66(e).

V. Miscellaneous:

A.

In most instances, the court will draft the order appointing the receiver.

B.

In theory, receivers must be on the court-approved receivers list maintained in each county. In practice, the receiver lists are often not up to date and sometimes lack attorneys who have expertise in distressed realty. The Court consequently will sometimes appoint someone who is not on the receiver list upon a showing of need.

Relevant Codes, Statutes or Case Law:

Mass. Sup. Ct. R. 66(e).

Massachusetts Rule of Civil Procedure 66; Altman v. Vogue Int'l, 366 Mass. 176, 180 (1974); Hampden Nat'l Bank v. Hampden R.R. Corp., 246 Mass. 404, 407 (1923).

Michigan

Foreclosure Summary

Security Instrument	Mortgage/ Trust Deed
Judicial	Yes
Non-Judicial	Yes
Initial Public Notice	Publication
Time Frame	60 days
Redemption Period	Judicial- 6 months Non Judicial 6 or 12 months
Deficiency	Varies, case by case

Receivership Summary

Ancillary Remedy Necessary	Yes
Ex-Parte	Typically No
Approximate Time for Appointment	1 day to 2 weeks
Who or What can act as Receiver	Company or Individual
Specific Receiver Requirements	No Restrictions Given
Is there any approval list for receivers	No, although some Judges have a short list
Out of State Receivers Allowed	Depends on the court and the Judge

Foreclosure:

I. General Information:

A. Michigan allows for both Judicial and Non-Judicial, or foreclosure by advertisement.

B. Michigan also allows for the right of Redemption. However, the mortgagor can waiver redemption, but only in writing after default.

C. Michigan enforces assignments of rent. However, if mortgagee bids full amount of debt (or amount bid by a third party is sufficient to satisfy the debt), the debt is deemed satisfied as of the time of the sale, and the assignment of rents terminates.

D. Foreclosure will terminate junior lien holders, including in certain circumstances leases of tenants.

II. Judicial Foreclosure Basics:

A. Complaint to foreclose

1. Need to name Mortgagor and all parties with liens junior to mortgage being foreclosed.
2. Can request appointment of Receiver in connection with a foreclosure sale.
3. Can be combined with suit on note and on guaranties.
4. Can be combined with foreclosure of personal property.
5. However, must conduct the foreclosure sale before enforcing money judgment on deficiency.

B. Cannot start to advertise foreclosure sale until the latter of entry of judgment of foreclosure or six months after filing suit.

C. Must advertise the sale for 6 weeks, with sale on the following, or 7th, week. May adjourn sale on a week to week basis through posting.

D. Court may set a minimum bid amount.

E. Must seek confirmation of sale.

F. Entitled to a judgment on any deficiency.

G. Mortgagor and all parties claiming under mortgagor has right to redeem for six months following sale. Redemption amount equals the amount bid, plus interest, plus any property taxes paid or insurance paid.

III. Non-Judicial Foreclosure Basics:

A. Mortgage must contain a power of sale.

B. Election of remedies:

1. Cannot foreclosure by advertisement if filed suit on the debt unless:
   a. Suit has been discontinued.
   b. Judgment entered and execution has been issued and returned unsatisfied.
2. May file suit against guarantors and foreclose by advertisement at same time.

C. Post property and advertise for 4 weeks.

D. Not required to "serve" mortgagor.

E. Not required to "serve" or otherwise notify junior lien holders.

F. Sale in fifth week.

G. May adjourn on a week to week basis by posting.

H. Required to bid the lesser of the debt or fair value of the property.

I. Can be combined with foreclosure of personal property and similar collateral.

J. Redemption is 6 or 12 months, with most commercial properties being 6 months.

K. Following sale, may file suit for a deficiency.

IV. Guidelines for Power of Sale:

The mortgage instrument must contain a power of sale to permit a non-judicial foreclosure.

V. Power of Sale Guidelines as Represented in the Security:

If the mortgage instrument does not contain a power of sale, mortgagee may foreclose judicially, only.

VI. Guidelines for Foreclosure when there is No Power of Sale:

No information provided.

VII. Foreclosure When Instrument Contains No Power of Sale:

No information provided.

VIII. Any Additional Satisfaction Permitted Under Continuing Power of Sale:

If mortgage covers more than one parcel, mortgagee must sell by lots until debt is satisfied, unless the mortgage provides that a sale of the whole is permitted.

IX. Sale by Power of Sale when the Instrument is Silent as to the Place or Terms of Sale:

A. Non-judicial sales:

1. Must be held in county where mortgaged property is located.
2. Mortgagee may "credit" bid, all others must pay cash on day of sale.

B. Judicial Sales:

1. Suit must be filed where property is located, unless more than one mortgage in more than one county secures the debt.
2. Mortgagee may "credit" bid, all others must pay cash on day of sale.

X. Notice of Sale and How Notice is Given:

A. Date and time of sale.
B. Set forth amount owed.
C. Identify the mortgagor, the mortgagee, and any assignee.
D. Identify the mortgage.
E. Identify the mortgaged property.
F. Set forth period of redemption.
G. Judicial Foreclosure:
   1. Must serve mortgagor and junior lien holders with summons and complaint.
   2. Must post notice of sale at property.
   3. Must advertise in newspaper with circulation in the county where property is located (typically a weekly or daily legal newspaper).

H. Non-judicial Foreclosure:
   1. Must post notice of sale at property.
   2. Must advertise in newspaper with circulation in the county where property is located (typically a weekly or daily legal newspaper).
   3. Not required to "serve" mortgagor or junior lien holders – unless the state or federal taxing authorities have filed a lien.

XI. Place and Time for Conducting Foreclosure by Power of Sale:

Sales are held in county where property is located. Typically, the sheriff will conduct the sale in the county courthouse in the mid-morning, once a week. This will vary from county to county.

Relevant Codes, Statutes or Case Law:
MCL 440.9607 (UCC Article 9, Section 607); MCL 600.3101, *et seq;* MCL 600.3240; MCL 600.3280.

Receivership:

I. General information:

A. Circuit Judges may appoint Receivers where allowed by law.
   1. To enforce assignment of rents.
   2. To prevent waste.

3. Due to non-payment of taxes and insurance, if so provided in the mortgage.
4. Construction lien foreclosures

B. There is no independent remedy for appointment of Receiver, but rather as ancillary relief.

C. Motion to appoint a Receiver is ancillary to judicial foreclosure action.

II. Appointing the Receiver:

A. The Basics:

Receivers are appointed by motion, supported by affidavit and documents. Typically, the Court will enter an order to show cause requested by an ex parte motion for show cause, with a hearing within 2 weeks. The Court appoints a Receiver in the exercise of its discretion.

B. Time Frame for Appointment:

This varies by the practice of the particular court and judge. Notice can be as short as a day, or longer than 2 weeks.

C. Can you go in Ex Parte?

Typically not.

III. Loans and Advances:

A. Borrowing money should be covered in the Order Appointing the Receiver, especially terms of the method and process for such advances.

B. If not in the Order, typically will need an order from the court and then borrow under a Receiver certificate.

IV. Sales During the Receivership:

In Michigan a receiver is authorized to sell real property post judgment with a special order of the Court pursuant to MCR 2.622 and MCL 600.6104. Once the receiver obtains a purchase agreement for the property, the receiver and Plaintiff file a motion seeking court approval of the sale. Sales of real property by a receiver can also be effectuated pre-judgment if the order appointing the receiver authorizes the receiver to sell the real property. In this instance, the process is the same but most title companies will require that the closing not occur until the appeal period has run (21 days). The title companies will also require a certified copy of the order appointing receiver and order authorizing the receiver to convey the property.

V. Liens Against Receivership Property:

A. General Information:

In Michigan, parties that supply labor and materials to a development can claim a lien for monies owed. Liens must be filed within 90 days of last providing labor or materials. Once recorded an action to foreclose the construction lien must be filed within one year of recording. All construction liens can trace their priority back to the date of the first physical improvement to the property. First physical improvement is broadly construed to include any physical work done on the property that would give notice to an outsider that development has commenced. Construction liens that predate the recording of a mortgage are senior liens. That is, if the site was cleared of grass and trees on day one, all contractors including a contractor that performed the electrical work on day 300 can claim a senior lien over a mortgage on the property recorded anytime after day one.

B. How have lien issues been dealt with when a Receiver is appointed?

The Construction Lien Act, MCL 570.1101 et seq, provides for the appointment of a receiver with the power to sell real property free and clear of construction liens with the liens attaching to sale proceeds to be distributed in accordance of priority as determined by the court.

VI. Owners Associations:

There are no specific statutes that deal with owners associations. Association dues continue to accrue and therefore may be an expense of the receivership. If the owner association is not self sustaining, the receiver may be required to operate the owners association and the lender may be required to fund any shortfall in the operation income.

VII. Construction Related to Receivership Property:

A receiver in Michigan, by order of the Court, may be empowered to complete construction. Typically contracts for construction are subject to Court approval.

VIII. Ending the Receivership:

To wind up the Receivership a Motion and hearing and Order Releasing the Receiver are required, following final accounting.

IX. Miscellaneous:

A.

In certain circumstances, the Court may permit the Receiver to sell real property.

B.

In certain circumstances, the Court may permit the sale of real property free and clear of liens.

Relevant Codes, Statutes or Case Law:
MCLA 600.2926 through 600.2927, and annotations; MCR 2.622

Smith v Mut Benefit Life Ins Co, 362 Mich 114; 106 NW2d 515 (1960)
National Lumberman v Lake Shore Machinery Co, 260 Mich 440, 245 NW 494 (1932)
Wayne County Jail Inmates v McNamera, 178 Mich App 634, 444 NW2d 549 (1989)
Boucher v Boucher, 34 Mich App 213, 222-23 (1971); *Michigan Midwest-Bank v DJ Raynaert, Inc*, 165 Mich App 630, 647 (1988); *In re Forfeiture of 19203 Albany*, 210 Mich App 337, 342 n3 (1995).

Minnesota

Foreclosure Summary

Security Instrument	Mortgage
Judicial	Yes
Non-Judicial	Yes
Initial Public Notice	Publication
Time Frame	
Redemption Period	Varies
Deficiency	In some situations

Receivership Summary

Ancillary Remedy Necessary	Yes
Ex-Parte	Yes
Approximate Time for Appointment	Few Weeks
Who or What can act as Receiver	No Restrictions Given
Specific Receiver Requirements	Must Give a bond and file inventory
Is there any approval list for Receivers	No
Out of State Receivers Allowed	Unknown

Foreclosure:

I. Foreclosure procedures:

A. Foreclosure by advertisement

In order to foreclose by advertisement, the mortgage must contain a power of sale. Additionally, a default must have occurred and there can be no action pending on the debt or any part thereof. The mortgage and any and all assignments must be recorded. A notice of the pendency of the foreclosure and power of attorney to foreclose mortgage must be recorded before the first publication of the statutory form of Notice of Foreclosure. The statutory form of Notice of Foreclosure must be published for at least six weeks preceding the sheriff's sale.

B. Foreclosure by action

This is the procedure that is conducted like any ordinary civil suit. A judgment is entered for the amount due and the sheriff is ordered to sell the mortgaged premises or some part thereof to satisfy the judgment. Additionally, the sale must be confirmed by the Court.

C. Voluntary Foreclosure

For a mortgage executed after August 1993, in default for at least one month, and the property is not classified as agricultural or homestead, the mortgagor and mortgagee may enter into a written agreement for the voluntary foreclosure of the mortgage. The procedures for a voluntary foreclosure are set forth in Minnesota Statute Section 582.32. In a voluntary foreclosure, the mortgagor's redemption period is reduced to two months, the mortgagee waives any right to deficiency or other claim for personal liability against the mortgagor, the mortgagor waives any right to surplus sale proceeds and to contest the foreclosure and waives any right to rents and occupancy during the period from the date of the agreement through the redemption period. The mortgagee must record the voluntary foreclosure agreement, or a memorandum of the agreement, within seven days of its effective date.

II. Length of Procedure:

Foreclosure by advertisement can take from eight to fifteen months, consisting of two weeks to draft the foreclosure notice and arrange for publication, six to eight weeks to publish the notice of foreclosure, and six or twelve month for the redemption period. Foreclosure by action takes a year or more depending on the applicable redemption period and whether the mortgagor contests in the litigation. The majority of mortgages are foreclosed by advertisement.

III. Redemption:

Except for voluntary foreclosures, Minnesota has a six or twelve month redemption period. By statute, a mortgagee can seek a court order reducing the redemption period to five weeks if the mortgaged premises is a nonagricultural, residential dwelling that has been abandoned. A twelve month period of redemption exists for mortgages in 6 specific circumstances as follows:

(i) the mortgage was executed prior to July 1, 1967
(ii) less than 2/3 of the original principal remains owing
(iii) the mortgage was executed before July 1, 1987 and is greater than ten acres
(iv) the mortgage was executed before August 1, 1994 and the premises exceed ten acres but was less than forty acres
(v) the premises exceed forty acres
(vi) the premises exceed ten acres but is less than forty acres and was in agricultural use when the mortgage was executed and the mortgage was executed on or after August 1, 1994.

If the foreclosure is not a voluntary foreclosure, the mortgagee has not obtained a court order reducing the redemption period to five weeks, and none of the above circumstances apply, the redemption period is six months.

IV. Deficiencies:

A deficiency judgment is not allowed if a mortgage is foreclosed by advertisement and has a redemption period of six month or if the redemption period is reduced to five weeks. Also, if a mortgagee forecloses by voluntary foreclosure, the mortgagee waives any right to a deficiency. However, the mortgagee is not precluded from reaching an agreement with the mortgagor regarding additional payment. Minnesota's anti-deficiency statute does not apply to an agreement between a guarantor and a mortgagee.

Receivership:

A new statute was passed in Minnesota to codify the power of the court in appointing receivers and to clarify the types of receiverships and the respective powers and duties of each. Any receivership which is based upon the enforcement of an assignment of rents or leases, or the foreclosure of a mortgage lien, mechanic's lien, or other lien pursuant to which the respondent or any holder of a lien would have a statutory right of redemption, shall be a limited receivership. §576.24.

A receiver may be appointed under §576 whether or not the motion for appointment of a receiver is combined with, or is ancillary to, an action seeking a money judgment. A mimited receiver may be appointed before judgment to protect any party to an action who demonstrates an apparent right to property that is the subject of the action and is in the possession of an adverse party, and that the property or its rents and profits are in danger of loss or material impairment.

The court may appoint a receiver upon a motion with notice to the respondent, to all other parties in the action, and to parties in interest and other persons as the court may require. §576.25. A receiver can be appointed on an ex parte basis or shortened notice on a temporary basis if it is clearly shown that an emergency exists requiring the immediate appointment. The new statute specifically states that the order appointing the receiver does not create a trust.

§576.26 sets out the qualifications for a receiver. Any person, whether or not a resident of Minnesota, may serve as a receiver, provided that the court, makes written conclusions based in the record that the person proposed as receiver is qualified to serve as receiver and officer of the court, and is independent as to the parties and the underlying dispute.

Mississippi

Foreclosure Summary

Security Instrument	Trust Deed/Mortgage
Judicial	Yes
Non-Judicial	Yes
Initial Public Notice	Publication
Time Frame	60 days
Redemption Period	None
Deficiency	No

Receivership Summary

Ancillary Remedy Necessary	Yes
Ex-Parte	Yes
Approximate Time for Appointment	24 hours- weeks
Who or What can act as Receiver	Individual is preferred but the Judge can approve a corporation
Specific Receiver Requirements	Best practice is to request the appointment of an individual as receiver and request that the receiver be given the authority to hire a management company
Is there any approval list for Receivers	No
Out of State Receivers Allowed	Yes

Foreclosure:

I. General Information:

Mississippi is by custom and practice a power of sale jurisdiction for foreclosures. Generally, the first action in a foreclosure is to obtain a substitution of trustee unless the original trustee is available and willing to serve. The substitution must appear of record prior to the first publication of the notice of sale. To avoid power, authority and doing business issues, an individual is the most common choice for a trustee. Although notice to junior lienors is not a statutory requirement, most lawyers will provide notice to any lien holder affected by the foreclosure sale. A title bring to date from the mortgagee title insurance policy is recommended in all cases.

II. Judicial Foreclosure Basics:

Judicial foreclosures in Mississippi are rare and are used only in the event of an error in the deed of trust or a defect in title. The suit is filed in the Chancery Court of the county or judicial district in which the property is located. The time involved depends on the court docket and the chancellor. Upon entering a judgment of foreclosure, the chancellor will appoint a special commissioner to hold the sale. The sale is held in the same manner as a power of sale foreclosure, and the special commissioner will report the sale back to the court for judicial confirmation. The suit is a civil suit, subject to the same delays and appeals as any other civil court case.

III. Non-Judicial Foreclosure Basics:

A non-judicial foreclosure is governed by statute, and the statute should be carefully followed. Section 89-1-55 of the Mississippi Code of 1972, as amended, contains the general provisions for a foreclosure sale.

IV. Power of sale foreclosure guidelines

The trustee or substitute trustee should hold the sale between the legal hours of 11:00 a.m. and 4:00 p.m. at the location where such sales are generally held at the courthouse of the county or judicial district in which the land is located. The notice is read in full and bids are made. The sale is made to the highest bidder, usually the lender. The trustee or substitute trustee will execute a Trustee's Deed, without warranty of title, to the purchaser. Excess funds, if any, are payable to junior lien holders and the balance to the debtor. A deficiency judgment may be available based on the difference between the debt and the fair market value of the property foreclosed as of the date of the sale.

V. Power of sale constitutes part of security

A properly drafted deed of trust will contain provisions governing a power of sale. Such a provision will carefully follow the statutory guidelines.

VI. No Power of sale foreclosure guidelines

In accordance with Section 89-1-57 of the Mississippi Code of 1972, as amended, if the document is silent as to the place and terms of sale and mode of advertising, the foreclosure sale is held in the same manner as a sheriff's sale. The provisions for a sheriff's sale of land in Section 13-3-63 of the Mississippi Code of 1972, as amended, are essentially the same as for a regular power of sale foreclosure.

VII. Foreclosure when instrument contains no power of sale.

If the instrument contains no provision for foreclosure, an argument can be made that the beneficiary of the deed of trust did not bargain for a power of sale and the grantor did not grant such a right. The foreclosure would proceed as a judicial sale.

VIII. Additional satisfaction permitted under continuing power of sale.

The lien of the deed of trust would not be automatically discharged until the full indebtedness is paid, and the power of sale would continue to be valid as to any lands remaining subject to the lien of the deed of trust.

IX. Sale under power where instrument silent as to place or terms of sale.

As stated in Paragraph VI above, the sale would proceed in the same manner as a sheriff's sale.

X. Notice of Sale and How notice of sale is given

The sale is advertised in a newspaper published in the county where the land is located, or if no paper is published in the county, publication is made in some paper having a general circulation therein. The notice contains the name of the grantor(s), the trustee or substitute trustee, recording data for the deed of trust and any assignments as well as for a substitution of trustee, if applicable, the identity of the note holder, the fact of default, a description of the property being foreclosed, notice of the times of sale (between 11:00 a.m. and 4:00 p.m.), and the location of the sale. A notice is also posted in the courthouse of the county or judicial district in which the sale is held. The notice of sale must be published and posted for three consecutive weeks preceding the date of the sale. Most lawyers publish a notice once each week for four weeks.

XI. Place and time for conducting foreclosure by power of sale.

The sale is held after expiration of three consecutive weeks of publication of a notice of sale (generally, once each week for four consecutive weeks) between the legal hours of 11:00 a.m. and 4:00 p.m. at the applicable door of the courthouse of the county or judicial district in which the land is located. The individual holding the sale should confirm the customary location for sales with the applicable Chancery Clerk, for example, the north front door of the courthouse.

Relevant Codes, Statutes or Case Law:
Sections 89-1-43; 89-1-49; 89-1-53; 89-1-55; 89-1-57; 89-1-59; 89-1-63 and 13-3-163, Mississippi Code of 1972, as amended.

Receivership:

I. General information:

Miss. Code Ann. §§ 11-5-151 through 11-5-167 set forth the general receivership provisions under Mississippi law. The statutes provide little guidance as to the circumstances justifying a receivership, the powers that may be granted to a receiver or the structure of the receivership. Therefore, such issues must be developed by judicial interpretations of the statutes. As the

Mississippi Court of Appeals has noted, however, "there is little Mississippi case law interpreting the receivership statutes."

II. Appointing the Receiver:

A. The Basics:

A receivership is an ancillary remedy that supports some other claim for substantive relief, such as a judicial foreclosure, damages for breach of contract, or reformation of instruments. Because a receivership is an ancillary remedy, it is usually requested initially as one count of a multi-count complaint. As a general rule, all entities with interests of record should be joined as parties.

The party seeking to have a receiver appointed must demonstrate a clear legal or equitable right to that relief. One example of such a right is a lien upon property coupled with danger of neglect, waste, misconduct or insolvency of the defendant. Additionally, the party seeking that relief must show a reasonable probability of success on the merits.

There is no absolute right to the appointment of a receiver. Whether a receiver is to be appointed (as well as who the receiver will be) is subject to the chancellor's discretion. Nevertheless, there is no prohibition against the plaintiff recommending in the Complaint a particular receiver and requesting that the receiver have specified powers. Unless a defendant challenges the receiver's credentials and/or the proposed scope of authority, the chancellor will often accept the plaintiff's recommendation.

A defendant may avoid appointment of a receiver by posting a bond, subject to the discretion of the chancellor. If a receiver is appointed, the receiver is not authorized to act until posting a bond payable to the state in an amount determined by the chancellor. The receiver's bond is subject to being reduced, cancelled or replaced upon petition heard on at least five days' notice if the chancellor finds that the bond is in excess of the value of the receivership estate and, therefore, is an unnecessary expense, or for other sufficient cause. The receiver's compensation and estate expenses are subject to court approval and are secured by a lien on assets of the receivership estate. A receiver must follow the orders of the court and may seek modification of prior orders. A receiver may be removed upon appropriate notice.

B. Time Frame for Appointment:

A receiver may not be appointed except upon at least five days notice to the opposing party. However, Mississippi's receivership statutes are antiquated. It is unclear how much of the statutory procedure is supplanted by the Mississippi Rules of Civil Procedure, which give a defendant 30 days from service of process to file a responsive pleading. Miss. R. Civ. Proc. 81 provides that the Rules apply to "all civil proceedings but are subject to limited applicability in the following actions which are generally governed by statutory procedures … proceedings brought under … sections 11-5-151 through 11-5-167 …, Mississippi Code of 1972." The comments to Rule 81 provide that the Rules govern where the "controlling statutes are silent as to a procedure…" However, the practitioner may well face difficult decisions as to how the statutes and the Rules may mesh in a given instance. In light of this uncertainty, plaintiffs seeking receiverships often include a count for a receivership in the complaint but contemporaneously with the filing of the complaint also file an emergency motion seeking appointment of receiver and injunctive relief under Miss. R. Civ. Proc. 65 to support the receiver. This kind of motion may include as an alternative form of relief a request for an interim receiver pending a full adjudication of the issues. Typically, the motion will mirror the receivership and injunction counts of the complaint and will set forth specific grounds justifying the appointment of a receiver and injunctive relief, a resume of the proposed receiver and a detailed recitation of the proposed scope of the receiver's powers. It is best practice for the motion to be verified by the plaintiff under oath.

C. Receiver's Action and Reporting:

Where a receivership is expected to last a long time, quarterly or annual reports may be required by the court. Where the receivership is expected to be of short duration, a final report may be all that is required. Where reports are required, they usually are filed with the clerk of the court.

D. Can you go in Ex Parte?

A receiver may be appointed without notice to the opposing party, but only for good cause shown.

III. Loans and Advances:

No. Any such matters must be addressed in court orders.

IV. Sales During the Receivership:

No specific guidance is provided. Sales of property and the procedures for same must be spelled out in the order. Care should be taken to prevent the order from setting forth a procedure that violates due process rights of creditors. For example, the order should not permit the receiver to sell property without notice to creditors with liens on the property to be sold.

V. Liens Against Receivership Property:

No. This must be addressed in the order. If there is a priority dispute among secured creditors or a challenge to proper perfection of a lien, the receiver may file an ancillary action asking the court to declare the rights of the parties or for other relief.

VI. Owners Associations:

No. Such matters must be addressed in a court order.

VII. Construction Related to Receivership Property:

This would have to be spelled out in the order.

VIII. Ending the Receivership:

Typically, an order is submitted by the receiver or plaintiff's counsel attaching the receiver's final accounting. The proposed order should ratify the receiver's actions, terminate the bond, and close the receivership estate.

IX. Miscellaneous

It is best practice is to record in the land records immediately after the filing of the complaint a *lis pendens* notice. The purpose of this notice is to place any subsequent interest holders on notice that they need to intervene in the receivership action or run the risk of their interest being adversely affected by the receiver.

Most foreclosures in Mississippi are handled non-judicially, and the time-period for such procedures is short. Because the non-judicial foreclosure process is quick, most lenders do not seek a receiver unless there are extraordinary circumstances (such as the need to capture a large amount of rent) or there is a need to judicially foreclosure or reform instruments (which can take months or years to bring to conclusion).

Because a receivership is a drastic remedy, some Mississippi courts require extensive testimony as to the grounds justifying a receivership and the qualifications of the proposed receiver – even if the defendant fails to appear and contest the relief requested.

Relevant Codes, Statutes or Case Law:
Miss. Code Ann. §§ 11-5-151 through 11-5-167; Miss. Code Ann. §9-5-103; Spectrum Oil, LLC v. West, 34 So.3d 1213, P18 (Miss. Ct. App. 2010); Engleburg v. Tonkel, 106 So. 447 (Miss. 1925); Clark v. Fleming, 94 So. 458 (Miss. 1923); Tishomingo Sav. Inst. V. Allen, 23 So. 305 (Miss. 1898); Perry Mason Shoe Co. v. Sykes, 17 So. 171 (Miss. 1895); Miss. R. Civ. Proc. 81.

Missouri

Foreclosure Summary

Security Instrument	Trust Deed/ Mortgage
Judicial	Yes
Non-Judicial	Yes
Initial Public Notice	Publication
Time Frame	45 Days
Redemption Period	Yes
Deficiency	No

Receivership Summary

Ancillary Remedy Necessary	Yes
Ex-Parte	Yes
Approximate Time for Appointment	3-10 Days
Who or What can act as Receiver	No Restrictions Given
Specific Receiver Requirements	No Restrictions Given
Is there any approval list for receivers	No
Out of State Receivers Allowed	Yes

Foreclosure:

I. General Information:

In Missouri, non-judicial foreclosure is the standard method of foreclosure. A three party deed of trust with power of sale is the common method of creating a lien on real property. A non-judicial foreclosure can be completed within 30-40 days. Missouri law does not require written notice of default or acceleration prior to foreclosure of a commercial loan, unless the loan documents require such notice. But it is recommended that the lender provide written notice of default and acceleration to the appropriate parties. (Notice of default is statutorily required where the loan was made primarily for personal, family or household purposes, prior to the lender being able to accelerate and foreclose its secured interest).

Missouri does not have a one- action rule or anti-deficiency statute. Missouri does grant borrower redemption rights, but the procedures for a borrower to redeem are impracticable given that the borrower whose property is being foreclosed is usually in financial distress. In order to exercise such redemption rights, either at the sale or within ten days before the sale, the borrower must provide written notice of borrower's intent to redeem and must, within 20 days from the date of the sale, give security to the circuit court in an amount that is not less than the costs, taxes, and interest that will accrue on the mortgage loan over the course of the one year immediately following the sale. Such security is often in the form of a redemption bond. Only if the borrower meets these requirements does the borrower have a one-year redemption period after the sale, and even then, the redemption right is contingent on the foreclosing lender being the purchaser at the sale. Redemption is very rarely exercised by borrowers in Missouri.

II. Judicial Foreclosure Basics:

Judicial foreclosure is rarely used in Missouri. A mortgage must be foreclosed by suit in Missouri. But the majority of real property in Missouri is secured by a three party deed of trust with power of sale. In those rare instances where real property is foreclosed judicially, the lender files suit and then seek summary judgment against the borrower, which judgment will direct the sheriff of the county to foreclose the property.

III. Non-Judicial Foreclosure Basics:

Non-judicial foreclosure provides the lender with a relatively inexpensive and effective process to foreclose its lien without the need to file suit or seek court approval. A court only becomes involved if the borrower challenges the foreclosure and seeks court intervention or if the borrower seeks to redeem and post a redemption bond. Non-judicial foreclosure, however, requires strict compliance with the law. A foreclosure sale may be set aside if the action taken by lender was not exercised with regularity, statutory conformity, or procedural fairness. The trustee under the deed of trust sends out a notice of trustee's sale 20 days prior to the foreclosure sale to the grantor, the current owner (as of 40 days prior to the sale), and others who record a request for notification of the sale. If there is an IRS lien, notice to the IRS must be provided 25 days prior to the sale. Notice of the Sale is published in a newspaper in the county where the property to be foreclosed is located. The notice must be published in a newspaper for 21 consecutive days or four consecutive weeks, depending upon the size of the county and the regularity of publication of the paper in which advertisement is to be made. The property is then sold at the foreclosure sale and the trustee records a trustee's deed.

IV. Power of sale foreclosure guidelines

A. The foreclosing lender should confirm that the deed of trust includes a power of sale.

B. The lender should identify the trustee. If it is more convenient to have someone different serve as trustee, the lender can sign a short form document appointing a successor trustee and have it recorded with the office of the recorder of deeds for the county in which the land is located. This must be done before written notice of the sale is sent out and before advertisement commences.

C. Provide written notice of foreclosure sale to required parties under the statute.

D. Publish notice of foreclosure sale as required by statute. E. Conduct foreclosure sale. There is no "sale confirmation" process in Missouri. The foreclosing lender should take care throughout the process to have title work that is as updated as possible so that it provides the proper parties with notice of the sale. The lender should also remain in contact with its title company through the sale process and obtain a commitment to insure, free of every exception possible, once the sale is completed in accordance with the statutory requirements.

V. Power of sale constitutes part of security

Generally, no. However, for lenders who consider selling their loans, there is no doubt that the loan asset itself will have far more value if the lender's deed of trust includes a power of sale than if the lender's deed of trust does not.

VI. No Power of sale foreclosure guidelines

File petition to foreclose security interest in the circuit court where the real property is located and obtain a judgment whereby the court sets forth the details of the sale process, including ordering the sheriff or another authorized person or entity to conduct the sale.

VII. Foreclosure when instrument contains no power of sale.

See above.

VIII. Additional satisfaction permitted under continuing power of sale.

Missouri has no clear case law regarding whether a power of sale is "exhausted" once exercised or whether it may be exercised more than once (in the case of error in connection with the initial sale or if a portion of the real estate secured by the deed of trust mistakenly was not included in the initial sale). Traditionally, lenders seeking to foreclose further, after having exercised their power of sale, have utilized judicial foreclosure to do so: one of the rare examples of when foreclosing lenders in Missouri opt for judicial foreclosure.

IX. Sale under power where instrument silent as to place or terms of sale.

At the main door or door designated by statute of the county courthouse in the county where the real property to be foreclosed is located.

X. Notice of Sale and how notice of sale is given

The notice of sale must include:

- **A.** the date the deed of trust was given;
- **B.** the book and page or instrument number of record of the deed of trust;
- **C.** the names of the grantors;
- **D.** the time of sale;
- **E.** the terms of sale;
- **F.** the place of sale; and
- **G.** a description of the property to be sold.

A written notice of foreclosure sale is sent to the appropriate parties, including the original borrowers, the owner of the property as shown by the records in the office of the county recorder of deeds as of 40 days before the sale, and any party who has filed a request for notice of sale in the prescribed form at least 40 days before the sale, by certified or registered mail at least 20 days prior to the foreclosure sale. If there is an IRS lien, notice must be provided to the IRS 25 days prior to the sale. A notice must also be published in a newspaper for 21 consecutive days or for four consecutive weeks, depending upon the size of the county and the regularity of newspaper publications within the county.

XI. Place and time for conducting foreclosure by power of sale.

The place of the foreclosure sale will be determined by the language in the deed of trust. Otherwise, the trustee's sale shall occur at the front door of the county courthouse in the county where the property to be foreclosed is located, which is usually the place identified in the deed of trust. A trustee's sale may be held between the hours of 9 a.m. and 5 p.m. The trustee may adjourn the sale up to one week without consent of the borrower. The borrower must approve in writing any longer extension for the extension to be valid. Otherwise, the foreclosing lender must recommence the notice and publication process anew.

Receivership:

I. General information:

In Missouri, the court has the power to appoint a receiver whenever such appointment shall be deemed necessary. The receiver's duty shall be to keep and preserve all property and protect any business or business interest entrusted to him or her pending any legal or equitable proceeding concerning the same, subject to the order of the court. A receiver should be appointed only when the court is satisfied that the appointment will promote the interests of one or both parties; it will prevent manifest wrong, imminently impending; and, the injury resulting will not be greater than the injury sought to be averted.

II. Appointing the Receiver:

A. The Basics:

The process begins with the filing of a petition in the circuit court, because it is essential to the appointment of a receiver that the applicant show either that he or she has a clear right or apparent right to or title in or to, the property itself, that he or she has some lien upon it, or that the property constitutes a special fund to which he or she has a right to resort for the satisfaction of his or her claim. Typically, the underlying action will be a suit on the note and guarantees. A foreclosure count is not necessary, since foreclosure in Missouri is non-judicial, and nothing precludes simultaneous prosecution of an action on the debt while conducting of the trustee's sale. A motion for appointment of a receiver is filed together with the petition on the note and guarantees.

Early case law states that the party seeking appointment of a receiver must show three things:

1. Immediate danger to the property;

2. A reasonable probability that the lender will prevail on the merits; and,
3. Insolvency of the borrower.

Other cases state that a receiver should not be appointed if a less drastic remedy can be invoked. Some cases interpreting the general statute have held that the courts have the power to appoint receivers to preserve property pending legal or equitable proceedings concerning the same, and the exercise of this power rests "within the sound discretion of the court."

B. Time Frame for Appointment:
3-10 days.

C. Can you go in Ex Parte?
Yes, the court has the authority to appoint ex parte under the right circumstances; however, it is unusual for the court to appoint a receiver ex parte, and the court will need to be convinced that some affirmative harm would result by informing the borrower or its counsel in advance of the motion. A court will appoint a receiver ex parte when there is an emergency and to prevent irreparable injury. An ex parte hearing, much like a temporary restraining order, will then be followed by a hearing conducted after notice to the adverse party.

III. Loans and Advances:

Case law provides that a receiver should receive court approval prior to entering into a contract to borrow. This can routinely be dealt with, however, in the order appointing the receiver, so as to render it a non-issue at the time the lender and receiver decide that the receiver will borrow from the lender.

IV. Sales During the Receivership:

No case law on the issue. The author, however, has effected receiver sales in Missouri.

V. Liens Against Receivership Property:

No case law on the issue.

VI. Owners Associations:

No case law on the issue.

VII. Construction Related to Receivership Property:

No case law on the issue.

VIII. Ending the Receivership:

An application for discharge must be made, notice of which should be given to all parties. The application for discharge should be accompanied by a final accounting of the receivership estate by the receiver.

Relevant Codes, Statutes or Case Law:
Mo. Rev. Stat. Chapter 515: Referees and Receiver; Mo. Rev. Stat. § 515.240; Appointment of receiver; Mo. Rev. Stat. § 515.250: Bond of receiver – powers; Mo. Rev. Stat. § 515.260: Compensation of receiver; Mo Rev. Stat. § 521.300: Authorizes circuit court to appoint receivers in aid of attachments "in a proper case." Mo. Rev. Stat. § 351.498: Receivership or custodianship (General and Business Corporation, Dissolution and Forfeiture); Sup. Ct. Rule 68.02 – Receivers in Circuit Courts.

Montana

Foreclosure Summary

Security Instrument	Trust Deed/ Mortgage
Judicial	Yes
Non-Judicial	Yes
Initial Public Notice	Notice of Sale
Time Frame	60 days to 6 months
Redemption Period	One year for financial disclosure
Deficiency	Only if Judicial

Receivership Summary

Ancillary Remedy Necessary	
Ex-Parte	Yes
Approximate Time for Appointment	Within 30 days
Who or What can act as Receiver	Individual or Company
Specific Receiver Requirements	No party, attorney, or person interested in an action can be appointed receiver therein without the written consent of the parties, filed with the clerk.
Is there any approval list for Receivers	Unknown
Out of State Receivers Allowed	Unknown

Foreclosure:

I. General information

There is only one action for the recovery of debt or the enforcement of any right secured by a mortgage upon real estate.

II. Judicial foreclosure

An injunction may be obtained to restrain the party in possession from injuring the property during foreclosure proceedings.

In an action to foreclose a mortgage of real property, the court must allow as a part of the costs a reasonable attorney's fee, which shall be fixed by the court, notwithstanding any stipulation in the instrument or any agreement between the parties to the contrary.

The purchaser of land at mortgage foreclosure is not entitled to the possession of the land as against the execution debtor during the period of redemption allowed by law while the execution debtor personally occupies the land as a home for the execution debtor and the debtor's family. It is unlawful to insert in any mortgage of real estate any provision intended to constitute a waiver by the owner of real estate personally occupying land as a home for the owner and the owner's family of the provision of this section or any provision intended to give the mortgagee possession of the land or premises prior to foreclosure upon default of tax, principal, or interest payments. The intention of which is to ensure to the owner the possession of the land prior to foreclosure and during the year of redemption.

Redemption period is one year. Written notice of redemption must be given to the sheriff and a duplicate filed with the county clerk

III. Non-judicial foreclosure

Non-judicial foreclosure is found in the Small Tract Financing Act of Montana Trust. Indentures are authorized for property not exceeding 40 acres to secure the performance of the grantor in the indenture to the beneficiary. A power of sale is conferred on the trustee be exercised after a breach of the obligation for which the transfer is security. A trust indenture may be foreclosed by advertisement or by juridical foreclosure. A power of sale may be exercised even without an express provision in the indenture.

A trust indenture is deemed a mortgage and the grantor is deemed the mortgagor and the beneficiary is deemed the mortgagee.

The trustee must be an attorney licensed to practice in Montana, a bank, trust company, or savings and loan association authorized to do business in Montana, or a title insurer or title insurance producer or agency authorized to do business in Montana.

The foreclosure of a trust indenture by advertisement and sale or by judicial procedure shall be commenced within the time, including extensions, provided by law for the foreclosure of a mortgage on real property.

In order to foreclose the trust indenture by advertisement, the indenture must be recorded and there must be a default by the grantor. The notice of sale must be recorded and must contain the names of the grantor, trustee and beneficiary, a description of the property, the book page where the indenture is recorded, the default, the sum owing on the obligation, the trustee or beneficiary's election to sell the property, the date of sale, which shall not be less than 120 days subsequent to the date on which the notice of sale is filed for record, and the time of sale, which shall be between the hours of 9 a.m. and 4 p.m., mountain standard time, and the place of sale which shall be at the courthouse of the county or one of the counties where the property is situated or at the location of the property or at the trustee's usual place of business if within the county or one of the counties where the property is situated.
On the date and time designated for the sale, the trustee must sell the property to the highest bidder. The property may be sold in one or separate parcels and the beneficiary can bid but the trustee cannot.

The proceeds of the trustee sale are applied first to the costs and expenses of exercising the power of sale and of the sale, including reasonable trustee's fees and attorney fees, then to the obligation secured by the trust indenture. Any surplus can be given to the person entitled to it or deposited with the clerk.

No deficiency judgment is allowed for a trust indenture if it is foreclosed by advertisement and sale.

IV. Power of sale foreclosure guidelines

Must advertise the real estate for sale at least 30 days before the date fixed for such sale, in a newspaper in the county in which such real estate is situated. Posting the notice of sale is also permitted if no newspaper is available. Notice of sale must be served personally at least 30 days before the date fixed for such sale upon the occupant of the property so advertised for sale and upon the mortgagor if within the state of Montana and upon every person or persons having or claiming an interest of record in the real estate so advertised for sale who may be found within the state of Montana.

Surplus may be paid to the person entitled to it and in the meantime, deposited with the court.

Same redemption rights as judicial foreclosure. Redemption period is 1 year.

V. Power of sale constitutes part of security

Yes, for small tract financing.

VI. Notice of Sale and How notice of sale is given

Notice of sale must be given at least 120 days before the date fixed for the sale and a copy of the notice of sale must be mailed by certified mail to the grantor, each person designated in the indenture to received notice, any person who has filed a request for a copy of the notice of sale, any successor in interest to the grantor whose interest and address appear of record, and any person with a lien or interest whose lien or interest and address appear of record.

Contributed By: Rebecca L. Mann of Gunderson Palmer Nelson Ashmore

At least 20 days before the date fixed for the trustee's sale, a copy of the recorded notice of sale must be posted in some conspicuous place on the property to be sold. A copy of the notice of sale must be published in a newspaper of general circulation published in any county in which the property or some part of the property is situated, at least once each week for 3 successive weeks. On or before the date of sale, there must be recorded in the office of the clerk and recorder of each county where the property or some part of the property is situated, affidavits of mailing, posting, and publication showing compliance with the requirements of this section.

Relevant Codes, Statutes or Case Law:
MCA 71-1-101 et seq. Mortgages – General Provisions
MCA 71-1-201 et seq. Mortgages of Real Property
MCA 71-1-301 et seq. Small Tract Financing
MCA 25-13-801 et seq. Redemption of Real Property

Receivership:

I. General information about your state:

In general, Montana has few statutes or case law on receivership. Each case is unique and the order for receivership should take into account the specific needs of that case.

A receiver may be appointed by the court in which an action is pending when the action is: (1) by a vendor to vacate a fraudulent purchase of property; (2) by a creditor to subject any property or fund to the creditor's claim; (3) between partners or others jointly owning or interested in any property or fund, on the application of the plaintiff or of any party whose right to or interest in the property or fund or the proceeds of the property or fund is probable and when it is shown that the property or fund is in danger of being lost, removed, or materially injured; (4) by a mortgagee for the foreclosure of the mortgagee's mortgage and sale of the mortgaged property and when it is shown that the mortgaged property is in danger of being lost, removed, or materially injured or that the condition of the mortgage has not been performed and the property is probably insufficient to discharge the mortgage debt; (5) after judgment, to carry the judgment into effect; (6) after judgment, to dispose of the property according to the judgment or to preserve it during the pendency of an appeal; or (7) for proceedings in aid of execution, when an execution has been returned unsatisfied or when the judgment debtor refuses to apply the judgment debtor's property in satisfaction of the judgment.

II. Appointment Process

Notice of an application for the appointment of a receiver in an action before judgment in the action must be given to the adverse party unless the party has failed to appear in the action and the time limited for the party's appearance has expired or unless it appears to the court that there is immediate danger that the property or fund will be removed beyond the jurisdiction of the court or lost, materially injured, destroyed, or unlawfully disposed of.

III. Receiver's action and reporting

A receiver cannot begin his duties until an oath and undertaking are performed.

The receiver has, under the control of the court, the power to: bring and defend actions in the receiver's own name, as receiver; take and keep possession of the property; receive rents, collect debts, and compound for and compromise the rents and debts; make transfers; and generally do acts respecting the property that the court may authorize.

IV. Loans and advances

The receiver has the power to do acts respecting the property that the court may authorize.

V. Sales During the Receivership

The receiver has the power to do acts respecting the property that the court may authorize. The order will control.

VI. Liens

The receiver has the power to do acts respecting the property that the court may authorize. The order will control.

VII. Owners Associations

No information provided.

VIII. Construction

N/A

IX. Ending the receivership

The court can remove the receiver at any time. Generally the order will control. It may require a motion and hearing to terminate receivership.

Relevant Codes, Statutes or Case Law:
MCA Chapter 27-20 Receivers

Nebraska

Foreclosure Summary

Security Instrument	Mortgage/Deed of Trust
Judicial	Yes
Non-Judicial	Yes, if power of sale is expressly provided for in deed of trust
Initial Public Notice	Petition for Judicial/Notice of Sale for Non-Judicial
Time Frame	180 days for Judicial; 80-90 days for Non-Judicial
Redemption Period	Yes, any time prior to confirmation of sale
Deficiency	Yes, in action separate from foreclosure proceeding

Receivership Summary

Ancillary Remedy Necessary	Yes
Ex-Parte	No
Approximate Time for Appointment	Minimum 5 days
Who or What can act as Receiver	Any person who is not a party, solicitor, counsel, or in any manner interested in the suit subject to objection by opposing party
Specific Receiver Requirements	Bond
Is there any approval list for Receivers	No
Out of State Receivers Allowed	Yes

Foreclosure:

I. Non-Judicial Foreclosure Basics:

Foreclosures in Nebraska may be accomplished non-judicially, if the deed of trust contains a power of sale, upon default of an obligation for which the trust property is conveyed as security. Mortgages and deeds of trust without a power of sale cannot be foreclosed non-judicially. The non-judicial foreclosure process takes far less time than a judicial foreclosure process and a non-judicial sale is made without a right of redemption. In order to commence a non-judicial foreclosure, the trustee must file a notice of default with the register of deeds. The notice of default provides the borrower with a 30 day right to cure the payments in arrears (without regard to acceleration). If the defaults are not timely cured, at least one month after the initial notice is filed (two months if farm property), the trustee must give written notice of the time and place of sale by publishing such notice, at least five times, once a week for five consecutive weeks. The beneficiary of the deed of trust must commence an action to recover any deficiency within three months after the sale of the property. A beneficiary of a deed of trust with a power of sale also may elect to proceed by the judicial foreclosure process, if necessary (for example, if the deed of trust needs to be reformed in some manner).

II. Judicial Foreclosure Basics:

An action to foreclose a mortgage in Nebraska is commenced by the filing of a complaint and a praecipe (a praecipe directs the clerk of the court to prepare or issue something and at the commencement of the case the praecipe should direct the clerk to prepare the necessary summons). The complaint should be filed in the district court in the county where the real property encumbered by the mortgage or deed of trust is situated. Service of the complaint and summons by certified mail is permitted in Nebraska. Although not absolutely necessary, it is good practice to attach copies of the core loan documents to the complaint. The complaint also should allege that no action at law has been had for the recovery of the debt secured by the mortgage or deed of trust.

Upon commencement of the foreclosure action, a lis pendens notice should be recorded with the register of deeds for the applicable county. The lis pendens should include the names of the parties, the object of the action, a legal description of the subject real property, the date of the mortgage, the parties to the mortgage and the recording information.

Within twenty (20) days after entry of a foreclosure decree, the owner of the subject real property can file with the court a request for a stay of a foreclosure sale (tenants and junior lien holders cannot request a stay). The stay is granted automatically and is generally for a period of nine (9) months. If the subject real property is residential real property of less than three (3) acres in size and the maturity date of the loan is more than twenty years from the date the foreclosure complaint was filed, the stay period is three (3) months; the stay period is six (6) months if the maturity date of the loan is between 10 and 20 years from the date the foreclosure complaint is filed. Only the owner of the real property can request a stay. A request for stay waives any right to claim errors in the foreclosure proceedings that may have occurred prior to the request for stay.

After expiration of the stay period, or twenty days after entry of the foreclosure decree, if no request for stay is filed, the plaintiff may file a praecipe for entry of an order of sale. Sales of real estate pursuant to an order of sale are conducted by the county sheriff, and the plaintiff's counsel should work closely with the sheriff's office in scheduling and publishing the notice of the sale. Notice of the sale must be published once a week for four consecutive weeks in a newspaper of general circulation within the county where the real property is situated. Notice also should be sent to all parties and an affidavit of mailing should be filed with the clerk of court's office.

Upon completion of the sale, the sheriff will file a return of sale with the court. Once the return is filed, the plaintiff or the winning bidder can file a motion to confirm the sale. If the sale is confirmed, the sale proceeds will be disbursed in conformity with the confirmation order.

At any time prior to confirmation of the sale, the owner may redeem the property by paying the amount of liens found due in the foreclosure decree plus interest thereon and costs and twelve (12) percent interest on the sheriff's sale purchase price from the date of the sale to the date of redemption if the plaintiff was not the purchaser at the sale. Redemption is limited to the owner of the subject real estate.

A separate action must be commenced for proceeding against the borrower on any deficiency.

Receivership:

I. General information:

A receivership is ancillary to the main action in Nebraska and therefore must be combined with another cause of action, such as a mortgage foreclosure. However, Nebraska state law provides that a Receiver can be appointed in connection with the exercise of the power of sale in a deed of trust after the filing of a notice of default. Because a receivership is an equitable remedy, the action must be filed in a Nebraska District Court, as opposed to the Nebraska County Courts which do not have equity jurisdiction.

II. Appointing the Receiver:

A. The Basics:

The plaintiff may seek appointment of a Receiver by complaint or through a motion. If the plaintiff wants the appointment of a Receiver when the action is commenced, the request for appointment of a Receiver should be included in the complaint. If the grounds for a Receiver arise after the complaint has been filed, appointment of a Receiver can be requested through a motion. Nebraska state law provides for the appointment of a Receiver, among other circumstances, in an action for the foreclosure of a mortgage or deed of trust and in connection with the exercise of the power of sale under a trust deed where the property subject to the trust deed is in danger of being lost, removed or materially injured or is probably insufficient to discharge the mortgage debt secured by the mortgage or trust deed.

Notice of the application for appointment of a Receiver must be served on the adverse party at least five days prior to the hearing concerning such application.

B. Time Frame for Appointment:

A receiver only may be appointed within the context of a pending suit. Although Nebraska law requires a minimum of five days notice of a receiver application prior to the hearing, the time frame for the hearing largely will depend upon the court's calendar. It generally will be a shorter time period if the case is pending in the greater Omaha area (Douglas or Sarpy Counties) or in Lincoln (Lancaster County) than in rural areas where judges are responsible for multiple counties.

C. Can you go in Ex Parte?

The appointment of a Receiver ex parte (or without notice) is prohibited under Nebraska law and any order appointing a receiver without notice is void. However, according to state law, the court may direct the county sheriff to take temporary possession of property pending the hearing on the application for appointment of a Receiver if the five-day notice period prior to a hearing is "hazardous to the rights of any party."

III. Loans and Advances:

The Nebraska statutes do not speak directly to the requirements for loans or advances. The Order of Appointment, however, will contain special directions with respect to a Receiver's powers and duties and may speak to the Receiver's authority to obtain loans or to issue advances.

IV. Sales During the Receivership:

No information provided.

V. Liens Against Receivership Property:

No information provided.

VI. Owners Associations:

No information provided.

VII. Construction Related to Receivership Property:

No information provided.

VIII. Ending the Receivership:

There are no specific requirements regarding the closing of the receivership. The closing of the receivership should be handled in the order of appointment.

Relevant Codes, Statutes or Case Law:

Neb. Rev. Stat. §§ 25-1081-25-1090 (receivership); Neb. Rev. Stat. §§ 76-1001-76-1018 (Nebraska Trust Deeds Act); Neb. Rev. Stat. §§ 25-1527-25-1531 (execution of foreclosure sale); Neb. Rev. Stat. §§25-2137-25-2155 (foreclosure process); Nev. Rev. Stat. §§ 25-1505-25-1514 (stay of execution)

Nevada

Foreclosure Summary

Security Instrument	Trust Deed
Judicial	Rarely
Non-Judicial	Yes
Initial Public Notice	Notice of Default
Time Frame	Approximately Four Months
Redemption Period	Trustee's Sale: No Judicial F/C: One Year
Deficiency	Yes

Receivership Summary

Ancillary Remedy Necessary	No
Ex-Parte	Yes
Approximate Time for Appointment	2-5 Weeks
Who or What can act as Receiver	Individual/Company
Specific Receiver Requirements	No
Is there any approval list for Receivers	No
Out of State Receivers Allowed	Yes, but local presence helpful

Foreclosure:

I. General Information:

Deeds of trust may be foreclosed by judicial or non-judicial means. Although rarely used, mortgages may only be foreclosed judicially. Mortgages are governed by chapter 106 of the Nevada Revised Statutes ("NRS"). Deeds of trust are governed by NRS chapter 107.

Nearly all foreclosure sales in Nevada are non-judicial foreclosure sales because they are generally less expensive and faster than judicial foreclosure sales. In contrast to judicial foreclosure sales, borrowers do not have a right of redemption following a non-judicial foreclosure sale. Unless otherwise stated, the information set forth in this section relates to non-judicial foreclosures via the exercise of a trustee's power of sale under a deed of trust.

II. Judicial Foreclosure Basics:

Judicial foreclosure is governed by NRS 40.430 through 40.450. Judicial foreclosure is rarely used, but is the exclusive method available to foreclose a mortgage. Nevada's form of the "one-action" rule is set forth in NRS 40.430. A judicial foreclosure is initiated by filing and serving a complaint upon the borrower and all other parties with an interest in or lien on the property. A complaint for judicial foreclosure results in a monetary judgment owing to the lender with a decree from the court directing a sheriff's sale of the property. Following the sheriff's sale, the borrower and certain other secured lienholders, have a one-year right of redemption in which to purchase the property by paying the amount bid for the property and other costs and charges, and, in certain instances, the amount owed to satisfy the lien of the foreclosing lienholder.

III. Non-Judicial Foreclosure Basics:

Non-judicial foreclosures are accomplished by the exercise of a trustee's power of sale under a deed to trust pursuant to NRS 107.080. If the loan is secured by both real and personal property, the lender may, under certain circumstances, use the non-judicial foreclosure process to conduct a unified sale of the real and personal property collateral. Generally, a non-judicial foreclosure can be completed within four months.

IV. Guidelines for Power of Sale:

A. Perfection of Interest in the Deed of Trust and Appointment of Trustee.

All assignments of the deed of trust must be recorded before the current holder can commence foreclosure. Further, any appointment of a new trustee is not effective until a substitution of trustee is recorded. The beneficiary under the deed of trust may not act as the trustee for purposes of exercising the power of sale.

B. The Notice of Default and Election to Sell.

A non-judicial foreclosure is commenced by recording a notice of default and election to sell (NOD) in the office of the county recorder in which the property is located and by service of the NOD upon the parties identified below. The NOD must specify the event of default, and, if permitted by the underlying loan documents, may declare the lender's intent to accelerate the debt if the event of default is not cured within the period prescribed by statute.

As of October 2011, an affidavit executed by the lender must be attached to and recorded with the NOD. This affidavit must attest to the lender's authority to exercise the power of sale, and state, among other items: (1) the name and address of the current trustee, the current holder of the debt and beneficiary of the deed of trust, and any loan servicers; (2) the name and last known address of any prior beneficiary of the deed of trust; (3) the date and recording information for every assignment of the deed of trust; and (4) the amount in default, the outstanding principal balance, and a good faith estimate all fees and charges to be imposed on the borrower as a result of the default.

The NOD must be sent via certified mail to the borrower, the record owner of the property, junior lienholders, guarantors, and other parties with an interest in the property or who have otherwise required notice. Additional notice requirements apply with respect to residential properties and certain licensed medical facilities.

C. Cure Period.

The borrower, the record owner of the property, a beneficiary under a subordinate deed of trust, or any other person who has a subordinate lien or encumbrance of record on the property, has 35 days from the date the NOD is recorded and mailed in which to cure the default set forth in the NOD. If cure is not made within this period, there is no further statutory right to cure.

D. Notice of Sale.

The notice of trustee's sale (NOS) will set the sale date, time and location, and describe the real property and personal property, where permitted, to be sold by the trustee. Once three months have elapsed from the date of the recordation of the NOD, the trustee may record the NOS and must provide notice of the sale by: (1) mailing a copy of the NOS by registered or certified mail to the borrower and all other persons entitled to receive notice, as identified above, (2) posting a copy of the NOS for 20 consecutive days, in a public place in the township or city in which the property is located, and (3) publishing a copy of the NOS three times, once a week for three consecutive weeks, in a newspaper of general circulation in the county in which the property is located. Again, additional notice requirements apply with respect to residential properties and certain licensed medical facilities.

E. Sale Date and Payment.

Non-judicial foreclosure sales are conducted as public auctions to the highest bidder. The sale must be held between 9:00 a.m. and 5:00 p.m. at a public location in the county in which the property is located that is designated by the governing body of the county for that purpose. The sale may be postponed three times by oral proclamation to a later date at the same time before a new NOS must be recorded, mailed, posted and published. The property is to be sold to the highest bidder. The beneficiary may credit-bid. The trustee generally has 30 days from the sale date in which to record the trustee's deed upon sale. Real property transfer tax is due at the time of recording the deed, even where the property reverts to the beneficiary.

F. Deficiency Judgment:
Any action for a deficiency judgment must be brought within six months of the foreclosure sale.

G. Special Local Considerations.
An ordinance passed by the City of Las Vegas in December 2011 requires, among other things, lenders foreclosing on vacant real property to register with the City of Las Vegas and to inspect and maintain the property until the foreclosure sale. Other local jurisdictions may adopt similar ordinances in 2012.

Relevant Codes, Statutes or Case Law:
NRS Chapter 40; NRS Chapter 106; NRS Chapter 107; City of Las Vegas Ordinance No. 6169 (Dec. 7, 2011).

Receivership:

I. General information:
State law provides that a receiver may be appointed in a variety of circumstances. The discussion below pertains to receivers appointed over real property (and related personal property) in connection with a borrower's default in the performance of an obligation secured by that real property. A receiver of a business entity may have additional powers and limitations not addressed below.

A. Judicial Foreclosure.
In connection with a judicial foreclosure, a receiver may be appointed where it appears that the property is in danger of being lost, removed or materially injured and that the property is probably insufficient to discharge the debt.

B. Non-Judicial Foreclosure.
In tandem with a non-judicial foreclosure, lenders will also often seek the judicial appointment of a receiver to stabilize, manage

and operate the secured property prior to the foreclosure sale. At any time after recording the NOD, the lender may apply to the state district court for the county in which the property or any part of the property is located for the appointment of a receiver of the property. A receiver is to be appointed where it appears "that personal property subject to the deed of trust is in danger of being lost, removed, materially injured or destroyed, that real property subject to the deed of trust is in danger of substantial waste or that the income therefrom is in danger of being lost, or that the property is or may become insufficient to discharge the debt which it secures."

C. Uniform Assignment of Rents Act.

In addition, appointment of a receiver may be sought pursuant to the Uniform Assignment of Rents Act, adopted as NRS chapter 107A. Specifically, NRS 107A.260 provides that a lender-assignee under an assignment of rents (including an assignment of rents granted in a deed of trust) is entitled to the appointment of a receiver upon the borrower-assignor's default in the performance of its obligations under the loan documents where, among other things, one or more of the following has taken place: (1) the borrower has agreed in a signed document to the appointment of a receiver in the event of its default; (2) it appears likely that the real property may not be sufficient to satisfy the secured obligation; and/or (3) the borrower has failed to turn over to the assigned proceeds that the lender is entitled to collect. Notably, the appointment of a receiver under NRS ch. 107A does not require the commencement of a judicial or non-judicial foreclosure.

D. Other Grounds.

A lender may also seek the appointment of a receiver where the property is affected by the presence of a hazardous substance. Other equitable grounds may also support the appointment of a receiver.

II. Appointing the Receiver:

A. The Basics.

The party seeking appointment must file a complaint and a motion setting forth sufficient facts in support of the appointment. Among other salient facts, the party seeking appointment will want to make specific reference to the factors outlined in state statutes, as applicable, in its motion for appointment of a receiver. State law does not require a receiver to post a bond; judges, however, have the discretion to require one. The receiver will be paid through the income generated by the receivership estate and by the lender to the extent that income from the property is insufficient. Most orders require larger expenditures, leases and other contracts to be approved by the lender, and require the receiver to remit excess cash flow to the lender to be applied per the loan documents.

B. Time Frame for Appointment.

Generally, it takes between two and five weeks to appoint a receiver in order to provide the borrower with notice and an opportunity to be heard. A borrower may also stipulate to the appointment of a receiver.

C. *Ex Parte* Appointments.

Depending on the exigency of the situation, a receiver may be appointed on an *ex parte* basis in less than one week. After such an appointment, further hearing will likely be required in order to provide the borrower with notice and an opportunity to be heard.

III. Loans and Advances:

Generally, the appointment order will permit the lender to provide advances to the receiver to fund operating expenses not otherwise covered by the rents and other income generated by the property. Any debts incurred by the receiver without court authorization may be the personal responsibility of the receiver.

IV. Sales During the Receivership:

While there is no express statutory authority, sales by receivers appointed in connection with a non-judicial foreclosure or pursuant to the Uniform Assignment of Rents Act are common in Nevada. A carefully drafted appointment order may permit the receiver to market and sell the property, subject to further court and lender approval and notice to the borrower and other lienholders. Generally, the ability of the prospective buyer to obtain title insurance is a driving factor and the proposed title insurer should be consulted early in order to determine any unique underwriting requirements.

V. Liens Against Receivership Property:

A. General Information.

Generally, a receiver is to resist any levy against the receivership estate and, depending on the circumstances, other creditors of the borrower—including owners associations—may not foreclose on property included as part of the receivership estate absent court approval. However, the receivership estate is subject to all valid and existing liens upon the property at the time of their appointment. Furthermore, a receiver, depending on the scope of the appointment order, may have the power to compromise lien claims and other litigation affecting the receivership estate.

B. Dealing with liens on Receivership property.

Generally, a receiver is a neutral party in disputes regarding competing interests among creditors in the receivership estate. Any party who seeks to recover receivership property must sue the receiver in the receiver's official capacity. As noted above, a receiver, depending on the scope of the appointment order, may have the power to compromise lien claims and litigation.

VI. Owners Associations:

The appointment order typically charges a receiver with taking any necessary action with respect to the maintenance and operation of the receivership property, which would normally include paying association fees out of any rents collected or other income of the receivership estate. In addition, to the extent the borrower is the "declarant" under the governing documents of the association, the appointment order should address any rights of the receiver to act in such capacity. As noted above, an association may need court approval to foreclose an association lien secured by property included as part of the receivership estate.

VII. Construction Related to Receivership Property:

Depending on the nature of the project, the appointment order should be broad enough to meet a receiver's anticipated functions, including any necessary construction duties.

VIII. Ending the Receivership:

In state court, the rules of civil procedure require a court order to dismiss any action where a receiver has been appointed. It is advised that the receiver apply to the court for a final distribution, file a final report and obtain an order to dismiss the receivership and to discharge the receiver. In federal court, the applicable rules provide that a receiver shall not be dismissed except by leave of court and upon notice to all parties.

Relevant Codes, Statutes or Case Law:
NRS chapter 32; NRS chapter 40; NRS chapter 106; NRS chapter 107; NRS chapter 107A, Nevada Rules of Civil Procedure, Rule 66 (Receivers); Federal Rules of Civil Procedure, Rule 66 (Receivers); Local Rules of Practice for the United States District Court for the District of Nevada, LR 66-1 (Receivers)

New Hampshire

Foreclosure Summary

Security Instrument	Mortgage/ Trust Deed
Judicial	Yes
Non-Judicial	Yes
Initial Public Notice	Notice of Sale
Time Frame	Varies by process; 60 days
Redemption Period	No
Deficiency	Yes

Receivership Summary

Ancillary Remedy Necessary	No
Ex-Parte	Yes
Approximate Time for Appointment	10-30days
Who or What can act as Receiver	Individual or trust Company
Specific Receiver Requirements	Must file a bond prior to commencing duties
Is there any approval list for Receivers	No
Out of State Receivers Allowed	Yes but you will need an in state agent for service of process

Foreclosure:

I. General Information:

New Hampshire is a "title" state, similar to what others states describe as trust deed, i.e., a deed of property immediately conveys title subject to performance of all obligations in the loan documents. Upon performance, the mortgage becomes void. While a breach can be cured prior to foreclosure, once the foreclosure is complete the borrower has no further right of redemption. The lender has several foreclosure options upon a default, although as a practical matter the power of sale option is used almost exclusively.

II. Judicial Foreclosure Basics:

New Hampshire has no statutory procedure for judicial foreclosure outside the context of a power of sale. If the mortgage instrument contains a power of sale, a court will, upon request of the mortgagee, declare that the property be sold subject to the power, after such notice and other acts as the court's ruling may require. Since the requirements of an extra-judicial sale under the power are not onerous, as a practical matter few mortgages avail themselves of the judicial decree procedure.

III. Non-Judicial Foreclosure Basics:

Apart from power of sale, New Hampshire allows foreclosure by entry and continued possession for one year. If the entry cannot be peaceably accomplished, it may be accomplished under process of law. If entry can be peaceably accomplished, a notice stating the time at which possession commenced must be accompanied by publication in some newspaper printed in the county or an adjoining county, for three consecutive weeks.

IV. Guidelines for Power of Sale:

New Hampshire has statutory guidelines for exercise of the power of sale, described below. If the mortgage instrument contains any mandatory provision concerning the conduct of, notice of, or other acts effecting a sale under the power, they must be followed unless inconsistent with a statutory requirement.

Contributed By: Frank P. Spinella &
Thomas W. Morse of Hall Morse

V. Power of Sale Guidelines as Represented in the Security:

A mortgage may be sold or assigned to a third party, and the sale or assignment carries with it any power of sale in the instrument.

VI. Foreclosure When Instrument Contains No Power of Sale:

Absent the words "statutory power of sale," the mortgage can only be foreclosed by entry and possession for one year.

VII. Any Additional Satisfaction Permitted Under Continuing Power of Sale:

Deficiency judgments are permitted in New Hampshire.

VIII. Sale by Power of Sale when the Instrument is Silent as to the Place or Terms of Sale:

If the instrument designates a place other than the mortgaged premises for conducting the sale, the designated place governs – but if the instrument is silent, the mortgaged premises must be the location of the sale. If the instrument recites no terms of the sale, the mortgagee is free to include any commercially reasonable terms.

IX. Notice of Sale and How Notice is Given:

A notice is sufficient if it sets forth:

A. the date, time and place of sale;
B. the location of the mortgages premises by street number and town;
C. the date of the mortgage and the volume and page of its recording at the registry of deeds in the county in which it lies;
D. the location where the original mortgage instrument may be examined; and
E. the terms of the sale (deposit amount, form of deposit, closing date).

It must also include the following language: "You are hereby notified that you have a right to petition the superior court for the county in which the mortgaged premises are situated, with service upon the mortgagee, and upon such bond as the court may require, to enjoin the scheduled foreclosure sale."

At least 25 days before the sale, the notice of sale must be sent by registered or certified mail to the mortgagor(s) and to each lienholder whose interest was on record thirty days prior to the scheduled sale date. It must also be published in a newspaper of statewide circulation or of general circulation within the town, once a week for three consecutive weeks, with the first publication at least 20 days prior to sale.

X. Place and Time for Conducting Foreclosure by Power of Sale:

Unless the mortgage instrument designates a place other than the mortgaged premises as the location for a foreclosure sale, it must be held at the mortgaged premises (or, if more than one parcel has been mortgaged and is being sold together, on either parcel specified in the notice). The designated date may be any date beyond 21 days after the notice is sent to all those entitled to same.

Relevant Codes, Statutes and Case Law:
N.H. RSA 479:6; N.H. RSA 479:18; N.H. RSA 479:19; N.H. RSA 479:22; N.H. RSA 479:25

Receivership:

I. General information:

The appointment of a Receiver is clearly within the equitable powers of the Superior Court. The appointment of a Receiver should be considered in a situation where immediate control of the property is necessary to preserve the collateral value and the borrower is not cooperating with a request to yield control and possession to the mortgagor. The appointment of a third party Receiver also has the advantage of protecting the lender from a lender liability claim based on unreasonable control exercised by the lender. The lender in bringing such a petition would need to identify a willing and able Receiver.

II. Appointing the Receiver:

A. The Basics:

New Hampshire process: If for a pending case, a party to the case seeking appointment of a Receiver does so by filing a Motion for Appointment of a Receiver. If there is no pending case, any person who can establish a legal or equitable interest in the property may file a Petition for Appointment of a Receiver. If the requested appointment is by Motion, a copy must be sent to the opposing party as well as filed with the court. If the appointment is by Petition, the same is filed with the court and a Order of Notice obtained, following which the same is served on the opponent. In addition, although third parties who may have possession of, or an interest in, the property to be seized need not be made parties to the case, they must be served with a copy of the motion or petition, and given notice of the time set for hearing.

The Motion or Petition is typically supported by sworn affidavits or is a verified petition with respect to each and every fact set forth. If the applicant wishes to suggest a particular person for the office of Receiver, this may be done, but the permission of the person as so sought for the appointment should be first obtained, and the Motion or Petition must so state that the person has so agreed to serve if appointed.

The court will always hold a hearing on the motion or petition to appoint a Receiver. The issues at the hearing will be: the need for a Receiver and the possibility of accomplishing the desired purpose by an alternative remedy; the scope of the Receiver's authority; the precise identity and location of the property to be taken and held; and the suitability of the person for the post. The decision to appoint or refuse to appoint a Receiver is discretionary on the part of the court. If the court decides to appoint a Receiver, this is done by a written commission in the form of an Order directed at the Receiver. The Order will specify the duties; term of office; and the property to be taken and held; the size of the bond required and any conditions to the time for posting same; the specification of any duties to account if different from the statutory periods for the same; and any other conditions the court deems appropriate. The Receiver will be sworn in and will assume duties immediately, without regard to whether there may be appeal filed to the Supreme Court.

B. Time Frame for Appointment:

This varies considerably, based substantially upon the requirement that there is a hearing, and the court's calendar. If by Motion, the opposing party must make objection within 10 days. If by Petition, the period for filing an Appearance and Answer by opposing party, is as set by the court in the Order of Notice, typically 30 days.

C. Can you go in Ex Parte?

The court may hear and grant the request for appointment of a Receiver on an ex parte basis, but when it does, the court will follow the procedures and guidelines established for temporary restraining orders.

III. Loans and Advances:

Allowed as ancillary proceedings, with court issuing same as supplemental orders; and the same may be obtained ex parte in an appropriate case.

IV. Sales During the Receivership:

No information provided.

V. Liens Against Receivership Property:

No information provided.

VI. Owners Associations:

No information provided.

VII. Construction Related to Receivership Property:

No information provided.

VIII. Ending the Receivership:

Upon completion, the Receivership is terminated by a Motion to Terminate Receivership. This motion typically requires supporting affidavits, and may be objected to by any other party within 10 days. The court will hold a hearing on the Motion to Terminate Receivership, and will at that time issue Orders returning the property to the original owners or distributed to such other persons as the court determines have a greater right to same, subject to all obligations incurred by the Receiver during the period of his appointment.

Relevant Codes, Statutes or Case Law:
NH RSA 401-B:11; NH RSA 498:1, RSA 498:12, NH Superior Court Rule 165, Ladd v. Harvey, 21 N.H. 514 (1850), Eastman v. Sav. Bank, 58 N.H. 421 (1878), Standard Oil Co. v. Nashua St. R.R., 88 N.H. 342 (1937), Munsey v. G.H. Tilton & Son Co. 91 N.H. 51 (1940), Petition of Keyser, 98 N.H. 198 (1953).

New Jersey

Foreclosure Summary

Security Instrument	Mortgage
Judicial	Yes
Non-Judicial	No
Initial Public Notice	Complaint
Time Frame	8-24 Months, depending on a variety of factors including county of venue and whether or not it is contested
Redemption Period	Limited to 10 days
Deficiency	Yes, restricted

Receivership Summary

Ancillary Remedy Necessary	Yes
Ex-Parte	No
Approximate Time for Appointment	If motion granted, 30-62- days after filing
Who or What can act as Receiver	No restrictions
Specific Receiver Requirements	No
Is there any approval list for Receivers	No
Out of State Receivers Allowed	Rare

Foreclosure:

I. General Information:

In New Jersey, foreclosures are accomplished only by the judicial foreclosure process. "Power of sale" clauses, which would otherwise authorize lenders to sell the mortgaged property if the borrower defaults on the subject loan, are not permitted. Instead, the lender must commence an action against the borrower before the Chancery Court in the county in which the property is located. Upon receiving a docket number and filing date, the plaintiff should promptly file a notice of *lis pendens* in the appropriate county office where real estate documents are recorded.

In 1995, the Legislature enacted the "Fair Foreclosure Act". The Act governs residential foreclosure practice, and establishes uniform procedures with respect to the conduct of a sheriff's sale. In sum, the Act requires residential mortgage lenders to provide the mortgagor with at least 30 days notice prior to taking any legal action for possession. The Act sets forth with particularity the required content of the notice. The Act also gives mortgagors the right to cure a default by paying all sums due (including attorney fees and costs). The Act also requires that the Complaint allege compliance with the Act.

II. Judicial Foreclosure Basics:

Prior to commencing a judicial foreclosure action, a lender must be able to demonstrate that it has legal standing to foreclose the mortgage. A lender has standing as the owner of the note and mortgage where it owns or controls the underlying debt, demonstrated by possession of the original note or proper assignment of the loan, prior to the commencement of the action.

In addition, in order to foreclose all junior interests to the mortgaged premises, the lender should obtain a foreclosure search of the mortgaged premises. Counsel to the lender will then prepare the initial pleadings, naming as party defendants the mortgagor, any other owners of the mortgaged premises, any guarantors of the loan, and all subordinate lienholders.

A mortgagee commences judicial foreclosure by filing a summons and foreclosure complaint with the Superior Court Clerk's Office, located in Trenton, but venue of the action is based upon the county in which the property is situated. After the filing of the complaint, the plaintiff must file a *lis pendens* in the office of the county clerk where the mortgaged premise is located.

A New Jersey foreclosure complaint may only assert "germane claims", that is, claims which affect the validity or invalidity of the mortgage itself. Thus, "non-germane claims" including claims under the mortgage note or guaranty are prohibited and will not be entertained by the Chancery Court as part of the foreclosure action. Typically, such claims are brought in a separate action pending in the Law Division.

In response to the foreclosure complaint, defendants can serve a contesting answer, a non-contesting answer, or a motion to dismiss the complaint. If a defendant fails to respond within the prescribed time, it will be deemed to have defaulted.

If the foreclosure action is uncontested, the foreclosing mortgagee may proceed immediately to entry of the final judgment of foreclosure. If the action is contested, as soon as the defendants' time to respond has lapsed and in compliance with any other court-issued case management orders, the plaintiff may file a motion for summary judgment seeking to have defendants' contesting answers deemed stricken and having the action referred back to the Office of Foreclosure for entry of final judgment.

To obtain a Final Judgment of Foreclosure, the plaintiff shall file a motion for final judgment, on notice to all parties who appeared in the action, by filing the following: notice of motion for final judgment; certification of amount due; certification regarding non-military status; certification authenticating documents, annexing true copies of the original note, mortgage, and assignments thereof; certification of costs and search fees; a proposed form of final judgment; a proposed form of writ of execution; any other orders required to be entered by the Office of Foreclosure; and, if applicable, any other notices and certifications required pursuant to the Fair Foreclosure Act.

If a defendant has a valid objection to the amount due as stated in the plaintiff's motion for final judgment, he or she may submit it to the court within ten (10) days of receiving the motion, and the Office of Foreclosure will transfer the case back to the vicinage judge, who will make a final determination on the matter, and transfer the case back to the Office of Foreclosure.

The Office of Foreclosure issues the Final Judgment, fixing the amount due to plaintiff, including interest, late charges, taxed costs and attorney fees. Late charges cannot be charged after the date of the filing of the complaint. Attorney fees are set by statute, and are a percentage, set on a sliding scale, of the amount adjudged to be owed to the plaintiff. Simultaneously, the Office of Foreclosure issues the Writ of Execution, instructing the sheriff to sell the property.

The plaintiff submits to the sheriff of the county in which the property lies, the Final Judgment, Writ, an Affidavit of Consideration, and the legal description for the property. The sheriff is required to schedule an auction sale of the property within 120 days of receipt of the Writ. The borrower is entitled to two (2) two-week extensions of the sale date.

The sheriff conducts a public auction sale of the mortgaged premises, and the property will be sold to the highest bidder. The borrower has a 10-day period following the foreclosure sale to redeem, for the full amount of the mortgage indebtedness plus costs of foreclosure, fees, costs of sale, and interest from the date of the sale. If the plaintiff is the successful bidder, upon expiration of the redemption period, the sheriff will prepare and issue the deed, which will be delivered within approximately 30 days of the sale. The sheriff is entitled to a fee and commission, calculated as a percentage of the struck off purchase price, and payable by the plaintiff even if the full purchase price is less than the entire indebtedness.

A lawsuit for a deficiency must be filed within three (3) months from the date of the foreclosure sale. The deficiency is a personal judgment against the borrower for the remaining balance on the loan after a foreclosure sale

III. Non-Judicial Foreclosure Basics:

Not applicable.

IV. Power of sale foreclosure guidelines

Not applicable.

V. Power of sale constitutes part of security

Not applicable.

VI. No Power of sale foreclosure guidelines

Not applicable.

VII. Foreclosure when instrument contains no power of sale.

Not applicable.

VIII. Additional satisfaction permitted under continuing power of sale.

Not applicable.

IX. Sale under power where instrument silent as to place or terms of sale.

Not applicable.

X. Notice of Sale and How notice of sale is given

Notice of sale must be posted on the property as well as in the county where the property is located. In addition, the notice of sale must be published in two (2) local newspapers for four (4) consecutive weeks. One of these publications must be in either the largest municipality in the county or the county seat.

Notice must be given to the property owner at least ten (10) days prior to the scheduled sale. The Sheriff is required to schedule an auction sale of the property within 120 days of receipt of the

Writ. The borrower is entitled to two (2) two-week extensions of the auction date.

Foreclosure sales are conducted as public auctions, overseen by the sheriff or another officer of the county. The property is awarded to the highest bidder. The borrower has a right to redeem during the ten (10) days following the sale. After the expiration of the redemption period, the sheriff will prepare and deliver the original deed, transferring ownership to the purchaser.

XI. Place and time for conducting foreclosure by power of sale.

Not applicable.

Relevant Codes, Statutes or Case Law:
N.J.S.A. 14A:12-7; N.J.S.A. 14A-14; N.J.S.A. 54:5-123; N.J.S.A. 2A:50-31; N.J.S.A. 2A:15-8; R. 4:42-10; R. 4:46-1; R. 4:46-2; R. 4:64-1; R. 4:64-5; R. 4:3-2; R. 4:53-1; R. 4:87; Notice to the Bar Re Foreclosure Matters, 110 N.J.L.J. 325 (Sept. 16, 1982); Crest Sav. and Loan Ass'n v. Mason, 243 N.J. Super 646, 650 (Ch. Div. 1990).

Receivership:

I. General information:

In New Jersey, the appointment of a rent receiver lies within the sound discretion of the Chancery Court, and a receiver will typically be appointed only upon a showing that there is a real danger of impairment of the lender's security and that the collateral is in a precarious or uncertain position. Courts will be less inclined to appoint a receiver if the borrower demonstrates that the security is more than adequate to meet the mortgage debt without sequestration of rents or that the land is worth more than the amount owed under the mortgage.

While the presence of a provision in the mortgage authorizing the immediate appointment of a receiver upon the borrower's default is to be considered by a judge in determining whether to appoint a receiver, such contractual language is not dispositive of the issue.

II. Appointing the Receiver:

A. The Basics:

A foreclosing mortgagee seeking the appointment of a receiver will set forth the request in a separate count of the complaint, and file a separate motion for the appointment of a rent receiver.

The determination of whether to appoint a receiver is factual and there is no single factor relied upon by the court in determining whether the lender's security is in jeopardy. Rather, the court will consider a number of factors, including: inadequacy of the property to satisfy the outstanding debt; inability of mortgagor to respond for deficiency; failure by mortgagor to pay real estate taxes and water rents; failure by mortgagor to keep property in good repair; failure by mortgagor to insure property; misappropriation of rents; decline in property value; and the presence of stipulations in the mortgage document consenting to the appointment of a rent receiver or the assignment of rents to the mortgagee upon default.

In addition to authorizing the receiver to forthwith take charge and enter into possession of the premises and collect rents and maintain the premises, typical receivership orders contain provisions empowering the Receiver to: commence, prosecute, defend and compromise all legal proceedings necessary for the protection and preservation of the mortgaged property; rent or lease any part of the mortgaged property; keep the mortgaged property insured; pay all taxes, sewer and water charges; make necessary repairs; otherwise to do all things necessary for the due care and proper management of the mortgaged property; and to employ such firms and persons, other than attorneys, as he deems necessary.

B. Time Frame for Appointment:

The lender may file a motion for the appointment of a receiver at any time. Typically, the lender will seek appointment of a receiver by motion on notice. Applications made by motion on notice must be filed and served at least 16 days prior to the anticipated return date. Hearing dates will be set by the Court and can be determined by checking the applicable Chancery Judge's motion schedule.

If the lender proceeds by order to show cause, the appointment a receiver could occur with 5-10 days. If the lender moves by notice of motion, it could take in excess of 30 days.

C. Can you go in Ex Parte?

No order appointing a custodial rent receiver under the general equity power of the court will be granted without consent of or notice to the adverse party, unless it appears from specific facts shown by affidavit or by the verified complaint that immediate and irreparable damage will result to the applicant before notice can be served and a hearing had thereon.

III. Receiver's Action and Reporting:

The order typically requires the receiver to issue a monthly report, and at the conclusion of the foreclosure action, the receiver must render an accounting to the court in connection with his or her discharge.

IV. Loans and Advances:

Loans and advances are typically addressed in the receivership order.

V. Sales During the Receivership:

New Jersey has a seldom-used sale *pendente lite* statute, that provides for the sale of mortgaged property, upon application of an interested party, through a receiver or a sheriff prior to the obtainment of a final judgment of foreclosure, when the property is likely to decrease in value, and the continuing preservation of the property is not feasible, given the diminishing potential return on the property. This is a drastic remedy and a powerful showing of danger to, or deterioration of, the collateral is necessary.

In accordance with the statute, any party to a foreclosure action may make an application for a *pendente lite* sale of the mortgaged premises prior to sheriff's sale. The statute provides that a *pendente lite* sale can occur if the property is likely to deteriorate in value or to make its care or preservation difficult or expensive pending the determination of the action. However, there is no set standard as to when the court will allow the sale of the property prior to sheriff's sale. Rather, the court must determine each application for a *pendente lite* sale on a case-by-case basis. Courts look at the totality of the circumstances and apply the facts of that specific case to determine whether it meets the purpose of the statute.

An application to sell the mortgaged property *pendente lite* can be accomplished by first seeking the appointment of a receiver to effectuate the *pendente lite* sale or by seeking to have the sheriff's office sell the property by court order prior to the final judgment of foreclosure.

The *pendente lite* sale remedy is provided for by N.J.S.A. 2A:50-31 as follows: When, in an action for the foreclosure or satisfaction of a mortgage covering real or personal property, or both, the property mortgaged is of such a character or so situated as to make it liable to deteriorate in value or to make its care or preservation difficult or expensive pending the determination of the action, the Superior Court may, before judgment, upon the application of any party to the action, order a sale of the mortgaged property to be made at public or private sale through a receiver, sheriff, or otherwise, as the court may direct.

Few published opinions have applied this statute, and only one opinion exists in which the court granted *pendente lite* sale relief. See Mortgage Electronic Registration Systems, Inc. v. Rothman, 2005 WL 280321 (N.J. Super. Ch. Div. January 12, 2005) (Unpublished).

VI. Liens Against Receivership Property:

Nothing specific to New Jersey regarding liens.

VII. Owners Associations:

Although condominium association liens are generally subordinate to prior recorded mortgages and other liens, N.J.S.A. 46:8B-21 provides that they can enjoy some limited priority over a prior recorded mortgage in limited circumstances.

VIII. Construction Related to Receivership Property:

Construction issues, including the payment of construction expenses, should be provided for and addressed in the receivership order incurred by the receiver.

IX. Ending the Receivership:

A receivership does not automatically terminate at the end of the foreclosure action, but instead is discharged by court order, typically obtained on motion by the lender. A hearing on the motion, however, may be waived if no parties object to the discharge.

The receiver must be discharged by formal court order discharging the receiver and cancelling the surety bond. The motion typically also seeks approval of the receiver's accounting and proposed distributions, and authority to cancel the receiver's bond.

X. Miscellaneous

A receiver will not be entitled to employ separate counsel, absent application to the court showing such employment is necessary to the proper conservation and administration of the mortgaged property.

Relevant Codes, Statutes or Case Law:
N.J.S.A. 14A:12-7; N.J.S.A. 14A-14; N.J.S.A. 54:5-123; N.J.S.A. 2A:50-31; N.J.S.A. 2A:15-8; R. 4:42-10; R. 4:46-1; R. 4:46-2; R. 4:64-1; R. 4:64-5; R. 4:3-2; R. 4:53-1; R. 4:87; R. 4:53-3; R. 1:6-3(a); C.J.S. Receivers § 118; Mortgage Electronic Registration Systems, Inc. v. Rothman, 2005 WL 280321 (N.J. Super. Ch. Div. January 12, 2005) (Unpublished).

New Mexico

Foreclosure Summary

Security Instrument	Mortgage
Judicial	Yes
Non-Judicial	Yes, but rarely if ever used.
Initial Public Notice	Complaint
Time Frame	90-120 days unless contested
Redemption Period	Yes, limited One month if provided in document, 9 months if not.
Deficiency	Yes

Receivership Summary

Ancillary Remedy Necessary	Yes
Ex-Parte	No
Approximate Time for Appointment	2 Weeks
Who or What can act as Receiver	Not limited
Specific Receiver Requirements	Oath
Is there any approval list for Receivers	No
Out of State Receivers Allowed	Yes

Foreclosure:

I. General Information:

Although New Mexico has a Deed of Trust Act, it is essentially never used. As a result, it has not been tested. Although deeds of trust specifically referencing the Deed of Trust Act may use the power of sale, no sale may occur sooner than 180 days after the notice of sale is recorded. During that time, the borrower can bring an action to delay the sale, assert lender liability claims, etc., causing all the delay of a judicial foreclosure. People simply do not use the cumbersome provisions of the Deed of Trust Act.

II. Judicial Foreclosure Basics:

Judicial foreclosure is the standard procedure. An answer is due 30 days after service. If contested, the normal summary judgment or trial procedures follow. The time involved depends on the schedule of the judge and the amount the borrower fights. Timing once judgment is obtained is that a sale may be held no sooner than one month after judgment. There is a 9 month redemption time which can be and usually is reduced to one month by a term in the mortgage/deed of trust.

A deficiency judgment is permitted, and foreclosure does not waive rights against other assets or guarantors to the extent the debt is not satisfied by the amount bid at foreclosure sale.

III. Non-Judicial Foreclosure Basics:

Non-Judicial Foreclosure is rarely ever used in the state of New Mexico.

IV. Notice of Sale and How Notice is Given:

For judicial foreclosure, notice must be publicized for 4 weeks after entry of judgment. Sale cannot occur sooner than one month after judgment.

Relevant Codes, Statutes or Case Law:
§ 48-10-1 et seq.

Receivership:

I. General information:

The New Mexico Statutes Annotated provides general guidelines for the appointment of a Receiver. Generally the legal support is as is provided in the mortgage. A showing of actual need, such as diverted cash, necessary repairs and/or other basis is useful if the receivership is contested.

II. Appointing the Receiver:

A. The Basics:

You will need to file a motion for appointment upon the filing of the complaint for foreclosure.

B. Time Frame for Appointment:

Generally the court will hold a hearing within a week or so after the motion has been filed.

C. Can you go in Ex Parte?

Generally no, not without a very strong showing of an actual emergency. In any event, the Court would hold a hearing within 10 days with notice to the borrower.

III. Loans and Advances:

No statutes or rules govern loans or advances, and the Order of Appointment will govern the Receiver's authority to obtain loans or to issue advances.

IV. Sales During the Receivership:

In New Mexico, receivers are to "collect and manage" and "operate, maintain and preserve the receivership estate". The general concept is that the receiver will maintain, preserve and protect the assets pending final resolution of the foreclosure. Sales of property are to be by the special master after judgment. As a result, receivers generally do not sell real property other than in the normal course of a business for which it is acting as receiver. The Distress Sales Act (§ 57-10-2) refers to sales of distress merchandise by receivers, and the receiver would in that case have to obtain the appropriate license from the municipality. The statutes (§ 42-9-24) create an exception that allows for

Contributed By: Paul Fish of Modrall Sperling

property of a perishable nature and liable to be lost or diminished in value pending final adjudication in attachment actions. In that case, the Court may order sale. The receiver would have to have authority to conduct any sale in the Order appointing the receiver or by subsequent application to the Court. The Distress Sales Act has a reference to sales of merchandise by receivers. Several very old cases discuss the sale of perishable property, including growing crops. Otherwise they do not.

Recently Receivers have become more aggressive in seeking to obtain and receiving court authority to sell receivership assets including real estate. Someone contemplating doing so should have advance discussions with the title insurance company.

V. Liens Against Receivership Property:

The rights of all holders of liens (including the mortgage holder) will be adjudicated in the final judgment and the proceeds of the special master sale will be paid to lienholders in their order of priority. Typically the foreclosing mortgage holder will not bid enough at the foreclosure sale to pay junior lienholders but will pay off any liens found to be senior.

VI. Owners Associations:

There are no codes, statues or case law relating to the Receiver and an owners association related to the property in the receivership estate.

VII. Construction Related to Receivership Property:

The power of the receiver to complete construction would be subject to the Order appointing the receiver. The argument would be that in order to protect the existing value of the property, the construction must be completed. The financing arrangement (presumably with the foreclosing creditor) would be subject to court approval.

VIII. Ending the Receivership:

There should be a final report and order approving the same and discharging the receiver to close out the receivership.

Relevant Codes, Statutes or Case Law:
§ 44-8-1 et seq., Rules 1-041.F.(1), 1-066, very little case law; § 44-8-1 et seq.

New York

Foreclosure Summary

Security Instrument	Mortgage
Judicial	Yes
Non-Judicial	Repealed in 2009
Initial Public Notice	Complaint
Time Frame	12-18 Months
Redemption Period	No
Deficiency	Yes

Receivership Summary

Ancillary Remedy Necessary	Yes
Ex-Parte	Yes
Approximate Time for Appointment	5-14 days
Who or What can act as Receiver	Individual
Specific Receiver Requirements	Yes
Is there any approval list for Receivers	Yes, but the court for good cause may appoint someone who is not on the list
Out of State Receivers Allowed	Yes

Foreclosure:

I. General Information:

In New York, foreclosure is typically accomplished by judicial foreclosure, with the commencement of an action in equity where the mortgaged premises is sold and the sale proceeds are distributed according to New York's Real Property Actions and Proceedings Law (RPAPL). In rare and exceptional circumstances, a purchaser or mortgagee may alternatively commence an action for strict foreclosure, seeking a judgment that he or she is the absolute owner of the mortgaged premises.

II. Judicial Foreclosure Basics:

Prior to commencing a judicial foreclosure action, a plaintiff must be able to demonstrate that it has legal standing to foreclose the mortgage. A plaintiff has standing as the owner of the note and mortgage where it is either the holder or assignee of the subject mortgage and the holder or assignee of the underlying note at the time the action is commenced.

In addition, in order to foreclose all junior interests to the mortgaged premises, the plaintiff should obtain a foreclosure search of the mortgaged premises. Counsel to the plaintiff will then prepare the initial pleadings, naming each borrower, guarantor, and subordinate lienholder as a defendant in the action. Tenants at the premises are not necessary parties to the action. However, the interests of tenants who are not named as defendants are not foreclosed.

Judicial foreclosure is commenced by the filing of the Summons, Complaint, and Notice of Pendency. The defendants' time to respond is triggered by service of process, which must be accomplished as prescribed under New York's Civil Practice Law and Rules (CPLR). There are specific personal service requirements which must be met in order to obtain a deficiency judgment. In response to the complaint, a defendant may serve a notice of appearance and waiver, a general notice of appearance, an answer, or a motion to dismiss the complaint. If a defendant fails to respond within the prescribed time, the plaintiff may move for default.

Contributed By: Evelyn H. Seeler, and
Vivian M. Arias of Thompson & Knight and
Bruce J. Zabaruskas of Crowell & Moring

Upon expiration of a defendant's time to answer or upon service of defendant's responsive pleading, the plaintiff moves for summary judgment and an order of reference seeking the appointment of a referee to determine the amount due on the mortgage. The plaintiff submits to the referee proof of the amount due on the mortgage, together with expenses incurred in protecting the lien, such as real estate taxes. Typically, plaintiff's counsel will prepare a referee's oath and report of amount due, to be completed, signed, and filed by the referee. Statutorily, a referee's hearing on the amount due may be required, but the formality of a hearing is frequently waived.

Once the referee has filed his oath and report of amount due, the plaintiff moves to confirm the report and file for a Judgment of Foreclosure and Sale. The Judgment will include the appointment of a referee to sell the premises, any award of legal fees to the foreclosing party, and a determination of whether a defendant will be liable for any deficiency remaining after the sale. The Notice of Pendency, which is typically filed at the commencement of the foreclosure action, and expires after 3 years, must be filed and in effect at least 20 days prior to entry of the Judgment of Foreclosure and Sale.

Prior to any sale, notice of the sale must be published and posted, fulfilling all statutory advertising requirements. Then, the referee conducts a public auction sale of the mortgaged premises, often at the courthouse of the county in which the premises lies. The successful bidder must deposit the amount as set forth in the terms of sale (usually 10%) with the referee, unless it is the plaintiff, in which case he may credit bid up to the amount due pursuant to the Judgment of Foreclosure and Sale. After the sale, the referee executes a deed to the winning bidder. The mortgagor has no right of redemption following the auction. After the deed is conveyed, a report of sale must be filed within 30 days. The report of sale is confirmed by motion, at which time, plaintiff must seek any deficiency judgment against defendants. There are specific time requirements for confirmation motions set forth in the RPAPL and a motion for deficiency judgment must be made within 90 days after conveyance of the deed.

III. Non-Judicial Foreclosure Basics:

Non-judicial foreclosure, or Foreclosure by Power of Sale, is no longer available in New York. Power of Sale mortgage foreclosure became statutorily effective in 1998, but was repealed on July 1, 2009, by its own terms when it was not renewed. Non- judicial foreclosures that were commenced prior to July 1, 2009 may proceed to conclusion, but unless the New York legislature acts to reinstate this remedy, mortgagees will be required to foreclose under the available methods of judicial foreclosure or strict foreclosure.

IV. Power of sale foreclosure guidelines

Not applicable.

V. Power of sale constitutes part of security

Not applicable.

VI. No Power of sale foreclosure guidelines

Not applicable.

VII. Foreclosure when instrument contains no power of sale.

Not applicable; see discussion of judicial foreclosure.

VIII. Additional satisfaction permitted under continuing power of sale.

Not applicable; see discussion of judicial foreclosure.

IX. Sale under power where instrument silent as to place or terms of sale.

Not applicable.

X. Notice of Sale and How notice of sale is given

Not applicable.

XI. Place and time for conducting foreclosure by power of sale.

Not applicable.

Contributed By: Evelyn H. Seeler, and
Vivian M. Arias of Thompson & Knight and
Bruce J. Zabaruskas of Crowell & Moring

Relevant Codes, Statutes or Case Law:
CPLR §§ 308, 311, 316, 507, 1006, 1007, 1012, 1013, 5011, 5015, 6501, 6511-6513, 6516; RPL § 254, 275; RPAPL §§ 231, 241, 1301(1), 1311, 1331, 1341, 1351, 1353, 1354(1)-(4), 1355(1)-(2), 1361(1)-(2), 1371(1)-(3), 1401-1408, 1410, 1411(3), 1414, 1415, 1417-1421; U.S. Bank, N.A. v. Collymore, 68 A.D.3d 752, 890 N.Y.S.2d 578; Wells Fargo Bank Minn., N.A. v. Mastropaolo, 42 A.D.3d 239, 837 N.Y.S.2d 247; Rodgers v. County of Monroe (In re Rodgers), 333 F.3d 64 (2d Cir. 2003).

Receivership:

I. General information:

The appointment of a receiver in a New York foreclosure action is generally governed by RPAPL § 1325(1) and N.Y. Real Property Law (RPL) § 254(10), which recognize the enforceability of mortgage provisions providing for the appointment of a receiver upon default without notice and without regard as to the adequacy of the mortgagee's security.

While ex parte relief is permissible, for strategic reasons, a plaintiff may wish to proceed on an expedited basis on notice to the defendant pursuant to an order to show cause because, in some counties, proceeding by order to show cause often results in the appointment of a receiver on a more expedited basis than by seeking ex parte relief. This is particularly true in New York City and the surrounding counties.

In the absence of a contractual right to a receiver under the mortgage, a plaintiff may resort to CPLR § 6401 which provides for the appointment of a receiver upon motion of "a person having an apparent interest in property which is the subject of an action in the supreme or a county court . . . where there is danger that the property will be removed from the state, or lost, materially injured or destroyed."

II. Appointing the Receiver:

A. The Basics:

The plaintiff may seek the appointment of a receiver by: (1) notice of motion, which would require a minimum of 8 days statutory notice (13 days if service is accomplished by mail), but in all likelihood would probably not be heard for at least 30 days; (2) order to show cause, which is New York's equivalent of a motion to shorten notice, and which could result in a hearing being held in approximately 5-10 days and interim relief; or (3) ex parte motion, to the extent provided for in the loan documents.

The appointment of a receiver is accomplished by the filing of a motion with the court following the commencement of the foreclosure action. Motion papers typically consist of an: (1) an affidavit of a representative of the plaintiff describing the loan and loan documents, including provisions governing the appointment of a receiver, the defendant's default, and the rent roll at the property; (2) an attorney affirmation setting forth the procedural history of the case (i.e., commencement of the action and filing of a notice of pendency); (3) a memorandum of law in support of the motion; (4) a proposed order appointing the receiver; and (5) a request for judicial intervention, if this is the first motion filed in the case.

If the plaintiff is proceeding by order to show cause, the supporting papers must also state: (1) the reasons why the plaintiff needs expedited relief and is proceeding by order to show cause, rather than by notice of motion; and (ii) that no prior motion seeking the same or similar relief has been previously made to any court. An allegation that expedited relief is necessary to protect rents from being misapplied or misappropriated is generally sufficient cause for an expedited hearing on a motion to appoint a receiver.

In addition to authorizing the receiver to forthwith take charge and enter into possession of the premises and collect rents and maintain the premises, typical receivership orders contain these provisions:

(i) authorizing the receiver to institute and maintain legal proceedings and to take such actions and effect such measures necessary for the protection of the premises;

Contributed By: Evelyn H. Seeler, and
Vivian M. Arias of Thompson & Knight and
Bruce J. Zabaruskas of Crowell & Moring

(ii) authorizing the receiver to commence eviction proceedings against tenants;

(iii) directing the defendant to deliver and turn over to the receiver, all keys to the premises, the proceeds and control of all bank accounts containing tenant security deposits, rental payments and other funds relating to the premises, possession of any and all documents, books, records and property which relate to construction upon the premises, including all leases, service, maintenance, and other contracts and agreements, all lists of vendors and records of transactions with vendors, all books of account, payroll records, accounts receivable and account payable lists, budgets and other financial records, all monies on deposit with vendors, service companies, utility companies or others, employment and union agreements and records relating to past and present employees, and all permits and licenses necessary for the operation of the premises;

(iv) directing the defendant to cooperate with the receiver;

(v) directing all tenants to attorney and to the receiver;

(vi) authorizing the receiver to rent or lease vacant units at the premises at the prevailing market rates and for terms not exceeding two (2) years, but only with the written consent of the plaintiff; and,

(vii) providing that the Receiver shall not retain professionals or make secondary appointments without prior court authorization on notice to the plaintiff.

The receivership order is required to contain these provisions: (1) requiring the receiver to promptly deposit funds collected by the receiver into a checking account or an interest- bearing account designated by the court; (2) providing that no funds may be withdrawn from the receiver's account unless directed by court order or the check is counter-signed by the receiver's surety. In addition, some courts require a provision that the receiver shall comply with Section 35-a of the Judiciary Law and 22 NYCRR Part 36, as well as a provision that plaintiff shall reimburse the receiver for fees, costs, and expenses, if the income generated from the property is insufficient to cover such amounts.

B. Time Frame for Appointment:

The plaintiff may file a motion for the appointment of a receiver at any time. Moving by notice of motion is rare in foreclosure cases. While CPLR provides that motions may be made on 8 days' notice (13 days if served by mail), a hearing on such motion is not likely to be held for at least 30 days. This is because the return date on an initial motion filed in a case is returnable to the Clerk's office. No hearing is held on the return date. Rather, on the return date, the Clerk's office assigns a judge to the case. After receiving the papers from the Clerk's office, the assigning judge will determine whether a hearing is necessary and will set the date for any such hearing.

By contrast, when proceeding by order to show cause, the Clerk's office will appoint a judge upon the filing of the motion, and will generally submit the papers to Chambers on the date of filing. Typically, the Court will sign the order to show cause within 2 days and will schedule a hearing on an expedited basis, usually within 5-10 days after filing of the motion.

While ex parte relief may be permissible under the loan documents, if the ex parte application is submitted to an Ex Parte Motion office, it may take up to 30 days for the ex parte motion to be ruled upon by a judge. This is especially true in New York City and the surrounding counties. Thus, in New York City and the surrounding counties, proceeding by order to show cause is sometimes more expeditious than proceeding on an ex parte basis.

If the plaintiff moves by notice of motion, the appointment of a receiver may take in excess of 30 days. If the plaintiff proceeds by order to show cause, the appointment of a receiver could occur within 5-10 days. If the plaintiff moves on an ex parte basis, the time frame may be the same as moving by order to show cause, with the exception of New York City and the surrounding counties.

C. Can you go in Ex Parte?

As set forth above, the ex parte appointment of a receiver is permissible to the extent provided in the mortgage.

D. Specific requirements for the Receiver

Unless appointed for good cause in a writing filed by the appointing judge with the fiduciary clerk, a receiver must be on the list of approved receivers which is maintained by the Chief Administrator. In order to qualify for this list, the appointee may not be: (1) a full-time or part-time judge or housing judge or relative or related by marriage to a full-time or part-time judge or housing judge; (2) a full-time or part-time employee of the Unified Court System; (3) the spouse, brother/sister, parent or child of a full-time or part-time employee of the Unified Court System at or above a salary grade JG24, or its equivalent in the judicial district in which such appointment is sought, or in a statewide district; (4) a person who currently or within the last two years has served as chair, executive director or the equivalent of a state or county political party, or the spouse, brother/sister, parent or child of such political party official, or an associate, counsel or employee of a law firm or entity with which such political party official is currently associated; (5) a former judge or housing judge who left office within the last two years and is seeking appointment in the district in which he presided, or the spouse, brother/sister, parent or child of such former judge; (6) a judicial hearing officer who is seeking appointment in the district where he serves; (7) an attorney who is currently disbarred or suspended in any jurisdiction; (8) a convicted felon for whom no certificate of relief from disabilities has been received; (9) a person convicted of a misdemeanor for which a sentence was imposed within the last five years and for which no certificate of relief from disabilities has been received, or waived by the Chief Administrator; and (10) a person who has been removed from an appointment list of the Chief Administrator for unsatisfactory performance or conduct incompatible with appointment. Additionally, in order to qualify to be appointed to the list, an applicant must complete a certified training course.

E. Receiver's Action and Reporting

Before taking any action, the receiver must qualify by signing and filing an oath, and posting a bond in an amount fixed by the order appointing the receiver. The receiver shall file an accounting with the Court "at least once a year." All monies received by the receiver are to be deposited into an account in the receiver's name, which shall also show the name of the case. No monies may be withdrawn from such account except as authorized by the Court, or the check is counter-signed by the receiver's surety. Orders typically require monthly reporting to the plaintiff.

III. Loans and Advances:

Loans and advances are governed by the order appointing the receiver. The order typically provides that the receiver shall not obtain loans or make advances beyond certain monetary limitations unless approved by the Court pursuant to a motion on notice to the parties.

IV. Sales During the Receivership:

A receiver is not permitted to sell property under New York law.

V. Liens Against Receivership Property:

Nothing specific to New York regarding liens.

VI. Owners Associations:

No provisions in New York relating to owners associations and a receiver.

VII. Construction Related to Receivership Property:

A receiver is not bound by the defendant's contracts concerning construction. Construction issues, including the payment of construction expenses, should be provided for and addressed in the receivership order.

VIII. Ending the Receivership:

A receivership is terminated by entry of an order authorizing such termination. The motion will seek approval of the receiver's accounting and proposed distributions, and authority to cancel the receiver's bond. In the alternative to a motion, the Court may approve a stipulation executed by all parties approving the receiver's accounting and proposed distribution, terminating the receivership and authorizing the cancellation of the receiver's bond.

Relevant Codes, Statutes or Case Law:
NY RPAPL § 1325; NY Real Property Law § 254; NY CPLR § 6401; Rules of the Chief Judge § 36.2, Uniform Rules for the New York State Trial Court § 202.52;
22 NYCRR Part 36; Meyer v. Indian Hill Farm, Inc., 258 F.2d 287 (2d Cir. 1958) (where mortgage provides for appointment of receiver upon default, "[p]roof of the inadequacy of the security and of the probability of success of the action is not required"); Union Chelsea Nat'l Bank v. Rumican 190 Corp., 228 A.D.2d 279, 643 N.Y.S.2d 586 (1st Dep't 1996) (affirming ex parte appointment of receiver pursuant to mortgage); In the Matter of Lowenthal, 199 A.D. 39, 191 N.Y.S. 282 (1st Dep't 1921) ("The receiver is not bound to adopt the contracts of the defendant"); Charles v. Charles, 22 Misc. 3d 1130A, 881 N.Y.S.2d 362, 2009 WL 580754 (Queens Cty. Sup. Ct. Feb. 27, 2009) ("A temporary receiver cannot be empowered to sell property to which the receiver has no title.")

North Carolina

Foreclosure Summary

Security Instrument	Deed of Trust, Mortgage
Judicial	Yes
Non-Judicial	Yes
Initial Public Notice	Notice of Sale
Time Frame	90-120 days
Redemption Period	10 Days
Deficiency	Varies

Receivership Summary

Ancillary Remedy Necessary	Yes
Ex-Parte	Yes
Approximate Time for Appointment	Varies county to county
Who or What can act as Receiver	None Given
Specific Receiver Requirements	Bond must be filed prior to Receiver commencing duties
Is there any approval list for Receivers	No
Out of State Receivers Allowed	Yes

Foreclosure:

I. Judicial Foreclosure Basics:

Judicial foreclosure is available and can be used when there is no power of sale clause in the security instrument or where there may be some defect in the security instrument that would preclude a non-judicial foreclosure.

II. Non-Judicial Foreclosure Basics:

Non-judicial foreclosure is available pursuant to N.C.G.S. §45-21.1 *et seq.*, provided that a power of sale is granted by the debtor to the creditor in the deed of trust.

III. Guidelines for Power of Sale:

Any foreclosure by power of sale should begin with a review of the loan documents and a title examination to ensure compliance with the loan documents and that the necessary parties receive notice. Even in the non-judicial foreclosures a hearing must be held before the clerk of court before any power of sale can be exercised. At the hearing, the party moving for foreclosure must show:

A. the party seeking foreclosure is the holder of a valid debt, see: In re David A. Simpson, P.C., 711 S.E.2d 165 (N.C. App. 2011);

B. default;

C. right to foreclosure under the instrument;

D. notice of the hearing was provided pursuant to all statutory and contractual requirements;

E. the loan is not a home loan (as defined by statute, or if it is a home loan, all statutory notice requirements specific to foreclosing a home loan have been satisfied); and

F. the sale is not barred by N.C.G.S. §45-21-12A, regarding a debtor in the military service.

Once approved by the clerk, the creditor may proceed with the sale and should make sure to follow requirements for contents, posting and publishing of the notice of sale. Upset bids are possible within ten (10) days after the initial sale and any other upset bid. The clerk of court will issue an order of possession after completion of the sale and all applicable upset and notice periods. Confirmation of the sale is not required.

IV. Guidelines for Foreclosure when there is No Power of Sale:

Regardless of the presence or absence of any guidelines in the security instrument, the statutory requirements must be complied. However, the guidelines in the instrument can certainly add requirements (notices, publication requirements, etc.).

V. Foreclosure When Instrument Contains No Power of Sale:

Without a power of sale, judicial foreclosure must be used.

VI. Any Additional Satisfaction Permitted Under Continuing Power of Sale:

A deficiency judgment is available unless prohibited by the loan documents. The debtor may rebut the evidence for the deficiency by showing that the fair market value at the time of the sale was equal to the debt, or that the amount bid was substantially less than the true value of the property. Deficiency judgments are not available if the mortgage represents part of the purchase price pursuant to a seller financing transaction.

VII. Sale by Power of Sale when the Instrument is Silent as to the Place or Terms of Sale:

When the deed of trust contains a power of sale provision, but is silent as to the place or terms of sale, the place and terms of the sale are set by the statutory requirements and are provided in the notice of sale.

VIII. Notice of Sale and How Notice is Given:

The notice of sale must comply with N.C.G.S. §45-21.16A and should describe:

A. the instrument pursuant to which the sale is to held, with recording data;
B. the date hour and place of sale;
C. the real property to be sold;
D. terms of the sale;
E. any requirements provided by the instrument;
F. if the property is being sold subject to taxes, subordinate rights, or other interests.

Pursuant to N.C.G.S. §45-21.17, the notice should be posted in the area designated for posting by the clerk for at least 20 days immediately preceding the sale and published at least once a week for two consecutive weeks in a newspaper in the county where the property is located.

IX. Place and Time for Conducting Foreclosure by Power of Sale:

Time and place of sale may be designated in the notice of sale. Pursuant to N.C.G.S. §45-21.23, the sale must occur within an hour of the time designated in the notice of sale and must be between 10:00 A.M. and 4:00 P.M. on any day other than Sunday or a legal holiday.

Relevant Codes, Statutes or Case Law:
N.C.G.S. §45-21.1 *et seq.*; N.C.G.S. §1-339.1 *et seq.*; : In re David A. Simpson, P.C., 711 S.E.2d 165 (N.C. App. 2011)

Receivership:

I. General information:

A receiver may be appointed in North Carolina before judgment in order to protect the property pending litigation or post-judgment in order to carry the judgment into effect or dispose of designated property. A receiver may also be appointed pending a sale via power of sale pursuant to N.C.G.S. §45-21.35.

II. Appointing the Receiver:

A. The Basics:

The holder of the debt will file a civil action in the county where the property is located seeking the appointment of a receiver in a proceeding that is ancillary to the non-judicial foreclosure. The receivership will typically remain pending until the property is conveyed pursuant to a foreclosure sale, a receiver's sale, or a deed-in-lieu of foreclosure.

B. Time Frame for Appointment:

This will vary from county to county depending on the access to a judge.

III. Loans and Advances:

There are no specific statutes or case law.

IV. Sales During the Receivership:

N.C.G.S. §1-505 provides for sale of the property by a receiver.

V. Liens Against Receivership Property:

No information provided.

VI. Owners Associations:

No information provided.

VII. Construction Related to Receivership Property:

No information provided.

VIII. Ending the Receivership:

The receivership can be closed as is specified in the order appointing the receiver. This could be upon sale or foreclosure of the property. However, typically a motion to discharge the receiver is filed and the court specifically approves the discharge.

Relevant Codes, Statutes or Case Law:
N.C.G.S. § 1-501 – 1-507

Cases: Lowder v. All Star Mills, Inc., 273 SE2d 247 (1981); In re Penny, 10 F.Supp. 638 (1935); Wachovia Bank and Trust Co., N.A., v. Carrington Development Associates, 495 SE2d 17 (1995); Barnes v. Kochhar, 633 SE2d 474 (2006); Woodall v. North Carolina Joint Stock Land Bank of Durham, 201 NC 428 (1931); Williams v. Liggett, 440 SE2d 331 (1994)

Contributed By: Jim Pulliam of
Kilpatrick Townsend & Stockton

North Dakota

Foreclosure Summary

Security Instrument	Mortgage
Judicial	Yes
Non-Judicial	No
Initial Public Notice	Complaint
Time Frame	90 days
Redemption Period	12 Months
Deficiency	Yes

Receivership Summary

Ancillary Remedy Necessary	No
Ex-Parte	Yes
Approximate Time for Appointment	No information provided
Who or What can act as Receiver	No restrictions
Specific Receiver Requirements	No restrictions
Is there any approval list for Receivers	No
Out of State Receivers Allowed	Yes

Foreclosure:

I. General Information:

North Dakota is a judicial, non-deficiency (for the most part) state. Foreclosures are filed in District Courts in the civil section and are treated as normal civil cases.

II. Judicial Foreclosure Basics:

All foreclosures in North Dakota are judicial with the exception of foreclosures by the state of North Dakota itself. North Dakota is rare in one sense. Statute requires that a "Notice Before Foreclosure" (NBF) be personally served on the record-title owner prior to commencing the action. It must be served thirty days prior to the filing the summons and complaint, and at least one defendant must be served within ninety days of service of the NBF.

The plaintiff in North Dakota foreclosures is the holder of the note and mortgage. A clear chain of title to the note and mortgage holder must be shown by the time of filing the summons and complaint. The defendants in North Dakota foreclosures are any person who may claim an interest in the property. The defendants typically include the owner of the property, the borrower, any other junior lien holders, and any person in possession of the property.

The interest holders are identified by a title commitment. The title commitment specifies any exceptions to the final title policy, which insures clear title to the Plaintiff, by listing any interest holders as exceptions. All exceptions must be met in order for the Plaintiff to obtain the final title policy. These exceptions are cured by listing all interest holders in the foreclosure action as defendants.

The judgment will provide that the property foreclosed on is to be sold at a Sheriff's Sale in the county where the property lies. Following the sale of the property there is a 60 day redemption period in which the borrower may redeem the property. After the redemption period has expired, a Sheriffs deed is issued to the highest bidder at the sale. If a foreclosure action has properly cured these exceptions to the final title policy (which is done so by listing the interest holders as defendants), the title company will issue a final title policy to the plaintiff insuring that the plaintiff has clear title.

X. Notice of Sale and How notice of sale is given

The judgment of the foreclosure must have an order for sale included in the language. A sale date is set after the judgment is entered. The sale is conducted by the sheriff of the county where the property lies. The notice of the sale must be delivered to all defendants as well as published in the local newspaper for three consecutive weeks.

Relevant Codes, Statutes or Case Law:
N.D.C.C. 32-19-01 through N.D.C.C.32-19-41; N.D.C.C. 28-24-01;N.D.C.C. 28-24-02; N.D.C.C. 28-24-04

Receivership:

I. General information:

Receivers can be appointed for a few different reasons, but the most important to the lender would be when it appears that the mortgaged property is in danger of being lost, removed, or materially injured or if the property is insufficient to discharge the mortgage debt. Because North Dakota is typically a non-deficiency state, receivers are rarely used in regards to foreclosure actions. Receivers are appointed at the discretion of the court.

II. Appointing the Receiver:

A. The Basics:

Receivers in North Dakota are appointed upon a Motion to the court where the action is pending or by the judge.

B. Time Frame for Appointment:

No information provided.

C. Can you go in Ex Parte?

Receivers can be appointed Ex Parte; however, the court may require the party to undertake sureties in an amount fixed by the court. These sureties are paid to the defendant if the defendant is damaged by the appointment of the receiver and the applicant procured the appointment wrongfully, maliciously, or without sufficient cause.

III. Receiver's Action and Reporting:

There are no specific rules for the receiver, other than it must obey all court orders. Rules pertaining to reporting are explained in the next section.

North Dakota Rules of Court, Rule 8.1 gives a few rules with regards to reports of Receivers. The first rule is in regard to timelines of reports. Receivers must file an annual report. The court may require special reports, and a final report must be completed at the termination for the receivership. The second rule is a very general rule which states that the court may prescribe a specific form for the reporting. The final rule in regards to reporting has to do with fees. Fees may only be applied for at the time the receiver files its report with the court.

IV. Loans and Advances:

In North Dakota there are a limited number of statutes and rules governing Receivers none of which specifically address loans and advances. No specific case law could be found regarding the same.

V. Sales During the Receivership:

No information provided.

VI. Liens Against Receivership Property:

No information provided.

VII. Owners Associations:

No information provided.

VIII. Construction Related to Receivership Property:

No information provided.

IX. Ending the Receivership:

Pursuant to North Dakota Rules of Civil Procedure, rule 66 states that in any action where a receiver has been appointed, a receiver may only be dismissed upon a court order.

The receiver must file a final report pursuant to North Dakota Rules of Court, Rule 8.1 and an order to dismiss the receiver must be entered by the court.

Relevant Codes, Statutes or Case Law:
N.D.C.C. 32-10-01 through N.D.C.C. 32-10-05
North Dakota Rules of Court, Rule 8.1
North Dakota Rules of Civil Procedure, Rule 66
North Dakota has hundreds of cases regarding receivers.

Contributed By: Casey Kosteleckty of Mackoff Kellogg

Ohio

Foreclosure Summary

Security Instrument	Mortgage
Judicial	Yes
Non-Judicial	No
Initial Public Notice	Complaint
Time Frame	150 days or more
Redemption Period	Until filing of confirmation order
Deficiency	Yes

Receivership Summary

Ancillary Remedy Necessary	Yes
Ex-Parte	Yes, if, in mortgage, mortgagor consents to appoint of receiver and waives hearing requirement
Approximate Time for Appointment	Several weeks
Who or What can act as Receiver	The receiver must be an individual, not an entity
Specific Receiver Requirements	The receiver must be an Ohio resident unless cause is established for appointment of non-resident
Is there any approval list for Receivers	Some judges make appointment from their own lists
Out of State Receivers Allowed	Yes, when cause is established

Foreclosure:

I. General Information:

To enforce the mortgage lien as to an Ohio real property interest, the mortgagee as plaintiff must file a court action, typically a complaint asserting claims seeking judicial foreclosure of the equity of redemption of the mortgagor/owner and incidental relief; unlike some other states, there is no out-of-court power of sale procedure. If the mortgagee is a named defendant in a court action commenced by another lienholder, that defendant mortgagee may also file a counterclaim/cross-claim. For the purposes of this discussion, it is assumed that the mortgagee files a court action as a plaintiff.

A. Judicial Foreclosure Basics:

Ohio statutory procedures and rules, common law rules and other local court rules set forth the required foreclosure procedures. This discussion focuses on Ohio statutory procedures and common law rules; therefore, before commencing a foreclosure action, plaintiff's attorney also needs to review and follow any local court rules that modify or supplement such statutory procedures and rules.

B. The complaint phase

1. **Title review**. To comply with statutory requirements, to identify all lienholders and to determine if there are any peculiar title issues that must be addressed as part of the foreclosure proceeding, the mortgagee must order a title report in the form of a title commitment or a preliminary judicial report.

2. **Court of filing.** The court action is typically filed in the general division of an Ohio trial court (or, occasionally, if diversity requirements are satisfied, in a federal district court) in the county (or district) where the subject real property is situated. If the

Contributed By: Jonathan S. Hawkins of Thompson Hine

court action involves properties located in more than one county, the court action for all properties can be filed in one county so long as a certified copy of the complaint is filed in the clerk's offices of each other relevant county.

3. The plaintiff. The named plaintiff in a foreclosure action must have standing requiring, at a minimum, that the plaintiff is the proper party to enforce the underlying secured obligation. Some Ohio districts have interpreted the standing requirement to mean that when the plaintiff is an assignee, the assignment of mortgage must be recorded before the filing of the complaint; otherwise, according to these courts, the assignee lacks standing. Other Ohio courts do not require that the assignment be recorded. However, regardless of the district, the plaintiff must be entitled to enforce the underlying obligation at or before the time the suit is filed.

4. The defendants. The named defendants typically include (a) each non-released obligor and any guarantor as necessary to recover a money judgment; (b) each property owner and spouse (to subject dower interest to sale); (c) lienholders perfected as of the date of the filing of the complaint (but if the plaintiff is a junior lienholder, a senior lienholder is only joined as a defendant if it consents to a sale free and clear of its lien); and (d) any tenants in possession prior to the recording of plaintiff's mortgage. Lienholders that perfect liens after the filing of the foreclosure complaint do not become part of the foreclosure proceeding because, by virtue of the lis pendens doctrine, such liens do not attach to the real property being foreclosed.

5. Confession of judgment/cognovit note. If a defaulting obligor defendant and/or guarantor defendant signed a promissory note or guaranty in connection with a commercial transaction that contains a provision whereby such person designates any attorney to act on its/his-her behalf to confess judgment and that contains a conspicuous statutory notice, and when a money claim is included in the complaint, the court has the statutory authority to grant an immediate judgment, without the necessity of service, the filing of an answer, or adjudication on the merits, so long as the obligor or guarantor, at the time of the signing of the note or guaranty, was an Ohio resident or executed the note or guaranty in Ohio. Ohio is one of a few states which still permits this accelerated proceeding; however, Ohio courts loathe this procedure and are quick to set aside the judgment if the obligor or guarantor files a timely motion and asserts viable defenses.

6. Recovery of attorney fees. If a note, guaranty and/or mortgage includes a provision requiring the obligor, guarantor or mortgagor to pay attorney fees that the mortgagee incurs to collect the indebtedness and if the indebtedness is $100,000 or more, the complaint may also include a claim to recover such fees.

7. Certification. Some local court rules require a certification as part of the complaint that acknowledges that the party seeking relief has examined the public records to determine property ownership and the parties claiming interests therein. The certification also typically opines that all parties claiming such an interest (except the named excluded parties) are joined in the action.

8. Mediation. At any stage of the foreclosure proceeding (typically prior to entry of a foreclosure decree), the court may require the parties to participate in mediation.

9. Filing title evidence. Within 14 days after the filing of the complaint, the plaintiff

Contributed By: Jonathan S. Hawkins of
Thompson Hine

must file with the court action the title commitment or preliminary judicial report that contains statutory required information and that is dated no more than 14 days before the complaint filing date. In addition, before filing the decree, the plaintiff must also file a final judicial title report that describes any activity through the complaint filing date.

10. Service of defendants. The complaint and summons must be served in accordance with the Ohio Rules of Civil Procedure.

C. The decree phase

1. The form of decree. In due course, if the plaintiff is entitled to relief, the court will enter a foreclosure decree in the form of (a) a default judgment if the mortgagor does not file an answer to the complaint; (b) a summary judgment if the mortgagor does file an answer but plaintiff files a summary judgment motion and establishes that there is no genuine issue of material fact and that it is entitled to judgment as a matter of law; or (c) a judgment after a trial of any contested issues.

2. Contents of decree. The filed decree will typically (a) include a money judgment (if the court has not previously awarded a cognovit judgment); (b) declare the validity and priority of all liens; (c) authorize foreclosure of the mortgagor's equity of redemption; (d) authorize the sheriff of each county where the real property is located to appraise, advertise and sell the subject property interest; (e) direct the property to be sold as a whole or in separate parcels and either free and clear of all liens or subject to senior liens, as applicable; and (f) also address unique issues raised.

D. The judicial sale phase

1. **Property appraisal**. Once directed by the plaintiff's attorney, the sheriff shall initiate the judicial sale phase by directing three disinterested freeholders that are residents of the county where the property is located to actually view that property so as to determine the true value thereof (i.e., the current market value thereof).

2. **Notices**. Once the freeholders determine the true value of the subject property, the sheriff will then set a sale date and publicly advertise sale terms in accordance with timing and other statutory requirements. In addition, at least seven days before the sale date, the plaintiff's attorney must send a written notice to each non-defaulting defendant advising each such party of the date, time and place of the sale. The plaintiff's attorney must then file a copy of that notice with the clerk of courts with proof of service noted thereon.

3. **Governmental inspection**. The municipal corporation or township where the subject real property is located may inspect such property prior to the judicial sale.

4. **Open house**. When the subject real property is abandoned, the sheriff may hold an open house. The date and time of this open house may be included as part of the public advertisement.

5. **Cancelling the sale**. If the plaintiff's attorney decides to cancel the scheduled sale, that attorney will typically file a motion (which in some counties require a showing of "cause") and the courts generally grant that motion.

6. **The sale**. The sheriff conducts the sale at the courthouse or other designated location in

the county where the action is proceeding. The opening bid must be in an amount at least two-thirds of the appraised value; provided, however, if the property interest being sold is subject to a senior lien, the opening bid must be an amount equal to two-thirds of the difference between the appraised value of the interest and the unpaid amount of the prior lien. If there is active bidding, the property interest must be sold to the highest bidder. A lienholder may credit bid its lien amount. If the successful bidder is not the mortgagee, such bidder, at the time of sale, typically must pay the sheriff a required deposit as required by local court rules or by custom in a particular county. The successful bidder may thereafter assign its bid to someone else.

7. **Effect of no bid/no sale**. If there is no bidding at the initial sale ("no bid/no sale"), the plaintiff may seek a second order of sale that directs a new appraisal, advertisement and sale. Alternatively, the motion may seek a second order of sale that fixes the amount as to which the property can be sold and that allows payment to be one-third cash at the time of sale, one-third nine months after such sale and one-third 18 months after such sale, with the deferred payments drawing interest at the rate of 6% per annum and secured by a mortgage as to the purchased property.

8. **Sheriff surrogate**. The court has the discretion to authorize a licensed auctioneer to step into the shoes of the sheriff and to carry out the sale steps in accordance with Ohio law. For an agreed-upon charge and a commission based on a percent of the sale proceeds, the auctioneer/broker will actively market the sale (and not just advertise in a newspaper of general circulation) and will typically conduct the auction at the property site; as a result, the surrogate procedure often results in higher sale prices. In addition, the auctioneer will be able to complete the sale process faster than the sheriff.

9. Purchaser information. After the sale, the successful bidder is required to provide certain information to the sheriff. If this does not occur, the court will set aside the sale upon motion of an interested party.

E. The sale confirmation phase

1. Bidder's opportunity to examine title. Some local court rules allow a successful bidder a period of time after the sale date to examine title. If the examination discloses title or procedural deficiencies, the local court rules then permit the successful bidder to file a motion within such examination period seeking to set aside the sale. In response, the court may allow additional time to correct the defects. The successful bidder may waive this examination period by signing the confirmation order.

2. Stay of confirmation of sale. The court may stay the confirmation of the sale to permit the property owner more time to redeem the property or for any other appropriate reason.

3. Confirmation of sale. After a completed sale, the sheriff must file its writ of execution reporting the sale. Within 30 days thereafter, if the court concludes that the sale conforms to statutory law, that court will direct the clerk of courts to make a journal entry stating that the court is satisfied with the legality of the sale and that the attorney must now prepare a deed to convey the property to the purchaser. The plaintiff's attorney typically initiates this confirmation step by filing a motion seeking entry of a confirmation order. The court will then sign a confirmation order that typically finalizes the sale, extinguishes the mortgagor's equity of redemption, determines lien priorities as required, cancels liens or, when appropriate, indicates that the transfer is subject to certain senior liens, directs the plaintiff's attorney to prepare and deliver to the sheriff a deed that will convey the property to the purchaser, directs the sheriff to distribute the sale proceeds and includes other conventional requirements.

4. Owner's exercise of redemption rights. The court will not enter a confirmation order and will instead terminate the proceedings if, prior to the filing of the confirmation order, the mortgagor exercises its right of redemption by fully paying the obligation owed to plaintiff, plus court costs, sheriff's fees and interest from the sale date to the redemption date.

5. Delivery of deed. Within seven days after the confirmation order is filed, the plaintiff's attorney shall deliver to the sheriff the deed to convey the subject real property to the purchaser.

6. Purchaser's payment of balance due. Within 30 days after the confirmation order is filed, the third party purchaser must pay to the sheriff the balance of the bid price. If the plaintiff, as a result of its credit bid, is the successful bidder, it must pay to the sheriff the amount necessary to satisfy liens senior to the plaintiff's position – the tax liens and any other senior liens that will be cancelled because the sale is free of clear of all liens, together with all court costs and sheriff's fees. If the purchaser does not timely make the required payment, the plaintiff has the right to seek an order of contempt. If the purchaser is found in contempt, that purchaser may forfeit the deposit paid at the conclusion of the sale to the extent that the mortgagee has sustained damages and the plaintiff may then initiate a second sale.

7. Property conveyed by deed; liens released; proceeds distributed. Within 14 days after the purchaser pays the required payment, the sheriff shall record the deed; the clerk of courts shall cause release of all liens as such liens affect the foreclosed property; and the sheriff shall distribute the sale proceeds in the order of priority. At the time of the sale, some counties also require a payment of a statutory conveyance fee (now up to $4.00 per $1,000 of bid price), while other counties treat the conveyance as exempt.

8. Collection of the deficiency judgment. If there is a deficiency judgment, the mortgagee typically attempts to collect that deficiency from any non-released obligor and/or guarantor.

Relevant Codes, Statutes or Case Law:
Ohio Rev. Code §§ 2329.01 et seq., § 2703.26; § 2103.041; § 2323.13; § 1301.21; § 2703.141; § 2323.06; § 2335.021.
Rules 3F, 4, 4.1 and 4.6, Ohio Rules of Civil Procedure

Receivership:

I. General information:

1. Legal and equitable grounds. When it appears that the property is in danger of being lost, removed or materially injured or a condition of the mortgage has not been performed and such property is probably insufficient to discharge the mortgage indebtedness, Ohio statutory law authorizes a judge to appoint a receiver to take possession of and manage the subject property. The judge also has the discretion to appoint a receiver consistent with "the usages of equity." Consistent with usages of equity, judges typically appoint a receiver when, as part of the mortgage, the mortgagor consents to such appointment even if the evidence does not otherwise establish material injury and insufficient value to discharge indebtedness. In addition, some local court rules expressly allow appointment of a receiver if the foreclosed property is income producing or if the mortgage embraces the property's rents and profits.

2. Ancillary to main action. A judge will only appoint a receiver incident or ancillary to another action – here, a foreclosure proceeding.

3. Receiver qualifications.

a. Residency requirement. Local court rules typically provide that the receiver must be a resident of Ohio or of the county where the property is located. However, some local rules do provide an exception for "cause." This exception enables the judge to appoint a non-resident if the judge is satisfied that this person will be able to perform the receivership duties, typically through a locally retained agent/employee and if the circumstances justify such an appointment, taking into consideration factors which include project size and specialized property use.

b. Disinterestedness requirement. The receiver must be disinterested unless the parties otherwise consent.

II. Appointing the Receiver:

A. The Basics:

A. Motion. To seek appointment of a receiver, the plaintiff will typically file a motion at the time of the filing of the foreclosure action seeking an order that approves such appointment. Ideally, the motion will include a copy of the mortgage authenticated by an affidavit of the movant.

B. Hearing requirements. Local court rules typically require that a hearing be set. However, judges will not require a hearing if the mortgage provides that the mortgagor consents to the appointment of a receiver upon default (or similar condition) and waives its right to a hearing. In such a circumstance, sufficient evidence should be in the record of the terms of the mortgage, through, for example the affidavit filed with the motion for appointment or in the form of a verified complaint. A hearing may also be waived if doing so is necessary to prevent irreparable loss. Despite this, some judges may still require a notice and a hearing. At such a hearing, the judge (and parties, with court permission) may inquire, formally or informally, on the receiver's qualifications and, consequently, the proposed receiver should be present at such a hearing. If the grounds for appointment of a receiver is not through a mortgage provision, evidence should be introduced at the hearing that establishes such grounds.

C. Selection of specific receiver by plaintiff or judge. Some judges will only permit appointment of a receiver that appears on the judge's approved list; other judges will defer to the plaintiff, particularly when the mortgagor does not object.

D. Timing. Depending on the caseload of the court, when the court requires a hearing, such hearing may be scheduled anywhere from several days to several weeks after the filing of the motion for the appointment.

E. Receiver order. Consistent with statutory provisions, the order appointing the receiver empowers a receiver to "take and keep possession of property, receive rents, collect, compound for and compromise demands, make transfers, and generally do such acts respecting the property as the court authorizes." The receiver order is frequently prepared by the party moving, and is the product of negotiation between the movant and the proposed receiver. The terms of the order typically grant more specific authority to a receiver and to include related provisions to address specific issues related to receivership income and expenses.

F. When receivership effective. The receivership is effective once the judge signs and files the receiver order and once the receiver complies with statutory requirements – i.e., the signing of an oath promising to faithfully perform his/her duties and to obey court orders and the posting of a bond in an amount that complies with any local court rule or the amount which the judge sets in his/her discretion. In lieu of requiring a bond, some courts allow substitution of a rider to the receiver's fidelity bond.

II. Post-Order Requirements

A. In general. While given broad discretion, so long as the receiver complies with the requirements of the receiver order, that receiver generally is not personally liable for his/her actions or inactions unless such actions or inactions constitute bad faith or fraud.

B. Local court rule requirements. Local court rules typically impose additional receiver requirements, such as the filing of periodic reports as part of the court proceedings. These reports generally detail receiver actions, income received and expenses incurred and paid, other financial information, condition of the premises and other relevant information.

C. Receiver loans and advances. There is no Ohio statutory law that regulates loan advances; however, the order appointing receiver may address this issue.

III. Receiver Sale Of Subject Real Property. With court authority, a receiver can sell the subject real property. To sell the property free and clear of all liens, the better view is that all lienholders must consent, particularly when any lienholder will not be fully paid. However, in a minority of jurisdictions, the court may grant a motion for the receiver's sale of property free and clear of liens over the objection of a junior lienholder if exigent circumstances are present.

IV. Concluding The Receivership. In Ohio, the receivership does not terminate automatically. To terminate the receivership, the attorney for the receiver will typically file a motion that (a) seeks termination of the receivership; (b) releases the receiver from any liability for performance of his/her services; (c) approves all compensation paid to the receiver; and (d) approves the receiver's final report (which the receiver submits concurrently with the filing of the motion).

V. Note On Potential Amendments To Ohio's Receivership Statute. At the time of this publication, the Ohio legislature is contemplating a major overhaul to Ohio's receivership statute, which would provide clarification of certain authorities that Ohio courts may provide to a receiver, including the sale of property free and clear of liens. The proposed legislation also would modify the circumstances under which receivers may be appointed and the qualifications an individual must have to act as receiver. The version of the bill to amend the receivership statute passed by the House may be found at http://www.legislature.state.oh.us/bills.cfm?ID=130_HB_9

Relevant Codes, Statutes or Case Law:
Ohio Revised Code §§ 2735.02-.

Contributed By: Jonathan S. Hawkins of Thompson Hine

Oklahoma

Foreclosure Summary

Security Instrument	Mortgage/Trust Deed
Judicial	Yes
Non-Judicial	Yes
Initial Public Notice	Complaint
Time Frame	90 days
Redemption Period	None
Deficiency	Yes, with time limitations on filing

Receivership Summary

Ancillary Remedy Necessary	
Ex-Parte	Yes, but in limited circumstances
Approximate Time for Appointment	24 hours to three weeks
Who or What can act as Receiver	Individual
Specific Receiver Requirements	No restrictions
Is there any approval list for Receivers	No
Out of State Receivers Allowed	Yes

Foreclosure:

I. General Information:

Mortgages are the primary instrument used to obtain a lien against real property in Oklahoma and are provided for in Title 16 of the Oklahoma Statutes. Both deeds of trust and contracts for deed are construed as mortgages in Oklahoma and are subject to the rules of mortgage foreclosures. Mortgages may be foreclosed through judicial foreclosure or through non-judicial power of sale foreclosure if the power of sale is granted to the mortgagee in the mortgage instrument itself. The majority of foreclosures in Oklahoma continue to be accomplished through the judicial foreclosure process.

II. Judicial Foreclosure Basics:

Judicial foreclosure is governed statutorily by various provisions in Title 12 of the Oklahoma Statutes, which is the civil procedure title of Oklahoma. The judicial foreclosure process is subject to the same procedural statutes and rules as any other civil action in Oklahoma. A judicial foreclosure may be completed in four to five months if the action is uncontested. If the action is contested, the judicial foreclosure process could carry on for six months or longer.

III. Non-Judicial Foreclosure Basics:

Non-judicial foreclosure by power of sale is permitted in Oklahoma, but must conform to the Oklahoma Power of Sale Mortgage Foreclosure Act set out by Okla. Stat. tit. 46, §§ 40-49. The power of sale must be expressly granted to the mortgagee in the mortgage instrument itself. Additionally, in order for the power of sale to be enforceable, the mortgage must include a statement in bold and underlined type containing substantially the following language: a power of sale has been granted in this mortgage. A power of sale may allow the mortgagee to take the mortgaged property and sell it without going to court in a foreclosure action upon default by the mortgagor under this mortgage.

Assuming the required notice can be served upon all interested parties in a timely manner, a non-judicial foreclosure by power of sale may be completed in three months. If the property is the mortgagor's homestead, certain additional statutory rights are granted to the mortgagor, including the right to elect (1) to avoid a deficiency judgment upon foreclosure by power of sale, or (2) to require judicial foreclosure. Because of the ease by which a residential mortgagor can derail the non-judicial foreclosure process, thus causing further delay, its use is generally only recommended on commercial foreclosures.

IV. Power of sale foreclosure guidelines

Prior to exercising a right to foreclose a mortgage by power of sale, the mortgagee must send the mortgagor, each guarantor and any other party obligated for payment or performance of the obligation secured by the mortgage written notice by certified mail of its intent to foreclose the mortgage by power of sale. The notice of intention to foreclose by power of sale must state: (1) the name and address of the mortgagee; (2) the nature of the claimed default with reasonable specificity; (3) that the mortgagor has 35 days to cure such default and reinstate the mortgage; (4) the amount of money or action necessary to effect the cure; (5) that if the default is not cured then the mortgagee may accelerate the debt and foreclose the mortgage; and (6) that the notice contains important information concerning legal rights under Oklahoma law and that the mortgagor should consult an attorney promptly if it has questions. The notice cannot be waived under Oklahoma law and must be provided prior to giving the notice of sale required under the Power of Sale Mortgage Foreclosure Act.

After the expiration of the 35-day cure period in the notice of intention to foreclose by power of sale, the mortgagee must provide a written notice of sale to the mortgagor, any holders of prior mortgages or liens on record, and all other parties whose interests in the mortgaged premises are to be foreclosed by the power of sale. The notice of sale must state the occurrence and general nature of the default, the election to use the power of sale, the date, time and place when the property will be sold, and the legal description of the property as it appears in the mortgage along with any street address of the property. The notice of sale must also advise the mortgagor and other interest holders of certain rights as set forth in the Power of Sale Mortgage Foreclosure Act, and must include an affidavit stating that the notice of intention to foreclose was properly sent. The notice of sale is to be personally served in the same manner as process in civil cases at least thirty days prior to the date of the sale. Additionally, the notice of sale must be published in a newspaper one day a week for four consecutive weeks, with the first publication occurring at least 30 days prior to the date of sale. The sale can be at any place in the county in which the mortgaged premises are located and at any time between 9:00 a.m. and 5:00 p.m. on any day other than a Sunday or legal holiday.

No minimum bids are required at the sale. Any person may bid, including both the mortgagee and the mortgagor. The mortgagee conveys title to the mortgaged premises by a deed executed by the mortgagee, without warranty, and such conveyance will be absolute and clear of all liens, claims or other interests as long as the proper parties were notified or served with appropriate process. The conveyance of the property by the mortgagee's deed terminates the mortgagor's right of redemption.

V. Power of sale constitutes part of security

The power of sale must be expressly granted to the mortgagee in the mortgage instrument itself.

VI. No Power of sale foreclosure guidelines

An action to judicially foreclose a mortgage in Oklahoma is commenced by the filing of a petition in the state district court of the county in which the mortgaged premises are located and is prosecuted under the same rules as other civil actions. A *lis pendens* should also be filed in the office of the County Clerk of that county. Upon obtaining a judgment, the mortgagee may apply to the Court Clerk to issue a writ of special execution and order of sale covering the mortgaged premises directing the sheriff of the county in which the mortgaged premises are located to advertise and sell the mortgaged premises at public auction within 60 days after the issuance of the writ of special execution. The mortgagee must have a written notice of sale executed by the sheriff containing the legal description and the date, time and place of sale mailed to the mortgagor and any other interest holder of record whose interest will be extinguished by the sale. Additionally, the mortgagee must cause public notice of the date, time and place of the sale published for two successive weeks in a newspaper in the county in which the property is located, and the sale may not occur less than 30 days after the date of first publication.

The foreclosure sale can occur with or without appraisement. Standard practice in Oklahoma is for the mortgage instrument to include a provision allowing the mortgagee to elect to sell the property with or without appraisement at the time judgment is entered in the foreclosure proceeding. If the foreclosure sale occurs subject to appraisement, then the sheriff will select three individuals from a pre-approved list to appraise the property, and the appraisal provided by these individuals will serve as the appraised value of the property for the purpose of setting the minimum bidding requirements. The appraised value will also constitute evidence of fair market value for determining any deficiency. If the mortgagee elects to sell the property with appraisement, then it must be sold for not less than two-thirds of the appraised value. If the mortgagee elects to waive appraisement, then the two-thirds minimum bid requirement will not apply to the sale. However, the writ of special execution and the order of sale cannot be issued until six months following the entry of judgment in the foreclosure action.

Any person may bid at the sheriff's sale. If the high bidder is someone other than the mortgagee and the high bidder fails to post cash or certified funds with the Court Clerk in an amount equal to ten percent of the amount bid within 24 hours after the sale, or otherwise fails to complete the sale, then the sheriff is authorized to accept the next highest bid. The mortgagee must file a motion with the court to confirm the sale and, upon confirmation, the sheriff will execute a foreclosure deed. The mortgagor may redeem the property from foreclosure by delivering payment in full of the judgment debt until entry of the order confirming the sale and the sheriff's deed, at which time the mortgagor's equity of redemption is extinguished.

The mortgagee may only obtain a deficiency judgment if it files a motion and notice within 90 days after date of the sheriff's sale. The deficiency will be determined by taking the amount of judgment with interest, plus costs and disbursements of action and amount owing on all prior liens and encumbrances with interest, less the market value as determined by the court or the sale price of the property, whichever is higher.

VII. Foreclosure when instrument contains no power of sale.

If the mortgage does not grant the mortgagee a power of sale, then the mortgage must be foreclosed through the judicial foreclosure process described above.

VIII. Additional satisfaction permitted under continuing power of sale.

To determine the highest bidder for property sold under a power of sale, any mortgagor present at the sale may suggest in writing the known lots, parcels, or divisions of the property in which the property should be sold. The mortgagee shall conditionally sell the property under each suggestion, and if the mortgagor offers no suggestion, then in such lots, parcels or divisions, or as a whole, may be determined by the mortgagee. The mortgagee shall determine which conditional sale or sales result in the highest total price bid for all of the property. The mortgagee may also postpone or continue the sale to another date and location by providing notice at the sale or by publication at least ten days prior to the new date of sale.

Additionally, the mortgagee may seek a deficiency against the mortgagor and any guarantors by commencing a judicial action for a deficiency judgment within 90 days of the sale date. In such action the mortgagor may establish that the fair market value of the mortgaged premises on the date of sale exceeded the sale price, which would reduce the amount of the deficiency accordingly.

IX. Sale under power where instrument silent as to place or terms of sale.

The foreclosure sale by power of sale may be held at any place in any county where part of the property to be sold is situated, on any day other than a Sunday or legal holiday, at any time between the hours of 9:00 a.m. and 5:00 p.m. The mortgagee can require that a successful bidder post at least ten percent of the purchase price within 24 hours and that the sale be completed within ten days or such longer reasonable time as agreed to by the mortgagee.

X. Notice of Sale and How notice of sale is given

In a non-judicial foreclosure by power of sale, the mortgagee must provide a written notice of sale to the mortgagor, any holders of prior mortgages or liens on record, and all other parties whose interests in the mortgaged premises are to be foreclosed by the power of sale. The contents required in the notice of sale are described in the guidelines above. The notice of sale is to be personally served in the same manner as process in civil cases at least thirty days prior to the date of the sale. Additionally, the notice of sale must be published in a newspaper one day a week for four consecutive weeks, with the first publication occurring at least 30 days prior to the date of sale.

In a judicial foreclosure, the mortgagee must have a written notice of sale executed by the sheriff containing the legal description and the date, time and place of sale mailed to the mortgagor and any other interest holder of record whose interest will be extinguished by the sale. Additionally, the mortgagee must cause public notice of the date, time and place of the sale published for two successive weeks in a newspaper in the county in which the property is located, and the sale may not occur less than 30 days after the date of first publication.

XI. Place and time for conducting foreclosure by power of sale.

The foreclosure sale by power of sale may be held at any place in any county where part of the property to be sold is situated, on any day other than a Sunday or legal holiday, at any time between the hours of 9:00 a.m. and 5:00 p.m.

Relevant Codes, Statutes or Case Law:
Okla. Stat. tit. 12, §§ 131, 686, 760-775; Okla. Stat. tit. 46, §§ 1, 1.1, 4, 40-49; Okla. Stat. tit. 16, § 11A.

Receivership:

I. General information:

Receiverships in Oklahoma are governed generally by Okla. Stat. tit. 12, §§ 1551-1559, but additional specific statutes governing receivers can also be found in Title 12 of the Oklahoma Statutes and scattered throughout other titles as well. Section 1551 provides for the appointment of a receiver in certain situations, including:

(1) In an action by a creditor to subject any property or fund to his claim where it is shown that the property or fund is in danger of being lost, removed or materially injured;

(2) In an action by a mortgagee for judicial foreclosure or in connection with a non-judicial foreclosure by power of sale under the Oklahoma Power of Sale Mortgage Foreclosure Act (a) where it appears that the mortgaged property is in danger of being lost, removed or materially injured, or (b) that a condition of the mortgage has not been performed, and that the property is probably insufficient to discharge the mortgage debt, or (c) that a condition of the mortgage has not been performed and the mortgage instrument provides for the appointment of a receiver;

(3) After judgment, to carry the judgment into effect;

(4) After judgment, to dispose of the property according to the judgment, or to preserve it during the pendency of an appeal, or in proceeding in aid of execution, when an execution has been returned unsatisfied, or when the judgment debtor refuses to apply his property in satisfaction of the judgment;

(5) In the cases provided by statute when a corporation has been dissolved, or is insolvent, or in imminent danger of insolvency, or has forfeited its corporate rights; or

(6) In all other cases where receivers have previously been appointed by courts of equity.

II. Appointing the Receiver:

A. The Basics:

The appointment of a receiver is governed by statute and may be obtained in an action ancillary to both judicial and non-judicial foreclosure of a mortgage. The appointment of a receiver must be ancillary to an existing action and a pleading solely requesting such remedy will not invoke the court's jurisdiction. While the appointment of a receiver may be requested in the foreclosure petition, the mortgagee must also file a motion seeking an order appointing the receiver and should include a brief in support and a proposed order. Notice of the motion should be provided to all parties named in the underlying action by the same means as any other motion, and generally will be served on the appropriate parties with the petition when the motion is filed contemporaneously.

If the court deems the appointment of a receiver to be an appropriate remedy, the selection of the person to serve as receiver is made at the court's discretion. In practice, however, the party seeking appointment of a receiver will nominate a person to serve as receiver in its motion and, if the court finds that such person is qualified, then the nominee is usually appointed. Upon entry of the order appointing the receiver, the receiver must post a bond and swear an oath with the court that the receiver will faithfully perform the duties set forth in the order. The amount of the bond will be based on the revenues to be managed by the receiver, and the bond premium and other receivership expenses may be recovered as a cost of the foreclosure proceeding.

The swearing of the oath and execution of the bond are mandatory prerequisites to appointment and must occur prior to the receiver commencing any duties under the order. The order appointing the receiver will establish the reporting requirements of the receiver. The receiver must file a final report prior to discharge.

B. Time Frame for Appointment:

A motion seeking the appointment of a receiver may be filed contemporaneously with the petition seeking foreclosure of the mortgage. Generally, notice of the appointment of a receiver is required to be provided to all interested parties. However, a receiver may be appointed without notice under circumstances establishing an emergency. In an emergency circumstance, the receivership hearing may be heard the same day as the filing of the petition and motion, subject to court availability, but more often the hearing can be held within days of the filing of the motion when the circumstances so justify an emergency. When no emergency is present, receivership hearings are set on a regular motion docket requiring 18 days in which the opposing party may have an opportunity to respond.

C. Can you go in Ex Parte?

In limited circumstances a receiver may be appointed on an emergency temporary basis, by standards akin to those required for a Temporary Restraining Order. However, those appointments are meant to be temporary and should remain only until an evidentiary hearing may be held.

D. Appeal of receiver.

Okla. Stat. tit. 12, § 993(C) allows for an immediate appeal of the appointment of a receiver and upon the appellant filing an appeal bond in an amount equal to the bond amount required of the receiver, to provide for the payment of all costs or damages that may accrue during the appeal, "**the authority of the receiver shall be suspended until the final determination of the appeal, and if the receiver has taken possession of any property, real or personal, it shall be returned and surrender to the appellant upon the filing and approval of the bonds.**"

III. Loans and Advances:

There is no Oklahoma statute specifically addressing loans in receivership. Under Oklahoma law, a receiver is given the power to bring and defend actions in his or her own name, to take possession of property, receive rent, collect debts, compromise debts, make transfers, and do any other acts with respect to the property which is in receivership as the court may authorize. In the event the receiver determines that obtaining a loan or advance is necessary for the preservation of the property or to otherwise carry out its duties, the receiver should seek the court's authorization by filing an application for approval of borrowing and issuance of a receiver's certificate, and a lien securing such indebtedness may be made a "priming" lien senior to the interests of the other secured creditors. A receiver should be cognizant of the interests of the secured creditors and the impact his or her actions may have on those interests. Specifically, the receiver must be careful not to take steps that cause a drop or diminution in the corpus of the receivership estate. The incurrence of any debt or other obligation must be accompanied by an increase in the value of the property by at least that same amount.

IV. Sales During the Receivership:

If authorized by the court, a receiver may sell property during the receivership. The receiver should seek an order from the court permitting the sale of the property. If authorized, the sale of the property must be conducted in all respects in the same manner as is provided for the sale of property upon execution. Prior to execution of the deed, the receiver must seek confirmation of the sale from the court.

V. Liens Against Receivership Property:

Liens against property subject to the receivership are not treated any differently than they would be outside of the receivership, and any issues related to priority or enforcement will be resolved as a part of the underlying action. Please note, however, that the costs and expenses of the receivership, including compensation for the receiver, counsel fees, and obligations incurred by the receiver in the discharge of its duties, will constitute a first charge against the property or funds in receivership. The court may authorize the sale of the property free and clear of any liens subject to court approval and notice to all parties in interest similar to a sale process under Section 363 of the Bankruptcy Code.

VI. Owners Associations:

There are no specific statutes with respect to receiverships and owners' associations. Liens valid under the owners' association statutes are entitled to the same treatment irrespective of the existence of a receivership.

VII. Construction Related to Receivership Property:

A receiver must obtain authorization of the court to complete construction.

VIII. Ending the Receivership:

The receiver should prepare a final report and file a motion seeking discharge of the receiver, release of the bond, allowance of the receiver's fee, and a release from any further liability or obligation to the court or any other parties. The receivership is terminated by entry of a court order Approving Report, Allowing Fee and Discharging Receiver.

IX. Miscellaneous

No party, attorney or person interested in an action may be appointed receiver except by consent of all parties. Additionally, a corporation cannot be a receiver in Oklahoma, with the exception of state banks and national banking associations in Oklahoma having trust powers, trust companies incorporated in Oklahoma having trust powers, and national banks and state banks and trust companies having trust powers located in states which reciprocally allow similar Oklahoma institutions to exercise trust and fiduciary powers therein under no greater restrictions than those imposed by Oklahoma.

Relevant Codes, Statutes or Case Law:

Okla. Stat. tit. 12, §§ 852-856, 861, 993, 1551-1559; Okla. Stat. tit. 6, § 1002.

 Contributed By: Robert Haupt, Joshua Edwards, and Andrew Chilson of Phillips Murrah

Ontario Canada

Foreclosure Summary

Security Instrument	
Judicial	Yes
Non-Judicial	Yes
Initial Public Notice	None
Time Frame	1-6 months
Redemption Period	Yes
Deficiency	

Receivership Summary

Ancillary Remedy Necessary	No
Ex-Parte	Generally, No
Approximate Time for Appointment	No Restrictions Given
Who or What can act as Receiver	No Restrictions Given
Specific Receiver Requirements	No Restrictions Given
Is there any approval list for Receivers	No
Out of State Receivers Allowed	Yes

Foreclosure:

I. General Information:

A. Ontario has two methods to enforce mortgages in default.

1. Action for foreclosure.
2. Power of Sale.

B. A foreclosure action is an action recovering the property, not the debt secured by the mortgage.

C. A Power of Sale action is an action recovering the debt under the mortgage.

D. A foreclosure action may be converted to a sale action by a Defendant who wishes a sale but does not want to defend the action. Request for Sale must be in the time stipulated for the delivery of a defence. The motion of any party made to the Court before Judgment will also convert a foreclosure action to a sale.

E. A Mortgagor has a right of redemption which must be served on the Mortgagee within the time prescribed for filing a Defence.

F. Where a request to redeem has been filed, the Mortgagee may require a reference whereafter the Registrar will sign Judgment; or a Mortgagee may elect not to have a reference, whereafter the Registrar will determine amounts due, priorities, and sign Judgment.

II. Judicial Foreclosure Basics:

A. Search Title.

1. Determine the identity of the current owner.
2. Ascertain details of all subsequent encumbrances who must be named as Defendants.
3. Conduct execution searches as against the owner to ascertain details of all subsequent encumbrances that must be named as Defendants.

B. Issue a Statement of Claim and serve.

C. Once the time for delivery of a Defence has elapsed, note default and proceed to obtain Judgment.

D. If a request to redeem has been filed,
1. Where no reference is required regarding subsequent encumbrancers, attend upon the Registrar, take accounts, determine priorities and obtain Judgment.
2. Where a reference is required regarding subsequent encumbrancers, attend before a Referee to determine priorities and sign Judgment.

E. Reference.
1. Prepare solicitor's affidavit as to title, subsequent encumbrancers, and executions.
2. Prepare a draft Notice of Reference to be served on all Defendants and subsequent encumbrancers, once approved by the Referee.
3. Attend on the Referee, who is either a Judge or Master of the Superior Court, first to approve the draft Notice, and then to have accounts taken, fix costs, ascertain parties entitled to redeem, and fix a date, if any, for redemption.
4. Report on the reference summarizing the amount and priorities of parties in attendance that proved their claims. Circulate to interested parties.
5. Re-attend on the reference to have the report signed.
6. Serve, file and enter the report in Court upon confirmation.
7. Upon the report, where no redemption was made in the time fixed, move for a final Order of Foreclosure.
8. The redeeming party in the time fixed may attend for a final order of foreclosure upon proof of payment into Court.
9. Enter the final Order of Foreclosure and register same on title to the property, calculate and pay land transfer tax.

F. Where a request for sale is filed.

1. If Defendants are noted in default, sign Judgment for immediate sale and other relief claimed, save foreclosure.
2. If the Defendants are noted in default, and a subsequent encumbrancer converts the foreclosure to a sale, sign Judgment conditional on the subsequent encumbrancer's proof of claim.
3. If the Defendants are noted in default in a sale action and no request to redeem has been filed, sign Judgment for immediate sale and relief sought save foreclosure.
4. If the Defendants are noted in default in a sale action and a request to redeem has been filed, sign Judgment with a redemption period and relief sought, save foreclosure and a Reference.

III. Guidelines for Power of Sale:

A. If no payment is made in the redemption period, apply for a final Order for Sale.
B. Prepare draft Notices of Reference for approval by the Referee.
C. Attend upon Referee to have the notices signed.
D. Serve the Notice of Reference and Judgment on all Defendants.
E. Prepare draft conditions of sale.
F. Obtain an appraisal. Prepare Affidavit of appraiser for submission on a Reference.
G. Attend on the Reference to settle the conditions of sale, method of sale and sale price or reserve.
H. Arrange for sale as settled on Reference.
I. Attend on the Reference with a draft interim report regarding the sale and proceeds having been circulated to all entitled parties, to settle the interim report.
J. Serve a copy of the interim report on all entitled parties. Enter the report at the Court office.
K. Following the sale, serve notice and attend on the Referee to fix costs, take accounts and settle the final report on sale.
L. Obtain confirmation of the final report, serve and file.

M. Apply to the Court for an Order paying the sale proceeds out of Court.

IV. Power of Sale Guidelines as Represented in the Security:

A. Search title and executions.

B. After the mortgage has been in default for at least 15 clear days, serve a Notice of Sale under Charge.
   1. During the notice period (45 days next), take no further proceedings under the mortgage without a Court Order.
   2. After expiry of the Notice of Sale, prepare statutory declarations of default, service of notice.
   3. If the property is vacant, take possession and preserve mortgaged property.
   4. If there is a tenant in possession, attorn rents and manage the property.
   5. If the mortgagor is in possession and vacant possession will not be surrendered, begin an action for possession in the Superior Court of Justice. Include a claim for payment under the mortgage.
   6. Follow the claim procedures set out in codes.

C. Claim for possession and payment.
   1. Prior to serving the Notice of Sale or following a lack of cooperation regarding vacant possession, commence an action for collection and possession under the mortgage.
   2. Subsequent encumbrancers need not be named.
   3. Serve the claim.
   4. If no Defence is filed in the required time, note default and proceed to Judgment.
   5. Upon obtaining Judgment, move without notice for a Writ of Possession.
   6. File the Writ of Possession with the Sheriff, complete an eviction form and pay the fee.
   7. Upon notice from the Sheriff, attend and take vacant possession of the mortgaged property.

D. Selling the Mortgaged Property.
   1. Obtain an appraisal.
   2. Select a method of sale.
   3. Any Agreement of Purchase and Sale must reflect that the property is sold under Power of Sale.
   4. Complete the sale transaction in the ordinary course.

E. Account for the sale proceedings.
   1. Prepare a full account of the sale proceeds and proposed distribution.
   2. Where there is question regarding the priority of claims, pay money into Court. Attend on a motion before the Superior Court for a determination of priorities and distribution.

F. Where there is a shortfall in proceeds of sale, commence an action in Superior Court. Where an action was pursued (see section III "C", *supra*), follow ordinary Judgment enforcement procedures: Garnishment, Writ of Seizure and Sale, and Judgment Debtor Examination.

Relevant Codes, Statutes or Case Law:
s. 35 of the *Mortgages Act,* R.S.O. 1990 c.M40.

Receivership:

I. General information:

A. Federal and Provincial Company and Secured Transaction laws in Canada govern receivership in the province of Ontario.
B. Liquidations are considered in receivership;
C. Restructurings are discussed in Canadian Federal Statute. The statute allows an insolvent company to rearrange its affairs and compromise claim, thereby allowing it to continue as a going concern.
D. If a Receiver is appointed, typically a corporation's business would stop immediately and the Receiver would merely collect the receivables and sell inventory and other assets with a view towards the expeditious liquidation of the corporation's property, assets and undertakings.

E. The recognition of a Receiver appointed by a foreign court will be granted as a matter of comity provided that three general criteria are met:
    1. Any relevant charge given by the debtor is enforceable in the jurisdiction where the property is situate;
    2. Foreign court was competent to make the appointment;
    3. Sufficient connection between the debtor and the jurisdiction in which the foreign Receiver was appointed to justify recognition of the foreign court's order outside the foreign court's jurisdiction.

II. Appointing the Receiver:

A. The Basics:

Receivers are appointed by motion or pursuant to security documentation to take possession or control of all or substantially all inventory, accounts receivable, or the other property of an insolvent person or bankrupt that was acquired for, or is used in relation to a business carried on by the insolvent person or bankrupt.

1. This appointment may occur by:
    a. Court Order
    b. Private Appointment
2. Immediately on appointment, a Receiver should give notice of its appointment to the debtor, so that the debtor can provide the Receiver with the names and addresses of all creditors as required by law.
3. No later than 10 days following its appointment, a Receiver must give notice of its appointment to the Superintendent as well as to the bankruptcy trustee, and all parties/creditors that the Receiver has been able to ascertain after making all reasonable efforts.
4. After taking possession or control, (whichever comes first) of the property of an insolvent person or bankrupt, Receiver must also send a provincement containing the name of each creditor, the amount owed to each creditor and the total amount owing to the creditors, the list of

assets in the possession or under the control of the Receiver and the book value of each asset and the intended plan of action of the Receiver during the receivership to the extent that such a plan has been determined.

5. Interim reports made at least every six months

B. Time Frame for Appointment:

There are no prescribed time periods for filing under the *BIA*.

C. Can you go in Ex Parte?

Generally not.

III. Loans and Advances:

There are no codes or statues on this so it is important to cover this issue in the receivership order in terms of the method and process for such advances. It is important to in receivership order.

IV. Sales During the Receivership:

A receiver has the authority to sell with permission of the inspectors. The steps in the process of the sale include:

A. The receiver should use his or her discretion to determine if the property in receivership should be sold as this power is discretionary;
B. The receiver obtains permission from the inspectors to conduct the sale of the property in receivership;
C. If the sale of the property is to a related person (including a corporation) the receiver must obtain court approval to see the property;
D. The duty of the receiver in selling the property in receivership is broader than selling the property at the best price;
E. The receiver should determine the best manner in which to sell the property;
F. The receiver should strive to obtain a fair market value for the property keeping market condition and individual circumstances in mind;

G. The sale should be expeditious as possible;
H. So long as the proper efforts to obtain offers have been made there is no reason for the receiver to reject a reasonable offer that is made;
I. The receiver may seek instruction from the court if he or she is unsure of what the proper process to follow in the sale of the property.

V. Liens Against Receivership Property:

There are no specific statutes relating to liens and the receivership. A lien holder is a secured creditor that has the right to realize on his or her security unless the trustee takes steps to postpone the realization of the security. A trustee or receiver may consider if there may be a realization on the security in excess of the amount owed to the secured creditor. He receiver has the ability to obtain more information regarding the security and the sale redemption of that security

VI. Owners Associations:

Case law provides that while a receiver/manager is not statutorily obligated, it is practical for the receiver/manager to consult with the owner's association, particularly when they are affected.

VII. Construction Related to Receivership Property:

The receiver and/or receiver manager may complete a construction project if the construction project is in the normal course of business of the bankrupt. There is no obligation on them to do so, however if the receiver and/or manager deems that it is in the best interest of the estate of the bankrupt he or she may take steps to complete the construction project.

VIII. Ending the Receivership:

In a court appointed receivership by court order, however in the case of a private appointment by way of submitting a final accounting of the Superintendent. Motion and hearing required following a final accounting.

IX. Miscellaneous:

A.

A Receiver appointed through a security agreement ensures that a fair sale is conducted of the assets covered by the security documents and that a proper accounting is made to the debtor.

B.

A more widely utilized approach to the liquidation of assets is through the enforcement by a secured creditor of its security.

Relevant Codes, Statutes or Case Law:
Bankruptcy and Insolvency Act, R.S.C. 1985, c. B.3; *Companies' Creditors Arrangement Act, R.S., c. C-2; Canada Business Corporations Act,* R.S.C. 1985, c. C.44.

Provincial:
Business Corporations Act, R.S.O. 1990, c. B.16; *Courts of Justice Act,* R.S.O. 1990, c. C. 43; *Personal Property Security Act,* R.S.O. 1990, c. P.10; *Ontario Court of Justice Act, R.S.O. 1990, c. C.43*

 Contributed By: John D. Leslie of Miller Canfield

Oregon

Foreclosure Summary

Security Instrument	Trust Deed/ Mortgage
Judicial	Yes
Non-Judicial	Yes
Initial Public Notice	Notice of Default
Time Frame	120-180 days
Redemption Period	Yes, but only with judicial foreclosure
Deficiency	Yes, but only with judicial foreclosure

Receivership Summary

Ancillary Remedy Necessary	Yes
Ex-Parte	Generally No
Approximate Time for Appointment	10-30 Days
Who or What can act as Receiver	Individual
Specific Receiver Requirements	Bond
Is there any approval list for Receivers	No
Out of State Receivers Allowed	Yes

Foreclosure:

I. General Information:

The nature of the loan instruments will determine the remedies that are available to a lender. In Oregon you have three methods for recovery action on the note, judicial foreclosure & non judicial foreclosure. The third option is not available with mortgages.

II. Judicial Foreclosure Basics:

A. Personal Property.

One significant consideration on what foreclosure process to employ is the personal property. Is the personal property essential to the value of the real estate or merely incidental thereto?

B. Real Property.

All mortgage foreclosures are judicial. With a purchase money mortgage (see above), no deficiency judgment will be available. With all other mortgage foreclosures a deficiency is available. A deficiency judgment will be available with a nonpurchase money mortgage on residential property. Contrast this with the trust deed statutes in which a deficiency judgment is not available after any kind of foreclosure of a residential property, except perhaps to foreclose other collateral after a judicial foreclosure.

Caveat: With a purchase money mortgage, an action on the note will result in waiver of the collateral. On the other hand, foreclosure of a purchase money mortgage will bar recovery of a deficiency. A purchase money mortgage is defined in the state laws as vendor financing secured by a mortgage or as financing that is less than $50,000 that is provided for the purchase of a primary or secondary residence. The loss of collateral caused by an action on the note alone does not apply to trust deeds. Thus it is possible in some instances, except with purchase money mortgages, to sue on the note, and if you are unable to recover all that is due on the judgment, then you may also foreclose the collateral. In the opinion of this author and most title insurers, any foreclosure after obtaining a judgment on the note or against a guarantor should be judicial.

Contributed By: Christine Kosydar of
Stoel Rives

The drawbacks to a mortgage foreclosure are:

a. the time required to complete the process;
b. the invitation to a borrower to assert defenses and counterclaims; and
c. the redemption rights that follow the sheriff's sale.

Because the process is judicial, the borrower has an easy forum to delay the process by asserting frivolous defenses or claims. In addition, state laws provide the grantor of the mortgage, *i.e.,* usually the judgment debtor, a 6-month redemption right and junior creditors a 60-day redemption right. The Internal Revenue Service (IRS) almost always has a 120-day redemption right after any foreclosure sale.

C. Issues with Redemption

Redemption rights impair the marketability of the property. Until the redemption rights expire, a sheriff's deed is not available and title insurance of a fee interest in the property cannot be obtained. Moreover, during the redemption period, even though the buyer at the sale is entitled to possession, it cannot recover any costs of improvements it may make, except perhaps to prevent waste. This means that the redemption period is not an opportunity to make improvements to increase the marketability of the property. Because the lender is usually the successful bidder at the foreclosure sale, redemption rights therefore increase significantly the time it takes for a lender to realize on its collateral. Lost time to redemption rights is not only lost money for a lender, it is also an additional opportunity for the borrower to file bankruptcy and delay the process a bit more. In bankruptcy the right to redeem will expire the later of either the scheduled expiration date or 60 days after bankruptcy is filed.

D. Trust Deed

The judicial foreclosure of a trust deed is identical to that of a mortgage. A deficiency judgment is available, except in residential cases. Although a judicial foreclosure is an opportunity to garner a deficiency judgment, it also results in redemption rights.

III. Non-Judicial Foreclosure Basics:

This process requires recordation, mailing, service and publication of notices with particular information within particular time frames.

Barring a bankruptcy filing or title issues that delay the process, a non-judicial foreclosure is typically completed within 130 to 150 days. The minimum time for notices to the grantor of the trust deed and those with an interest shown on title is 120 days. There are no redemption rights available, except for the IRS. Thus the process is swift and because the lender is not in court seeking relief, there is no open invitation to the borrower to respond with defenses and counterclaims. The burden is on the borrower to file an action or bankruptcy if it wishes to delay the process.

One disadvantage to the non-judicial process is that the lender may not recover a deficiency, except to foreclose other collateral. This means that the lender will be precluded from pursuing individuals on guarantees if there is a deficiency, except that lender may pursue collateral given for a guarantee.

Another significant disadvantage to the non-judicial process is that the borrower has up to five days before sale to reinstate the loan. Thus, some borrowers take advantage of this right, and immediately after reinstatement, they default on the loan again. These borrowers operate as if they are on a semiannual payment plan. However this problem can be remedied once and forever. The lender can accelerate the loan, foreclose judicially and end the maddening cycle of default and reinstatement. In some instances, the lender will choose the disadvantages of the judicial process simply to end the borrower's abuse of its reinstatement right under the non-judicial foreclosure statutes.

IV. Comparison of Judicial & Non Judicial

	Advantages	Disadvantages
Judicial	1) Deficiency judgment 2) No right to reinstate	1) Time - redemption rights - bankruptcy opportunity - slower process - invitation to claims 2) Cost
Non-judicial	1) Time - no redemption rights - no invitation to claims - faster process 2) Cost	1) No deficiency 2) Right to reinstate

V. The Foreclosure Process:

A. Personal Property:

Personal property may be foreclosed either judicially or by a non-judicial Uniform Commercial Code (UCC) process. Judicial foreclosure of the personal property is easily combined with a judicial foreclosure of the real estate. On the other hand, in a non-judicial foreclosure of the real estate, a separate judicial or non-judicial sale of the personal property is advisable. This is because Oregon's trust deed and forfeiture statutes, ORS 86.705, *et seq.,* and ORS 93.905, *et seq.,* do not clearly provide for a unified non-judicial foreclosure of real and personal property.

B. Judicial Foreclosure of Real Property:

The lender will need to retain an attorney to file an action in state court. The process is instituted with the filing a complaint and recordation of a *lis pendens*. Often the proceedings include claims to foreclose both real and personal property and for damages against the guarantors. If a Receiver is sought, at or shortly after the filing of the complaint, the lender's counsel will file a motion requesting the appointment of Receiver.

C. Non-Judicial Foreclosure of Real Property:

The following is a checklist available from the Oregon State Bar Continuing Legal Education materials:

Number of Days before Sale by Trustee		Action
	1.	Order and examine trustee's sale guaranty; prepare and record substitution of lender's attorney for trustee.
140	2.	Fix date, time and place of sale; prepare and record notice of default and election to sell.
	3.	Order and examine supplemental sale guaranty to cover date of recording notice of default.
130	4.	Mail or serve notices of sale on parties listed in ORS 86.740 (120 days notice required).
130	5.	Personally serve notice of sale on occupants (when required) (120 days notice required).
60	6.	Commence publication of notice of sale (four weeks).
30	7.	Recheck for federal tax liens and mail notices to occupant to vacate after foreclosure.
10	8.	Record affidavits showing proof of: •Mailing or service on each party entitled to notice under ORS 86.740 •Service on occupant(s) or nonoccupancy of property •Publication of notice of sale •Mailing notice of non-judicial sale to District Director of IRS (if applicable).
5	9.	Prepare statement of amount due on sale; last day for reinstatement of loan – five days before sale.
0	10.	Sale of property by trustee and payment to trustee of amount bid by purchaser.
	11.	Prepare trustee's deed and deliver to purchaser within 10 days; record certificate of nonmilitary service.

Note that typically the attorney for the lender is also the trustee and conducts the sale in the county where the real property is located, often on the courthouse steps.

Relevant Codes, Statutes or Case Law:
Beckhuson v. Frank, 97 Or App 347, 349, 775 P2d 923 (1989); ORS 88.040
ORS 23.560 and ORS 23.540; IRC § 7425(d); ORS 86.770; ORS 88.075; 11 USCA § 108(b) (1993); ORS 86.705, *et seq;* ORS 86.770; ORS 86.753(8)

Contributed By: Christine Kosydar of Stoel Rives

Receivership:

I. General information:

Oregon Statute Provides for two types of Receiverships that would be relevant to lenders: Corporate and General

A. Corporate Receivership: To wind up and liquidate the business and affairs of a corporation through a judicial dissolution process.

1. Process: Show cause process with five days' notice.
2. Qualifications: Receiver must be authorized to transact business in Oregon and court may require bond.
3. Powers and authority: Very broad—to dispose of assets at public or private sale, sue and defend, exercise all powers of corporation either through or in place of the board and officers in the best interests of the shareholders and creditors.

B. General Receivership. To protect cash collateral, complete construction, prevent waste, sell property, and resolve partnership, divorce or other dissolution disputes. Most commonly used by a secured lender:

1. Real Property: Covers all properties - apartments, retail, residential, etc.
2. Businesses: Assisted care or nursing home facilities, golf courses and hotels; provided lender holds a security interest in the business and its income, not just the hard assets.

II. Appointing the Receiver:

A. The Basics:

A formal complaint for the appointment of a Receiver is required together with a motion seeking the appointment of a Receiver. Alternatively, a Receiver may be sought in a pending action by the filing of a motion and asking that the affected parties appear before the court to show cause why a Receiver should not be appointed.

Generally a notice of the hearing must be served at least 5 days prior to the scheduled date.

B. Time Frame for Appointment:

Generally 10 to 30 days depending on the court's calendar. Expedited consideration is possible with as little as 2 days notice, but the circumstances need to be extreme and the court's calendar open.

C. Can you go in Ex Parte?

Generally not available.

III. Loans and Advances:

Advances may be obtained without notice if the order so provides, but Receivers typically send notice to all interested parties regardless of an anticipated need. Alternatively, if the order does not provide for lender advances, the lender may file a motion with the court requesting that it be permitted to loan money to the Receiver with the loan to be added to the debt balance and secured by its collateral.

IV. Sales During the Receivership:

Except in a corporate receivership, Oregon law does not provide authority for a receiver to dispose of real property. Such a sale without consent of all interested parties would circumvent redemption rights and likely not be insurable.

V. Liens Against Receivership Property:

A receiver's lien for its fees and costs has priority.

VI. Owners Associations:

This is a complex subject. If the "turnover" has not been completed, the receiver may find that he or she is in control of the homeowners' association.

Contributed By: Christine Kosydar of Stoel Rives

VII. Construction Related to Receivership Property:

If a court order provides authority for a receiver to complete improvements, then the receiver may proceed accordingly. The order should provide for advances. See above.

VIII. Ending the Receivership:

A receivership may be terminated only upon the filing of a motion with 10 days notice. Typically a final accounting is submitted with the request. If approved, the court will enter an order terminating the receivership duties and exonerating the bond.

Relevant Codes, Statutes or Case Law:
ORCP 80; *Investors Syndicate v. Smith*, 105 F2d 611(9 Cir. 1939); ORS 60.667.
See ORCP 80; ORS 60.667; ORCP 80 (B) 6 and 7; ORS 86.010

Pennsylvania

Foreclosure Summary

Security Instrument	Mortgage
Judicial	Yes
Non-Judicial	No
Initial Public Notice	Complaint
Time Frame	90 days
Redemption Period	No
Deficiency	Yes

Receivership Summary

Ancillary Remedy Necessary	Yes
Ex-Parte	Motion for Receiver is typically filed on an emergency basis
Approximate Time for Appointment	7-10 days
Who or What can act as Receiver	No Restrictions Given
Specific Receiver Requirements	No Restrictions Given
Is there any approval list for Receivers	No
Out of State Receivers Allowed	Yes

Foreclosure:

I. General Information:

Pennsylvania is a judicial foreclosure state. Sales are conducted by a Sheriff. There are two ways to complete the foreclosure:

A. a complaint for foreclosure, or
B. entry of a confession of judgment followed by execution proceedings.

Trustee sales pursuant to a deed of trust do not discharge junior liens. Hence, deeds of trust are rarely seen in Pennsylvania. Pennsylvania is not an election of remedies state. Borrowers have no right of redemption after the Sheriff's Sale.

If the mortgaged premises are residential property, certain notices must be sent to the borrower before the commencement of foreclosure.

II. Judicial Foreclosure Basics:

A. Complaint for Foreclosure:

A judicial foreclosure may begin in Pennsylvania with the filing and service of a complaint. Most counties limit the complaint to one count in foreclosure which means generally a mortgagee cannot foreclose multiple mortgages in one action. The only necessary parties are the mortgagee, mortgagor and property owner (if different from the mortgagor). Subordinate lienholders are not named as parties.

Only a Sheriff may serve the complaint on Pennsylvania residents and entities. Non-Pennsylvania residents and entities may be served by certified mail or a process server.

Depending on the existence and form of any opposition, judgment is entered by default, summary judgment or judgment after a trial. After judgment is entered, the sale process begins. The Prothonotary (equivalent to a county clerk) issues a Writ of Execution. The date of the Writ of Execution ("Writ") is important because (i) all lienholders as of the date of the Writ must receive notice of the sale, and (ii) lienholders subsequent to

Contributed By: Christopher P. Schueller
of Buchanan Ingersol & Rooney PC

the date of the Writ are barred from claiming an interest in the premises.

A Sheriff conducts the sale and is paid poundage of 2% to 3% of the bid price. In major counties, sales are conducted monthly. Sheriffs in rural counties hold sales less frequently. Lienholders as of the date of a Writ must receive a Sale Notice at least 30 days prior to the sale. The Sheriff has 30 days after the sale to post a schedule of distributions. Sheriffs usually issue a deed within 30 to 60 days after a sale. Depending on the county, an uncontested foreclosure should be completed in 6 to 9 months.

In most counties, a mortgagee does not pay transfer taxes if the mortgagee is the successful bidder. However, if the mortgagee assigns its bid to a special purpose entity after the Sheriff's Sale and the special purpose entity takes title, the mortgagee must pay a transfer tax.

B. Confessions of Judgment:

Foreclosure through a confession of judgment is the preferred process because it usually takes less time. If the loan documents contain a confession of judgment clause, the mortgagee simply enters judgment *ex parte* upon commencement of the action. The mortgagee then sends the mortgagor a Notice of Intention to Execute upon Confessed Judgment. The mortgagor then has the burden to, within 30 days, petition to strike or open the judgment. If the judgment remains undisturbed, the mortgagee obtains a Writ, and follows the process set forth in Section II above. Depending on the county, the entire process should be completed within 3 to 5 months.

C. Deficiency Judgments:

To obtain a deficiency judgment the mortgagee must file a Petition to Fix Fair Market Value of Real Property within 6 months after the Sheriff issues a deed.

III. Non-Judicial Foreclosure Basics:

Non-Judicial Foreclosure is not available in Pennsylvania.

Receivership:

I. General information:

Pennsylvania permits the appointment of a real estate Receiver pursuant to:

A. clear language in the loan documents which authorizes the appointment, or in the alternative;
B. based on principles of equity.

It goes without saying that to avoid a litigation quagmire, it is best to proceed based on loan documents if that is possible.

II. Appointing the Receiver:

A mortgagee must seek the appointment of a Receiver on notice to the borrower. The mortgagee typically files the motion on an emergency basis and usually receives a hearing date within a week to ten days.

III. Loans and Advances:

Pennsylvania does not have any pre-set laws, codes or case law on such matters. Loans and advances are possible with court approval.

IV. Sales During the Receivership:

No information provided.

V. Liens Against Receivership Property:

No information provided.

VI. Owners Associations:

No information provided.

VII. Construction Related to Receivership Property:

No information provided.

VIII. Ending the Receivership:

The receivership does not terminate automatically in Pennsylvania upon a Sheriff's sale. The mortgagee will need to obtain an order terminating the receivership.

Relevant Codes, Statutes or Case Law:

Metropolitan Life Ins. Co. v. Liberty Center Venture, 437 Pa.Super. 544, 650 A.2d 887 (1994) (court may appoint a Receiver upon the occurrence of a default without the necessity of equitable reasons for the appointment; also, the Receiver may make distributions to the mortgagee in excess of the amounts deemed necessary by the Receiver for the ongoing operations of the mortgaged property).

Pa. R.C.P. 1533 (permits a court to appoint a Receiver "if required by the exigencies of the case").

Pa. R.C.P. 3118(a)(3) and (6) (permits a court to enter an order directing the defendant or any other party to take such action as the court may direct to preserve a security interest or granting other necessary relief).

Pa. R.C.P. 3125 (permits a court to make an order for the sale, preservation or disposition of perishable property).

Contributed By: Christopher P. Schueller
of Buchanan Ingersol & Rooney PC

Rhode Island

Foreclosure Summary

Security Instrument	Mortgage/ Trust Deed
Judicial	Yes
Non-Judicial	Yes
Initial Public Notice	Legal Advertisement
Time Frame	Typically 60 Days
Redemption Period	No
Deficiency	Yes

Receivership Summary

Ancillary Remedy Necessary	Yes
Ex-Parte	Yes
Approximate Time for Appointment	1-60 days
Who or What can act as Receiver	Generally drawn from approved receiver list
Specific Receiver Requirements	No Restrictions Given
Is there any approval list for Receivers	Yes
Out of State Receivers Allowed	No

Foreclosure:

I. General Information:

Rhode Island General Laws § 34-27-1 *et seq.* governs foreclosures in Rhode Island.

II. Judicial Foreclosure Basics:

Rhode Island General Laws § 34-27-1 permits judicial foreclosure. However, mortgage holders rarely use this procedure.

III. Non-Judicial Foreclosure Basics:

Non-judicial foreclosure is the primary method whereby mortgage holders affect foreclosure in Rhode Island. The subject mortgage must contain statutory power of sale language in order to foreclose in this manner.

IV. Guidelines for Power of Sale:

Rhode Island General Laws § 34-27-4 provides the procedure for non-judicial foreclosure, and is discussed in greater detail in Sections X-XII, below.

V. Power of Sale Guidelines as Represented in the Security:

Assignees may exercise the power of sale in the same manner as original mortgagees.

VI. Guidelines for Foreclosure when there is No Power of Sale:

Mortgage holders must foreclose through the judicial foreclosure process if the mortgage lacks statutory power of sale language.

VII. Foreclosure When Instrument Contains No Power of Sale:

Mortgage holders must file a Complaint to Foreclose in the Superior Court of the county in which the subject realty lies in order to foreclose in the absence of statutory power of sale language. Rhode Island General Laws § 34-27-1 governs judicial foreclosure.

VIII. Any Additional Satisfaction Permitted Under Continuing Power of Sale:

The terms of the mortgage control whether additional satisfaction is permitted. If the mortgage contains language allowing the mortgagee to foreclose on its collateral in whole or in part without waiver of its foreclosure rights as to other collateral, the mortgagee may foreclosure at a later date on collateral unaffected by an earlier partial foreclosure. In the absence of such language, sale of some but not all of the encumbered property may waive the right of the mortgagee to seek foreclosure of additional encumbered property.

IX. Sale by Power of Sale when the Instrument is Silent as to the Place or Terms of Sale:

The foreclosure sale occurs at the property that is the subject of the sale.

X. Notice of Sale and How Notice is Given:

Rhode Island General Laws § 34-27-4 governs the Notice of Sale. That statutory section requires Notice of Sale by publication in a public newspaper at least once a week for three consecutive weeks before the sale, with the first publication occurring at least twenty-one days before the date of sale. The notice must contain the date and time of sale and a description of the property consistent with the requirement of Rhode Island General Laws § 34-27-5.

Notice must also be given to the mortgagor by certified mail at least twenty days before the date of publication of the first legal notice, in the case of a mortgagor other than an individual consumer mortgagor, and at least thirty days prior to the first legal notice with respect to an individual consumer mortgagor. The notice must contain the time and date of the foreclosure sale.

XI. Place and Time for Conducting Foreclosure by Power of Sale:

The foreclosure sale may occur at the subject property at any commercially reasonable time.

Relevant Codes, Statutes or Case Law:
Rhode Island General Laws § 34-27-1 *et seq*. controls foreclosures in Rhode Island.

Receivership:

I. General information:

Receivers for distressed commercial properties are available by two means: (1) petition for a receiver for the collateral property (and not the borrower) pursuant to the terms and conditions of the loan documents; or (2) petition for a receiver of the borrower entity (so long as the borrower is not an individual) under the applicable Rhode Island receivership statutes.

The availability of former method turns on the specific language of the mortgage. So long as the mortgage provides for appointment of receiver as one of the remedies upon default, the court will likely appoint a receiver for the operation and management of the collateral property. However, the mortgage will define the extent of the receiver's power. For instance, the receiver will not be able to exercise the power of sale for the property without additional court permission if the mortgage does not contain sufficient language for the receiver to do so.

The other option is to petition the borrower entity into receivership based upon its insolvency. Creditors regularly use Rhode Island state court receiverships to liquidate or reorganize failing debtors. There are few rules guiding the conduct of receiverships. Equitable considerations, recognized local practice, and the use of bankruptcy principles as persuasive precedent consequently govern most receiverships.

II. Appointing the Receiver:

A. The Basics:

The procedure for appointment of a receiver is straightforward. A creditor files a petition for receivership and assigns the matter for hearing for appointment of a temporary receiver. That assignment may be made with as little as one day notice. The petitioning party may suggest a receiver to the Court from the receivership list; however, the Court retains the right to select whatever receiver the Court deems appropriate for a given matter.

Contributed By: Armando Batasini of
Nixon Peabody

The order appointing the temporary receiver stays collection of all debts of the entity or property subject to the receivership. A hearing on appointment of a permanent receiver must occur within twenty-one days of the appointment of the temporary receiver.

B. Time Frame for Appointment:

The court may appoint a temporary receiver with as little as one day notice; the hearing on appointment of a permanent receiver will occur within twenty-one days of the appointment of the temporary receiver, unless extended by the court upon a showing of good cause.

C. Can you go in Ex Parte?

Under limited circumstances, a party may seek a temporary receiver on an *ex parte* basis upon the showing that Rhode Island Superior Court Rule 66(b) requires, including the need for maintenance of the status quo until such a time as notice can be provided to interested parties. In practice, the petitioner must generally demonstrate why it was unable to provide notice prior to seeking an *ex parte* appointment.

III. Loans and Advances:

No information provided.

IV. Sales During the Receivership:

The receiver has the ability to sell property in any manner that will capture the maximum reasonable value in the receiver's best business judgment, subject to court approval. The prevailing method is for the receiver to engage in a competitive bidding process. The receiver must seek court approval of the sale through filing a Petition to Sell Free and Clear of Liens, with notice to all creditors.

Rhode Island General Laws § 7-1.2-1316 allows a corporate receiver to liquidate corporate assets, including realty, as part of the corporate dissolution process subject to court supervision and approval. There are no statutes that govern the sale of property wherein a receiver is appointed for the property only.

V. Liens Against Receivership Property:

The receiver may generally sell property free and clear of liens, with the exception of government liens.

VI. Owners Associations:

No information provided.

VII. Construction Related to Receivership Property:

No information provided.

VIII. Ending the Receivership:

A receivership may only be discharged upon court order after notice and hearing.

IX. Miscellaneous:

A.

Rule 66(e) requires receivership reports once every thirty (30) days. This requirement is generally waived, and receivers file their reports at their discretion.

B.

There is a standard form of order for appointment of temporary and permanent receivers.

C.

With respect to an order appointing a receiver to take control of collateral property, the order must track the mortgage language regarding the powers of the receiver.

Relevant Codes, Statutes or Case Law:
Rhode Island General Laws § 7-1.2-1314 *et seq.*; Rhode Island Superior Court Rule of Civil Procedure 66; Reynolds v. E&C Assoc., 693 A.2d 278 (R.I. 1997); Leonard Levin Co. v. Star Jewelry Co., 175 A. 651 (R.I. 1934).

Contributed By: Armando Batasini of Nixon Peabody

South Carolina

Foreclosure Summary

Security Instrument	Mortgage
Judicial	Yes
Non-Judicial	No
Initial Public Notice	Lis Pendens
Time Frame	Varies
Redemption Period	No
Deficiency	Yes

Receivership Summary

Ancillary Remedy Necessary	Yes
Ex-Parte	Rare
Approximate Time for Appointment	10-30 days
Who or What can act as Receiver	No Restriction Given
Specific Receiver Requirements	None
Is there any approval list for Receivers	None
Out of State Receivers Allowed	Yes

Foreclosure:

I. General Information:

South Carolina only allows for Judicial Foreclosures.

II. Judicial Foreclosure Basics:

A. Notice Of Default/Acceleration

1. Notice of default/acceleration is not required for commercial loans, where a provision in a note authorizes acceleration of the mortgage balance without notice upon failure of payment, a mortgagee. Lender is not required to give notice to the mortgagor of his election to exercise his option to accelerate the balance due on the note prior to suit.
2. Service of the summons and complaint will satisfy the notice requirement in the context of commercial loans.
3. There are no statutory rights to cure with respect to commercial loans.

B. Commencing the Action

1. As soon as the decision has been made to commence a foreclosure action, a *lis pendens* should be filed. A *lis pendens* gives notice of pendency of action for twenty days.
2. In addition to the borrowers and guarantors, in actions brought to determine adverse claims to real property the plaintiff must also name "all other persons, known or unknown claiming any right, title, estate, interest in or lien upon the real estate".
3. Incorporated or unincorporated homeowners associations having liens for assessments, such as those established in Master Deeds for condominiums or restrictive covenants should also be served.
4. Most counties will allow uncontested foreclosure cases to be heard on the basis of prepared testimony submitted by counsel for the Plaintiff and accompanied by a letter of authorization executed by an authorized officer of the plaintiff.

5. The court, in its discretion, may grant a personal judgment against the debtor prior, at or after the sale of the property if a deficiency judgment is requested.
6. The "One Action Rule". The South Carolina Supreme Court has held that a judgment on the underlying obligation has no effect upon the mortgage or its lien and does not merge into it, and there is no inconsistency in pursuing two remedies.
7. South Carolina law is clear that guaranties of payments should not be treated as guaranties of collection. In other words, the court should not delay resolution of any suits against any guarantors on the grounds that the lender must first liquidate its collateral.

III. Deficiency Actions:

South Carolina does not have an anti-deficiency statute. Lenders may waive the right to a deficiency judgment to obtain other rights (*e.g.*, shorten or extinguish redemption rights, expedite the foreclosure sale). Foreclosure sales where a lender seeks a deficiency judgment must remain open until the 30th day after such sale, during which time any person other than the highest bidder at the initial sale may enter a higher bid complying with the terms of the sale. Bids are reopened at a second sale generally held on the 30th day after the initial sale. By waiving the right to a deficiency, the foreclosing lender eliminates this second sale.

IV. Redemption Rights

There are no statutory redemption rights, but there is a "fair value" limitation on the deficiency (*e.g.*, the deficiency is calculated based on the difference between the judgment amount and the "true value of the property as of the date of sale" rather than the amount of the successful bid at the foreclosure sale). However, a borrower or guarantor may waive the right to a statutory appraisal in certain commercial loan transactions by signing a statement "during the transaction."

V. Choice of Law:

There is no clear answer as to the effect of a choice of law provision in the loan documents on the applicability of deficiency laws. South Carolina grants the parties a contract latitude in selecting the law that is to govern their dealings, and it is therefore likely that South Carolina would not apply a choice of law provision.

VI. Non-Judicial Foreclosure Basics:

Non-Judicial Foreclosure is not allowed in South Carolina.

Relevant Codes, Statutes or Case Law:
Extensive case law exists for this section please contact contributor for more information

S.C. Code Ann. § 12-24-40 (2000); S.C. Code Ann. § 12-37-250; S.C. Code Ann.§ 12-45-180 (2000); S.C. Code Ann. § 12-51-40; § 12-51-90 (2006); S.C. Code Ann § 14-11-85 (2006 Supp.); S. C. Code Ann. § 15-11-10 (2005); S.C. Code Ann. § 15-29-60 (2005); S.C. Code Ann. § 15-35-540 (2005); S.C. Code Ann. § 15-39-650 (2005); § 15-39-660 (2005); § 15-39-680 (2005); § 15-39-690 (2005); § 15-39-690 (2005); § 15-39-700 (2005); § 15-39-720 (2005); § 15-39-760 (2005) S.C. Code Ann. § 15-65-10(1) (2005); § 15-65-20 (2005); § 15-65-30 (2005); § 15-65-50; S.C. Code Ann.§ 15-67-40 (2005); S.C. Code Ann. § 15-69-140 (2005); S.C. Code Ann. § 15-7-10; S.C. Code Ann.§ 18-9-170 (1976 & 2006 Supp.); S.C. Code Ann. § 27-31-210 (2007); S.C. Code Ann. § 29-3-620 (2007); § 29-3-650 (1991); § 29-3-660 (2007); § 29-3-680 through § 29-3-770 (2006); S.C. Code Ann. § 36-1-105(1); S.C. Code Ann. § 36-9-308(d) (2003); S.C. Code Ann. § 37-1-301(11); S.C. Code Ann. § 37-3-104 through § 37-3-105 (2006) ; S.C. Code Ann. § 37-5-110(2) (2006); § 37-5-111 (2002); § 37-5-111(1) (2006); § 37-5-111(2) (2006)

Receivership:

I. General information:

Appointment rests in the court's discretion regardless of the standard provision in most mortgages calling for the appointment of a receiver as a matter of right. Language in some cases suggests that the appointment of a receiver is a drastic remedy, to be exercised with great circumspection. As a practical matter, circuit court judges routinely appoint receivers where there is an assignment of leases, a provision in a mortgage authorizing the appointment of a receiver as a matter of right and an issue relating to rents or to the condition of the property. Other factors important in evaluating the decision to appoint a receiver are:

A. actual physical deterioration of the estate's assets;
B. impairment of security;
C. character of the property; and

D. inadequacy of the value of the assets in proportion to the debt.

II. Appointing the Receiver:

A. The Basics:

1. Notice of motion for appointment of receiver can be served with summons and complaint or at any later time. Ordinarily, four days notice must be given to the owner and any party to the action in possession of the property claiming an interest therein under any contract, lease or conveyance from the owner. If the owner cannot be found, notice to the party in possession is sufficient. If no one is in possession, notice is not necessary and person claiming property may be served by publication.
2. No temporary injunction or temporary restraining order will be granted without notice of motion to the adverse party unless it clearly appears from specific facts shown by affidavit or verified complaint that immediate and irreparable injury, loss or damage will result to the applicant before notice can be served and a hearing held.
3. An appeal is immediately available to the State Supreme Court of an order appointing or refusing the appointment of a receiver. An order appointing a receiver cannot be stayed during the period after its entry or during the pendency of an appeal. If the judgment appealed from directs the assignment or delivery of documents or personal property, the execution of the judgment will only be stayed by appeal if the appellant files a bond with at least two sureties in such amount as the court directs.
4. If the judgment appealed from directs the possession of real property, the judgment will not be stayed unless a written undertaking by the appellant, with two sureties, to the effect that during possession by appellant he will not commit or allow any waste thereon and that if the judgment is affirmed he will pay the value of the use and occupation of the

property, not exceeding a sum to be fixed by the court.

B. Time Frame for Appointment:

Motions must ordinarily be heard only upon giving at least 10 days notice. Supporting affidavits must accompany the motion except as otherwise provided in Rules of Civil Procedure. Additional or opposing affidavits may be served no later than two (2) days before the hearing, unless the Court permits them to be served at some later time.

C. Can you go in Ex Parte?

Ex parte orders appear to be authorized; however, the practicality of ex parte orders is limited.

II. Loans and Advances:

A. A receiver has no authority to borrow money unless specifically authorized by the court; however, the power of the court generally is extensive enough to authorize the receiver to borrow money necessary for the preservation and management of the property in receivership.

B. Receivers may borrow to complete construction projects which comprise the fund in the hands of the receiver and which, without completion, are of little or no value but the priority of these advances is open to question.

C. The court may allow a receiver contract to finish construction and to borrow additional funds and secure payment by receiver's certificates or judicial lien having priority over all other liens except costs.

D. In a case in which the money is required, not for the purpose of operating the business, but for the purpose of saving the property from destruction, the receiver may borrow funds and issue Receiver's Certificates.

E. The expenses of a receiver appointed to preserve property from destruction and waste are a "first charge" against the property, and creditors who contribute to the completion of a construction project which without completion is of little or no value, have priority over preexisting liens.

F. Where a receiver is appointed to operate property for the benefit of the lien holder, the operating expenses are a "first charge", not only on the current earnings, but on the receivership estate.

IV. Sales During the Receivership:

Possible, but generally frowned upon since the receiver is charged with maintaining the status quo.

V. Liens Against Receivership Property:

No information provided.

VI. Owners Associations:

No information provided.

VII. Construction Related to Receivership Property:

No information provided.

VIII. Ending the Receivership:

After the purchaser has received a deed the receiver should file a petition for discharge and prepare a final accounting. After the final accounting has been accepted by the court the receiver may be discharged and his bond exonerated.

IX. Miscellaneous:

A.

Appointment of a Receiver before judgment is possible if the moving party establishes an apparent right to the property which is the subject of the action, the subject property is in the possession of an adverse party, and the property or its rents and profits are in danger of being lost, materially injured or impaired.

B.

Lender does not assume any mortgagee-in-possession liability if a receiver is appointed but does if the lender takes possession of the property.

Relevant Codes, Statutes or Case Law:
S.C. Code Ann. § 15-65-10(1) (2005); S.C. Code Ann. § 15-65-20 (2005); S.C. Code Ann. § 15-65-30 (2005); S.C. Code § 15-65-40 (1976); S.C. Code Ann. § 15-69-140 (2005); S.C. Code Ann. § 15-65-50 (2005); S.C. Code Ann. § 18-9-150 (1976 and 2006 Supp.); S.C. Code Ann. § 18-9-170 (1976 and 2006 Supp.);

55 Am. Jur. 2d Mortgages § 972 (1971); 55 Am. Jur. 2d Mortgages § 989-93 (1971); 65 Am.Jur.2d Receivers § 136 (1971); 66 Am.Jur. 2d Receivers § 205 (1973), 66 Am.Jur.2d Receivers § 378, et seq. (1973); 75 C.J.S. Receivers, § 175(a) (1952); 75 C.J.S., Receivers, § 292(d)(3)(cc) (1952) (citing as authority Guimarin v. Southern Life & Trust Co., 100 S.C. 12, 84 S.E. 298 (1915)).

Andrick Dev. Corp. v. Maccaro, 280 S.C. 103, 311 S.E.2d 95 (Ct. App. 1984)
Ex parte Citizens Exch. Bank of Denmark, 140 S.C. 471, 139 S.E. 135 (1927)
Truesdell v. Johnson, 144 S.C. 188, 142 S.E. 343, 345 (1928)
Whisenhunt v. Sandel, 177 S.C. 207, 181 S.E. 61 (1935)
Ex Parte Simons, 289 S.C. 1, 344 S.E.2d 151 (1986).
Gadsden v. Whaley, 14 S.C. 210 (1880)
Hannon v. Mechanics Building & Loan Ass'n, 177 S.C. 153, 180 S.E. 873 (1935)
In re Fifty-Four First Mortgage Bonds, 15 S.C. 304 (1881)
J.P. Ludington, Annotation, Propriety of Appointing Receiver, at Behest of Mortgagee, to Manage or Operate Property During Foreclosure Action, 82 A.L.R.2d 1075 (1962)
Jeffcoat v. Morris, 300 S.C. 526, 389 S.E.2d 159 (Ct. App. 1989)
Kirven v. Lawrence, 244 S.C. 572, 137 S.E.2d 764 (1964)
Pelzer v. Hughes, 27 S.C. 408, 3 S.E. 781, 785 (1887)
Receivers § 292(d)(3)(bb) (1952)
South Carolina Appellate Rules 225(b)(2) and (3)
South Carolina Nat'l Bank v. Florence Sporting Goods, 241 S.C. 110, 127 S.E.2d 199 (1962)
Truesdell v. Johnson, 144 S.C. 188, 142 S.E. 343 (1928)
Virginia-Carolina Chem. Co. v. Hunter, 84 S.C. 214, 66 S.E. 177 (1909)

South Dakota

Foreclosure Summary

Security Instrument	Mortgage
Judicial	Yes
Non-Judicial	Yes
Initial Public Notice	Complaint
Time Frame	1 month for non-judicial/ 9 months from service of Complaint to sale if contested
Redemption Period	One year; 180 days in some cases
Deficiency	Yes

Receivership Summary

Ancillary Remedy Necessary	Yes
Ex-Parte	Yes
Approximate Time for Appointment	Typically 30 days; 1 to 2 days for ex parte
Who or What can act as Receiver	No restrictions given
Specific Receiver Requirements	Oath must be filed prior to commencing duties
Is there any approval list for Receivers	No
Out of State Receivers Allowed	No restrictions given

Foreclosure:

I. General Information:

All foreclosure sales must be made in the county where the property is situated.

Jurisdiction is appropriate in the circuit court for the county where the property or some portion is situated. Service by publication is allowed for nonresidents or residents that cannot be found after due diligence.

A judicial foreclosure action, including a short-term redemption mortgage foreclosure, is complete extinguishment, satisfaction and payment of the debt secured by the mortgage, unless the mortgage holder is granted a deficiency judgment. A foreclosure action is not considered satisfaction of an assignment of rents agreement under the mortgage.

The owner, mortgagor, judgment debtor, or the successors of either, having any interest in the property sold and the holders of any lien, legal or equitable, subsequent and junior to that from which redemption is to be made, on the property sold, or any part thereof, or any share or interest therein, shall have the right of redemption.

Redemption period is 1 year except under 180-day redemption mortgages.

II. Judicial Foreclosure Basics:

In an action for foreclosure, the complaint must state whether any proceedings have been had for the recovery of the debt and if so, whether any and what part has been collected. If a judgment has been obtained for the moneys demanded in the complaint, no proceedings can be had unless an execution against the property of the defendant is unsatisfied and the defendant has no property to satisfy the execution. Once a foreclosure action is commenced and pending, no other proceedings for the recovery of the debt can be had.

The defendant can cure the default and the complaint must be dismissed if the defendant brings into court before entry of

Contributed By: Rebecca Mann of
Gunderson Palmer Nelson Ashmore

judgment the principal and interest due, with costs and disbursements. However, the cure statute does not apply to 180-day redemption mortgages. The defendant can also cure by paying the principal and interest, with costs and disbursements, before the sale which will stay the proceedings until a further default occurs. If a subsequent default occurs, the court may enforce by order the collection of the subsequent installment due.

If the property can be sold in parcels without injury to the interests of the parties, only so much of the property can be sold which will be sufficient to pay the amount due with costs. The judgment will remain as security for any subsequent default at which time the court can direct the sale of so much of the property to sufficient to satisfy the subsequent default using the first judgment. If the property is such that sale of the whole property will be most beneficial to the parties, the judgment must be entered for the sale of the whole premises.

The mortgage holder can bid on the property at the foreclosure sale so long as he bids fairly and in good faith. In no event will the mortgage holder be required to bid a sum in excess of the debt adjudged by the court to be due with costs and disbursements taxed in the action and costs and expenses of the sale. If the mortgage holder is not willing to bid the full amount of the judgment debt, he must establish at trial the fair and reasonable value of the property and the court shall determine the same in its decree. The court can find the fair and reasonable value to be less than the balance due and authorize the mortgage holder to bid that amount. If a deficiency remains after the sale, the mortgage holder is entitled to a general execution for the deficiency only upon application to the court in which the judgment was entered.

The proceeds of the sale of the property must be applied first to payment of the costs and expenses of the sale, then to the payment of costs and disbursements taxed in the foreclosure action, and then to discharge the debt adjudged by the court to be due. If there is a surplus, it shall be paid into the court for the use of the defendant or person entitled thereto subject to the order of the court. If the surplus remains in the court for three months without being applied for, the court may direct the surplus to be put out at interest for the benefit of the defendant, his representatives or assigns subject to the order of the court.

The person making the sale must give the purchaser a certificate of sale which must contain a recital of the sale, the legal description of the property, the price bid for each parcel and the whole price paid.

If no redemption is made within the redemption period, a deed must be transferred to the purchaser. If crops have been sown before the issuance of the sheriff's deed, the mortgagor is entitled to the crops and has the right to enter the property to harvest the crops after the issuance of the deed. However, the lien priority of a secured party in crops shall be determined by South Dakota's uniform commercial code.

III. Non-Judicial Foreclosure Basics:

Non-judicial voluntary foreclosure may be done by written agreement between mortgagor and mortgagee. A non-judicial foreclosure may be done by doing all of the following: The mortgagor must convey to the mortgagee all interest in the property subject to the mortgage and the mortgagee must accept the conveyance and waive any rights to a deficiency judgment. The mortgagee must receive immediate possession of the property. The mortgagor and mortgagee must file a jointly executed document with the register of deeds stating they have elected to follow the voluntary foreclosure procedures. The mortgagee must send by certified mail a notice of the election to all junior lien holders stating that the junior lien holders have 60 days to exercise any rights of redemption and the sum necessary to redeem.

On the same day of the written agreement, the mortgagee must furnish a "Disclosure and Notice of Cancellation" which must advise the mortgagor that he is waiving his right to redemption by voluntarily foreclosing; that the mortgagor will not be liable for any deficiency but is also forfeiting any surplus; that the voluntary foreclosure may be canceled without penalty or obligation within 5 business days from the date of the agreement;

Contributed By: Rebecca Mann of
Gunderson Palmer Nelson Ashmore

that the agreement is entirely voluntary and that the mortgagor is not required to sign the agreement; that the agreement will become final unless the mortgagor signs and delivers the notice of cancellation before midnight on the proper date (which date is to be provided in the form); and a place to sign for cancellation.

A junior lien holder may redeem the property by paying the purchase price plus any other amounts paid by the purchaser to protect his interest within 60 days from the notice of election of voluntary foreclosure. If a junior lien holder fails to redeem, his lien is released.

The mortgagee possesses the property until the completion of the foreclosure subject to the liens of record at the time of the conveyance from the mortgagor. The mortgagee's lien is prior to any junior liens at the time of the conveyance.

IV. Power of sale foreclosure guidelines

Power of sale foreclosure is referred to as "foreclosure by advertisement" in South Dakota.

If the mortgage contains the power of sale, the mortgage can be foreclosed by advertisement upon default. A mortgage containing a power of sale must be duly recorded in the county where the property is situated for the power of sale to be effective. The power of sale does not become operative until a default in the condition of the mortgage has accrued. Without a default, there is no entitlement to foreclosure by advertisement. A foreclosure by advertisement is not allowed if an action has been instituted to recover the debt, unless the action has been discontinued or the execution of judgment returned unsatisfied.

If the mortgagee has commenced foreclosure by advertisement, the mortgagor or any other lien holder may require the mortgagee to foreclose by action by presenting to the court an application for such. Upon such application, the court shall enjoin the mortgagee from foreclosing by advertisement and direct all further proceedings be had in circuit court.

If the property consists of distinct farms, tracts or lots, only such lots can be sold as necessary to satisfy the amount due.

The mortgagee can, fairly and in good faith, purchase the property. If the mortgagee purchases the property and then requests a deficiency judgment, he must prove to the court that the amount he paid for the property was at or above market value. If the purchase price was less than the market value, the difference between market value and the purchase price is deducted from any deficiency judgment. A party foreclosing by advertisement is entitled to costs, disbursements and attorney fees out of the proceeds of the sale.

Like a foreclosure by action, the proceeds of the sale of the property must be applied first to payment of the costs and expenses of the sale, then to the payment of costs and disbursements taxed in the foreclosure action, and then to discharge the debt adjudged by the court to be due. Any surplus is paid to the clerk of court and notice is given to the mortgagor and junior lien holders of the surplus deposit.

The certificate of sale must contain a recital of the fact of the sale, stating the time and place and name of purchaser; a particular description of the property sold; the price bid for each distinct lot or parcel; and the whole price paid. The certificate of sale must be recorded within 10 days from the date of sale. A sheriff's deed is given to the purchaser if the property is not redeemed during the redemption period. Crops sown before the issuance of the sheriff's deed belong to the mortgagor who has the right to enter the property and harvest the crop.

V. Power of sale constitutes part of security

Yes

VI. No Power of sale foreclosure guidelines

No information provided.

VII. Foreclosure when instrument contains no power of sale.
No information provided.

VIII. Additional satisfaction permitted under continuing power of sale.
No information provided.

IX. Sale under power where instrument silent as to place or terms of sale.
No information provided.

X. Notice of Sale and How notice of sale is given
Notice must be published at least once per week for four successive weeks specifying the names of the mortgagor and mortgagees; the date of the mortgage; the amount claimed due at the date of the notice; a description of the mortgage premises which conforms substantially to that contained in the mortgage; the time and place of sale; a description of the default; that the mortgagor can apply for foreclosure by advertisement; and the name and address of all persons claiming a lien, encumbrance or other recorded ownership interest in the property.

The foreclosing creditor must serve a written copy of the notice of foreclosure sale at least 21 days before the sale on the mortgagor and any other lien holder whose interest in the property being foreclosed would be affected by the foreclosure.

XI. Place and time for conducting foreclosure by power of sale.
A sale for foreclosure by advertisement must be made at a public auction between 9 a.m. and 5 p.m. in the county where the property is situated by the sheriff or his deputy and sold to the highest bidder. The sale can be postponed by inserting a notice of the postponement in the newspaper in which the original notice was published and continuing to be published until the postponed sale date at the expense of the party requesting postponement.

XII. Short-Term Redemption Mortgages (aka 180 Day Redemption Mortgage)

A mortgage on property not more than 40 acres which contains a power of sale can, upon default, be foreclosed as a "short-term redemption mortgage" as an alternative to foreclosing by action or by advertisement. In order to foreclose as a short-term redemption mortgage, the mortgage must contain in capital letters: "THE PARTIES AGREE THAT THE PROVISIONS OF THE ONE HUNDRED EIGHTY DAY REDEMPTION MORTGAGE ACT GOVERN THIS MORTGAGE" and must be titled "MORTGAGE-ONE HUNDRED EIGHTY DAY REDEMPTION". The mortgage cannot contain a provision excluding the mortgagor from the property during the redemption period.

A short-term redemption mortgage can contain terms advantageous to the mortgage holder such as allowing the mortgage holder to recover attorney fees and disbursements actually incurred; allowing the parties to agree that taxes and insurance will be collected in installment payments and held in escrow, in an account with the mortgagee, until the due dates; allowing the mortgagor to assign all his rights and interest to income from the property during the redemption period; requiring the mortgagor to pay the difference between the net proceeds of the sale and total debt due; allowing the mortgagor to call the entire balance due within 60 days if the property is sold without its consent; in a foreclosure by action, the purchaser may apply to the court for a reduction of the redemption period of the property has been abandoned by the mortgagor.

A real estate mortgage in any form is authorized to be a short-term redemption mortgage.

If the mortgage debt is secured by other evidence of debt of any other person other than the mortgagor, the plaintiff may make such other persons a party to the action and the court may render judgment for the balance of such debt and enforce it. As with foreclosure by action, the complaint must state whether any proceedings have been held for the recovery of the debt and if

Contributed By: Rebecca Mann of
Gunderson Palmer Nelson Ashmore

so, whether any part has been collected. If a judgment has been obtained for the debt, no proceedings can be commenced unless an execution has been returned unsatisfied and the defendant has no other property to satisfy the execution. Once the foreclosure action is commenced, no other proceedings can be had for the recovery of the debt while the action is pending.

A defendant must answer within 30 days after service of the summons.

A notice of sale of the property must be published a least once a week for two successive weeks in the county where the property is located and must specify the name of the mortgagor, the amount claimed to be due, the date of the mortgage, a description of the property as described in the mortgage and the time, manner and place of sale.

The mortgage holder can purchase the property at the foreclosure sale if he bids the full amount of the judgment less the sum of the balance due on any prior liens. In no event will the mortgage holder be required to bid a sum in excess of the debt adjudged due plus costs of the action and costs of the sale.

Court may restrain commission of waste upon application of the purchaser or judgment creditor during the period for redemption.

The judgment debtor or junior lien holder have the right to redeem the property during the redemption period by paying the purchaser the purchase price plus any sums paid by the purchaser to protect his interest in the property such as taxes or insurance with interest. The redemption period is 180 days from the recording of the certificate of sale or 60 days if the property is abandoned. Redemption may not be extended beyond 180 consecutive days.

A written notice of redemption must be served on the purchaser and the person making the sale and recorded with the register of deeds. Upon redemption, the person making the sale must execute and deliver to the redeemer a certificate of redemption which must be recorded with the register of deeds.

Relevant Codes, Statutes or Case Law:
SDCL Ch. 21-47 Foreclosure by Action
SDCL Ch. 21-48 Foreclosure by Advertisement
SDCL Ch. 21-48A Nonjudicial Voluntary Foreclosure
SDCL 21-49 Short-Term Redemption Mortgages
SDCL Ch. 21-52 Redemption

Receivership:

I. General information:

In general, South Dakota has few statutes and case law on receivership. Each case is unique and the order for receivership should take into account the specific needs of that case.

A receiver may be appointed by the court when an action is pending in any of the following actions: (1) by a vendor to vacate a fraudulent purchase of property; (2) by a creditor to subject any property or fund to his claim; (3) between partners or others jointly owning or interested in any property or fund; or (4) by a mortgagee for the foreclosure of his mortgage where it appears that the property is in danger of being lost, removed, materially injured or the property is insufficient to discharge the debt; (5) where a corporation has been dissolved or is insolvent, in imminent danger of insolvency, has forfeited its corporate rights or is unable to exercise its corporate functions because of continued dissension between or neglect by its shareholders, directors and officers.

A receiver may be appointed after judgment (1) to carry the judgment into effect; (2) to dispose of property according to the judgment or to preserve it during the pendency of an appeal; (3) in proceedings to aid an execution when the execution has been returned unsatisfied; or (5) when the judgment debtor refuses to apply his property in satisfaction of the judgment.

A short-term mortgage may include a provision that in the case of foreclosure, the mortgage holder can appoint a receiver to take possession of the property if the property has been abandoned.

II. Appointing the Receiver:

A. The Basics:

Applicant makes a motion for the appointment of a receiver

B. Time Frame for Appointment:

It all depends on the court's calendar. Generally, the motion could be heard and appointment made within 30 days. An ex parte appointment could be made within 1-2 days.

Notice and filing is controlled by general rules of civil procedure. A written motion must be served no later than 10 days before the time specified for the hearing. A response is due 5 days before the hearing and a reply is due 2 days before the hearing.

C. Can you go in Ex Parte?

Yes. The court may require an undertaking from the ex parte applicant.

III. Loans and Advances:

The receiver can do such acts respecting the property as the court may authorize.

IV. Sales During the Receivership:

The receiver has the power to do such acts respecting the property as the court may authorize. SDCL § 21-21-9. Likely the order would provide the authority to sell the property if necessary.
There is no statutory process for sales during the receivership.

V. Liens Against Receivership Property:

No information provided.

VI. Owners Associations:

No information provided.

VII. Construction Related to Receivership Property:

No information provided.

VIII. Ending the Receivership:

Generally the order will indicate how the receivership is ended.

Relevant Codes, Statutes or Case Law:
SDCL Ch. 21-21 Receivership

Contributed By: Rebecca Mann of
Gunderson Palmer Nelson Ashmore

Tennessee

Foreclosure Summary

Security Instrument	Trust Deed/ Mortgage
Judicial	Yes (Rare)
Non-Judicial	Yes
Initial Public Notice	Publication
Time Frame	60 days
Redemption Period	Yes- for non judicial foreclosure
Deficiency	Yes

Receivership Summary

Ancillary Remedy Necessary	Yes
Ex-Parte	No
Approximate Time for Appointment	45 days
Who or What can act as Receiver	No Restrictions Given
Specific Receiver Requirements	Receiver will need to post a bond
Is there any approval list for Receivers	No
Out of State Receivers Allowed	Typically No

Foreclosure:

I. General Information:

Tennessee allows for both Judicial and Non-Judicial Foreclosure.

II. Judicial Foreclosure Basics:

While allowed for in a mortgage or a deed of trust, because Tennessee law permits foreclosure by power of sale and the process is simple and quick, judicial foreclosures are rarely done; therefore, the judicial process will not be reviewed here.

III. Non-Judicial Foreclosure Basics:

Non-judicial proceedings are almost always preferred because they can be completed in less time than is allowed for answering a complaint in a judicial proceeding and there can be a significant cost advantage. The mortgagee may have to bear the cost of a judicial foreclosure if it chooses this method over a power of sale.

IV. Guidelines for Power of Sale:

ALL OF THE FOLLOWING PROCEDURES ARE SUBJECT TO OTHER ADDITIONAL REQUIREMENTS AS CONTAINED IN THE DEED OF TRUST.

A. Order foreclosure reference or abstract.

B. Determine if any tax liens have been filed on the property and, if so, send out appropriate notices to applicable tax authority at least (25) days prior to the sale.

C. Conduct appraisal and environmental audit. [Not required, but often done.]

D. Determine if the Deed of Trust provides for the appointment of a substitute trustee for the purpose of exercising the power of sale under the instrument.

E. The appointment of successor trustees should be filed for recording before the first date of publication. If the name of the

Contributed By: John Rowland & Courtney Gilmer of Baker Donelson substitute trustee is not included in the first publication check with the statute on what should be done.

F. If the trustee is not a resident of the state of Tennessee, the notice shall include the name and address of a registered agent of the substitute trustee who is located in the state of Tennessee. The mailing of this notice is evidenced by the substitute trustee recording an affidavit to that effect prior to the recording of the deed evidencing the sale or by recitation on the substitute trustee's deed.

G. Note that the deed of trust may contain its own provisions regarding substitution of trustee and if the deed of trust has more stringent requirements than the statute, those requirements should be followed.

H. Please note that if the loan is a "home loan"* as defined by the Home Loan Act, notice is different.

I. Notify the insurance company prior to the initiation of foreclosure proceeding.

J. Prior to the first publication of the notice of foreclosure sale, send notice of the foreclosure sale to debtor and any co-debtor.

K. While not required by the statute, also send notice to any holder of a junior lien or encumbrance.

L. After sending notice to debtor, any co-debtor and holder of prior liens, advertise three (3) times with the first advertisement to appear at least twenty (20) days before the sale. Place three advertisements in a newspaper published in the county where the sale is to be made. When the advertisement cannot be made in a newspaper thirty (30) days' written notice posted in at least five (5) public places (including the courthouse door, the neighborhood of the defendant, and, if realty, in the civil district where the land lies). If the property is subject to a tax lien, special language identifying the lien must be included in the notice. State statue tells us that the notice must give the names of the plaintiff, defendant and other parties interested; describe the land in brief terms, including the street address; mention the time and place of the sale; identify each lien or claimed lien of the United States and/or of the state of Tennessee; and, for each lien, affirmatively state that the notice has been timely given according to applicable law, stating that for each such lien the sale of land thus advertised will be subject to the right of the United States to redeem.

V. Power of Sale Guidelines as Represented in the Security:

In Tennessee, the power of sale is constituted as part of the security.

VI. Guidelines for Foreclosure when there is No Power of Sale:

If debtor executes a mortgage, rather than a deed of trust, where there are no power of sale provisions and no trustee, while there is no case on point, we doubt that it could be enforced as a deed of trust.

VII. Any Additional Satisfaction Permitted Under Continuing Power of Sale:

If additional satisfaction is needed, then we suggest a suit for judgment for deficiency balance remaining on note be brought after foreclosure under power of sale.

Even if there is no evidence of irregularity, misconduct, fraud or unfairness on the part of the mortgage (beneficiary) in a suit for the deficiency, the debtor can still challenge the presumption that the value of the property at the time the foreclosure was equal to the sale price by proving the sale price was grossly inadequate. There are no specific limitations based on method of foreclosure (judicial versus nonjudicial), type of collateral (residence versus commercial), or type of loan.

VIII. Sale by Power of Sale when the Instrument is Silent as to the Place or Terms of Sale:

No reported cases to discuss.

IX. Notice of Sale and How Notice is Given:

Notice must be sent to the debtor and any co-debtor on or before the first date of publication of the notice of foreclosure sale by certified mail at least thirty (30) days prior to the first publication date. State statue details the exact process. Note that, if deed of trust imposes additional requirements, these must be followed.

XI. Place and Time for Conducting Foreclosure by Power of Sale:

Absent more stringent requirements in the deed of trust, can be accomplished within 45 to 60 days.

Relevant Codes, Statutes or Case Law:

See Franklin v. The Duncan, 133 Tenn. 472, 182 S.W. 230 (1916); *Irvin v. Shrum*, 97 Tenn. 186, 36 S.W. 1089 (1896); *Clark v. Jones*, 93 Tenn. 488, 27 S.W. 1009; *Duke v. Daniels*, 660 S.W.2d 793 (Tenn. App. 1983); *U.S. Bank, N.A., as servicer for Tennessee Housing Development Agency, v. Tennessee Farmers Mutual Insurance Company*, W2006-COA-R3-CV (Tenn. Ct. App. 2007); *Lost Mountain v. King*, 2006 WL 3740791 (Tenn. Ct. App. 2006) ("*Lost Mountain*").

26 U.S.C. § 7425(b); Tenn. Code Ann. § 67-1-1433(b)(1); Tenn. Code Ann. § 35-5-114; Tenn. Code Ann. § 35-1-101

Receivership:

I. General information:

Grounds for the appointment of a Receiver are:

A. if the property is being so misused, wasted, or neglected by the defendant that it is greatly endangered and likely to be lost or rendered inadequate, especially if the debtor fails to keep taxes paid;

B. if the defendant has abandoned the property;

C. if the defendant is insolvent or if the mortgage debt is overdue and the land mortgaged is inadequate security.

A court of equity will appoint a Receiver where there is danger of the property upon which the petitioner has a lien being misused or some injury done to it.

II. Appointing the Receiver:

A. The Basics:

File an application in chancery court. The defendant is entitled to notice and a hearing before the appointment. On an emergency basis, the hearing can be held as part of a "show cause." The standard to be met on a “show cause” basis is the same as obtaining an injunction.

B. Time Frame for Appointment:

If uncontested, forty-five (45) days unless emergency justifies a "show cause" proceeding.

C. Can you go in Ex Parte?

No.

III. Loans and Advances:

Tennessee does not have any preset laws, code or case law regarding loans and advances during a receivership.

IV. Sales During the Receivership:

No information provided.

V. Liens Against Receivership Property:

No information provided.

VI. Owners Associations:

No information provided.

VII. Construction Related to Receivership Property:

No information provided.

VIII. Ending the Receivership:

Tennessee requires a motion and hearing to end a receivership.

Contributed By: John Rowland &
Courtney Gilmer of Baker Donelson

Relevant Codes, Statutes or Case Law:
Tennessee Code Annotated ("T.C.A.") § 29-1-103, § 29-1-104 and § 29-6-140
Bidwell v. Paul, 64 Tenn. 693 (1875); *Pugh v. Burton*, 116 S.W.2d 624 (Tenn. App. 1942).

Texas

Foreclosure Summary

Security Instrument	Deed of Trust/ Mortgage
Judicial	Yes
Non-Judicial	Yes
Initial Public Notice	Publication
Time Frame	41 days from Notice of Default to foreclosure; process typically begins 60 - 90 days after default
Redemption Period	No
Deficiency	Yes

Receivership Summary

Ancillary Remedy Necessary	Yes
Ex-Parte	Yes
Approximate Time for Appointment	Few days
Who or What can act as Receiver	Individual or Texas Corporation
Specific Receiver Requirements	Must be a citizen of Texas and maintain a residence
Is there any approval list for receivers	No
Out of State Receivers Allowed	In some cases

Foreclosure:

I. General Information:

Real Property foreclosures in Texas are outlined under Section 51.002 of the Texas Property Code (the "Code") and a properly prepared deed of trust or mortgage.

Texas courts have adopted a "lien theory" as opposed to a "title theory" of mortgages. In Texas, a Deed of Trust is customarily utilized to secure the payment of the indebtedness and the timely performance of ancillary obligations. A Deed of Trust does not pass legal title to Trustee; equitable title is conveyed to a beneficiary and the legal title is retained by the grantor. In addition, the beneficiary is not entitled to rentals or profits from the mortgaged property unless grantor has executed a properly-crafted assignment of leases and rents. If the proper assignment has been executed, beneficiaries can generally take possession of rentals and profits after default if all statutory notice requirements are satisfied. In Texas, a Deed of Trust has the legal effect of a mortgage with the power to sell upon default.

II. Judicial Foreclosure Basics:

A judicial foreclosure proceeding in Texas is conducted in a court having jurisdiction over the mortgaged property. While judicial foreclosure is available in Texas, few lenders utilize it in light of the comparatively expedited non-judicial foreclosure procedures. The filing of a suit and entry of an order directing foreclosure may be more desirable if problems exist with conducting a non-judicial foreclosure or with respect to foreclosure of certain property specifically governed by statutory procedures. Judicial foreclosure may be preferable to non-judicial foreclosure if there is a question as to the occurrence of an event of default under the loan documents, or if there are issues related to notice, the organization of grantor, or authorization of grantor's signatories. If the existence of an event of default is contested, a judicial determination of default prevents a later suit for damages or rescission for wrongful foreclosure. If the mortgaged property is not subject to dissipation or loss and is of a value sufficient to satisfy a judgment for principal, interest, and attorneys' fees, the longer and more elaborate judicial procedure may be advisable. If dissipation or loss of the mortgaged property is feared during pendency of the suit, relief enjoining any sale or disposition of the mortgaged property is available until a final and non-appealable judgment in entered. A lender initiates either action by the service of legal pleadings upon:

A. all parties having a fee interest in the mortgaged property;

B. all parties having an interest of record in the real property; and

C. all parties in possession of the property, under leases or otherwise.

III. Non-Judicial Foreclosure Basics:

If an event of default remains uncured beyond the applicable cure period(s) contained in the loan documents, and the mortgagee opts to exercise its right to non-judicially foreclose under the power of sale clause in the deed of trust, the date, time and place of the foreclosure sale are governed by Section 51.002 of the Code. The mortgagee may cause the property to be sold at public auction to the highest bidder, between 10:00 a.m. and 4:00 p.m. on the first Tuesday of any month after default, after having given notice of the time, terms and place of such sale and the property to be sold and having posted such notice in such places and in such manner as so designated in the deed of trust, at least twenty-one (21) days prior to the sale.

A senior lienholder is not required under Texas law to notify junior lienholders of a foreclosure of its lien unless an agreement between the parties dictates otherwise. Absent an agreement, following the valid foreclosure of a senior lien, junior lienholders do not have a right of redemption, and their liens, if not satisfied from the proceeds of the sale, are extinguished. But if a notice of a federal tax lien has been filed more than thirty (30) days before the proposed sale, a notice in compliance with Section 7425(c)(1) of the U.S. Tax Code must be given to the Internal Revenue Service ("IRS") at least twenty-five (25) days prior to the date of the foreclosure or the foreclosure will transfer the foreclosed property subject to any federal tax lien filed against grantor (in the county where the mortgaged property is located). The IRS takes the position that the twenty-five (25) day period commences to run on the date the IRS receives the notice. Pursuant to Section 7425(d)(1) of the Tax Code, if proper notice is given, the IRS has one hundred twenty (120) days after the date of the foreclosure sale to redeem the property upon payment of the bid price to the purchaser.

IV. Guidelines for Power of Sale:

A. Default.

Before the mortgagee may exercise its remedies, including, without limitation, foreclosure, it must be determined that the mortgagor is in default. "In the absence of default of the debt owed mortgagee, there can be no foreclosure of the lien." Neither the Uniform Commercial Code nor the Code defines the term "default." To determine whether the mortgagor is in default, one must consult the loan documents entered into between the parties. For example, the note, the deed of trust or mortgage and/or the security agreement will contain defined events of default (which may or may not be subject to notice and cure periods in favor of mortgagor); such loan documents will also provide the mortgagee with remedies in the event of default by mortgagor and outline the procedures required to be followed by mortgagee in exercising such rights and remedies. Once it has been determined that an event of default has in fact occurred, it is imperative to examine the underlying agreements to ensure compliance with the applicable cure periods, demand and/or notice provisions contained therein. It is also important to determine whether a mortgagee has forfeited its rights to foreclose or exercise other remedies by waiving such rights due to simultaneous or subsequent oral modifications of the operative documents. It is also possible for a mortgagee to be estopped from exercising its rights at law or under the deed of trust if actions of mortgagee and mortgagor subsequent to the default indicate modification of the operative documents.

B. Demand and Acceleration:

While the deed of trust may contain provisions waiving any notice of default and/or acceleration, it is prudent practice for the mortgagee to give twenty (20) days (prior to acceleration and posting for foreclosure) notice of default and intent to accelerate and to provide mortgagor with an opportunity to cure the default during this twenty (20) day period. Upon expiration of the twenty (20) day notice period, the mortgagor should then give notice that the debt has been accelerated. The notice of acceleration can be provided simultaneously with the notice of foreclosure; therefore, it must be given at least twenty-one (21) days prior to the date of the sale.

C. Procedures to Follow Prior to Foreclosure:

A mortgagee planning a foreclosure sale should follow the following procedures prior to proceeding with the sale:

1. Title and Survey Review:

Once provided with a title down date and an updated survey showing items of record subsequent to the filing of the deed of trust, it is necessary to determine the effects of such new items on the property;

2. State Tax Lien Search:

General tax liens are subordinate to a secured first lien deed of trust, while ad valorem taxes have priority to almost all preexisting liens; therefore a state tax lien search should be conducted;

3. Federal Tax Lien:

If a federal tax lien is filed more than thirty (30) days before the proposed foreclosure sale, then the notice must be given, by certified mail, at least twenty-five (25) days prior to the foreclosure sale to the IRS. If this notice is properly given, the IRS has one hundred twenty (120) days following the foreclosure sale to redeem the property. This can be avoided, however, by obtaining formal consent from the IRS to the foreclosure sale free of the tax lien (*e.g.*, the equity is not in excess of the secured debt). Note, however, that if the Notice is not properly given, the tax lien survives. Mortgagee should send its Notice to*:

Northern Texas:	Southern Texas:
IRS, Attn: Collection Advisory Group Manager	IRS, Attn: Collection Advisory Group Manager
1100 Commerce Street	300 E. Eight Street
Mail Code 5028 DAL	MS 5021 AUS
Dallas, Texas 75242	Austin, Texas 78701
214-413-5349 - telephone	512-499-5241 - telephone
214-413-5654 - fax	512-499-5993 - fax

*See IRS Publication 4235.

4. Appraisal and Bid Price:

An updated appraisal on the property is necessary to assist in constructing the bid price. As for the bid price at the foreclosure sale, the "reasonably equivalent value" for the foreclosed property is the price in fact received at the sale, so long as the foreclosing party has complied with the requirements of the state's foreclosure laws.

5. Administration of Foreclosure:

A mortgage servicer may administer the foreclosure of property on behalf of a mortgagee if the mortgage servicer and the mortgagee have entered into an agreement granting the current mortgage servicer authority to service the mortgage; and the default and foreclosure notices disclose (i) that the mortgage servicer is representing the mortgagee under a servicing agreement, (ii) the name of the mortgagee and (iii) the address of the mortgagee or the address of the mortgage servicer.

6. Trustee; Appointment of Substitute Trustee:

After notice of default and demand of payment, notice of intent to accelerate and subsequent acceleration and notice of foreclosure, as applicable, in accordance with the previous subsection of this paper, the mortgagee must again look to the deed of trust to determine the identity of the party who is to foreclose — either the trustee named in the deed of trust or a substitute trustee. The deed of trust typically provides the method by which such party is appointed if the trustee is not available to conduct the foreclosure sale.

7. Conducting the Sale

On the first Tuesday of the month in which the foreclosure sale is to occur, the trustee or substitute trustee should conduct the foreclosure sale in the area designated for foreclosures of the county courthouse in the county in which the subject property is located. If there is not such a designated area in the county courthouse, the Statutory Notice must state the area of the courthouse, or such other location a commissioners court of the county may designate for conducting foreclosures, where the sale covered by the Statutory Notice will take place, and on the date of the sale, the sale must occur in the place so designated in the Statutory Notice. The trustee or substitute trustee will commence by reading the Statutory Notice and presenting a foreclosure speech that states the terms of the sale, including, without limitation, recitals describing the deed of trust and its terms and mortgagor's default thereunder. Bidding is open to the public, and the trustee or substitute trustee shall give the highest bidder a reasonable amount of time to obtain cash in the amount of the purchase price. Texas law permits the mortgagee to "credit bid" for the property and take the property as a credit to the indebtedness. The mortgagee also has the right to seek a deficiency judgment against the mortgagor and/or any full recourse guarantors, as discussed below.

After conducting the sale and executing a Trustee's Deed or Substitute Trustee's Deed in favor of the highest bidder at the public auction and same is filed with the office of the county clerk in the county in which the property is located, to provide evidence that the sale was in compliance with the deed of trust and the Code, it is advisable to file an Affidavit of Foreclosure, which describes the sale in detail, with the office of the county clerk in the county in which the property is located.

V. Power of Sale Constitutes Part of Security

A typical grant clause will read: "For this purpose, Borrower irrevocably grants and conveys to Trustee, in trust, with power of sale, the following described property located in the __________ of ______________:"

Contributed By: Brigitte Kimichik and David Ortigoza of Andrews Kurth

VI. Guidelines for Foreclosure when there is No Power of Sale:

When no power-of-sale clause is included in the mortgage or deed of trust, judicial foreclosure is the only method available.

VII. Foreclosure When Instrument Contains No Power of Sale:

The foreclosure is administered by the court. The lender files suit against the borrower to obtain a court order to foreclose on the property. Once the court orders a foreclosure, the property is scheduled for public sale.

VIII. Any Additional Satisfaction Permitted Under Continuing Power of Sale:

Deficiency Judgments: Lenders may obtain deficiency judgments, but they are limited to the difference between the sale price of the property and the balance of the loan in default. After a non-judicial foreclosure sale, suit must be filed recover a deficiency against the borrower or a full-recourse guarantor. The person against whom the judgment is sought is entitled to present evidence of the fair market value of the property; if the court finds that the fair market value is greater than the sales price, then the amount of the deficiency will be reduced accordingly. There is a 2-year statute of limitations that does not apply to deficiencies remaining after repossession and sale of personal property unless the personal property was sold incidentally to a real estate foreclosure sale.

IX. Notice of Sale and How Notice is Given:

Notice of the sale ("Statutory Notice") must be given twenty-one (21) days prior to conducting the public foreclosure sale. The Statutory Notice must include a statement of the earliest time the sale will begin, and the sale must, in fact, commence at that time or within three (3) hours thereof. The Statutory Notice should be posted at the courthouse door of each county in which the property is located, filed in the office of the county clerk of each county in which the property is located, and a copy of the notice should be sent by certified mail to each debtor who is obligated to pay the debt to which the power of sale is related. In addition to the statutory requirements, it is imperative that the mortgagee look to the deed of trust to determine whether any additional notice requirements exist (*i.e.*, advertising notice in the public notice section of the newspaper that services the county in which the subject property is located). It is also necessary for the mortgagee to look to the deed of trust for guidance regarding any other parties to whom notice of default and/or foreclosure is required.

The Statutory Notice must also include:

A. description of the deed of trust lien, matured debt, and property to be sold (attach legal description);

B. statement that an event of default exists;

C. statement that the holder of the secured debt has authorized enforcement of the power of sale granted in the deed of trust;

D. statement of the date and location of the sale;

E. statement that the property will be sold at public auction to the highest bidder for cash;

F. statement that such notice of sale is not intended to violate any stay in bankruptcy; and

G. contain a statement that is conspicuous, printed in boldface or underlined type, and substantially similar to the following: "Assert and protect your rights as a member of the armed forces of the United States. If you are or your spouse is serving on active military duty, including active military duty as a member of the Texas National Guard or the National Guard of another state or as a member of a reserve component of the armed forces of the United States, please send written notice of the active duty military service to the sender of this notice immediately."

In addition to the above, the mortgagee should consult the deed of trust regarding the notice to be provided to ensure that mortgagee is not required to include any additional items in the Statutory Notice.

After posting and filing the Statutory Notice, the party who conducted the posting and filing should execute an Affidavit of

Posting that should be filed of record in the office of the county clerk in each county in which the property is located. In addition, subsequent to mailing the Statutory Notice, the trustee, substitute trustee or other party who caused the Statutory Notice to be mailed should execute an Affidavit of Mailing and such Affidavit of Mailing should be filed of record in the office of the county clerk in each county in which the property is located. These two affidavits will serve as proof of compliance with the Code in the event that the foreclosure sale is contested at a later date.

Relevant Codes, Statutes or Case Law:

Chapter 64 and Sections 51.0001, 51.002, and 51.003 of the Code

Receivership:

I. General information:

Texas has multiple statutes that allow for the appointment of a Receiver.

Chapter 64 of Texas's Civil Practice & Remedies Code (the "CPRC") contains the general provisions governing receivership.

Sections 11.403 and 11.404 of the Texas Business Organizations Code (the "TBOC") allows a court to appoint a Receiver for property of corporations, limited liability companies, limited partnerships, and certain other entities.

Those situations in which a Receiver may be appointed, under Chapter 64 of the CPRC or Sections 11.403 and 11.404 of the TBOC, likely to be of most interest to a lender include:

A. in an action by a creditor to subject any property or fund to his claim;

B. in an action by a mortgagee for the foreclosure of the mortgage and sale of the mortgaged property; or

C. for a corporation that is insolvent, is in imminent danger of insolvency, has been dissolved, or has forfeited its corporate rights.

Section 11.410 of the TBOC allows a court to appoint a Receiver for all property, in and outside of Texas and its business in Texas and its business if the court determines, in accordance with ordinary usages of equity that circumstances exist that necessitate the appointment of a Receiver.

Under Section 31.002(b)(3) of the CPRC, a court may, in the aid of execution of a judgment, appoint a Receiver with the authority to take possession of the nonexempt property, sell it, and pay the proceeds to the judgment creditor to the extent required to satisfy the judgment.

Contributed By: Monica Blacker of Andrews Kurth

II. Appointing the Receiver:

A. The Basics:

The party seeking the receivership must file an action in a court of competent jurisdiction seeking appointment of a receivership.

B. Time Frame for Appointment:

Time to appoint would depend on the facts of the case and degree of emergency. In an appropriate case, a Texas court would give expedited consideration to a motion for appointment of a Receiver, possibly within a few days.

C. Can you go in Ex Parte?

Texas civil procedure requires that at least three days notice for the hearing be given for a Receiver to be appointed to take charge of property which is fixed and immovable.

Otherwise, a Receiver may be appointed *ex parte* only in "exceptional and extreme cases." Also, *ex parte* appointment should occur "only where the right thereto Receiver is clearly shown, and then in exercise of great caution by the court."

III. Loans and Advances:

There are no set laws but one statute does reference it.

IV. Sales During the Receivership:

Sales may occur during the Receivership if authorized by the Court.

V. Liens Against Receivership Property:

No information provided.

VI. Owners Associations:

No information provided.

VII. Construction Related to Receivership Property:

No information provided.

VIII. Ending the Receivership:

Under Texas law, the duration of the receivership and its termination are normally within the sound judicial discretion of the appointing court; however, Section 11.403(d) of the TBOC states that if the condition necessitating the appointment of a receiver under this section is remedied, the receivership shall be terminated immediately, and the receiver shall redeliver to the domestic entity all of the property remaining in receivership. Receiverships generally end upon a motion. However, Texas's Civil Practice & Remedies Code limits corporate receiverships to three (3) years, although the court may extend the receivership to up to five (5) years beyond the original three (3) years if (a) litigation prevents the court from winding up the affairs of the corporation or (b) the Receiver is operating the corporation as a going concern.

The following steps will typically be pursued to wind up the receivership:

A. A final accounting submitted by the Receiver and approved by the court and the filing of the amount of the Receiver's fees and ordering them paid.

B. Restoration of the property held by the Receiver to the owner of the property.

C. An order entered by the trial court discharging the Receiver.

IX. Miscellaneous:

A.

Texas courts are generally protective of creditor rights.

B.

Under Chapter 64 of Texas's Civil Practice and Remedies Code:

Section 64.021 of Texas's Civil Practice & Remedies Code requires that a Receiver: (1) be a citizen and qualified voter of Texas at the time of appointment, (2) not be a party, attorney or other person interested in the action for appointment of a Receiver, and (3) maintain actual residence in Texas during the receivership. But under the provisions of the TBOC, the requirement that a Receiver be a citizen of Texas may not apply.

Section 11.406(a) of the TBOC requires that a Receiver for a corporation: (1) be (a) a citizen of the United States or (b) a corporation or other entity authorized to act as Receiver, which corporation may be a domestic corporation or a foreign corporation authorized to transact business in this State, and (2) give such bond as the court may direct with such sureties as the court may require.

Relevant Codes, Statutes or Case Law:

Chapter 64 and Section 31.002(b)(3) of the Civil Practices and Remedies Code; Texas Business Organization Code §§ 11.403, 11.404; Texas Rules of Civil Procedure 695, 695a; Texas Fam. Code § 6.502(5), 6.709(3)

Case Law
Associated Bankers Credit Co. v. Meis, 456 S.W. 2d 744, 750 (Tex. App. -- Corpus Christi 1970, no writ); *North Side Bank v. Wachendorfer,* 585 S.W.2d 789 (Civ. App.--Houston [1st Dist.] 1979, no writ); *Wilkenfeld v. State*, 189 S.W.2d 80 (Civ. App.--Galveston 1945, no writ); *Krumnow v. Krumnow*, 174 S.W. 3d 820, 829 (Tex. App -- Waco 2005, pet. denied); *Gilles v. Yarbrough,* 224 S.W.2d 720 (Civ. App.--Fort Worth 1949, no writ)
Hammond v. Hammond, 216 S.W.2d 630 (Civ. App.--Forth Worth 1948, no writ)
Humble Exploration Co., v. Walker, 641 S.W.2d 941, 945 (Tex. App.--Dallas 1982, orig. proceeding).

Utah

Foreclosure Summary

Security Instrument	Trust Deed/ Mortgage
Judicial	Yes
Non-Judicial	Yes
Initial Public Notice	Notice of Default
Time Frame	Typically about 120 days from Notice of Default if by trust deed foreclosure; varies if by judicial foreclosure
Redemption Period	Yes (6 mos from sale) if judicial foreclosure; No if trust deed foreclosure
Deficiency	Yes for difference between decree and sale price, of judicial foreclosure; Yes for difference between debt and greater of FMV or bid amount, if sold at trust deed sale

Receivership Summary

Ancillary Remedy Necessary	No
Ex-Parte	Possible, w/ cause; otherwise after notice
Approximate Time for Appointment	15 – 30 days
Who or What can act as Receiver	Individual or entity
Specific Receiver Requirements	Must swear oath before performing duties; bond
Is there any approval list for Receivers	No
Out of State Receivers Allowed	Yes

Foreclosure:

I. General Information:

Utah permits the foreclosure of an interest in real property by either a judicial foreclosure or by private sale, if the security is in the form of a Deed of Trust, but requires a judicial foreclosure if the security is a mortgage. Mortgages are rarely used in modern commercial lending practice in Utah, and virtually all security agreements on land are Deeds of Trust.

II. Judicial Foreclosure Basics:

Judicial foreclosure provides a forum for resolution of any disputes about the nature, validity and priority of liens and claims, provides a forum for the borrower to assert defenses and affirmative claims, and provides a forum for resolution of all claims. It can also be used as a vehicle for obtaining equitable remedies, such as injunctions or appointment of a receiver.

The sale procedures after entry of Decree of Foreclosure and following required notices and posting involve an auction by a Sheriff, who will sell only enough of the real property to satisfy the judgment. The defendant may direct the order in which the property is to be sold. The Sheriff delivers the Certificate of sale to the buyer.

A right of redemption exists for 180 days after the sale, and applies to all real property, except unexpired leasehold of less than 2 years. The borrower / defendant or any junior lienholder may redeem. If the defendant redeems, the effect of the sale is terminated and defendant is restored to the original ownership estate.

In general, the price to redeem is the sale price plus 6%, and subsequent redemptions are at the redemption price plus 3%. Taxes, assessments, insurance, maintenance, repairs or other liens paid by holder, plus 6% or 3% as applicable.

Special rules apply for rents, profits, and waste.

An automatic deficiency judgment is issued for any difference between the Decree and the sale amount.

III. Non-Judicial Foreclosure Basics:

If the obligation is secured by a Deed of Trust and not by a mortgage, the alternative remedy of a private trustee sale is available. A Deed of Trust also can be foreclosed judicially as if it was a mortgage, but a mortgage cannot be foreclosed by private sale as if it was a Deed of Trust.

The defendant has the opportunity to the cure the default for a period of three months after the filing and recording of a Notice of Default.

Following failure to cure, and the required notice and posting requirements, a public auction is scheduled, and is conducted by the trustee, successor trustee or attorney for the trustee. A substitution of trustee, if not previously recorded, must be filed concurrently with the Notice of Default. In situations involving condominium or community associations, a unit owner can demand a judicial foreclosure. The borrower may direct the order in which the trust property is sold if the property consists of several known lots or parcels which can be sold separately.

The Beneficiary (lender) under the Deed of Trust may credit bid at the sale up to the unpaid amount of principal, accrued interest, expenses (taxes, insurance, maintenance, etc.), costs and attorney's fees. The conveyance to the purchaser is by a Trustee's Deed and is without any right of redemption.

Utah has a One Action Rule that applies to both mortgages and Deeds of Trust. It requires that, where a debt is secured solely by a mortgage or Deed of Trust, the lender must first foreclose before pursuing the borrower for a deficiency. The One Action Rule does not apply to an association or unit owners' judicial or non-judicial foreclosure of a unit. Since guarantors are entitled to the protections of the limited deficiency rule with respect to private sales under Deeds of Trust (see below), they indirectly also are protected somewhat by the One Action rule.

IV. Deficiency Actions

In a judicial foreclosure action, the amount of the deficiency is the difference between the amount of the debt specified in the court's decree of foreclosure and the sale price. In a private sale under a Deed of Trust, the deficiency is the difference between the greater of the "fair market value" of the property on the date of sale or the sale price, and the amount of the debt on such date. Guarantors are entitled to the protections of the limited deficiency rule with respect to private sales under Deeds of Trust. The purpose of this rule is to prevent the lender from obtaining a double recovery in a non-judicial foreclosure where there is no right of redemption, i.e. a creditor otherwise could purchase the property for a low credit bid at a private sale, sue the debtor for a large deficiency, and then resell the property for a higher price, thus collecting part of the deficiency from both the property and the debtor.

This limited deficiency rule does not apply to a "sold-out" junior lienholder which loses the collateral as a result of a sale by a senior lender. In such a situation the sold-out junior creditor is not pursuing a "deficiency judgment" but a direct action on the underlying obligation. The value of the property on the date of the private sale, therefore, is not relevant to a sold-out junior lien creditor.

An action to recover a deficiency must be brought within 3 months after any sale of the property under a Deed of Trust. The suit must set forth the amount of the indebtedness, the sale price, and the alleged fair market value on the date of sale.

Relevant Codes, Statutes or Case Law:
§ 57-1-19 to -44 UCA § 57-8-48 ti 8a-303 UCA § 78-37-1, UCA, Rule 69, URCP

George v. Simon, 5 Cal. Rptr. 2d 428 (Cal. Ct. App. 1992
G. Adams, Ltd. v. Durbano, 782 P.2d 962 (Utah 1989); First Security Bank of Utah, N.A. v. Felger, 658 F.Supp. 175, 181-84 (D. Utah 1987); First Southwestern Financial Services v. Sessions, 875 P.2d 553, 555 (Utah 1994).; APS v. Briggs, 927 P.2d 670, 673 (Utah App. 1996).; City Consumer Services, Inc. v. Peters, 815 P.2d 234, 236 (Utah 1991).

Receivership:

I. General information:

There are very few published decisions in Utah on receivership proceedings, and those cases that have been published generally recognize the broad, equitable power of the trial court to structure appropriate relief in a wide variety of situations.

Grounds for appointment of a receiver:

A. When a property is in danger of being lost, removed, damaged or insufficient to satisfy a judgment, order or claim;
B. To carry a judgment into effect, dispose of property according to the judgment and to preserve property during the pendency of an appeal;
C. Upon a writ of execution which has been returned unsatisfied or when the judgment debtor refuses to apply property in satisfaction of the judgment;
D. When a corporation has been dissolved, insolvent, in imminent danger of insolvency, or has forfeited its corporate rights;
E. In all other cases in which receivers have been appointed by courts of equity

Courts in Utah also have appointed receivers in situations where misappropriation of corporate assets by insiders is asserted, or at the request of stockholders, suing individually or derivatively, to protect the company's assets.

II. Appointing the Receiver:

A. The Basics:

There are no rules or official forms governing the appointment process. Typically, a plaintiff will file a separate action seeking the appointment, or seek the appointment as a separate claim in an action that also seeks other forms of relief, i.e. judicial foreclosure of a lien. The Plaintiff typically files a separate motion, with a supporting memorandum, declaration and a proposed form of order, obtains a hearing date from the court, and serves the Complaint, Summons, Motion, Memorandum, Declaration, Proposed Order and Notice of Hearing on the defendant.

Powers of a receiver (determined by the scope of the order):

A. Bring and defend actions;
B. Seize property;
C. Collect, pay and compromise debts;
D. Invest funds;
E. Make transfers and "take other actions as the court authorizes."

B. Time Frame for Appointment:

Plaintiff also may file a separate ex parte motion for a separate "procedures order" shortening times for the filing of opposing memoranda and declarations, and fixing the hearing date, both of which also would be served on the defendant with the other papers. Usually special circumstances, or "cause" must be shown to obtain ex parte relief. Absent such an ex parte motion and order, the matter may be set on the normal motion calendar, in which case opposing memoranda are due in 10 business days, plus 3 additional calendar days, if the pleadings are served by mail.

If the appointment is sought without notice to the defendant, then the applicable procedures for granting temporary injunctive relief without notice will govern. Usually a showing of the 4 tests for injunctive relief will be required:

A. Sufficient legal basis
B. Irreparable injury
C. A balance of harm in favor of the plaintiff
D. Absence of a public injury or interest

In addition, for orders without notice the plaintiff also must make a clear showing that some immediate and irreparable injury, loss, or damage is likely to occur before notice can be given to the plaintiff. Courts are reluctant to appoint receivers without notice in a commercial context, unless there are egregious circumstances, i.e. evidence the waste, destruction or improper disposition of collateral is in process. In addition, courts are more likely to require a plaintiff's bond when relief is sought without notice. Thus, it is more common for plaintiffs to seek an expedited hearing, than to seek appointment of a receiver without notice.

E. Can you go in Ex Parte?

Yes.

III. Loans and Advances:

No information provided.

IV. Sales During the Receivership:

No information provided.

V. Liens Against Receivership Property:

No information provided.

VI. Owners Associations:

No information provided.

VII. Construction Related to Receivership Property:

No information provided.

VIII. Ending the Receivership:

No information provided.

IX. Miscellaneous

A. Security

The court may require security from a receiver in connection with pre and post-judgment writs of attachment, replevin, garnishment and execution, in an amount the court deems adequate.

The court also may relieve a party of the necessity to provide security if it appears that none of the parties will incur damages, costs or attorney fees as a result of the receiver being wrongfully obtained. The amount of security does not establish or limit the amount of damages, costs or attorney fees recoverable if the appointment is wrongfully obtained.

The court may consider objections to the nature or amount of any proposed security or surety, and proceedings on objections are expedited.

B. Payment of taxes.

Before the receiver may sell, transfer or pledge personal property, the receiver shall pay applicable taxes and shall file receipts showing payment of taxes. If there are insufficient assets to pay the taxes, the court may authorize the sale, transfer or pledge with the proceeds to be used to pay taxes.

C. Real Property.

Before a receiver is vested with real property, the receiver must file a certified copy of the appointment order in the office of the county recorder of the county in which the real property is located.

Relevant Codes, Statutes or Case Law:
Rule 66, URCP, Rule 7, URCP 65, URCP
Interlake Co. vs. Von Hake, 697 P.2d 238
Shaw vs. Robinson, 537 P.2d 487 (Utah 1975),
Inland Empire Insurance Co. vs. Freed, 239 F.2d 289 (10th Cir. 1956)
Pusey & Jones Co. vs. Hanssen, 261 U.S. 491
Jau-Fei Chen vs. Jau-Hwa Stewart, 100 P.3d 1177 (Utah 2004),

Vermont

Foreclosure Summary

Security Instrument	Mortgage
Judicial	Yes, judicial strict or judicial sale foreclosures available
Non-Judicial	Yes
Initial Public Notice	Complaint
Time Frame	210 Days
Redemption Period	Yes
Deficiency	Yes

Receivership Summary

Ancillary Remedy Necessary	Yes
Ex-Parte	Rare
Approximate Time for Appointment	15-30 days
Who or What can act as Receiver	No Restrictions Given
Specific Receiver Requirements	No Restrictions Given
Is there any approval list for Receivers	No
Out of State Receivers Allowed	Will most likely favor in state Receiver

Foreclosure:

I. General Information:

Vermont has three mortgage foreclosure procedures: Strict judicial, judicial sale and non-judicial sale.

II. Judicial Foreclosure Basics:

Vermont judicial foreclosures take the form of civil suits in equity in Superior Court. The foreclosing party serves a civil summons and complaint on the mortgagor and junior encumbrancers. Any of these defendants may plead facts in defense. If the Court finds for the plaintiff, it will enter a decree providing each defendant an opportunity to redeem up to a certain deadline. If no defendant redeems within this period of redemption, the Court will order either a public auction of the property or a direct conveyance of title to the plaintiff without a public sale. There is no post-sale redemption; once approved by the court and not appealed from, the sale is final.

III. Non-Judicial Foreclosure Basics:

Non-judicial foreclosure is available for all properties except for farms and private residences and as long as it is provided for in the mortgage deed.

IV. Guidelines for Power of Sale:

The procedure for non-judicial power-of-sale and judicial power-of-sale foreclosures are detailed in the state statute.

V. Power of Sale Guidelines as Represented in the Security:

Vermont has a title theory of mortgages. The power of sale is a contractual right that amounts to additional security beyond the basic conditional title that every mortgagor conveys to his/her mortgagee.

VI. Guidelines for Foreclosure when there is No Power of Sale:

Even if the mortgage deed lacks a power-of-sale clause, the court in a judicial foreclosure will order a sale if there may be equity in the property. If the plaintiff can show that there is no equity, the court may waive the sale and transfer title directly to the plaintiff if the defendants do not redeem.

VII. Foreclosure When Instrument Contains No Power of Sale:

Private foreclosure sale is not authorized by statute unless the mortgage deed contains a power of sale.

VIII. Any Additional Satisfaction Permitted Under Continuing Power of Sale:

There is no case law or statute in Vermont on this topic.

IX. Sale by Power of Sale when the Instrument is Silent as to the Place or Terms of Sale:

In the case of non-judicial sale, the statute specifies the procedure but allows the foreclosing party to set the terms and place of sale. In judicial sale, the court establishes terms and place by decree.

X. Notice of Sale and How Notice is Given:

Vermont has a form for the notice of sale that can be altered as circumstances require.

A. Judicial foreclosure: notice to mortgagor by mail; notice to public by legal advertisement.

B. Non-judicial foreclosure: Sixty-day notice served on or mailed to mortgagor, recorded in land records and published three times.

XI. Place and Time for Conducting Foreclosure by Power of Sale:

According to state statute, the sale shall be held on the premises where the real estate is located unless directed by the court or, in the case of non-judicial foreclosure, agreed to in writing by the mortgagor and the mortgagee not less than 60 days or more than 90 days before the sale.

Relevant Codes, Statutes or Case Law:
Title 12 VSA Sec. 4522 – 4533a.

Contributed By: Douglas Riley of Lisman Leckerling, P.C.

Receivership:

I. General Information:

Receivership is a remedy within the Vermont courts' inherent equitable powers. Various statutes provide for the appointment of Receivers by the courts, but none applies specifically to lenders or servicers. The remedy is however clearly available in the secured-lending context.

II. Appointing the Receiver:

A. The Basics:

A court, on its own initiative or upon application of a party to the civil action, may appoint a Receiver.

B. Time Frame for Appointment:

If requested in the complaint that commences the action, the answer is due within 20 days of service; the relief may be granted by default after that if no defense has been pleaded. If the relief is requested by later motion, the response time is 15 days. If a party opposes the relief, a hearing will be necessary, adding up to several weeks to the process.

C. Can you go in Ex Parte?

Vermont courts will hear motions *ex parte* in compelling circumstances only (e.g. a rapidly wasting asset). A lender may take control of an abandoned property as mortgagee in possession without court approval, but it takes certain risks and lacks the powers of a court officer in that case.

III. Loans and Advances:

Yes, there are Vermont statutes governing future advances and various lien priorities.

IV. Sales During the Receivership:

There is no procedure specified by rule or statute in Vermont. The receiver must apply to the Court for permission to sell. However, the receiver may enter into contracts (presumably including sales contracts) regarding the property, but only with court permission.

V. Liens Against Receivership Property:

A receiver takes subject to vested liens.

Existing, perfected liens are undisturbed by receivership. No reported cases deal with post-receivership liens, but Vermont courts generally regard the receiver as standing in the shoes of the legal owner, and therefore subject to that owner's obligations regarding the property.

VI. Owners Associations:

There are no reported Vermont cases on this point. Vermont courts can be expected to adhere to the general principle that the receiver stands in the shoes of the legal owner, with the same privileges and obligations regarding an owners' association.

VII. Construction Related to Receivership Property:

The receiver must apply for and obtain the appointing court's permission to proceed.

VIII. Ending the Receivership:

The court has the power to act on its own, but will ordinarily expect a motion by a party. Decision on the motion will be without a hearing if there is no objection.

Relevant Codes, Statutes or Case Law:
Vermont Rule of Civil Procedure 66; *Munty v. Allen*, 71 Vt. 377 (1899); *Underhill v. Rutland RR Co.*, 90 Vt. 462 (1916); Clifford v. W. Hartford Creamery Co., 103 Vt. 229; 153 A. 205 (1931); Baldwin v. Spear Bros., 79 Vt. 43; 64 A. 235 (1906); Clifford v. W. Hartford Creamery Co., 103 Vt. 229; 153 A. 205 1931).

Virginia

Foreclosure Summary

Security Instrument	Trust Deed / Mortgage
Judicial	Yes
Non-Judicial	Yes
Initial Public Notice	Publication
Time Frame	60 days
Redemption Period	Varies
Deficiency	Yes

Receivership Summary

Ancillary Remedy Necessary	Yes
Ex-Parte	Yes
Approximate Time for Appointment	No Restrictions Given
Who or What can act as Receiver	No Restrictions Given
Specific Receiver Requirements	Must post a bond before performing duties
Is there any approval list for Receivers	No
Out of State Receivers Allowed	Yes

Foreclosure:

I. General Information:

While mortgage instruments are allowed in Virginia, the primary means of obtaining a lien against real estate is the deed of trust. A deed of trust conveys legal title to the real estate to a trustee, in trust, to secure the noteholder's indebtedness. The lender, upon default of the loan and the occurrence of any applicable conditions precedent to foreclosure contained in the deed of trust, can utilize non-judicial foreclosure under the deed of trust to instruct the trustee to sell the property.

II. Judicial Foreclosure Basics:

There is no requirement for judicial foreclosure of deeds of trust. Most frequently, judicial involvement in the foreclosure process under the deed of trust is limited to the review and approval of the trustee's account of sale by the commissioner of accounts. Judges also become involved when an owner or other interested party seeks to enjoin a scheduled foreclosure. Judicial foreclosures principally are used when no power of sale is present in the deed or mortgage.

III. Non-Judicial Foreclosure Basics:

Non-judicial foreclosure is the common way for a lender to address a default on a loan secured by real estate in Virginia. Prior to the trustee taking possession of the property, the trustee must be informed of the default and must be requested by the trust beneficiary to initiate foreclosure. In many situations, a substitute trustee is appointed to perform the actual foreclosure process. Virginia statute requires that trustees and substitute trustees be residents of the Commonwealth. Similarly, corporate trustees must be chartered under the laws of the Commonwealth or the laws of the United States and have their principal office within the Commonwealth.

IV. Guidelines for Power of Sale:

Upon default or violation of any covenant in the deed of trust by the borrower, and after receiving foreclosure instructions from the beneficiary of the deed of trust, the trustee may take possession and sell the property at auction to satisfy the

Contributed By: John G. McJunkin of McKenna Long & Aldridge LLP borrower's debts after expiration of any cure or reinstatement rights provided for by the deed of trust. Such a sale must meet certain minimum notice requirements under Virginia statutory law.

V. Power of Sale Guidelines as Represented in the Security:

By statute, deeds of trust are construed to confer upon the trustee the power to sell in the event of default and request by the beneficiary. A trustee has no vested contract right in the enforcement of the deed of trust.

VI. Foreclosure When Instrument Contains No Power of Sale:

If there is no provision for power of sale in the deed of trust, the lienholders may file a bill of complaint with any court with jurisdiction over the subject property to decree a sale of the property, if they can show that such action will promote their interests and that such sale will not violate the interests of other lienholders. All others claiming an interest or lien on the property shall be named and served as defendants to insure that their interests will not be violated.

If the bill of complaint statutory procedure is not followed, and a trustee sells the property or makes any other conveyance, the subject transfer will be deemed valid after a period of thirty years has lapsed if the transfer is properly recorded and there are no adverse claims during that time.

VII. Any Additional Satisfaction Permitted Under Continuing Power of Sale:

Within six months after the foreclosure sale, the trustee is required to make an account of sale to the commissioner of accounts of the court where the instrument was first recorded. On the account of sale, the trustee should indicate any amount remaining due on the indebtedness after the foreclosure sale. The deficiency amount may be recovered through personal judgment against the debtor. The action on the debt can be brought independent of the foreclosure remedy before the foreclosure is completed.

VIII. Place and Terms for Conducting Foreclosure by Power of Sale:

A. Generally:

The place and terms of sale are determined by the terms of the deed of trust.

B. When Instrument is Silent to Place or Terms:

If the deed of trust does not otherwise provide for a place of sale, the trustee may choose from a list of potential locations. The sale may take place on the premises of the property, in front of the circuit court building or at such other place in the city or county where the property is located, or in the corporate limits of any city surrounded by or immediately bordering the county where the property is located. If the land on which the property sits has been annexed, the sale may also take place in the county where the land was formerly located.

As to the terms of sale, the trustee is given broad discretion with respect to deposit requirements imposed upon bidders, whether to recess the sale or postpone the sale (postponement requires a new advertisement, but not a new notice) and whether to sell on cash or credit terms, absent a contrary provision in the deed of trust. The Virginia Code does not provide requirements for time of sale, but it is a generally accepted practice that the sale should occur during normal business hours.

IX. Notice of Sale and How Notice is Given;

The trustee or the lender shall provide written notice of the foreclosure to six defined parties: the present property owner, any subordinate lienholder holding a note against the property secured by a deed of trust recorded at least 30 days prior to the sale, any assignee of the subordinate lienholder whose assignment was likewise recorded within 30 days prior to the sale, and to the extent that a lien is filed in their favor, any condominium owners' association, any property owners' association, and any proprietary lessees' association. A condominium owners' association, property owners' association, and proprietary lessees' association must have established their note or lien against the deed of trust 30 days before the proposed sale. The notice must include the time, date, and place of the sale, and also certain documentation regarding the appointment of the trustee or substitute trustee. The notice must be delivered to the owner 14 days prior to the sale by certified or registered mail; the other defined parties may receive the notice by ordinary mail at least 14 days prior to the sale. Notice is not required for guarantors or tenants. When written notice is properly issued, it creates a rebuttable presumption that the lienholder has complied with the requirement to provide notice of default contained in the deed of trust.

The trustee or the lender must comply with any specific condition precedents under the Deed of Trust (e.g., notice and providing an opportunity to cure) prior to the noticing the foreclosure sale in order to acquire the right of acceleration. The failure to properly serve notice will not invalidate a foreclosure sale.

X. Advertising Requirements:

The trustee shall place an advertisement in a newspaper having general circulation in the city or county where the property is sold, subject to additional statutory provisions. Among other things, the provisions provide that if the deed of trust is silent to number of newspaper advertisements, then the trustee shall advertise once a week for four successive weeks. Even if the deed of trust addresses this issue, advertisements must be published not less than once per week for two weeks, or once a day for three days. The advertisement must be placed in the section of the newspaper where legal notices appear or where the type of property being sold is generally advertised for sale. Like the notices of sale, the advertisements must include the time, date, and place of sale, along with information regarding the property to be sold. If a trustee fails to comply with the mandatory time periods set forth in the advertisement requirements, the sale of the property is voidable.

Relevant Codes, Statutes or Case Law:

Va. Code § 64.2-1206 (2012); § 64.2-1308; Va. Code § 55-58.1(2); Va. Code § 55-59(7), (9); Va. Code §§ 55-59.1 to -59.4; Va. Code § 55-61.
Paul K. Campsen et al., Basics of Foreclosure Seminar 43 (Virginia CLE 2006).

Mathews v. PHH Mortg. Corp., 283 Va. 723, 730, 724 S.E.2d 196, 1999 (Va. 2012)
Bayview Loan Servicing, LLC v. Simmons, 275 Va. 114, 121, 654 S.E.2d 898, 901 (Va. 2008)
Pollack v. Allen, 266 Va. 118, 122, 581 S.E.2d 198, 200 (Va. 2003)
Gallant v. Deutsche Bank Nat'l Trust Co., 766 F. Supp. 2d 714 (W.D. Va. 2011)

Receivership:

I. General Information:

Virginia has two types of receivers: general receivers and special receivers. A general receiver, who may be the clerk of court, may be appointed by any circuit court. The duty of a general receiver is "to receive, take charge of and hold all moneys paid under any judgment, order or decree of the court, and also to pay out or dispose of same as the court orders or decrees." A special receiver, on the other hand, is appointed based on the necessity of a particular situation. Generally, receivers are appointed to oversee the liquidation or dissolution of an entity.

II. Appointing the Receiver:

A. The Basics:

A party requesting a receiver should set out in its initial pleadings why the appointment is necessary and proper. The requesting party must show some potential for loss or misappropriation of the property. Courts are directed to use great caution in appointing a receiver and should only do so when there is a strong showing of necessity.

B. Time Frame for Appointment:

In normal, non-emergency situations, the court is required to designate the time and place for a hearing on the receivership application, and must provide enough time for "reasonable notice thereof to be given to the defendant, and to all other parties having a substantial interest, either as owners of or lienors of record and lienors known to the plaintiff, in the subject matter." Thus, the time period between filing the application and holding a hearing on the application is court driven. It is incumbent on the party requesting a receiver to provide the court with material information relating to parties having a substantial interest in the subject property.

C. Can You Go in Ex Parte?

Ex parte motions for the appointment of receivers will be granted in emergency situations where the appointment is necessary to preserve the property. The emergency appointment will not last longer than 30 days. During those 30 days, notice must be given to all parties having a substantial interest in the subject matter concerning any request to extend the receivership beyond the emergency period. There is a bond requirement for the applicant to protect and save harmless the owners, lienors and creditors of the subject property.

III. Loans and Advances:

Under Virginia law, a special receiver should first obtain authority from the court to enter into loans or to draw down on loans secured by the subject property.

IV. Sales During the Receivership:

No information provided.

V. Liens Against Receivership Property:

After the appointment of the receiver, all property is sequestered by the court. The receiver, acting on behalf of the court, administers the estate in the best interest and for the protection of all parties in interest.

The appointment of the receiver does not affect vested rights or the order of existing liens.

VI. Owners Associations:

No information provided.

VII. Construction Related to Receivership Property:

No information provided.

VIII. Ending the Receivership:

While there does not appear to be a requirement for a motion to terminate the receivership, the better practice is to make such a motion to clarify the termination of the receivership. Thus, the receivership can end when the receiver's office terminates by necessity, by motion, upon removal by the court, or if the order appointing the receiver is wholly reversed on appeal.

IX. Miscellaneous:

A.

Once appointed, the receiver is required to prepare a list of all of the creditors with an interest in the subject property. This list is then used to notify each of the creditors that a receiver has been appointed. A court shall not order the sale of any assets under receivership until all the creditors on this list have been notified by mailing.

B.

The receiver must provide a bond and security for the faithful discharge of her duties. Likewise, there are provisions for the keeping of accounts and confirmation of this accounting by the court or an appointed commissioner in chancery. The receiver must present an accurate copy of all receipts and disbursements to the commissioner in chancery within four months of distributing the receivership's assets, unless the court provides otherwise.

Relevant Codes, Statutes or Case Law:

Va. Code § 8.01-582 (2012), Va. Code § 8.01-588, §§ 8.01-591 to -599, § 8.01-617
C.F. Trust, Inc. v. First Flight LP, 140 F. Supp. 2d 628 (E.D. Va. 2001).
S. W. Rawls, Inc. v. Forrest, 224 Va. 264, 295 S.E.2d 791 (1982).
15 Michie's Jurisprudence of Virginia and West Virginia, Receivers (1998 & Supp. 2007).

Washington

Foreclosure Summary

Security Instrument	Deed of Trust
Judicial	Yes
Non-Judicial	Yes
Initial Public Notice	Notice of Trustee's Sale
Time Frame	Typically 120 days
Redemption Period	None
Deficiency	Yes

Receivership Summary

Ancillary Remedy Necessary	Yes
Ex-Parte	Yes
Approximate Time for Appointment	7-10 days
Who or What can act as Receiver	Individual of Corporation
Specific Receiver Requirements	No Restrictions Given
Is there any approval list for Receivers	No
Out of State Receivers Allowed	Yes

Foreclosure:

I. General Information:

Washington is a "lien-theory" state. In Washington, mortgages and deeds of trust do not convey title or possession to the holder. These instruments are securities that create a lien on the property they encumber. Once recorded, these instruments preserve a holder's priority over all unrecorded and all other subsequently recorded liens, deeds of trust and mortgages. To this end, these instruments secure the payment of a debt or performance of some other obligation that can be reduced to a money judgment. Where a debtor defaults on his, hers or its obligation secured by one of these instruments, a creditor may seek to enforce his, hers or its rights as a substitute for performance by foreclosure and sale as permitted law.

II. Judicial Foreclosure Basics:

All foreclosures in Washington are governed by statute. Chapter 61.12 of the Washington Code Revised ("Wash. Rev. Code" or RCW") provides the primary source of substantive law applicable to judicial foreclosure proceedings. The remedy of foreclosure is limited to the property mortgaged in the absence of any agreement to the contrary.

A judicial foreclosure action commences with the filing of a complaint in the superior court. Upon filing, a mortgagee may record a *lis pendens* in the county auditor's office where the subject property, or a part of it, is located. Any defendant who defaults forfeits the opportunity to contest the foreclosure action on its merits. Following the entry of a default, the plaintiff mortgagee may move for an order and subsequently a default judgment, which will negatively affect that non-appearing party's legal rights.

Once a plaintiff mortgagee obtains a final judgment and sale order, he, she or it becomes a judgment creditor. The judgment creditor may then proceed to execute on the judgment and sale order. The documents are transmitted to the sheriff of the county where the property or a part of it is located, who conducts an auction sale of the mortgaged property. Subject to any redemption rights, the sheriff provides a certificate of sale to the successful bidder at the auction. The successful bidder must then seek judicial confirmation of that sale. Following confirmation and the expiration of any applicable redemption period, the sheriff conducting the auction will issue a "Sheriff's Deed" to the successful bidder.

III. Non-Judicial Foreclosure Basics:

RCW Chapter 61.24 provides the primary source of substantive law applicable to "non-judicial" foreclosures of statutory deeds of trust. To obtain priority and to facilitate any foreclosure rights, a deed of trust must be recorded in each county where the land secured is located.

A non-judicial foreclosure commences with a default in an obligation embodied within a recorded deed of trust, containing a valid power to sale pertaining to land that is not used principally for agricultural or farming purposes.

IV. Guidelines for Power of Sale:

Judicial foreclosure is the exclusive method of foreclosing upon a straight mortgage. Statutory deeds of trust, containing a power of sale, may be foreclosed upon non-judicially through a trustee's sale or, alternatively, through the judicial foreclosure process.

A default by the grantor or the grantor's assignee is a prerequisite to the non-judicial foreclosure process. That default renders the trust deed's power of sale operative.

A. Notice of Default:

Following that default, the beneficiary or trustee will prepare and serve a Notice of Default upon the grantor or the grantor's assignee. Once service of the Notice of Default is completed, the grantor or the grantor's assignee has thirty ("30") days to cure the default. The Notice of Default must disclose the sums necessary to "cure" the default.

B. No Concurrent Debt Recovery Actions:
Similar to mortgage law principles, no beneficiary may maintain any separate action to satisfy any obligation secured by a deed of trust. This provision, however, does not apply to any action to enforce other liens or other security interests on commercial property, secured by a deed of trust. Neither does it apply to actions to appoint a receiver.

C. Notice of Sale/Notice of Foreclosure:
If the debtor fails to cure the identified default, the beneficiary may take the next step in the process (1) "Notice of Trustee's Sale" and (2) "Notice of Foreclosure" Delivery of these notices must occur at least 90 days prior to the sale date. Unlike the Notice of Trustee's Sale, which is delivered to multiple parties, the Notice of Foreclosure is only served upon the grantor and borrower.

D. Date of Foreclosure Sale:
At its earliest, a trustee's sale may not occur any earlier than 190 days from the date of default, as identified in the earlier served Notice of Default.

E. Cure of Default Prior to Trustee's Sale:
After delivery of the Notice of Trustee's Sale, any eligible person may halt or discontinue the trustee's sale by curing the default up eleven (11) days before the sale. Persons eligible to cure the default include: (a) the grantor or the grantor's assignee; (b) the beneficiary of any subordinate deed of trust; or (c) the holder of any subordinate lien, mortgage or other recorded encumbrance. This cure includes paying the trustee the entire amount then due, excluding any accelerated portion of the debt, as well as the trustee's actual expenses and attorneys' fees.

F. Stays of Sale Proceedings:
A trustee's sale may be stayed by an order from a U.S. Bankruptcy Court, or an order from a state superior court. A Washington superior court may similarly issue a stay order to temporarily halt a trustee's sale.

G. Purchaser's Interest at the Trustee's Sale:
As the successful bidder, the purchaser must forthwith pay the purchase price to the trustee. The trustee then provides the purchaser a deed, which while without warranties, recites the pertinent facts pertaining to the Notice of Trustee's Sale and that the sale was conducted in accord with the statute. The trustee's deed will not cut off the interest of any individual or entity to which the trustee did not provide notice of the sale. The successful bidder is entitled to possession of the property purchased within twenty ("20") days after the trustee's sale and the payment of purchase price. Following the twentieth ("20th") day after a foreclosure sale, the purchaser has the right to evict the grantor and any occupants claiming through him by commencing unlawful detainer proceedings.

H. Distribution of Proceeds from the Trustee's Sale:
Washington's non-judicial foreclosure statutes provide the framework for the distribution of proceeds from the trustee's sale. Following receipt of payment from the successful bidder, the proceeds are paid to cover the sale's expense. Next in the statutory framework, the sale proceeds are used to satisfy the obligation secured by the deed of trust. After these obligations are satisfied, any remaining funds are "surplus." The trustee deposits the surplus with the clerk of the superior court for the county where the property is located, together with copies of the notices that the trustee earlier prepared and served on all interested parties. This act is somewhat analogous to an interpleaded action. The trustee serves notice of the deposit upon all interested parties, the deposit is indexed on the records of the court and the trustee receives a discharge from the court. This discharge terminates the trustee's responsibilities for the surplus. Any person or entity claiming an interest in the surplus may then file a noticed motion with evidentiary support for its claim to the surplus.

I. Setting Aside the Trustee's Sale:
Some parties may present post-sale challenges to "set aside" the trustee's sale.

V. Power of Sale Guidelines as Represented in the Security:

Deeds of trust are a relatively recent creation of law in Washington and have existed in statutory form since 1965. Upon an obligor's default and consistent with statute, a trustee has power to foreclose upon the encumbered real property by a nonjudicial sale.

VI. Guidelines for Foreclosure when there is No Power of Sale:

See section below.

VII. Foreclosure When Instrument Contains No Power of Sale:

Judicial foreclosure actions are subject to the same rules of civil procedure applicable to all other civil lawsuits. Unlike other civil actions, however, a mortgagee as a foreclosure plaintiff cannot concurrently prosecute any other action on the same obligation.

A. Mortgage Default:

A mortgagee may commence a judicial foreclosure action only upon a mortgagor's default in the performance of any condition contained in a mortgage.

B. Action Commencement:

A judicial foreclosure action is commenced by filing an action in the County Superior Court where the land or portion of that land is located.

C. Parties to Action:

To the extent possible, the complaint initiating the foreclosure action should name all parties necessary to afford complete relief to the mortgagee.

D. Service of Process:

Following service of process, the named defendants must appear and respond to the complaint within 20 days.

E. Stay of Foreclosure Proceedings:

A plaintiff mortgagee should also be aware that any party to a judicial foreclosure action retains the power to stay foreclosure proceedings, both before and after entry of judgment.

F. Acceleration:

Judicial foreclosures preserve the benefits of any acceleration clause contained within a mortgage document. However, the provisions of RCW § 61.12.130 do not apply where a default triggers the acceleration of all subsequent mortgage installment payments. Where an existing acceleration clause is triggered upon a mortgagor's default, Washington's common law requires that the mortgagee must provide clear and unequivocal written notice of the acceleration.

G. Concurrent Actions and Alternative Remedies:

Foreclosure proceedings are prohibited where a mortgagee is concurrently pursuing any other action for the same debt or matter secured by the mortgage in question.

H. Deficiency Claims:

Deficiency judgments are enforced in the same manner as any other money judgment, after the foreclosure sale. However, that right may be waived if the mortgagee's complaint does not specifically seek a deficiency judgment.

I. Judgment:

In ordering that sale the court may also, upon application, determine a minimum price below which the sale may not be made or confirmed. The foreclosure judgment should also state whether a deficiency will be allowed and define any redemption period. The judgment should also declare whether the property should be sold as a whole or in parcels.

J. Foreclosure Sale - In General:

After the mortgagee successfully obtains a judgment through motion or trial, the mortgagee becomes a judgment creditor. As such, they must prepare a proposed written order, which if entered, directs the Clerk of the Superior Court to issue an order of sale and specifies the contents of that order. After the five (5) day appeal period expires the clerk issues the order of sale, which serves as a writ of execution. The order of sale is valid for a period of sixty ("60") days. Following the receipt of whatever additional fees, bonds or instructions the individual county may require, the sheriff sets in motion the procedure to conduct a foreclosure sale.

K. Post Judgment Payments:

Even after entry of a foreclosure judgment, at any time before a court-ordered sale, any party may satisfy the judgment by the payment of the mortgage debt, together with interest and costs accrued.

L. Conduct of Sale:

Such sales are made by the sheriff, at public auction occurring during regular business hours, at the front door of the courthouse in the county where the property is located. The sheriff sells the property to the highest bidder. --The county sheriff is empowered with the discretion to postpone auction sales. The auction may be postponed in one-week increments, where the sheriff deems that there are too few bidders present or for other sufficient reason. With written consent of the plaintiff, now judgment creditor, the sheriff may also postpone the sale from time to time, not to exceed 30-days.

Prior to conducting the sale, a written notice must also be provided to various individuals and correspondingly posted on the subject property. Both the judgment creditor and the county sheriff have separate notice obligations. Four weeks prior to the sale, the sheriff must post at least two notices- One on the courthouse door where the property will be sold, and the other is to be posted on the property to be sold. The sheriff must also publish notice of the forthcoming sale in a qualified newspaper, designated by the judgment creditor, once a week, for a four week period prior to the sale.

M. Terms of Sale:

Upon application by the judgment creditor and following a hearing on that application, the court in ordering the sale may set a minimum or upset price to which the mortgaged premises must be bid or sold. Sale terms may additionally be set subsequent to the sale, where a court has not previously set a minimum or upset price. If the court's fair value, when applied to the mortgage debt, discharges it, a judgment creditor may not receive a deficiency judgment.

N. Report of Sale:

Following the sale, tender of the purchase price and all applicable fees, the sheriff delivers a certificate of sale to the successful purchaser, with a copy to court clerk. The certificate describes the sale particulars, including the bid price and the property description. The clerk of the court issuing the judgment enters a record of the sale and provides notice of the sale to all parties appearing. A successful bidder is entitled to receive an order confirming the sale and commencing the running of the redemption period from the date of the sale. After a 20-day waiting period following the mailing of sale notice, the successful bidder may file motion requesting an order confirming the sale. Any objections to confirmation must be filed and served within the 20-day period following the clerk's sale notice. Following a hearing on the requested confirmation, if the court determines that no irregularities occurred in connection with the sale, the court will confirm the sale.

O. Redemption:

After the sale, Washington law affords eligible persons a limited period of time to redeem the property from the purchaser. Only two groups have redemption rights. Group One consists of the borrower and his, her or its assignee. Group Two consists of "redemptioners," who are creditors who have a legally recognizable interest in the subject property, or their assignees, who hold liens subsequent in priority to that being foreclosed.
During this period, the purchaser or any subsequent redemptioner is entitled to possession.

P. Conveyance:

After the applicable redemption period expires, a successful bidder receives a "sheriff's deed." Once the sheriff's deed is delivered and recorded, the judicial foreclosure process is complete.

Q. Satisfaction of Deficiency Judgment:

The successful bid amount or "upset price" (if an "upset price" was established in the judgment), is subtracted from the total judgment, yielding the amount of the deficiency. --Once a deficiency is established, the balance due may be satisfied from any property of the judgment debtor. In this regard, satisfaction of a deficiency judgment is similar in all respects to the recovery of any judgment.

R. Disposition of Proceeds of Sale:

Sale proceeds are paid to the judgment creditor on the principal, interest and costs due on the judgment.

S. Surplus Money Proceedings:

If there is any surplus following satisfaction of the foreclosed mortgage debt and the properly adjudicated debt of junior encumbrances, the judgment debtor is entitled to any surplus.

VIII. Any Additional Satisfaction Permitted Under Continuing Power of Sale:

A trustee's non-judicial foreclosure satisfies the obligation secured by the deed of trust. No deficiency decree or other judgment may be obtained on that obligation. The "no deficiency" rule does not appear to preclude a creditor from concurrently pursuing other separate security given for obligation, such as a surety or personal guaranty. However, to avoid issues pertaining to the "no deficiency" rule, creditors should consider pursuing alternative remedies against sureties or personal guarantors, prior to exercising any non-judicial foreclosure.

IX. Sale by Power of Sale when the Instrument is Silent as to the Place or Terms of Sale:

Under Washington law, the Notice of Trustee's Sale must disclose the location of the sale. The trustee is free to sell the property in gross or in parcels as he, she or it may deem the most advantageous. Though the trustee's sale is a non-judicial foreclosure, it is a public auction sale to the highest bidder. However, the trustee may not bid at the auction.

X. Notice of Sale and How Notice is Given:

See section above.

XI. Place and Time for Conducting Foreclosure by Power of Sale:

The date for the trustee's sale must be on a Friday; and if that date is a legal holiday, then the date will default to the following Monday. The sale must occur between the hours of 9:00 a.m. and 4:00 p.m. Moreover, while the trustee's sale is non-judicial, it is considered a "public" sale and accordingly must be held in any public place in the county where the property is located.

Relevant Codes, Statutes or Case Law:
Chapter 61.12 RCW & RCW § 61.24.040
American Federal Savings and Loan v. McCaffrey, 107 Wash. 2d at 181, 728 P. 2d at 155. Ameresco Independence Funding, Inc. v. SPS Properties, LLC, 129 Wash. App. 532, 119 P. 3d 884 (2005). Beal Bank, SSB v. Sarich, 161 Wash. 2d 544, 167 P. 3d 555 (2007). Cox v. Helenius, 103 Wash. 2d 383, 693 P. 2d 683 (1985), Donovick v. Seattle-First National Bank, 111 Wash. 2d 413, 757 P. 2d 1378 (1988). Koegel v. Prudential Mut. Savings Bank, 51 Wash. App. 108, 752 P. 2d 385 (1988). People's National Bank v. Ostrander 6. Wash. App. 28, 491 P. 2d 1058 (1971). Seattle Medical Center v. Cameo Corporation, 54 Wash. 2d 188, 194-195, 339 P. 2d 93, 97-98 (1959). Steward v. Good, 51 Wash. App. 509, 754 P. 2d 150 (1988); Washington Mutual Savings Bank v. United States, 115 Wash. 2d 52, 58, 793 P. 2d 969, 972, as clarified by 800 P. 2d 1124 (1990).

Receivership:

I. General Information:

Receivership law is a vital part of Washington jurisprudence. In 2004 the Washington legislature repealed all prior state statutes regarding receiverships. In their place, it enacted a new comprehensive set of receivership statutes to create a more streamlined and cost-effective set of procedures applicable to proceedings in which the property of a person is administered by Washington courts for the benefit of creditors and persons having an interest in that property.

Washington's all-embracing statutory scheme covers the field of receivership topics ranging from, but not limited to, the appointment of receivers, receiver bonds, reports, powers, duties, automatic stays, utility service, financing, personal liability, receiver's actions, claim allowance and rejection, priorities, property dispositions, interest on claims and receivership terminations.

Under Washington law, the appointment of a receiver is a provisional remedy. Receivers cannot be appointed unless the court determines that the appointment is reasonably necessary and that the applicant's legal remedies are either inadequate or unavailable. Receiverships are uniquely suited to function in a wide ranging set of case scenarios, including where a lender has commenced a foreclosure (judicial or non-judicial) and finds that the appointment of a receiver is necessary to collect rents and profits, or to preserve a real property asset from the immediate danger of dissipation, loss, damage or destruction resulting from the actions of others.

Washington law recognizes two independent authoritative bases for the appointment of a receiver, namely: appointment by contractual right, for example, arising out of a mortgage, deed of trust or assignment; and, alternatively, the appointment by right of statute.

II. Appointing the Receiver:

A. The Basics:

As a predicate to the presentation of a valid application for the appointment of a receiver, the applicant must possess an interest in the subject property in dispute. The application may take the form of a noticed motion, or an *ex parte* application with a corresponding application for an order to show cause.

In addition to the written notice, which will be provided to the subject property's owner and all parties to the action, an applicant's moving papers should contain a memorandum of points and authorities, a proposed order and supporting affidavits setting forth factual matters, including: (1) facts demonstrating the court's jurisdiction over the property; (2) the basis for the moving party's probable right or interest in the subject property; (3) that the subject property is in the possession of an adverse party; and (4) that the subject property or its income-producing potential is in danger of being lost or materially injured or impaired. The moving party's supporting affidavits should also demonstrate that the receiver's appointment is reasonably necessary and that any other remedy is inadequate or not available.

In preparing an appointment application, consideration should be given whether the retention of professionals such as outside counsel will be necessary. Court approval is required before a receiver may retain any professional to assist him or her. If it is known at the outset that legal counsel will be required, for example, the application for appointment of a receiver should state this fact, identify the qualifying professional sought to be retained, identifying the facts pertaining to the proposed retention, including the fees charged by the professional, and request specific authority to retain the professional identified.

Where the request for the appointment of a receiver is to be made in connection with the filing of a lawsuit, the facts supporting the appointment of a receiver should be set forth in the body of the proposed complaint. This document should be concurrently filed with the receiver appointment application. Among the relevant facts to be included in the proposed complaint are the bases for the appointment, whether statutory or contractual. If contractual, then the proposed complaint should also identify the specific contractual right, together with a description of those documents containing that right. If no such contractual right exists, then the complaint should describe those facts demonstrating the applicant's right to the appointment of a receiver. The proposed complaint should also include in the prayer for relief a request for the appointment of a receiver and an articulation of the appropriate powers sought for the receiver, as well as a description of the property over which the receiver is to take charge.

B. Time Frame for Appointment:

The time for the appointment of a receiver is roughly the same via a noticed motion and a request for an order to show cause, which is minimally 7 days, with additional time added if service is affected by mail. That minimum time period, however, may be adjusted depending upon the calendar constraints of the individual court assigned to hear the application for the appointment of the receiver. The minimum time period, may also be enlarged or expanded upon good cause shown by an opponent of the application.

C. Can you go in Ex Parte?

While an application for the appointment of a receiver is generally made on notice, Washington courts are empowered by statute to appoint a receiver on *ex parte* application. However, while a court may on *ex parte* application appoint a receiver where an emergency is shown, any appointment under such circumstances is temporary. The moving party will need to return to the court for an order confirming the receiver.

III. Loans and Advances:

Washington receivership law contemplates that receivers may seek two types of financing in relation to the receivership estate. In the ordinary course of business, receivers are authorized to seek without leave of court, unsecured credit and incur unsecured debt to operate the business as an administrative expense of the receiver. For indebtedness other than in the ordinary course of business, after notice to all interested persons and a hearing on the matter, the court may allow the receiver to mortgage, pledge, hypothecate or otherwise encumber receivership property for the repayment of any indebtedness that the receiver may incur.

IV. Sales During the Receivership:

No information provided.

V. Liens Against Receivership Property:

No information provided.

VI. Owners Associations:

No information provided.

VII. Construction Related to Receivership Property:

No information provided.

VIII. Ending the Receivership:

Receiverships in Washington may only be terminated upon noticed motion. This rule applies to all scenarios, be it a motion by an interested party to remove and/or replace a receiver, or the court's own motion to remove and/or replace the receiver. Termination may proceed upon the distribution or disposition of all receivership property, of the completion of receiver's duties with respect to the estate.

Relevant Codes, Statutes or Case Law:

Washington Laws, 2004 c. 165 § 1. , Wash. Rev. Code § 7.60.005. RCW 7.60.015 RCW 7.60.025, RCW 7.60.035, RCW 7.60.045, RCW 7.60.055, RCW 7.60.060, RCW 7.60.070, RCW 7.60.080, RCW 7.60.090, RCW 7.60.100, RCW 7.60.110, RCW 7.60.120, RCW 7.60.130, RCW 7.60.140, RCW 7.60.150, RCW 7.60.160, RCW 7.60.170, RCW 7.60.180, RCW 7.60.190, RCW 7.60.200, RCW 7.60.210, RCW 7.60.220, RCW 7.60.230, RCW 7.60.240, RCW 7.60.250, RCW 7.60.260, RCW 7.60.270, RCW 7.60.280, RCW 7.60.290, RCW 7.60.300,

West Virginia

Foreclosure Summary

Security Instrument	Deed of Trust, Mortgage
Judicial	Yes (uncommon)
Non-Judicial	Yes
Initial Public Notice	At least 20 days
Time Frame	Typically 60 days
Redemption Period	No
Deficiency	No

Receivership Summary

Ancillary Remedy Necessary	Yes
Ex-Parte	No Restrictions Given
Approximate Time for Appointment	No Restrictions Given
Who or What can act as Receiver	No Restrictions Given
Specific Receiver Requirements	No
Is there any approval list for Receivers	No
Out of State Receivers Allowed	Yes

Foreclosure:

I. General Information:

West Virginia allows for both judicial and non-judicial foreclosure, but non-judicial foreclosure is more common.

II. Judicial Foreclosure Basics:

A judicial foreclosure is a lawsuit which is commenced with the…? A judicial foreclosure is initiated by filing a complaint for defaulting on the loan. Before the lender may proceed with foreclosure, the court has to confirm the default and issue an order at which time the property is sold by public auction.

Judicial foreclosure is only used when the underlying loan documents do not include a "Power of Sale" clause, pursuant (may want to use different word) to which a lender is entitled to pursue non-judicial foreclosure.

III. Non-Judicial Foreclosure Basics:

If the underlying loan documents include a "Power of Sale" clause, the lender is authorized to sell the property, pursuant to an event of default, out of court.

IV. Guidelines for Power of Sale:

Power of sale foreclosure guidelines follow terms of deed of trust.

V. Power of Sale Guidelines as Represented in the Security:

If no terms are prescribed in the deed of trust, the following guidelines apply:

A. A Notice of Sale must be served on the borrower and all lien holders at least 20 days before the sale. The Notice of Sale must also be posted at the courthouse in the county where the property is located, at the property and two other public places in the same county. The notice must contain

1. the date, time and place of the sale;
2. parties to the deed;
3. date the deed was signed and recording information;

Contributed By: Christopher P. Schueller
of Buchanan Ingersoll & Rooney PC

4. property description;
5. terms of the foreclosure sale

B. The Notice of Sale must be advertised in the newspaper once a week for at least four weeks prior to the sale.

C. The sale must take place at the time listed in the notice. Winning bidder has to pay 1/3 of his bid in cash at the time of the sale, unless the deed of trust specifies otherwise, 1/3 (with interest) within the first year after the date of sale and the remainder (with interest) within two years of the date of sale.

VI. Foreclosure When Instrument Contains No Power of Sale:

If there is no power of sale, then the lender must follow judicial foreclosure procedures.

VII. Any Additional Satisfaction Permitted Under Continuing Power of Sale:

West Virginia does not permit a lender to file for deficiency claims.

VIII. Notice of Sale and How Notice is Given:

Under West Virginia Code 38-1-4, the Notice of Sale must contain:

A. the date, time and place of the sale;
B. parties to the deed;
C. date the deed was signed and recording information;
D. property description;
E. terms of the foreclosure sale

Notice of sale must be served on the borrower and all lien holders at least 10 days before the sale date by certified mail, return receipt requested. Notice of sale must also be posted at the courthouse located in the county where the property sits, at the property and at two other public places in the county.

Notice of Sale must also be advertised once a week for at least four weeks prior to the sale. This is repetitive… all items are already listed above.

IV. Place and Time for Conducting Foreclosure by Power of Sale:

Public auction is scheduled by the lender or the trustee authorized to conduct the sale.

Relevant Codes, Statutes or Case Law:
West Virginia Code Chapter 38 Section 1 (Trust Deed Liens)

Receivership:

I. General information:

West Virginia permits the appointment of a real estate Receiver pursuant to West Virginia Code §53-6-1 by a court of equity in a pending case upon a showing that there is a danger of loss or misappropriation of the subject property, including any rents or profits to which Mortgagee may be entitled. The petitioner must show a clear right to the property or a lien on such property, i.e. must be secured.

II. Appointing the Receiver:

A. The Basics:

A Mortgagee must file an application for appointment of Receiver with the court. West Virginia requires that the borrower/Mortgagor receive notice of the application.

The application must contain a specific prayer that a receiver be appointed.

B. Time Frame for Appointment:

No information provided.

C. Can you go in Ex Parte?

No information provided

III. Loans and Advances:

Yes, with court approval.

Contributed By: Christopher P. Schueller
of Buchanan Ingersoll & Rooney PC

IV. Sales During the Receivership:

The court may appoint a receiver and direct the sale of the property.

V. Liens Against Receivership Property:

Not applicable.

VI. Owners Associations:

Unknown.

VII. Construction Related to Receivership Property:

Yes, with court approval.

VIII. Ending the Receivership:

A Mortgagee is required to obtain an order terminating the receivership.

Relevant Codes, Statutes or Case Law:
West Virginia Code Section 53-6-1

Wisconsin

Foreclosure Summary

Security Instrument	Mortgage/ Trust Deed
Judicial	Yes
Non-Judicial	No
Initial Public Notice	Complaint
Time Frame	Varies (90 days - 12 months)
Redemption Period	Yes, but it would be considered a Cure Period in other states
Deficiency	Yes, unless waived

Receivership Summary

Ancillary Remedy Necessary	Yes
Ex-Parte	Court's Discretion
Approximate Time for Appointment	10-21 days unless expedited
Who or What can act as Receiver	Company or Individual
Specific Receiver Requirements	Generally required to post Bond but this can be waived
Is there any approval list for Receivers	No
Out of State Receivers Allowed	Yes

Foreclosure:

I. General Information:

A non-judicial, power of sale, foreclosure action has been statutorily abolished. Judicial foreclosure is available with respect to either monetary or non-monetary defaults.

II. Judicial Foreclosure Basics:

A judicial foreclosure action is commenced in a Circuit Court for the County in which the real property is located. Prior to commencing suit, a title report or foreclosure title policy is obtained to determine what junior liens, if any, are filed against the property so that those lien claimants may be named as parties in order to clear title. Most foreclosures proceed on a default basis following expiration of a 20-day period for answering the complaint. Default foreclosure hearings may be held "on affidavit", i.e., without formal hearing, depending on each Circuit Court's practices. Where a commercial property is generating rents (e.g., apartment buildings, shopping centers), a Receiver may be appointed to collect the rents and manage the property.

Upon entry of foreclosure judgment, a statutory redemption period begins to run, the length of which is determined by the type of property. A foreclosure sale cannot be held until the redemption period has expired. For example, commercial properties have a 6-month redemption period, while single-family residential properties have a 12-month redemption period. In either case, if the parties expressly so elect in the mortgage, the mortgage holder may shorten the redemption period by one half if it waives any deficiency claim against the borrower. That election is made by an allegation in the complaint, and is quite common, especially where the borrower/mortgagor has no other assets. There is a two month redemption period if the mortgage holder can demonstrate that the property has been "abandoned" within the meaning of the statute. Note that Wisconsin foreclosure procedure differs from that in some other states where the redemption period begins to run after the sale is held.

A Notice of Foreclosure Sale must be published in a local newspaper for six consecutive weeks and the publication may commence within two months prior to the expiration of the redemption period. The notice of foreclosure sale is also posted in public places, locally, by the county Sheriff.

A foreclosure sale is conducted by a Sheriff's Deputy and the mortgage holder is usually permitted to enter a bid by mail. If a deficiency is waived, the mortgage holder frequently bids the full amount owing. A third party bidder is required to deposit 10% of the bid in cash at the sale. The foreclosing creditor is typically the only bidder at the foreclosure sale and may credit bid some or all of the amount owing.

Transfer of title is by Sheriff's Deed following confirmation of the foreclosure sale by the Court, which typically occurs ten days to two weeks after sale, and upon notice to the parties. In addition to confirming the sale, the confirmation order may award a deficiency judgment, if that claim is reserved, and approve a Receiver's Report and discharge the Receiver.

The Court may confirm a foreclosure sale if it determines that the bid was for "fair value." This value is determined usually with reference to appraisals (if available), tax assessment information, or realtor estimates of value, or a combination. The standard is not "fair market value" since the Court considers that the property is being liquidated in a forced sale where prices are usually depressed from what the fair market value might otherwise be. As a rule of thumb, bids within 70% of a relatively current "fair market" appraisal will be confirmed. If a third party is a successful bidder, it is required to pay the balance of the amount bid within 10 days of confirmation of sale, failing which, the deposit is forfeited and another sale is scheduled following with new publication and posting of the Notice.

If the Court refuses to confirm the sale, it has the options of requiring a new sale, or setting an amount that it determines to be "fair value" which would be credited against the loan secured by the mortgage.

III. Non-Judicial Foreclosure Basics:

Wisconsin does not allow for non-judicial foreclosures.

Receivership:

I. General information:

Receivers may be appointed under a variety of circumstances and under several different sections of the Wisconsin Statutes. A "Supplementary Receiver" may be appointed in connection with enforcing remedies supplementary to execution. Unlike the § 813.16 Receiver and the Chapter 128 Receiver, a § 816.04 Receiver may be appointed by a judicial court commissioner rather than a judge.

The § 813.16 Receiver is typically appointed where there is an interest in property and the property or its rents and profits are in danger of being lost or materially impaired (e.g., in a foreclosure context).

Other grounds include an appointment by or after a judgment to carry it into effect or to dispose of property according to the judgment, or when a corporation has been dissolved or is insolvent or in imminent danger of insolvency, or has forfeited its corporate rights.

A Chap. 128 Receiver may be appointed involuntarily, in a proceeding commenced under Chapter 128, Wis. Stats. (entitled "Creditors' Actions"). Grounds for appointment include when an execution against a judgment debtor is returned unsatisfied in whole or in part, or when a corporation has been dissolved or is insolvent or is in imminent danger of insolvency, or has forfeited its corporate rights.

II. Appointing the Receiver:

A. The Basics:

A Receiver can only be appointed upon motion. A motion for appointment of a Receiver may be sought on an expedited basis and there is no specific outside deadline for having a Receiver appointed. A motion for appointment of a Receiver is typically filed immediately following the filing of the complaint.

B. Time Frame for Appointment:

The time period between filing a motion for appointment of a Receiver and obtaining an Order, generally depends on the calendar of the judge to whom the case is assigned. If the motion is to be heard on less than seven days' notice, evidence must be presented to the Court, usually in affidavit form, justifying expedited treatment (e.g., the property is in immediate danger of loss or other dissipation). In the absence of a showing of urgency, a hearing may typically be held within ten days to three weeks of filing.

C. Can you go in Ex Parte?

There is no express prohibition against the *ex parte* appointment of a Receiver, however most courts will require some type of notice to the opposing parties, even where a motion is to be heard on an expedited basis.

III. Loans and Advances:

No statutes or rules govern loans or advances, and the Order of Appointment will govern the receiver's authority to obtain loans or to issue advances.

IV. Sales During the Receivership:

A Chapter 128 Receiver must get permission from the Court approving sales of property. A § 813.16 Receiver must obtain similar permission. In virtually all types of receivership in Wisconsin, the Receiver must apply to the court and obtain authorization to sell property.

V. Liens Against Receivership Property:

Liens are dealt with based on priority irrespective of whether a receivership is in place. A Receiver is subject to prior liens. A Chapter 128 Receiver has the power to avoid liens as preferential transfers.

VI. Owners Associations:

This issue has not been dealt with in any reportable fashion and there are no statutes relating to the issue.

VII. Construction Related to Receivership Property:

A Receiver would have to get permission from the court to complete construction, usually in the order appointing the Receiver.

VIII. Ending the Receivership:

A Receiver can be discharged only upon motion and hearing, unless by stipulation of opposing parties, following submission of the Receiver's final account.

Relevant Codes, Statutes or Case Law:
§ 128.08, Wis. Stats; § 813.16, Wis. Stats; § 816.04, Wis. Stats.

American Medical Services Inc. v. Mutual Federal Savings & Loan Assn., 52 Wis. 2d 198, 188 N.W.2d 529 (1971); Community National Bank v. Medical Benefit Administration, 242 Wis. 2d 626, 626 N.W.2d 340, (Ct. App. 2001)
Chapter 128 Wis. Stats; Northridge Bank v. Community Eye Care Center, 91 Wis. 2d 298, 282 N.W.2d 632, (Ct. App. 1979); Wisconsin Brick and Block Corp v. Vogel, 54 Wis. 2d 321, 195 N.W.2d 664 (1972)

Wyoming

Foreclosure Summary

Security Instrument	Mortgage
Judicial	Yes
Non-Judicial	Yes
Initial Public Notice	Complaint/Publication
Time Frame (non-judicial)	180 days
Debtor's Redemption Period	3 months or 12 months depending on property size and location
Deficiency	Yes

Receivership Summary

Ex-Parte	No
Approximate Time from for Appointment	30-60 days
Who or What can act as Receiver	Individual or Company
Specific Receiver Requirements	Must swear an oath, post bond, and publish notice of appointment
Is there any approval list for Receivers	No
Out of State Receivers Allowed	Yes

Foreclosure Section:

I. General information

Wyoming is a lien theory state. Title to the property is deemed to remain with the mortgagor. The mortgagee only has a lien on the property and has no interest in the title. The mortgagee only has a right to foreclose in the event of a default. Wyoming's lien theory is a creation of the Wyoming Supreme Court.

A mortgage must be recorded in the office of the registrar of deeds (county clerk) in the county where the property is located. Wyoming is a race-notice state. The effect is that a properly recorded mortgage is constructive notice to any and all third parties, and such mortgage takes precedence over any subsequent purchaser, mortgagee, or lien claimant. An unrecorded mortgage is void as to a subsequent good-faith purchaser who gives valuable consideration, whose conveyance shall be first duly recorded. The burden of proving good faith and valuable consideration is on the purchaser of the property.

It is a prerequisite to foreclosure that when a mortgage has been assigned to a third party, that foreclosing third party must have a recorded assignment. It is important to note that the recording of the assignment of a mortgage, shall not in itself, be deemed notice of such assignment to the mortgagor, his heirs or personal representatives, so as to invalidate any payment made by them or either of them to the mortgagee.

If the mortgaged premises consist of distinct tracts or lots, the foreclosing mortgagee may sale the distinct tracts or lots as a whole, or the foreclosing mortgagee may offer for sale separately sufficient tracts or lots necessary to satisfy the amount due on the mortgage on the date of the notice of sale.

Contributed by: Lindsay A. Woznick and
Ronald J. Lopez
Hirst Applegate, LLP

A judicial or nonjudicial foreclosure sale may be rescinded at any time after the sale, but before the sheriff's deed has been recorded. If the purchaser at the foreclosure sale was the foreclosing mortgagee, then the foreclosing mortgagee may rescind the sale for any reason by executing and recording a notice of foreclosure sale rescission in the office of the county clerk of the county where the real estate is located. Similarly, if the purchaser at the foreclosure sale was not the foreclosing mortgagee, then the foreclosing mortgagee and the certificate holder (the party holding the certificate of sale) may agree to rescind the foreclosure sale for any reason. The foreclosing mortgagee must refund to the certificate holder either an amount agreed upon, or the foreclosure sale bid amount, plus ten (10%) per annum. A notice of rescission, signed by the foreclosing mortgagee and the certificate holder, must be recorded in the office of the county clerk of the county where the real estate is located. Should the purchaser at the foreclosure sale be a party other than the foreclosing mortgagee, and the certificate holder does not agree to rescind the sale, the foreclosing mortgagee may still rescind the foreclosure sale if the foreclosure sale did not comply with the applicable federal or state law. In such an instance, a refund of the certificate holder's bid amount, plus interest, is the certificate holder's only remedy notwithstanding any other provision of law. Upon the recording of a notice of foreclosure sale rescission, the following occurs: (1) the mortgage and all rights thereunder, as well as all junior liens are revived as if no foreclosure sale had taken place; (2) the certificate of sale is rendered null and void as if the foreclosure sale had not taken place; and (3) the mortgagor's indebtedness to the foreclosing mortgagee is revived as of the date of the foreclosure sale, as if no foreclosure sale had taken place, or as otherwise agreed to by the mortgagor and mortgagee.

II. Judicial foreclosure

Judicial foreclosure is an *in rem* proceeding; proper venue is in the county where the land is situated. Any person with an interest in the land, which is junior or subject to the mortgage, is a necessary party defendant. A party who acquires an interest *during* the course of the proceedings is not a necessary party. If a junior lien holder is not made a party to the foreclosure, the junior lien holder can foreclose on the property himself as if the foreclosure had never taken place. A foreclosure will not affect a senior interest, and the purchaser will take subject to such senior interest.

The typical form of judgment in Wyoming gives a judgment to the mortgagee for the entire amount of the debt, and then orders that the property securing the debt be sold, with the proceeds of the sale applied in satisfaction of the debt. A judicial foreclosure results in a public auction conducted by the sheriff. Notice of the time and place of the sale, the names of the plaintiff and defendant, and a description of the property must be advertised in a newspaper of general circulation in a county where the property is located for 4 successive weeks before the sale. The property is sold at a public auction to the highest bidder; however, the mortgagee may bid at the sale and is often the only bidder present because the mortgagee can credit bid up to the value of the debt without having to pay any money. The purchaser, at the foreclosure sale, receives a certificate of purchase, which is executed by the sheriff conducting the sale, stating the amount of the bid and that the purchaser is entitled to a sheriff's deed at the end of the period of redemption, unless the property is redeemed. This certificate of purchase is to be recorded.

The purchase price at the foreclosure sale establishes the redemption price and also determines the deficiency. If the foreclosure sale is properly conducted, the purchaser at the sale takes title free and clear of all junior interests joined in the foreclosure action and of unrecorded conveyances or mortgages. If the property sells for less than the amount of the judgment, there is a deficiency judgment for the difference, which is the personal obligation of the mortgagor.

III. Non-judicial foreclosure/power of sale foreclosure guidelines:

The following are prerequisites for a non-judicial foreclosure:

- **(a)** The mortgage must contain a power of sale provision;
- **(b)** The mortgage must have been recorded;
- **(c)** There must have been a default;
- **(d)** No suit has been instituted to recover the debt secured by the mortgage; and
- **(e)** That written notice of intent to foreclose the mortgage by advertisement and sale has been served upon the record owner and the person in possession of the mortgaged premises, if different than the record owner and the person in possession at least 10 days before commencement of publication of notice of sale. Proof of compliance with this requirement shall be by affidavit.

In Wyoming, the purpose of the advertisement and sale foreclosure is to avoid the expense and delay of a judicial proceeding. Unless the mortgage provides otherwise, advertisement and sale foreclosures must be conducted in accordance with the statutory procedures.

Written notice of intent to foreclose by advertisement and sale must be served by certified mail, return receipt requested, and mailed at least 10 days before commencement of publication of notice of sale. The notice of intent must be mailed to the last known address of the record owner and the party in possession of the property, if different than the record owner. Strict compliance is required. Thereafter, A Notice of Sale must be published for 4 successive weeks in a newspaper of general circulation in the county where the property is located. The statute specifies the form and contents of the Notice. The sheriff, or a person appointed for that purpose, conducts the. The property is sold at a public auction to the highest bidder; however, the mortgagee may bid at the sale and is often the only bidder present because the mortgagee can credit bid up to the value of the debt without having to pay any money. The purchaser, at the foreclosure sale, receives a certificate of purchase, which is executed by the sheriff conducting the sale, stating the amount of the bid and that the purchaser is entitled to a sheriff's deed at the end of the period of redemption, unless the property is. This certificate of purchase is to be recorded.

The purchase price at the foreclosure sale establishes the redemption price and also determines the deficiency. If the foreclosure sale is properly conducted, the purchaser at the sale takes title free and clear of all junior interests joined in the foreclosure action and of unrecorded conveyances or mortgages. If the property sells for less than the amount of the judgment, there is a deficiency judgment for the difference, which is the personal obligation of the mortgagor.

A defective sale may be set aside by the mortgagor, and the mortgagor is not required to redeem, although a *bona fide* purchaser from the foreclosure purchaser generally takes title free of any defects in the sale. If the property sells for less than the debt, the mortgagee may seek a judgment against the mortgagor for the deficiency, even if the mortgage does not provide for a deficiency judgment.

IV. Right of Redemption after a Foreclosure Sale:

A mortgagor has a statutory right to redeem the property after the mortgage has been foreclosed upon and the property has been sold at a foreclosure sale. The certificate of purchase, which is presented to the successful bidder at the foreclosure sale, is only a lien against the property. Actual legal title to the property still remains with the mortgagor until the statutory redemption period has expired. Wyoming classifies property as either non-agricultural or agricultural real estate in terms of redemption. Agricultural real estate includes any parcel of land in excess of 80 acres lying outside the boundaries of an incorporated city, town or subdivision. Non-agricultural real estate may be redeemed within 3 months after the date of the sale. Agricultural real estate may be redeemed within 12 months after the date of the sale.

The amount to be paid to exercise the right of statutory redemption is based upon the price paid at the foreclosure sale. The mortgagor must pay either an amount agreed upon by the purchaser and the redemptioner, or the purchase price plus 10-percent interest, plus the amount of any taxes, assessments, or liens paid by the purchaser. In redeeming non-agricultural real estate, the mortgagor is entitled to possession, rents, and profits for the 3-month period during which he may redeem. For agricultural real estate, the mortgagor is entitled to possession, rents, and profits for the 12-month period during which he may redeem.

Contributed by: Lindsay A. Woznick and Ronald J. Lopez Hirst Applegate, LLP

If the mortgagor does not redeem, junior parties, including judgment creditors and any grantee or mortgagee of the real estate or any person holding a lien on the property, may redeem within thirty (30) days after the expiration of the mortgagor's redemption period. The junior lien holders must pay the purchase price plus 10 percent interest, plus the amount of any taxes, assessments, or liens paid by the purchaser, plus any senior lien held by the purchaser or by a senior lien holder who has redeemed.

If the mortgagor redeems, junior liens are revived because redemption renders the foreclosure sale null and void. A mortgage given to secure the redemption money has priority over any junior liens that might be revived. There is a split of authority as to whether redemption cancels the right to a deficiency judgment against the mortgagor; however, a judgment lien for any deficiency attaches to the property.

V. Foreclosure When Instrument Contains No Power of Sale:

If the mortgage does not contain a power of sale provision, the mortgagee must foreclose by means of judicial foreclosure as described above.

VI. Sale Under Power Where Instrument Silent As To Place Or Terms Of Sale:

Foreclosure sales are conducted in the county where the real property is located. State statues requires that the sale be conducted at a public venue, between the hours of 10:00 a.m. and 5:00 p.m. at the front door of the courthouse, or the place of holding the district court of the county within the county in which the real property to be sold is located, and shall be made by the sheriff or deputy sheriff of the county, to the highest bidder. The sale must be conducted in accordance with Wyoming's statutory guidelines described above.

VII. Notice Of Sale And How Notice Of Sale Is Given:

Written notice of intent to foreclose by advertisement and sale must be served by certified mail, return receipt requested, and mailed at least 10 days before commencement of publication of notice of sale. The notice of intent must be mailed to the last known address of the record owner and the party in possession of the property, if different than the record owner. Strict compliance is required. A Notice of Sale is also mailed to the mortgagor and must be published for 4 consecutive weeks in a newspaper of general circulation in the county where the property is located. The statute specifies the form and contents of the notice.

VIII. Place and Time For Conducting Foreclosure By Power Of Sale:

Generally, foreclosure sales take place at the front door of the courthouse, or the place of holding the district court of the county within the county in which the premises to be sold, or some part of them, are situated, and is conducted between the hours of 10:00 am and 5:00 pm.

Relevant Codes, Statutes or Case Law:
Wyoming Statute §§ 1-18-101 et seq. and 34-4-101 et seq. contain Wyoming's foreclosure and redemption statutes.

Receivership Section:

I. General Information About Your State:

A receiver may be appointed by the district court in the following actions or cases:

(a) By a vendor to vacate a fraudulent purchase of property;

Contributed by: Lindsay A. Woznick and Ronald J. Lopez Hirst Applegate, LLP

(b) By a creditor to subject any property or fund to his claim;

(c) By a partner or other person jointly owning or interested in any property of fund whose right to or interest in the property or fund or the proceeds thereof is probably and where it is shown that the property or fund is in danger of being lost, removed or materially injured;

(d) By a mortgagee for the foreclosure of his mortgage and sale of mortgaged property where it appears that the mortgaged property is in danger of being lost, removed or materially injured, or that a condition of the mortgage has not been performed and the property is probably insufficient to discharge the mortgage debt;

(e) After judgment to carry the judgment into effect;

(f) After judgment to dispose of the property according to the judgment or preserve it during the pendency of an appeal, or when an execution has been returned unsatisfied and the judgment debtor refuses to apply the property in satisfaction of the judgment;

(g) When a corporation has been dissolved or is insolvent or in imminent danger of insolvency or has forfeited its corporate rights; and

(h) In all other cases where receivers have been appointed by courts of equity.

II. Appointment Process

A. The Basics:

A receiver is appointed by a district court, generally after a petition or application is made to the court. The petition or application is usually made in the form of a motion. As a general rule, a receiver should not be appointed until after notice is provided to the defendant or any other interest party.

B. Time Frame for Appointment:

This will largely depend on the docket of the court and whether the motion is contested or uncontested. Generally, uncontested motions to appoint a receiver are granted within 30-60 days of filing the motion.

C. Can you appoint Ex Parte?

No.

III. Loans and advances

There are no rules or statutes that govern loans or advances in the context of a receivership, however WYO. STAT. ANN. § 1-33-104 provides that, a "receiver under control of the court, may bring and defend actions in his own name as receiver, take and keep possession of the property, receive rents, collect, compound for and compromise demands, make transfers and generally do acts respecting the property as the court may authorize." Generally, a court order governs whether a receiver is able to make loans or advances.

IV. Sales During the Receivership

Generally, a court order is required for a sale of receivership property.

Property may also be sold when permitted by Court order.

Contributed by: Lindsay A. Woznick and Ronald J. Lopez Hirst Applegate, LLP

V. Liens Against Receivership Property:

The Wyoming Supreme Court has previously held that "[t]he receiver, by his appointment, succeeded only to the title of the judgment debtor and as to property incumbered [sic] by liens he has only such rights as the judgment debtor had at the time of the appointment." *James S. Jackson Co. v. Meyer*, 677 P.2d 835, 838 (Wyo. 1984) (citations omitted).

There is very little guidance in Wyoming on this issue. Wyoming has one statute that may provide some direction for lien issues when a receiver is appointed. WYO. STAT. ANN. § 1-17-414 states: "[i]f it appears that the judgment debtor has an interest in real estate in the county in which proceedings are had, as mortgagor, mortgagee or otherwise, and his interest can be ascertained as between himself and any person holding the legal estate or having a lien or interest therein, without controversy, the receiver may be ordered to sell and convey the real estate, or the interest of the debtor. The sale shall be conducted as provided for the sale of real estate upon execution, and before execution of the deed, the proceedings of sale shall be approved by the court in which the judgment was rendered or the transcript filed."

The Wyoming Supreme Court has held that a lien holder may not disturb the receivership to foreclose on its lien without first obtaining permission from the court. Specifically, "[i]t is stated in 53 C. J. 111-112 that the rule against interference with the receiver's possession applies even though a claimant's lien is paramount to the right of the receiver. In 53 C. J. 131, 132, the general rule is stated that when property has passed into the hands of a receiver, it is not subject to execution. Cases are cited from about twenty different jurisdictions. All the authorities, without exception, seem to be agreed that no holder of a lien, paramount or otherwise, can, without the court's authority, disturb the receiver's possession. . . . The proper remedy, as stated by High on Receivers, (2nd Ed.) Sec. 141, 'for a judgment creditor, who desires to question the receiver's right to the property, is to apply to the court appointing him to have the property released from the receiver's custody, in order that he may proceed against it under judgment.'" *Tibbals v. Graham*, 50 Wyo. 277, 298-299 (Wyo. 1936).

VI. Owners Associations

This issue has not been addressed in Wyoming.

VII. Construction

This issue has not been addressed in Wyoming; however, a receiver would most likely be required to obtain court authorization prior to completing any construction.

VIII. Ending the receivership

Wyoming Rule of Civil Procedure 66 provides that an action wherein a receiver has been appointed shall not be dismissed except by order of the court. Accordingly, a court order is needed to end the receivership.

IX. Miscellaneous:

A.

Items generally included in the order are the legal description of the property, the reason a receiver is being appointed, the name and contact information of the receiver, the time frame that the receivership will be in effect (if known), compensation to be paid to the receiver, a requirement that the receiver post bond in accordance with Wyoming Statute, a requirement that the receiver comply with the notice requirements and other requirements set forth in Wyoming's receivership statutes, and a list of items, tasks, and powers that the receiver is authorized to do or utilize.

Contributed by: Lindsay A. Woznick and Ronald J. Lopez Hirst Applegate, LLP

B.

Any person having a claim against the person, company, property, corporation or partnership for which the receiver is appointed must exhibit his or her claim to the receiver within four (4) months from the date of the first publication of the notice of appointment of receiver, and if the claims are not made within that time frame, they are forever barred from participation in the assets of the receivership. If a properly filed claim is rejected by the receiver, or if allowed by the receiver and rejected by the court, the holder of the claim must bring suit against the receiver within four (4) months after the date upon which he is given notice of the rejection, otherwise the claim is forever barred.

Relevant Codes, Statutes or Case Law:
Receiverships are governed by WYO. STAT. ANN. §§ 1-33-101 to 1-33-110. Some of the Wyoming cases that have dealt with receivers include: *O'Donnell v. First Nat'l Bank*, 9 Wyo. 408, 94 P. 337 (Wyo. 1901); *Barber v. Barber*, 349 P.2d 198 (Wyo. 1960); *Barrett v. Green River & Rock Springs Livestock Co.*, 28 Wyo. 379, 205 P. 742 (Wyo. 1922); *State ex. Rel Avenius v. Tidball*, 35 Wyo. 496, 252 P. 499 (Wyo. 1927); *Grieve v. Huber*, 38 Wyo. 223, 266 P. 128 (Wyo. 1928); *Anderson v. Riddle*, 10 Wyo. 277, 68 P. 829 (Wyo. 1902); *State Bd. Of Law Exmrs. v. Goppert*, 66 Wyo. 117, 205 P.2d 124 (Wyo. 1949); *Stockmen's Nat'l Bank v. Calloway Shops*, 41 Wyo. 232, 285 P. 146 (Wyo. 1930); *Krist v. Aetna Cas. & Sur.*, 667 P.2d 665 (Wyo. 1983).

UCC And Related Issues In Enforcing Defaulted Loans Secured By Real And Personal Property

1. Why should a CRE lender care about the UCC?

Most commercial real estate (CRE) loans are secured in part by personal property, both tangible and intangible. Consensual liens on personal property (also called security interests) are generally governed by Article 9 of the Uniform Commercial Code (UCC). A secured lender who ignores Article 9 is probably leaving money on the table by failing to pursue assets that might improve its loan recovery or by failing to use remedies that might speed its loan resolution.

2. Does Article 9 of the UCC apply to all consensual liens on personal property?

No. Although Article 9 of the UCC applies to many such liens, Article 9 specifically excludes certain liens from its coverage. Chief among these excluded liens are assignments of leases and rents. Whether a real property owner's interest in leases and rents is treated as real property or as personal property may vary from state to state. In California, for example, a real property owner's interest in leases and rents is treated as personal property. No matter how such interests are classified, however, enforcement of an assignment of leases and rents will generally be governed by law other than the UCC.

3. Does Article 9 of the UCC cover any transactions that might surprise a secured lender?

Yes: note sales. Although Article 9 has historically applied mainly to security interests intended to secure an obligation, since 2001, Article 9 has also covered sales of promissory notes (whether or not the promissory notes qualify as "negotiable instruments" under Article 3 of the UCC).

Although this change in the law might seem a bit strange, it has proved to be good news for secured lenders:

A. First, Article 9 provides that the sale of a promissory note automatically carries with it all related liens (*e.g.*, mortgages and deeds of trust) and all related supporting obligations (*e.g.*, guaranties and indemnities). This rule is particularly useful to a lender who bought a promissory note in a "lightly documented" transaction (*i.e.*, a transaction in which the note was indorsed by the prior lender to the current lender but no assignment of loan documents was executed).

B. Second, Article 9 provides the buyer in a "lightly documented" note sale who wishes to enforce a mortgage or deed of trust non-judicially with a special procedure that enables the buyer to become, in effect, the beneficiary of record.

4. Must a lender whose loan is secured by both real and personal property foreclose on the personal property separately from the real property collateral?

No. Article 9 of the UCC generally permits a secured lender (a) to conduct a "unified sale" of both the real property and the personal property under the real property rules or (b) to proceed separately as to the personal property under the Article 9 rules without prejudicing the secured lender's rights with respect to the real property under the real property rules. In California, Article 9 is even more flexible: the secured lender may proceed as to some or all of the personal property under the Article 9 rules and, together with the real property, some or all of the personal property under the real property rules.

5. How does a lender enforce its rights in a borrower's deposit account that is subject to a deposit account control agreement among the lender, the borrower and the bank?

Assuming that the deposit account control agreement is properly drafted, enforcement is generally a two-step process. First, the lender should send the bank a "notice of exclusive control" or similar instruction to cut off the borrower's access to the funds in the deposit account and to ensure that the bank will no longer comply with any instructions regarding the deposit account that the bank may receive from the borrower. Second, the lender should direct the bank to transfer some or all of the funds in the deposit account to an account designated by the lender. Note: under Article 9 of the UCC, once the funds in the deposit account are transferred to the lender's account, such funds must be applied to the secured obligation (*i.e.*, the borrower's outstanding indebtedness).

6. In many secured loan transactions, the lender holds borrower funds in a deposit account established in the lender's name. How does the lender enforce its rights in such a deposit account?

Assuming that the borrower has no access to the deposit account (*i.e.*, no ability to withdraw or transfer funds from the deposit account), enforcement is even easier. There is no need for the first step described in the answer to Question 5 above: the lender already has exclusive control. All that is necessary is for the lender to transfer the funds in the deposit account to the lender's account. As before, once the funds in the deposit account are transferred to the lender's account, such funds must be applied to the secured obligation.

7. Do all bank accounts constitute deposit accounts under Article 9 of the UCC?

No. Some bank accounts (particularly those in CMBS deals where funds must be invested in "permitted investments") constitute "securities accounts" rather than "deposit accounts" under Article 9 of the UCC. Different rules apply to security interests in securities accounts, not only to the creation and perfection of such security interests but also to the enforcement of such security interests. For more information on how to deal with that type of collateral, consult a UCC expert.

8. If some of the contracts that are part of the collateral package for a secured loan have anti-assignment clauses, are the lender's liens on these contracts invalid?

No, not necessarily. Article 9 of the UCC has special rules that may, in some cases, wholly or partially override contractual anti-assignment clauses. For example, franchise agreements often have anti-assignment provisions that purport to make a collateral assignment or other transfer of the franchisee's rights without the franchisor's consent a default entitling the franchisor to terminate the franchise agreement. If a franchisee collaterally assigns its rights under a franchise agreement to a lender as security for a loan, Article 9 provides that the collateral assignment does not constitute a default and that the lender's security interest is valid. While Article 9 limits the lender's ability to enforce its security interest in the franchise agreement against the franchisor, the lender still benefits significantly from these special rules. If the franchisee's rights under the franchise agreement are later sold to a third party (whether pursuant to a section 363(f) sale in bankruptcy or as part of a consensual sale outside of bankruptcy), the lender's security interest will attach to the sale proceeds and will be fully enforceable at that point.

9. A CRE lender has a first lien on all of the borrower's real and personal property and, as additional collateral, a first priority security interest in all of the equity interests in the borrower. To save time, should the lender enforce its loan by pursuing a UCC sale of the equity interests rather than a foreclosure sale of the borrower's real and personal property?

Absolutely not (unless proper waivers have been obtained). In most cases, a UCC sale of equity interests is structured as a public sale so that the lender can participate in the sale. In part because the lender has the right to credit bid its debt, the winning bidder in a UCC sale of equity interests will almost invariably be the lender. The problem is this: a full or partial credit bid may result in the sponsor party pledging the equity interests having a reimbursement claim against the borrower for the amount of the bid. In addition, a full credit bid may result in the sponsor party being subrogated to (*i.e.*, acquiring by operation of law) all of the lender's rights against the borrower under the lender's loan and security documents. In the latter scenario, the lender and the sponsor party would effectively switch positions, with the lender becoming the owner of the equity interests and the sponsor party acquiring a first lien against the borrower's real and personal property. Bottom line: before proceeding under these circumstances, consult with an experienced finance attorney who is knowledgeable not only about enforcing liens on real and personal property but also about dealing with suretyship rights and defenses.

Common Foreclosure Terms

Accelerate

an option given to lenders through an "acceleration" clause in the mortgage or deed of trust requiring the borrower to pay the entire balance of the loan all at once if their loan is in default.

Affidavit

A voluntary declaration of facts written down and sworn to by the declarant before an officer authorized to administer oaths, such as a notary public. A great deal of evidence is submitted by affidavit, esp. in pretrial matters such as summary-judgment motions.

Appraisal

The determination of what constitutes a fair price; valuation; estimation of worth.

Appreciation

An increase in an asset's value, usu. because of inflation.

Assignment

The transfer of rights or property.

Bid

A buyer's offer to pay a specified price for something that may or may not be for sale.

Certificate of Sale

A document given to the winning bidder at a foreclosure sale stating their rights to the property once the borrowers redemption period has expired.

Clear Title

A title free from any encumbrances, burdens, or other limitations.

Credit Bid

A bid on behalf of the lender at a foreclosure sale. The bid amount must be less than or equal to the balance of the loan in default.

Decree

A court's final judgment.

Deed

A written instrument by which land is conveyed.

Deed-in-lieu of Foreclosure
A deed by which a borrower conveys fee-simple title to a lender in satisfaction of a mortgage debt and as a substitute for foreclosure.
Deed of Trust
Deed conveying title to real property to a trustee as security until the grantor repays a loan. This type of deed resembles a mortgage.
Default
A mortgage of deed of trust is said to be in default when the borrower fails to make the payments as agreed to in the original promissory note.
Deficiency Judgment
A judgment against a debtor for the unpaid balance of the debt if a foreclosure sale or a sale of repossessed personal property fails to yield the full amount of the debt due.
Equitable Title
A title that indicates a beneficial interest in property and that gives the holder the right to acquire formal legal title.
Fair Market Value
The price a property would sell for on the open market.
Foreclosure
A legal proceeding to terminate a mortgagor's interest in property, instituted by the lender (the mortgagee) either to gain title or to force a sale in order to satisfy the unpaid debt secured by the property.
Free & Clear
Unencumbered by any liens; marketable.
Judicial Foreclose
A costly and time-consuming foreclosure method by which the mortgaged property is sold through a court proceeding requiring many standard legal steps such as the filing of a complaint, service of process, notice, and a hearing. • Judicial foreclosure is available in all jurisdictions and is the exclusive or most common method of foreclosure in at least 20 states.
Lien
A legal right or interest that a creditor has in another's property, lasting usu. until a debt or duty that it secures is satisfied.

Legal Description
A formal description of real property, including a description of any part subject to an easement or reservation, complete enough that a particular piece of land can be located and identified. The description can be made by reference to a government survey, metes and bounds, or lot numbers of a recorded plat.
Lender
A person or entity from which something (esp. money) is borrowed.
Lis Pendens
A notice, recorded in the chain of title to real property, required or permitted in some jurisdictions to warn all persons that certain property is the subject matter of litigation, and that any interests acquired during the pendency of the suit are subject to its outcome.
Mortgage
A conveyance of title to property that is given as security for the payment of a debt or the performance of a duty and that will become void upon payment or performance according to the stipulated terms.
Non-Judicial Foreclosure
A foreclosure process by which, according to the mortgage instrument and a state statute, the mortgaged property is sold at a nonjudicial public sale by a public official, the mortgagee, or a trustee, without the stringent notice requirements, procedural burdens, or delays of a judicial foreclosure A foreclosure method that does not require court involvement.
Notary
A person authorized by a state to administer oaths, certify documents, attest to the authenticity of signatures, and perform official acts in commercial matters, such as protesting negotiable instruments.
Notice of Sale
A notice giving specific information about the loan in default and the proceedings about to take place. This notice must be recorded with the county where property is located and advertised as stated in the security document or as dictated by state law.

Personal Property
Any movable or intangible thing that is subject to ownership and not classified as real property.

Posting
To publish, announce or advertise by physically attaching a notice to an object.

Postponement
To put off to a later time.

Right of Redemption
A borrower's right to reacquire a property lost due to a foreclosure.

Request for Notice
A recorded document requiring a trustee send a copy of a Notice of Default or Notice of Sale concerning a specific deed trust in foreclosure to the person who filed the document.

Subject to
The purchase of a property with an existing lien against the title without assuming any personal liability for the liens payment.

Title
The instrument that is evidence of a person's right in real.

Trustee
A person appointed by the U.S. Trustee or elected by creditors or appointed by a judge to administer the bankruptcy estate during a bankruptcy case.

Trustee sale
An auction of real property conducted by a trustee. Also known as a Sheriff's Sale.

Upset Bid
A bid in a judicial sale made for more than the purchaser's bid so that the sale will be set aside.

Writ
A court's written order, in the name of a state or other competent legal authority, commanding the addressee to do or refrain from doing some specified act.

Common Receivership Terms

Affidavit
A voluntary declaration of facts written down and sworn to by the declarant before an officer authorized to administer oaths, such as a notary public.

Ancillary Jurisdiction
A court's jurisdiction to adjudicate claims and proceedings related to a claim that is properly before the court.

Bankruptcy
A statutory procedure by which a (usu. insolvent) debtor obtains financial relief and undergoes a judicially supervised reorganization or liquidation of the debtor's assets for the benefit of creditors; a case under the Bankruptcy Code.

Bond
A written promise to pay money or do some act if certain circumstances occur or a certain time elapses; a promise that is defeasible upon a condition subsequent; esp., an instrument under seal by which (1) a public officer undertakes to pay a sum of money if he or she does not faithfully discharge the responsibilities of office, or (2) a surety undertakes that if the public officer does not do so, the surety will be liable in a penal sum.

Complaint
The initial pleading that starts a civil action and states the basis for the court's jurisdiction, the basis for the plaintiff's claim, and the demand for relief.

Ex Parte
Done or made at the instance and for the benefit of one party only, and without notice to, or argument by, any person adversely interested; of or relating to court action taken by one party without notice to the other, usu. for temporary or emergency relief.

Federal Jurisdiction
The exercise of federal-court authority.

Foreclosure
A legal proceeding to terminate a mortgagor's interest in property, instituted by the lender (the mortgagee) either to gain

title or to force a sale in order to satisfy the unpaid debt secured by the property.

Franchise Agreements

The contract between a franchisor and franchisee establishing the terms and conditions of the franchise relationship. State and federal laws regulate franchise agreements.

Jurisdiction

A court's power to decide a case or issue a decree.

Liability

The quality or state of being legally obligated or accountable; legal responsibility to another or to society, enforceable by civil remedy or criminal punishment.

Receiver

A disinterested person appointed by a court, or by a corporation or other person, for the protection or collection of property that is the subject of diverse claims.

Receiver's Certificate

An instrument issued by a receiver as evidence that the holder is entitled to receive payment from funds controlled by the bankruptcy court.

Receivership Estate

The totality of the interests that the receivers of an association in one or more states are appointed to protect.

Receivership Sale

A sale conducted under the authority of a judgment or court order, such as an execution sale.

Remedy

The means of enforcing a right or preventing or redressing a wrong; legal or equitable relief.

Rents & Profits Receivership

The total income or profit arising from the ownership or possession of property.

Secured Creditor

A creditor who has the right, on the debtor's default, to proceed against collateral and apply it to the payment of the debt.

Security

Collateral given or pledged to guarantee the fulfillment of an obligation; esp., the assurance that a creditor will be repaid (usu. with interest) any money or credit extended to a debtor.

Subject Matter Jurisdiction
Jurisdiction over the nature of the case and the type of relief sought; the extent to which a court can rule on the conduct of persons or the status of things.
Unsecured Creditor
A creditor who, upon giving credit, takes no rights against specific property of the debtor.

About our Authors

Alabama

Jason Woodard has extensive experience in the representation of creditors in distressed debt situations, typically secured creditors in the bankruptcy, receivership, foreclosure and out-of-court workout arenas.

Burr & Forman LLP• 420 North 20th Street, Suite 3400•Birmingham, Alabama 35203
PhonePhone (205) 458-5188 • FaxFax (205) 244-5722 •
jwoodardjwoodard@burr.comcom

Alaska

Foreclosure Section:

Trigild Staff

TrigildTrigild • 9339 Genesee Ave #130 • San Diego CA 92121
PhonePhone (858) 242-1197 • david.wallace@trigild.com

Receivership Section:

Erin Eliasen is an associate practicing in the Corporate practice group. She has experience in the areas of corporate governance, mergers and acquisitions, venture capital, credit finance, secured transactions and bankruptcy practice. Erin has also advised and assisted numerous clients in forming, capitalizing and maintaining corporations, limited liability companies and partnerships. Her experience also includes representation of creditor and equity committees, debtors and trustees, bank agents and financial sponsors.

Stoel Rives LLP •600 University St, Suite • Seattle, WA 98101
PhonePhone (206) 386-7605 • FaxFax (206) 386-7500 •
eleliaseneleliasen@stoel.comcom

Richard Goldfarb practices primarily in the commercial, banking, corporate, and securities law areas. He is experienced in complex commercial transactions, including foreign and domestic sales; secured transactions for banks, other financial institutions and borrowers; and in essentially all aspects of the Uniform Commercial Code. Rick also serves as a general corporate counselor. He is a fellow of the American College of Commercial Finance Lawyers.

Stoel Rives LLP •600 University St, Suite • Seattle, WA 98101
PhonePhone (206) 386-7639 • FaxFax (206) 386-7500 •
rlgoldfarbrlgoldfarb@stoel.comcom

Arizona

JeffreyJeffrey S. Pitcher is a partner in the Real Estate Department and Practice Leader of the Commercial Real Estate Recovery Group. His practice focuses on the areas of distressed real estate and real estate development, finance, and leasing. Mr. Pitcher represents clients on a variety of distressed projects, including master-planned and mixed-use developments, retail and office centers, multifamily developments, hotels, industrial properties, and other types of commercial real estate.

Ballard Spahr LLP. • 1 East Washington St Suite 2300 • Phoenix, Arizona 85004-2555
PhonePhone (602) 798-5462 • pitcher@ballardspahr.com

Andrew A. Harnisch is an associate in the Litigation Department and a member of the Bankruptcy, Reorganization and Capital Recovery Group. His practice is focused on commercial bankruptcy, insolvency, corporate reorganization, and related federal and state court litigation. Mr. Harnisch is experienced in representing creditors, debtors, and trustees in a variety of bankruptcy court matters, and frequently litigates receiverships and other creditors' rights cases in state and federal courts.

Ballard Spahr LLP. • 1 East Washington St Suite 2300 • Phoenix, Arizona 85004-2555
PhonePhone (602) 798-5458 • harnischa @ballardspahr.com

Daniel N. Weber is an associate in the Real Estate Department and a member of the Real Estate Development, Commercial Real

Estate Recovery, Finance, and Leasing Groups. Mr. Weber concentrates his practice on commercial real estate and transactional work with an emphasis on loan transactions, real estate workouts, acquisitions, leasing and the representation of lenders generally.

Ballard Spahr LLP. • 1 East Washington St Suite 2300 • Phoenix, Arizona 85004-2555
PhonePhone (602) 798-5446 • weberd@ballardspahr.com

Arkansas

MelissaBandyMelissa L. Bandy has a B.A. in English from Davidson College, Davidson, North Carolina, and a J.D. with high honors from the University of Arkansas at Little Rock. She is an associate at Mitchell, Williams, Selig, Gates & Woodyard, P.L.L.C. in Little Rock, Arkansas and practice in the areas of commercial transactions, finance, and real estate.

Mitchel Williams.• 425 West Capitol Ave Suite 18001800 • Little Rock, Arkansas 72201
PhonePhone (501) 688-8865 • mbandy@mwlaw.com

California

Maura O'Connor is the managing partner of O'Connor Cochran LLP, a real estate boutique firm based in Los Angeles, California. She is the former Chairman of the Los Angeles County Economic Development Corporation. Ms. O'Connor writes the national real estate industry law blog, Practical Counsel, for www.GlobeSt.com, the premier national commercial real estate web portal. Maura was named one of the top 10 real estate lawyers in Southern California by Real Estate Southern California.

O'Connor Cochran LLP • 515 South Flower St, 36th36th Floor • Los Angeles, CA 90071
Phone (213) 236-3624 • moconnormoconnor@oconnorcochran.comcom

Jim Cochran is a partner with O'Connor Cochran LLP in Los Angeles. Jim has extensive experience advising clients in workouts and restructurings involving complex collateral packages and multiple jurisdictions. He has represented secured lenders, distressed debt investors, special servicers and other clients in connection with secured loan restructurings (including consolidations), structured asset dispositions, collateral "take backs," note sales and similar matters as well as lien enforcement proceedings (including judicial and non-judicial foreclosures of retail, office, hotel and other properties and UCC sales of limited liability company and partnership interests).

O'Connor Cochran LLP • 515 South Flower St, 36th36th Floor • Los Angeles, CA 90071
Phone (213) 236-3624 • jcochranjcochran@oconnorcochran.comcom

---

Colorado

Lino Lipinsky de Orlov is a litigation partner in the Denver office of McKenna Long & Aldridge LLP, an international law firm. His practice emphasizes representation of clients in real estate, trade secrets, creditor's rights, employment, and contract cases. Among his notable matters, he represented the defendant in one of the largest age discrimination cases filed in the District of Colorado, a national financial services corporation in multi-million dollar trade secrets litigation, and a Fortune 500 retailer in complex real estate cases. In addition to handling state and federal litigation, Mr. Lipinsky counsels clients and writes on legal issues relating to technology. He is a member of the firm's Cybersecurity Practice Group and the E-Discovery Committee of the United States District Court for the District of Colorado. Among his honors, Mr. Lipinsky was selected by his peers to be included in *The Best Lawyers in America, 19th edition,* for his work in commercial litigation. In addition, he has been recognized as a "Colorado Super Lawyer" by the publishers of Law and Politics and a "Legal Luminary" by the American Constitution Society. Mr. Lipinsky is President of the Faculty of Federal Advocates, a member of the Public Affairs Council of the Denver Metro Chamber of Commerce, and a co-founder of the Colorado Chapter of the American Constitution Society. He received his A.B. degree, *magna cum laude*, from Brown University and his J.D. degree from New York University School of Law, where he was a member of the *New York*

University Law Review. He is a member of the Colorado, District of Columbia, and New York bars.

McKenna Long & Aldridge LLP • 1400 Wewatta Street, Suite 700 • Denver, CO 80202
Phone (303) 634-4336 • Fax (303) 634-4400 • llipinsky@mckennalong.com

Charles Swanson is an associate in the Denver office of McKenna Long & Aldridge LLP, an international law firm. His practice focuses on commercial and government contracts litigation, with specific experience in contract disputes (both in the private commercial context and in the federal contracting arena), in trade secret issues, and in the federal False Claims Act. During law school, Mr. Swanson interned with Senior Judge John L. Kane of the United States District Court for the District of Colorado and Judge Dennis A. Graham of the Colorado Court of Appeals. Charles graduated from the University of Colorado Law School, *Order of the Coif*, and received a B.A. from Rice University.

McKenna Long & Aldridge LLP • 1400 Wewatta Street, Suite 700 • Denver, CO 80202
Phone (303) 634-4337 • Fax (303) 634-4400 • todiltodil@mckennalong.comcom

---

Connecticut

TimothyFierstTimothy J. Fierst is a partner with Rosenberg & Estis, PC and is a member of the Litigation Group. He represents numerous lenders, servicers and lien holders with respect to residential and commercial transactions, secured loan workouts, REO transactions, loan restructures and a wide range of banking, real estate, corporate and commercial finance issues in New York and Connecticut, including mortgage related litigation, judicial and non-judicial foreclosures and bankruptcy proceedings.

Rosenberg & Estis PC • 733 3rd3rd Ave • New York, NY 10017
Phone (212) 551-1203 • Fax (212) 551-8484 • tfiersttfierst@rosenbergestis.comcom

JamieJamie C. Krapf isis of counsel with Rosenberg & Estis, PC and is a member of the Litigation Group. She represents numerous lenders, servicers and lien holders with respect to residential and commercial transactions, REO transactions, loan restructures and a wide range of banking, real estate and commercial finance issues in New York and Connecticut, including mortgage related litigation and judicial and non-judicial foreclosures.

Rosenberg & Estis PC • 733 3rd Ave • New York, NY 10017
Phone (212) 551-1235 • Fax (212) 551-8484 • jkrapfjkrapf@rosenbergestis.comcom

---

Delaware

Foreclosure Section:

Trigild Staff

TrigildTrigild • 9339 Genesee Ave #130 • San Diego CA 92121
PhonePhone (858) 242-1197 • david.wallace@trigild.com

Receivership Section:

Henry J. Jaffe is a partner in the Wilmington office of Pepper Hamilton LLP. He represents debtors, trustees, creditors' committees and other claimants, and defends and prosecutes avoidance actions nationwide. He frequently writes and lectures on bankruptcy topics.

Pepper Hamilton LLP •1313 North Market Street, Suite 5100 • Wilmington, DE 19899
Phone (302) 777-6575 • Fax (302) 421-8390 • jaffehjaffeh@pepperlaw.comcom

---

Florida

Joseph E. ("Ed") Foster is a senior partner at Akerman Senterfitt, a 500+ lawyer and consultant firm with offices throughout Florida, and in several other states. He is listed in Best Lawyers in America in four categories, Commercial Litigation; Litigation-

Banking & Finance; Litigation-Bankruptcy, and Litigation-Real Estate. He was also ranked in Chambers USA 2006-2012 for General Commercial Litigation in Florida.

Akerman Senterfitt • 420 South Orange Avenue Suite 1200 • Orlando, FL 32801-3336
Phone (407) 423-4000 • Fax (407) 843-6610 • eded.foster@akerman.comcom

---

Georgia

Gary Marsh focuses on general commercial litigation and bankruptcy, workouts and debtor/creditor law. He represents creditors and debtors in Chapter 11 reorganization proceedings, out of court restructurings and debtor/creditor litigation. He also represents court appointed receivers, examiners and trustees.

McKenna Long & Aldridge LLP • 303 Peachtree St, NE Ste 5300• Atlanta, GA 30308
Phone (404)-527-4150 • (Fax) 404-527-4198 • gmarshgmarsh@mckennalong.comcom

---

Hawaii

Steve Iwamura counsels the mortgage banking industry on commercial and residential loans, including foreclosures, bankruptcies, regulatory compliance, workouts, and lender liability.

Clay Chapman Iwamura Pulice & Nervell • 700 Bishop St, Ste 2100 • Honolulu, HI 96813
Phone (808) 535-8406 • Fax (808) 536-1141 • iwamuraiwamura@paclawteam.comcom

---

Idaho

Brad Dixon is a Partner in the Boise office of Stoel Rives LLP's Litigation practice group. He has a broad range of trial and litigation experience representing clients in disputes involving complex commercial litigation, employment, insurance coverage, products liability, title insurance, foreclosure and bankruptcy trial practice. In addition, Brad provides governmental affairs services to firm clients before the Idaho

State Legislature and state regulatory agencies and is a member of the firm workout and restructuring group.

Stoel Rives • 101 S. Capitol Boulevard, Suite 1900 • Boise, ID 83702-5958
Phone (208) 387-4284 • Fax (208) 389-9040 • bjdixonbjdixon@stoel.comcom

---

Illinois

John Collen is a partner in the Chicago office of Tressler, LLP, where he heads the firm's Insolvency, Restructuring and Workouts practice. He is an adjunct professor in the Bankruptcy LLM Program at St. John's Law School in New York, and a widely published author and frequent speaker. He is a fellow of the American College of Bankruptcy, and is included in Illinois Super Lawyers®, and in Marquis Who's Who in American Law.

Tressler LLP • 233 South Wacker Drive, 22nd22nd Floor • Chicago, IL 60606
Phone (312) 627-4193 • Fax (312) 627-1717 • jcollen@tresslerllp.com

---

Indiana

Jim Vantine

Miller, Canfield, Paddock and Stone, P.L.C. • 277 S. Rose St, Ste 5000 •Kalamazoo, MI 49007 • vantine@millercanfield.com

Lori Purkeyu

Miller, Canfield, Paddock and Stone, P.L.C. • 277 S. Rose St, Ste 5000 •Kalamazoo, MI 49007 • purkey@millercanfield.com

---

Iowa

Jeffery Wegner

Kutak Rock LLP • 16501650 Farnam Street •Omaha, NE 68102-21862186
Phone: (402) 346-6000 • Fax: (402) 346-1148 •
JeffreyJeffrey.Wegner@KutakRock.comcom

Kansas

John L. Snyder represents banking institutions and loan servicers on commercial loan transactions, workouts, and foreclosures; represents real estate funds and other buyers of distressed assets and debt; represents developers and companies on complex real estate projects, including development, land use, financing and economic incentives; represents landlords and tenants on lease negotiations. Snyder is licensed in Kansas and Missouri.

SNR Denton US LLP • 4520 Main St, Suite 1100 • Kansas City, Missouri 64111
Phone (816) 460-2668 • Fax (816) 531-7545 • john.snyder@snrdenton.com

Kentucky

James R. Williamson

Stites & Harbison PLLC • 400 W. Market St., Suite 1800 • Louisville, KY 40202
Phone (502) 681-0444 • Fax (502) 799-8283 • jwilliamsonjwilliamson@stites.comcom

Louisiana

Susan M. Tyler is a member of Jones Walker with over twenty years of practice concentrated in the areas of real estate and commercial business transactions, including extensive experience in workouts, restructurings and foreclosures in federal and state courts. She is also a licensed title agent and was recently selected for inclusion in Woodward White's Best Lawyers in America for Real Estate Law and as a Louisiana Super Lawyer in Real Estate. Ms. Tyler is located in the firm's New Orleans office.

Jones Walker Waechter, Poitevent, Carrère & Denègre, L. L. P. • 201 St. Charles Avenue, 50th Fl • New Orleans, LA 70170
Phone (504) 582-8298 • Fax: (504) 589-8298 • styler@joneswalker.com

Maine

Fred W. Bopp III is a shareholder and director of Perkins Thompson, and a member of the Firm's Executive Committee. Mr. Bopp's practice focuses on bankruptcy, reorganizations, the pursuit and enforcement of creditors' and debtors' rights, and the representation of various parties in a wide range of insolvency and reorganization proceedings and out-of-court workouts, including the representation of financial institutions and other secured and unsecured creditors inside and outside of bankruptcy cases. Mr. Bopp has appeared before the bankruptcy courts in the Districts of Maine, Massachusetts, New Hampshire, and New York. His practice experience also includes significant commercial collections, evictions, and repossessions.

Perkins Thompson PA • One Canal Plaza PO Box 426 • Portland, ME 04112-0426 •
Phone (207) 774-2635 x8111 • Fax (207) 871-8026 • fbopp@perkinsthompson.com

Lauren Weliver

Perkins Thompson PA • One Canal Plaza PO Box 426 • Portland, ME 04112-0426 •
Phone (207) 400-8118 • lweliver@perkinsthompson.com

Stephanie A. Williams

Perkins Thompson PA • One Canal Plaza PO Box 426 • Portland, ME 04112-0426 •
Phone (207) 400400-8122 • swilliams@perkinsthompson.com

Maryland

MatthewCheneyMatthew W. Cheney is a partner in Crowell & Moring's Washington, DC office. Matt's practice includes bankruptcy and creditors' rights matters, commercial transactions, loan workouts and distressed debt matters.

Crowell & Moring •1001 Pennsylvania Ave, N.W. • Washington, DC 20004
Phone (202) 624-2903 • Fax (202) 628-5116 • mcheneymcheney@crowell.comcom

MoniqueMonique Almy is a partner in Crowell & Moring's Washington, DC office and is a member of the Bankruptcy, Corporate and Financial Services practice groups. Monique's practice focuses primarily on corporate bankruptcy, restructuring, and on other insolvency related matters, with an emphasis on creditors' rights.

Crowell & Moring •1001 Pennsylvania Ave, N.W. • Washington, DC 20004
Phone (202) 624-2935 • Fax (202) 628-5116 • malmymalmy@crowell.comcom

---

Massachusetts

Armando Batastini is a partner at Nixon Peabody, LLP, and is a member of the Real Estate Litigation Team. A large portion of his practice is devoted to representing special servicers and lenders in work-outs, foreclosures, receiverships and litigation related to commercial property throughout the Northeast.

Nixon Peabody LLP • 100 Summer Street • Boston, MA 02110• One Citizens Plaza, Suite 500 • Providence, RI 02903
Phone (617) 345-1116 • (401) 454-1015 • Fax (866)-680-8453 • abatastini@nixonpeabody.com

---

Michigan

Steven A. Roach applies his more than 20 years of commercial transaction and litigation experience in restructuring lending relationships and enforcing loan transactions. His unique perspective as both a trial and transactional lawyer allows him to service the firm's financial institution clients, whether the loan transaction is complex, multi-jurisdictional, or international, and also when borrowers or guarantors are confrontational. Steve primarily represents lenders in the restructure, work out and enforcement of distressed loans, both in and out of court.

Miller, Canfield, Paddock, and Stone, P.L.C • 150 W Jefferson Ste 2500 • Detroit, MI 48226
Phone (313) 963-6420 • FaxFax (313) 496-8454 • roachroach@millercanfield.comcom

Minnesota

Trigild Staff

TrigildTrigild • 9339 Genesee Ave #130 • San Diego CA 92121
PhonePhone (858) 242-1197 • david.wallace@trigild.com

Mississippi

Jeff Barber is a partner in the Business & Commercial Litigation Practice Group of Jones, Walker, Waechter, Poitevent, Carrère & Denègre L.L.P. and practices from the firm's Jackson office. He is also the office head for the firm's three Mississippi locations. He focuses his practice on bankruptcy and creditors' rights and is a frequent lecturer on bankruptcy and creditors' rights matters. He regularly represents clients in bankruptcy proceedings, state and federal receiverships and assists them in restructurings. In addition, he has served as an adjunct professor of Debtor-Creditor Law at the Mississippi College School of Law and is the author of several published works.

Jones, Walker, Waechter, Poitevent, Carrere & Denegre LLP • 190 E Capitol St Suite 800 • Jackson MS 39201 Phone (601) 949-4765 • jbarber@joneswalker.com

Missouri

Brett D. Anders enforces the rights and remedies of secured lenders in state, federal and bankruptcy courts across the nation. One of his specialties is the use of receivership proceedings to manage, operate and ultimately sell collateral as an alternative to traditional foreclosure and bankruptcy sales. He also represents CMBS and institutional lenders in lender liability, prepayment and intercreditor cases.

Polsinelli Shughart PC • 700 W. 47th St Ste 1000 • Kansas City, MO 64112
Phone (816) 360-4267• Fax (816) 753-1536 • bandersbanders@polsinelli.comcom

Montana

Rebecca L. Mann is an associate at Gunderson, Palmer, Nelson and Ashmore, LLP in Rapid City, South Dakota. A native of South Dakota, Rebecca earned her J.D. from the University of South Dakota and is licensed in South Dakota, North Dakota and Montana. Her practice areas include family law, insurance defense, debtor creditor relations, employment law and general civil litigation.

Gunderson Palmer Nelson Ashmore LLP • 506 Sixth St • Rapid City, SD 57701
Phone (506) 719-3486 • Fax (605) 342-9503 • rmannrmann@gpnalaw.comcom

Nebraska

Jeffery Wegner

Kutak Rock LLP • 16501650 Farnam Street •Omaha, NE 68102-21862186
Phone: (402) 346-6000 • Fax: (402) 346-1148 •
JeffreyJeffrey.Wegner@KutakRock.comcom

Nevada

David Barksdale is a partner in Ballard Spahr Andrews & Ingersoll, LLP's Las Vegas office. He is Co-Chair of the firm's Distressed Real Estate Initiative.

Ballard Spahr Andrews & Ingersoll LLP • 100 City Pkwy Ste 1750 Las Vegas, NV 89106
Phone (702) 387-3086 • Fax (702) 471-7070 •
barksdaledbarksdaled@ballardspahr.comcom

New Hampshire

ThomasThomas W. Morse

Hall Morse Anderson Miller & Spinella • 14 Centre Street • Concord, NH 03302-2289
Phone (603) 225-6655 • Fax (603) 228-52205220 • tmorsetmorse@hallmorlaw.comcom

FrankFrank P. Spinella, Jr.

Hall Morse Anderson Miller & Spinella • 14 Centre Street • Concord, NH 03302-2289
Phone (603) 225-6655 • Fax (603) 228-52205220 •
spinellaspinella@hallmorlaw.comcom

New Jersey

Mark Lictenstein is a partner with the New York office of Crowell & Moring LLP. He concentrates his practice on a broad range of bankruptcy matters, including bankruptcy litigation and the acquisition of assets in bankruptcy cases, as well as out of court restructurings and workouts, creditors' rights litigation and general commercial litigation. Mark also has extensive experience providing bankruptcy advice in connection with commercial transactions and the rendering of opinions in connection therewith.

Crowell & Moring • 590 Madison Ave, 20th20th Floor • New York, NY 10022
Phone (212) 895-4267 • Fax (212) 223-4134 • mlichtenstein@crowell.com

William M. O'Connor is a Partner and Co-Chair of the Real Estate Capital Markets Practice Group at Thompson & Knight LLP in New York. He is a nationally recognized leader in the special servicing of commercial mortgage backed securities (CMBS) and related aspects of loan workouts. He is licensed to practice in New York and New Jersey and has been named to the *New York Super LawyersLawyers*® and *Irish Legal 100* by *Irish Voice*. In addition to his Trigild membership, he is a founding member and chairman of the High Yield Debt and Investment Forum at CREFC.

Thompson &Knight LLP • 900 Third Ave 20th20th Floor • New York, NY 10022
Phone (212) 751-3001 • William.oconnor@tklaw.com

Vivian M. Arias is an Associate at Thompson & Knight LLP in New York. She focuses her practice on representing institutional lenders, including national banks, special servicers, and investment banks, in creditors' rights litigation, insolvency, and Chapter 11 bankruptcy proceedings, as well as loan restructurings and workouts. She his licensed to practice in New York and New Jersey and previously served as a Legal Intern for Judge Donald C. Pogue in the Court of International Trade.

Thompson &Knight LLP • 900 Third Ave 20th20th Floor • New York, NY 10022
Phone (212) 751-3001 • Vivian.arias@tklaw.com

New Mexico

Paul M. Fish is a shareholder of the Albuquerque law firm of Modrall Sperling Roehl Harris & Sisk, P.A., where his practice focuses on commercial litigation, including creditor representation in commercial bankruptcy proceedings. Mr. Fish is a member of the State Bar of New Mexico (past chairman, Bankruptcy Law Section), is a fellow of the American College of Bankruptcy, was named "Best in the Bar" in 2010 in bankruptcy, has been repeatedly named a "SuperLawyer" and has been listed in every edition of the Best Lawyers in America. He is a frequent speaker on creditor's rights in bankruptcy, foreclosure and lender liability law.

Modrall Sperling Roehl Harris & Sisk, P.A • 500-4th St., NW, Ste 1000 • Albuquerque, NM 87102
Phone (505) 848-1871 • Fax (505) 848-1882 • pfishpfish@modrall.comcom

---

New York

Vivian M. Arias is an Associate at Thompson & Knight LLP in New York. She focuses her practice on representing institutional lenders, including national banks, special servicers, and investment banks, in creditors' rights litigation, insolvency, and Chapter 11 bankruptcy proceedings, as well as loan restructurings and workouts. She is licensed to practice in New York and New Jersey and previously served as a Legal Intern for Judge Donald C. Pogue in the Court of International Trade.

Thompson &Knight LLP • 900 Third Ave 20th20th Floor • New York, NY 10022
Phone (212) 751-3001 • Vivian.arias@tklaw.com

Evelyn H. Seeler is a Partner at Thompson & Knight LLP in New York. She has more than 20 years of experience representing Wall Street institutions, national and regional banking institutions, hedge funds, mortgage lenders, and servicers. She maintains a diverse practice that includes general commercial and creditors' rights litigation, loan workouts and restructurings, bankruptcies, foreclosures, receiverships, lien enforcement, condemnation, and landlord-tenant litigation at both the state and federal levels.

Thompson &Knight LLP • 900 Third Ave 20th20th Floor • New York, NY 10022
Phone (212) 751-3001 • evelyn.seeler@tklaw.com

Bruce Zabaruskas

Crowell & Moring • 590 Madison Ave, 20th20th Floor • New York, NY 10022
Phone (212) 895-4200 • bzabaruskas@crowell.com

North Carolina

JamesJames H. Pulliam

Kilpatrick Townsend & Stockton LLP • 214 North Tryon Street Suite 2500 • Charlotte, NC 28202
Phone (704) 338-5288 • Fax (704) 371-83118311
jpulliamjpulliam@kilpatricktownsend.comcom

North Dakota

Casey Kosteleckty

Mackoff Kellogg • 38 Second Ave E • E Dickinson, ND 58601
Phone (701) 227-1841 • Fax (701) 227-4739 •
ckosteleckyckostelecky@mackoff.comcom

Ohio

Jonathan Hawkins is an attorney in Thompson Hine LLP's Business Restructuring, Creditors' Rights & Bankruptcy Practice Group in Dayton, Ohio, and he frequently represents secured lenders in non-judicial work-outs and in Ohio's federal, state and bankruptcy courts.

Thompson Hine LLP 2000 • Courthouse Plaza, N.E. 10 W. Second St • Dayton, Ohio 45402
Phone (937) 443-6625 •Fax (937) 443-6635 •
LarryLarry.Burick@ThompsonHine.comcom

Oklahoma

Robert J. Haupt is a director/shareholder of Phillips Murrah P.C. practicing primarily in the areas of commercial bankruptcy and bankruptcy litigation, with a particular focus in hospitality related companies. In addition to serving on the editorial board of the American Bar Association's Bankruptcy Litigation journal, Haupt has authorized numerous professional articles involving bankruptcy, including among others, "*When is a Farmer a 'Family Farmer'—an Analysis of Chapter 12 Qualifications*" (Oklahoma City Univ. Law Review, Fall 2004, reprinted, The Natl. Agricultural Law Center, Univ. of Arkansas Law School); "*Net Present Discount Valuation and Application in Bankruptcy*" (Bankruptcy Litigation, Winter 2009); and "*Is it a raft or a shark? (11 U.S.C. § 523(a)(19) Application to denial of discharge to securities law violators -- broad or narrow construction?*" (Bankruptcy Litigation, Summer 2009). Haupt has led a number of successful Chapters 11 and 12 bankruptcies through plan confirmation.

Phillips Murrah P.C. • 101 N Robinson Ave #1300 •Oklahoma City, OK 73102
Phone (405) 235-4100 • Fax (405)235-4133 • rjhaupt@phillipsmurrah.com

Joshua L. Edwards is an attorney in the Oklahoma City office of Phillips Murrah P.C. and practices primarily in the areas of Commercial Finance, Real Estate and Securities. Josh also works closely with the firm's Bankruptcy and Creditor Rights practice group with respect to real estate and UCC issues arising in bankruptcies, foreclosures and workouts. Josh co-authored the Oklahoma chapter to *Commercial Lending Law: A State-By-State Guide* published by the American Bar Association and has written extensively on the UCC.

Phillips Murrah P.C. • 101 N Robinson Ave #1300 • Oklahoma City, OK 73102
Phone (405) 235-4100 • Fax (405)235-4133 • jledwards@phillipsmurrah.com

Andrew R. Chilson is an attorney in Phillips Murrah P.C.'s litigation section focusing on disputes involving commercial clients, with a concentration in the areas of bankruptcy, foreclosure, and debtor/creditor law. In addition to working to achieve the best resolution for clients through either non-judicial workouts and reorganizations or court-aided restructuring, he represents creditors and debtors in Chapter 11 reorganization proceedings, with a special emphasis on clients in the hospitality industry.

Phillips Murrah P.C. • 101 N Robinson Ave #1300 •Oklahoma City, OK 73102
Phone (405) 235-4100 • Fax (405)235-4133 • archilson@phillipsmurrah.com

---

Ontario, Canada

John D. Leslie

Miller, Canfield, Paddock and Stone LLP • 161 Bay St, 27th Fl •Toronto, ON M5J 2S1
Phone (519) 561-7422 • Fax (519)977-1565 • leslieleslie@millercanfield.comcom

---

Oregon

Christine Kosydar is a partner of the firm focusing her practice in bankruptcy, real estate and creditors' rights and remedies law with a focus on workouts, security interests in real and personal property, lien priority and title analysis and litigation, construction claims and related lien disputes, plus landlord and tenant lease enforcement matters, collections and executions. When the economy is healthy, Chris also devotes a considerable part of her practice to commercial loan and lease transactions and title underwriting analysis. She is an experienced arbitrator certified by ICM. She also has over 25 years experience successfully handling significant and complex commercial litigation in her focus area, including foreclosures, receiverships, commercial evictions and recoveries, fraudulent transfers and related bankruptcy cases.

Stoel Rives LLP • 900 SW Fifth Ave., Suite 2600 • Portland, OR 97204
Phone (503) 294-9533 • Fax (503) 220-2480 • cakosydarcakosydar@stoel.comcom

---

Pennsylvania

Christopher P. Schueller is a shareholder with Buchanan Ingersoll & Rooney PC. Chris regularly handles real estate workouts throughout the country. He is admitted to practice in Pennsylvania, New York, Ohio and West Virginia.

Buchanan Ingersoll & Rooney PC • 301 Grant St, 20th Fl • Pittsburgh, PA 15219-1410
Phone (412) 562-8432 • Fax (412) 562-1041 • schuellercpschuellercp@bipc.comcom

---

Rhode Island

Armando Batastini is a partner at Nixon Peabody, LLP, and is a member of the Real Estate Litigation Team. A large portion of his practice is devoted to representing special servicers and lenders in work-outs, foreclosures, receiverships and litigation related to commercial property throughout the Northeast.

Nixon Peabody LLP • 100 Summer Street • Boston, MA 02110• One Citizens Plaza, Suite 500 • Providence, RI 02903

Phone (617) 345-1116 • (401) 454-1015 • Fax (866)-680-8453 •
abatastiniabatastini@nixonpeabody.comcom

South Carolina

Morris A. Ellison is a principal in the law firm of Buist Moore Smythe McGee PA, 5 Exchange Street, Charleston, South Carolina 29401, where his practice includes commercial real estate transactions, commercial litigation and banking law. Mr. Ellison is a fellow in the American College of Real Estate Lawyers and the American College of Mortgage Attorneys. He is also the South Carolina member of the American Property Tax Counsel.

Womble Carlyle Sandridge & Rice PLLC. • 5 Exchange St. • Charleston, SC 29401
PhonePhone (843) 720-4614 • FaxFax (843) 723-
7398 • mellisonmellison@buistmoore.comcom

South Dakota

Rebecca L. Mann is an associate at Gunderson, Palmer, Nelson and Ashmore, LLP in Rapid City, South Dakota. A native of South Dakota, Rebecca earned her J.D. from the University of South Dakota and is licensed in South Dakota, North Dakota and Montana. Her practice areas include family law, insurance defense, debtor creditor relations, employment law and general civil litigation.

Gunderson Palmer Nelson Ashmore LLP • 506 Sixth St • Rapid City, SD 57701
Phone (506) 719-3486 • Fax (605) 342-9503 • rmannrmann@gpnalaw.comcom

---

Tennessee

John H. Rowland, shareholder in the Nashville office of Baker, Donelson, Bearman, Caldwell & Berkowitz, concentrates his practice in the areas of commercial litigation and business reorganization. Listed in The Best Lawyers in America® since 2005 for Bankruptcy and Creditor-Debtor Rights Law, John has extensive experience representing secured lenders in workouts and out-of-court restructurings.

Baker, Donelson, Bearman, Caldwell & Berkowitz, PC • 211 Commerce St. Ste 1000 • Nashville, TN 37201
Phone (615) 726- 5544 • Fax (615) 744-5544 • jrowlandjrowland@bakerdonelson.comcom

CourtneyCourtney H. Gilmer, shareholder in the Nashville office of Baker, Donelson, Bearman, Caldwell & Berkowitz, concentrates her practice in the areas of bankruptcy, creditors' rights, restructuring and commercial litigation. She has extensive experience in the representation of creditors sued for the return of preference or avoidance payments, creditors with claims in complex bankruptcy cases and related contested bankruptcy issues. Ms. Gilmer also has experience representing lenders and businesses in the many areas of commercial litigation.

Baker, Donelson, Bearman, Caldwell & Berkowitz, PC • 211 Commerce St. Ste 1000 • Nashville, TN 37201
Phone (615) 726-5747 • Fax (615) 744-5544 • cgilmercgilmer@bakerdonelson.comcom

---

Texas

Foreclosure Section:

Brigitte G. Kimichik is a partner at the law firm of Andrews Kurth LLP and has experience in all areas and with all types of commercial real estate (including shopping centers, hotels, office buildings, industrial parks, and franchised properties). She advises clients with respect to real estate portfolios of multiple properties in multiple states, emphasizing lending, leasing, sales and acquisitions, sale-leaseback transactions, note sale transactions, and restructuring and workouts of defaulted loan transactions. Her specialty at the firm involves financing and sale leaseback transactions secured by multiple fast food restaurants, gas stations and convenience stores. She received her J.D. in 1986 from Southern Methodist University Dedman School of Law and her B.B.A., *with honors*, from The University of Texas in 1983 where she was a member of the Dean's List and Golden Key Honor Society; She earned her Abitur in 1980 from the Gymnasium Osdorf, in Hamburg, Germany (German Highschool).

Andrews Kurth LLP • 1717 Main Street Suite 3700 • Dallas, TX 75201
Phone (214) 659-4441 • Fax (214) 659-4777 •
bkimichikbkimichik@andrewskurth.comcom

Jason S. Brookner is a partner in the Dallas office of Andrews Kurth LLP. His practice concentrates on transactional, restructuring and litigation matters, both in and out of court. Jason has broad experience representing debtors, trustees, committees, individual creditors, sellers/purchasers of assets and other constituents. Jason received his BA in 1991 from the State University of New York at Binghamton and his JD in 1994 from Hofstra University of Law where he was an Articles Editor on the Hofstra Property Law Journal. After law school, Jason served as law clerk for the Honorable Charles N. Clevert, Jr., Chief United States Bankruptcy Judge for the Eastern District of Wisconsin. From 2005 through 2011 Jason has been profiled as one of the leading bankruptcy/restructuring lawyers in Texas in *Chambers USA, America's Leading Lawyers for Business*. For the past two years, Jason has served as one of the Co-Chair's for the American Bankruptcy Institute's Commercial Fraud Committee and was the Committee's Educational Director for the two preceding years. In 2007 Jason was the Chair of the Dallas Bar Association's Bankruptcy and Commercial Law Section. Jason has also written multiple articles, and is a frequent speaker, on chapter 11 issues.

Andrews Kurth LLP • 1717 Main Street Suite 3700 • Dallas, TX 75201
Phone (214) 659-4418 • Fax (214) 659-4887
• jbrooknerjbrookner@andrewskurth.comcom

Receivership Section:

Monica Blacker's practice includes representation of debtors, secured and unsecured creditors, and creditors' committee in Chapter 11 bankruptcy proceedings. Monica's practice focuses on out-of-court workouts and in-court bankruptcies. In the recent years, her focus has been on real estate cases, representing major lending institutions. Monica's recent cases have included NextMedia Group, Inc., BroadStar Wind Systems Group, LLC, DBSI, Inc., M.B.S. Properties and Kitty Hawk, Inc. Monica received her J.D., cum laude, in 1996 from Southern Methodist University Dedman School of Law and her B.B.A., cum laude, in 1993 from James Madison University.

Andrews & Kurth, L.L.P. • 1717 Main Street Suite 3700 • Dallas, TX 75201
Phone: (214) 659-4576 • Fax: (214) 659-4844 •
monicablackermonicablacker@andrewskurth.comcom

Utah

David E. Leta; partner at Snell & Wilmer, L.L.P.; practice concentrates on bankruptcy litigation, business reorganizations and creditor rights; has represented creditors, debtors, committees and trustees in a wide variety of commercial settings; continuously recognized in Woodward/White, Inc. as one of the Best Lawyers in America.

Snell & Wilmer L.L.P. • 15 West South Temple, Suite 1200 • Salt Lake City, Utah 84101
Phone (801) 257-1928 • Fax (801) 257-1928 x1800 • dletadleta@swlaw.comcom

Vermont

Douglas Riley is a transactions partner at Lisman Leckerling, P.C. of Burlington, Vermont. Mr. Riley is a member of the Vermont and Connecticut Bars.

Lisman Leckerling, P.C. • 84 Pine Street, 5th Floor • Burlington, VT 05401
Phone (802) 864-5756 • Fax (802) 864-3629 • drileydriley@lisman.comcom

Virginia

John G. McJunkin's practice focuses on loan workouts, business bankruptcies and commercial litigation. Mr. McJunkin works extensively with creditors in protecting their rights during workouts, litigation, foreclosures, and bankruptcy. His commercial litigation experience includes the prosecution and defense of numerous lawsuits and arbitrations arising out of disputes related to various lending issues as well as contractual matters, real estate disputes, franchise issues, title insurance matters and business torts. He has been recognized as one of *America's Leading Lawyers* for Bankruptcy Litigation by *Chambers USA*.

McKenna Long & Aldridge, LLP • 1900 K Street, NW • Washington, DC 20006
Phone: 202-496-7312 • Fax: 202-496-7756 • Email: jmcjunkinjmcjunkin@mckennalong.comcom

Craig Rust is an associate practicing as a member of the McKenna Long & Aldridge's Litigation Team. Prior to joining MLA, he clerked for the Honorable Samuel G. Wilson of the U.S. District Court for the Western District of Virginia. He graduated magna cum laude from George Mason University School of Law.

McKenna Long & Aldridge, LLP • 1900 K Street, NW • Washington, DC 20006
Phone: 202-496-7312 • Fax: 202-496-7756 • Email: crust@mckennalong.com

---

Washington

Terry Highan currently practices in the Santa Monica office of McLean & McLean, LLP, representing and advising clients throughout California and the United States. His practice areas include: commercial/business liability; receiverships and insurance related litigation.

McLean & McLean LLP • 3001 2nd2nd Street Suite E • Santa Monica, CA 90405
Phone (310) 450-9353 • Fax (310) 581-8006

Washington, D.C.

Matthew W. Cheney is a partner in Crowell & Moring's Washington, DC office. Matt's practice includes bankruptcy and creditors' rights matters, commercial transactions, loan workouts and distressed debt matters.

Crowell & Moring •1001 Pennsylvania Ave, N.W. • Washington, DC 20004
Phone (202) 624-2903 • Fax (202) 628-5116 • mcheney@crowell.com

MoniqueMonique Almy is a partner in Crowell & Moring's Washington, DC office and is a member of the Bankruptcy, Corporate and Financial Services practice groups. Monique's practice focuses primarily on corporate bankruptcy, restructuring, and on other insolvency related matters, with an emphasis on creditors' rights.

Crowell & Moring •1001 Pennsylvania Ave, N.W. • Washington, DC 20004
Phone (202)624-2935• Fax (202) 628-5116 • malmymalmy@crowell.comcom

---

West Virginia

Christopher P. Schueller is a shareholder with Buchanan Ingersoll & Rooney PC. Chris regularly handles real estate workouts throughout the country. He is admitted to practice in Pennsylvania, New York, Ohio and West Virginia.

Buchanan Ingersoll & Rooney PC • 301 Grant St, 20th Fl • Pittsburgh, PA 15219-1410
Phone (412) 562-8432 • Fax (412) 562-1041 • schuellercpschuellercp@bipc.comcom

---

Wisconsin

Roy L. Prange, Jr., is a Partner with Quarles & Brady LLP, and practices in the areas of commercial litigation, lender liability defense and creditors rights/bankruptcy. Mr. Prange is a former Chair and Director of the State Bar of Wisconsin Bankruptcy, Insolvency and Creditors Rights Section. He is a Fellow of the American College of Bankruptcy.

Quarles & Brady LLP • 33 East Main Street Suite 900 •Madison, WI 53703
Phone (608) 283-2485 • Fax (608) 294-4920 • rlprlp@quarles.comcom

---

Wyoming

Lindsay A. Woznick is a partner at Hirst Applegate, where she has practiced law since 2005. Prior to joining Hirst Applegate, Lindsay attended the University of Wyoming College of Law where she graduated with honors, Order of the Coif, and Order of the Barristers. She obtained her bachelor's degree in Education from the University of Wyoming, graduating with honors, *Summa Cum Laude.* Her practice is focused primarily in the areas of trust and estate planning and administration, oil and gas, real estate, creditors' rights and commercial litigation.

Hirst Applegate, LLP • 1720 Carey Ave, Suite 400 • PO Box 1083 • Cheyenne WY 82003-10863
Phone (307) 632-0541 • Fax (307) 632-4999 • lwoznicklwoznick@hirstapplegate.comcom

Ronald J. Lopez is an associate at Hirst Applegate, where he has practiced law since 2010. Prior to joining Hirst Applegate, he attended the University Of Wyoming College Of Law where he graduated with honor, and was awarded the Excellence in Advocacy Award. While at the University of Wyoming he competed on the winning team of the Rothgerber Trial Competition and went on to compete regionally. His practice is focused primarily on corporate/LLC law, real estate law, creditors' rights, and estate planning and administration.

Hirst Applegate, LLP • 1720 Carey Ave, Suite 400 • PO Box 1083 • Cheyenne WY 82003-1086
Phone (307) 632-0541 • Fax (307) 632-4999 • rlopezrlopez@hirstapplegate.comcom

---

UCC and Related Issues

Jim Cochran is a partner with O'Connor Cochran LLP in Los Angeles. Jim has extensive experience advising clients in workouts and restructurings involving complex collateral packages and multiple jurisdictions. He has represented secured lenders, distressed debt investors, special servicers and other clients in connection with secured loan restructurings (including consolidations), structured asset dispositions, collateral "take backs," note sales and similar matters as well as lien enforcement proceedings (including judicial and non-judicial foreclosures of retail, office, hotel and other properties and UCC sales of limited liability company and partnership interests).

O'Connor Cochran LLP • 515 South Flower St, 36th36th Floor • Los Angeles, CA 90071
Phone (213) 236-3624 • jcochranjcochran@oconnorcochran.comcom

---

Federal Receivership Basics

Kay Standridge Kress is a partner in the Detroit Office of Pepper Hamilton LLP. She concentrates in corporate restructuring, insolvency and bankruptcy matters and has been involved in numerous federal receivership actions.

Pepper Hamilton LLP • 100 Renaissance Center, Suite 3600 • Detroit, MI 48243
Phone (313) 393-7365 • Fax (313) 557-0656 • kresskkressk@pepperlaw.comcom

State Receivership Basics

Robert A. Hammeke is a partner in the Kansas City, Missouri office of Husch Blackwell LLP and he is licensed in Missouri and Kansas. His practice includes all aspects of creditor/debtor relationships, with a concentration on loan enforcement, workout, and restructuring, including enforcement of ancillary remedies such as pre-judgment attachment, injunctions, replevins, and state and federal court receiverships. Bob represents banks and other financial institutions, private lenders, distressed debt purchasers, and special servicers seeking to maximize recovery from distressed and defaulted loans or loan portfolios. His representations include out-of-court workouts and enforcement actions in state court and federal district and bankruptcy courts.

Husch Blackwell Sanders LLP • 4801 Main Street, Suite 1000 • Kansas City, MO 64112
Phone (816) 983-8342 • Fax (816) 983-8080 •
robertrobert.hammeke@huschblackwell.comcom

BuchalterNemer
A Professional Law Corporation

California Non-Judicial Foreclosure Flow Chart

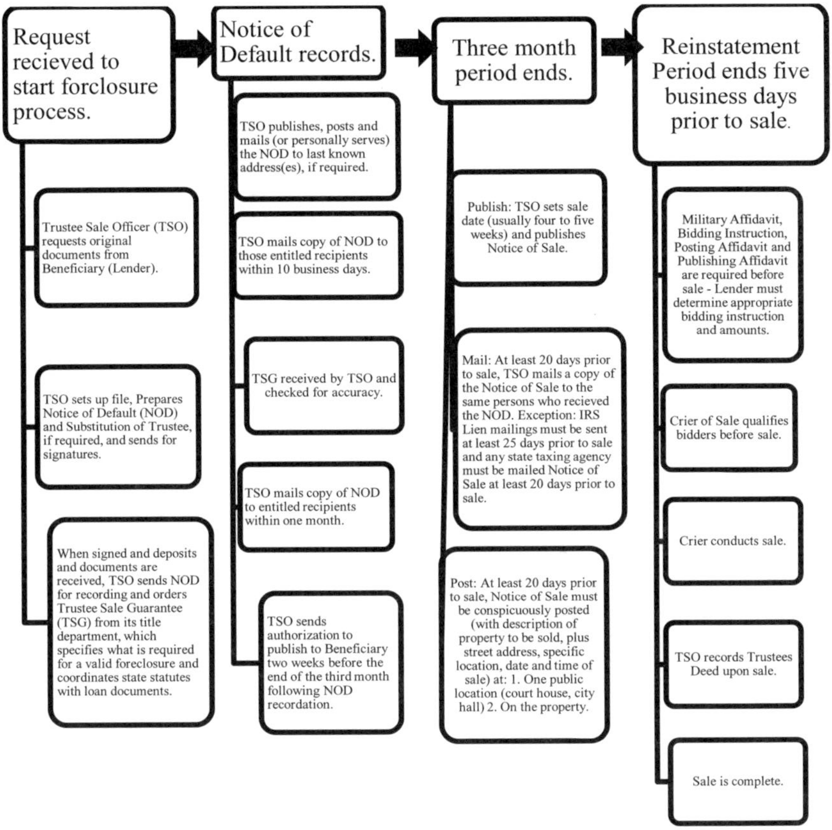

Items may occur in tandem

*This flow chart which was prepared by the law firm of Buchalter Nemer, is not intended to provide specific legal advice or to establish an attorney-client relationship. Consult an appropriate professional for advice about your particular situation.

Contact
Sharon Morrissey
Buchalter Nemer
55 Second Street
San Francisco, CA 94105
Telephone: (415) 227-3502

NOTES